Preface

Big data has transformed the businesses of the digital era. It encompasses an exciting new set of tools, techniques, frameworks, and platforms for modern, data-powered applications to generate business value. Hadoop has evolved as a de-facto for data management and acts as an operating system for big data distributed storage and parallel computation. However, data evangelists, data managers, data scientists, and analysts who are new to big data ecosystem may feel that big data ecosystem tools and techniques are programming oriented rather than analytically oriented. This is because a fundamental shift needs to occur in thinking about how we manage, control, compute, and analyse data to generate business value.

This book proposes to fill the current gaps in the thinking shift of the data stakeholders such as data evangelists, data managers, data scientists, and analysts to leverage big data tools, techniques, frameworks, and platforms to generate business value. The book prepares data stakeholders of the digital era for that shift in thinking by providing elaborative discussions on big data ecosystems, fundamentals, management, and analytics in a readable and direct manner. Business leaders, analysts, data engineers, and scholars will be the primary beneficiaries of this pristine book, which aims at enriching the journey of big data management and analytics through a very pragmatic approach.

The book consists of three major parts, as follows:

In ***Part I***, the readers will understand the need for the analytics driven culture, big data architecture, information pioneered product, and ethics framework for big data ecosystem. Readers will get to know the principles behind organizational and business shift in leveraging big data for generating its business value. An ethical framework is also introduced to ensure that data stakeholders involved in the data product address the ethical dilemma and execute the appropriate ethical strategy to harness the data ethically.

In ***Part II***, big data management principles, fundamentals, components, and architecture of HADOOP ecosystem are described at length. Each subsequent chapter addresses the challenge for an organization to use the HADOOP components in totality. Topics such as MapReduce, HIVE, HBase, PIG, SQOOP, and FLUME are discussed in detail.

In ***Part III***, the reader will understand how to generate value through big data business leadership model, analytics platform, and frameworks. An introduction to R and RStudio is also provided here. The supervised and unsupervised learning techniques are elaborated in detail covering all the leading methods such as Regression, Clustering, Classification, Decision Trees, Random Forests, etc. This will help the reader to delve deeply into the spectrum of practical analytics. All the working problem examples are solved and presented using R (RStudio). The big data business leadership model will enable industries to develop their own big data journey—pathways, competencies, and competitiveness.

Each chapter is supported by appropriate examples, business case, and exercise set for the readers.

The book aims to provide benefits to the readers, as it

- considers the appropriate and balanced way of addressing the topics in a lucid and readable fashion;
- adopts a user-friendly approach and an easy-to-understand language;
- provides reliable, concise information on the real benefits, usage, and operationalization aspects of big data business leadership;
- covers realistic vignettes, case studies, exercises, and examples;
- explores the capabilities and opportunities that Hadoop ecosystem provides
- contains coverage of topics such as MapReduce, HIVE, HBase, PIG, SQOOP, FLUME, and R;
- elaborates the principles to identify the value of the data before investing in the infrastructure and resources for the data lookout;
- develops a thinking mind-set to understand and generate business value through data.

I hope this book provides an enriched experience to the readers.

Nitin Upadhyay

Dedicated
To
Avatar Meher Baba

"I have come to sow the seed of love in your hearts, so that, in spite of all the superficial diversity which your life in illusion must experience and endure, the feeling of Oneness, through Love, is brought about amongst all nations, creeds, sects and castes of the world"

Meher Baba

BIG DATA

MANAGEMENT & ANALYTICS

NITIN UPADHYAY

Chair and Head of the Centre for Innovation,
Goa Institute of Management, Goa.
Chair of Cloud SLAs, Cloud Computing Innovation Council of India.

CENGAGE

Australia • Brazil • India • Mexico • Singapore • United Kingdom • United States

CENGAGE

BIG DATA: Management & Analytics

Nitin Upadhyay

Cover Image: © Thinkstock

ISBN-13: 978-93-87994-20-1
ISBN-10: 93-87994-20-1

Cengage Learning India Pvt. Ltd.
418, F.I.E., Patparganj
Delhi 110092

Cengage Learning is a leading provider of customized learning solutions with office locations around the globe, including Australia, Brazil, India, Mexico, Singapore, United Kingdom, and United States. Locate your local office at:
www.cengage.com/global

Cengage Learning products are represented in Canada by Nelson Education, Ltd.

For product information, visit **www.cengage.co.in**

Acknowledgements

To my wife, Dr Shalini Upadhyay, I owe my indebtedness for always supporting me in my ups and downs. Her never-ending and unconditional love cannot be expressed in words. I am thankful to her for teaching me the virtues of perseverance, dedication, and determination.

I am beholden to my sweet little angel and dearest daughter, Ms Meherika Upadhyay, for making my life so beautiful with her smile, laughter, and innocence. For every night asking me "*will you study and write chapters for your book*?", which showed that even in this tender age she understood the significance of my work and that she was concerned about me. Not only am I indebted to her but also apologetic for stealing her time in order to realise this work. A special thanks to my dog "Brownie" for spending endless hours with me during the project and showing love, care; and bringing energy.

I am thankful to all the reviewers who have provided necessary and appropriate comments for making this book as apt as possible. I acknowledge my students, fellow colleagues, peers, and researchers for their healthy discussions, suggestions, and necessary co-operation towards the completion of this work.

I am thankful to the Director, Goa Institute of Management, Goa, for providing me the conducive environment necessary to accomplish such a project.

Quite importantly, I would like to express my deep gratitude towards Cengage Learning, publishers, for providing me with an opportunity to write a book on such an essential topic, and for monitoring the progress and providing valuable suggestions for the improvement of the chapters from time to time.

Finally, I express my gratitude to all those who have directly and indirectly helped me in my this project.

Nitin Upadhyay

Brief Contents

Detailed Contents

PART II

PART III

Part I

The Age of Information Pioneered Product

1

"All revolutions are impossible till they happen, then they become inevitable."

—Albie Sachs

Learning Objectives

On completing this chapter, you will be able to:

LO 1 Comprehend the driving force towards the information revolution

LO 2 Summarize the big data dimensions and characteristics

LO 3 Examine the information pioneered product

LO 4 Understand the analytics revolution

LO 5 Describe the big data management architecture

CASE STUDY: Underdog Women to Silver Medallist

The amalgamation of sports and big data has emerged as a silver bullet to the sports ecosystem. The enormous and effective usage of data helped OAthelete project to deliver high impact performance and raise the bar of US women's cycling team. The team later went from underdogs to silver medallists at the 2012 London Olympics.

Fig. 1.1 Women cyclists

Sky Christopherson and his team started the OAthelete project after getting disillusioned from the doping culture in sports. Christopherson held a world record for 200 m velodrome sprint in the 35+ category. This he achieved by following a performance-enhancing regime based on personalized digital health approach inspired by Dr Eric Topol.

A 'Dream Team' project was started prior to the 2012 London Olympic Games. Christopherson led this in collaboration with other thought leaders from sports, medicine, and technology, including a pioneer in digital medicine (Dr Eric Topol). The main mission of the OAthelete project was to create a sustainable performance using 'Data not Drugs' philosophy. The OAthelete technology platform became the lifeblood for the sports performance of the cyclists. The platform effectively integrates wearable technology, digital health, and a wireless sensor ecosystem for high-performance training. This, in turn, generates key measurements for individual athlete to keep a check on various parameters that include genetics, environment, physiology, psychology, etc. Closely working with the women's cycling team who were using the technology platform, Christopherson could create individual's high-performance training regimes. He stated that one could achieve 'breakthrough performance' by drilling to 'individual optimal zones' based on parameters such as diet, sleep patterns, environment, and training intensity.

Data turned out to be wealth and the fuel for tailoring and customizing high-performance personalized training programs. Various structured and unstructured data were utilized to create personalized custom-made training programs. For example, time series data—blood sugar level, pulse rate (bpm), and skin level; environmental data—sunlight, level of SpO2, temperature, time of day, and weather (based on public data); sleep patterns data through ECG; video data of the athlete; and stress data were utilized and analysed for actionable decisions. Christopherson partnered with the San-Francisco based firm Datameer having specialization in data analytics and visualization. The Hadoop on the cloud was utilized to store the data and Datameer's impactful visualizations detailed out the precise patterns. In the case of Sarah Hammer, the data displayed the vitamin D deficiency, and thus the training for her was customized to cover up the vitamin D deficiency, which includes practice in the sunlight. In another notable incidence, it was identified that the sleep pattern has a significant performance impact on the cyclist. Jenny Reed seemed to perform better during the training when she slept in the night at a lower temperature a day before the scheduled training. As per the directions, she started using the water-cooled mattress, which helped her to perform better as she could maintain her body temperature throughout the night before the training.

Some of the benefits and temptations to use performance-enhancing drugs by the athletes are to avoid injuries, increase strength, improve recovery rate, reduce fatigue, increase endurance, and increase performance results which otherwise are not possible. Christopherson revealed that big data solution could give early warnings of injury; so, one can avoid pushing an athlete for overtraining and notifications could be achieved in case an athlete is under trained. Thus, the philosophy of 'Data not Drugs' worked well and he advocates it very well. He got the benefit and based on his coaching the US women's cycling team demonstrated high performance by winning the silver medal in the 2012 London Olympics.

Questions

1. Which problem is big data helping to solve here?
   Tip: Identify usage of data in sports.
2. How is big data applicable in practice in sports?
   Tip: Identify use cases of data in sports. Further, categorize the type of data that is relevant.
3. Which data is important for the sports stakeholders?
   Tip: Identify the context of data usage. Further, prioritize the use cases to gather the important type of data.
4. Which technology is being used to handle the sports data?
   Tip: Identify the primary, secondary, support, and other technological solutions.

5. What challenges do cyclists need to overcome?

   Tip: Identify the journey of the cyclists. Further, map the journey with the milestones, goals, and setbacks.

6. Which patterns are effective for high-performance training regimes?

   Tip: Identify the primary, secondary, support, and other use cases contributing to the underpinning assumption of 'Data-not-Drugs' principle.

References

https://www.crunchbase.com/organization/oathlete#/entity [accessed April 26, 2017];
http://peds.weebly.com/advantages.html [accessed April 26, 2017];
http://www.oathelete.com/#intro [accessed April 26, 2017];
https://vimeo.com/48833290 [accessed April 26, 2017]

> *"A revolution is coming – a revolution which will be peaceful if we are wise enough; compassionate if we care enough; successful if we are fortunate enough–but a revolution which is coming whether we will it or not. We can affect its character; we cannot alter its inevitability."*
>
> *[Report to the United States Senate on his trip to Latin America and the Alliance for Progress, May 9-10 1966]*
>
> —Robert F. Kennedy

Fig. 1.2 We are living in a digital age.

LO 1 *Comprehend the driving force towards the information revolution*

Ours is a digital age generation that acts as a driving force towards the information revolution. We are witnessing the Information Renaissance that is transforming society, culture, academia, research, and business and most importantly us all into both consumers and producers of a new valuable material—data. Unlike traditional revolutions such as the automobile, electricity, and the computer, the Internet revolution has surpassed its expectations. It took 38 years for radio broadcasters and 13 years for television to reach an audience of 50 million, but the Internet did it in just four years (Gallup, 2017). The present information revolution has not just only driven by the change in the communication, but also in scale, speed, and variety. During 1993, World Wide Web (WWW) hosted and served around 50 web pages. Today, it is very difficult to measure the full coverage of the density of WWW. Roughly, the size of the indexed World Wide Web is around 45 billion pages as of 24 April, 2017 (*Source*: http://www.worldwidewebsize.com/), see Fig. 1.3. The WWW is the single largest and most widely used source of information, with nearly 3.2 billion users (Wikipedia). The human race is creating on an average 2.3 million Terabytes (TB) of data every day, so much that 90 percent of the data in the world today has been created in the last two years alone. As per CISCO, the human has entered into the Zettabyte (ZB) era, and data created by Internet of Everything (IoE) devices will reach 507.5 ZB per year (42.3 ZB per month) by 2019, up from 134.5 ZB per year (11.2 ZB per month) in 2014 (Cisco.com). It also forecasted that the data would reach 247 EB by 2020, up almost 10-fold from 25 EB in 2015. Big data alone will represent 27 percent of data stored in data centers by 2020, up from 15 percent in 2015.

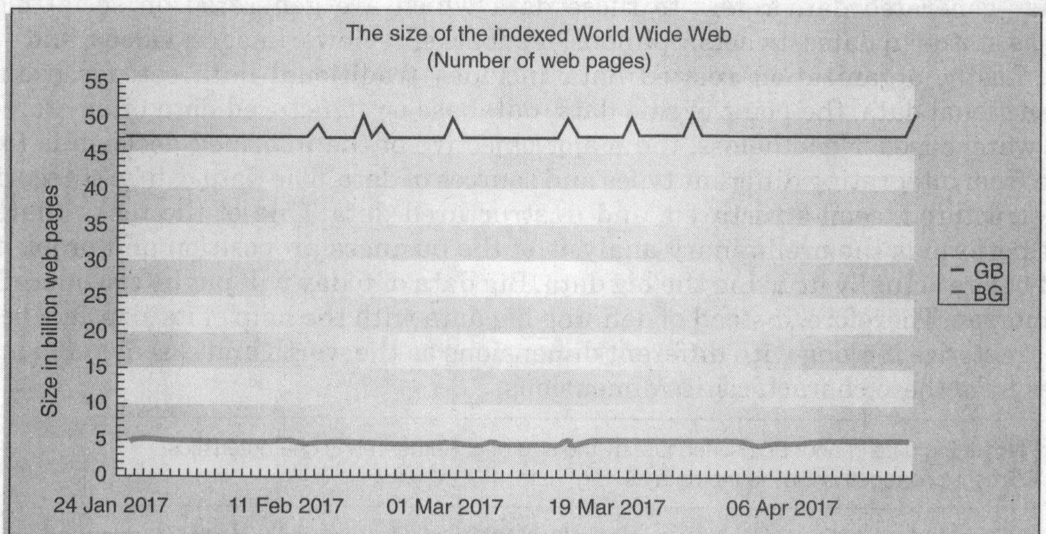

Fig. 1.3 Size of the indexed World Wide Web [GB = Sorted on Google and Bing and BG = Sorted on Bing and Google]

The data comes from everywhere—connected devices, physical sensors, browsing and click patterns, social media interactions, audio and video streams, transaction records, and telecommunication signals to name a few. Thus, business and people must be equipped with the right infrastructure and resources to fully capitalize on such valuable material—data. This progression and change will be accomplished only when they are made aware of analytics ecosystem, data storage and management platform, and strategic and decision-making capabilities. Our world is becoming more complex due to the rapid and agile availability of abundance data sets. The banks would like to understand the behaviour of a person or a company's goodwill before they lend a loan. They also would like to know whether a person or a company could repay the loan. This information is critical as none of the banks would like to fall into the trap of loss in finances. A new product in the context of big data is referred to as the information pioneered product which is becoming a survival and competing strength for the companies to perform effectively.

1.1 HOW BIG IS BIG

LO 2

Summarize the big data dimensions and characteristics

The big data era is witnessing a big torrent of data flowing from the variety of sources. These sources could be machines, people, and organizations. Your mobile device monitors your step counts, calorie burnt, and other health-related measures to update you on your health status on a regular basis. This information is possible with the help of various sensors deployed on the machines, here, mobile device. Human-generated data refers to those data which are generated on social media such as status updates, tweets, opinions, feedbacks, reviews, images, videos, and voice calls. Lastly, organization related data includes traditional data set; for example transactional data, the point of sale data, database or structured data often stored in data warehouses. Nonetheless, the major objective of the informed decision is to get value from integrating different types and sources of data. The data can be categorized into structured, semi-structured, and unstructured data. One of the tasks that one must perform is the preliminary analysis of the business proposition and problem at hand before actually utilizing the big data. Big data of today will not be considered big of tomorrow. Therefore, instead of defining big data with the help of its size, it is better to characterize it along with different dimensions as the worth and essence of big data comes from these characteristics/dimensions.

Note: Big data cannot be defined just by the size of it. Rather many characteristics/ dimensions together define the data as 'Big' data.

It is worth looking at the statistics that 90% of the world's data is created in the last two years (IBM, 2018). The various dimensions that make big data are defined as follows:

- **Volume:** It represents the scale of the data. Ben Walker estimates that 2.5 Quintillion bytes are created every day. He also suggests that 'around 216,000 Instagram posts are posted every minute, 204,000,000 emails are sent in a minute, around 12 hours of footage is uploaded to YouTube and 277,000 tweets are posted on Twitter per minute'. The data size is huge.
- **Variety:** Big data can be of any type. It can be structured data, unstructured data, and semi-structured data. Structured data are specified by rule or pre-defined format, can be like the relational data stored in the relational database. Unstructured data does not have a data model or any defined proper format. It includes books, journals, documents, metadata, health records, audio, video, analog data, images, files, and unstructured text such as the body of an e-mail message, web page, or word-processor document. Semi-structured data model is the model behind the Web. Mostly, they are arranged in the tree format.
- **Velocity:** In massive and critical applications, sometimes, a 1-minute delay is dangerous. Velocity refers to the speed of the data. IBM suggests that 'for time-sensitive processes such as catching fraud, big data must be used as it streams into your enterprise to maximize its value'.
- **Veracity:** Data normally does not come clean. Typically, the biases, noise, and abnormality associated with the data refer to veracity. One of the biggest challenges for a big data team is to store and mine clean and process data for further analysis.
- **Valence:** In big data, valence represents the interconnectedness of the data. The complexity of the analysis increases with more connections. In the real world, this works in a very handy fashion. For example, if you would like to go out for your first date, there might be a chance that you would like to know about your prospective partner before you meet him/her. First things first, you will try to establish relationships—his/her social media presence, his/her professional and friend circle. The more you establish relationships and connections among the set of data more complex and meaningful is the relationship model.
- **Value:** The real benefit of the mashup of five Vs comes to realization only if true value is the outcome. Are you able to decide on the development of new product line, economized measure, or an opportunity for acquisition based on the actionable insights from your data?

> **Note:** Do not work with data just for the sake of some technological satisfaction. Every big data project must generate some true value, i.e., actionable insights.

1.2 INFORMATION PIONEERED PRODUCT

LO 3 *Examine the information pioneered product*

> *Any product that combines the capability of incorporating data and intelligent processes to generate meaningful and valued actionable decisions and associated information* is considered as an **information pioneered product.**

In a very trivial term, *any product that combines the capability of incorporating data and intelligent processes to generate meaningful and valued actionable decisions and associated information* is considered as an **information-pioneered product**. This data can come from anywhere—for example, from your browsing and search history on Amazon websites; your likes or status messages on the Facebook site; and your movement trail through GPS sensors. The moment you type your desirable product on the Amazon search bar you might find that Amazon smartly recommends the products to you. Now, this is based on your past search history, your current browsing pattern, and based on similar purchase behaviours of other users. In this case, order and search history information is combined with the '*recommended*' intelligent processes (termed as recommendation algorithm) to predict what you might purchase in the future.

On the similar lines, LinkedIn recommends potential professional relationships based on prospective candidate's skill set, profile, and search or browsing pattern. These examples are certainly revolutionary in their respective domains of usage and market share—and are information pioneered products. Eduardo (2016) clearly cites that '*LinkedIn is still one of the most solid social networks out there. The data it has about professional users and their connections is second to none*'. This opens a new fact that LinkedIn, an information pioneered product, not only has the combination of information and intelligent processes to provide meaningful and valued actionable decisions, such as potential professional partner/employer, but also generates associated information, which becomes fuel for its engine. Thus, information pioneered product derives value from the information and in turn generates more valuable and meaningful information by creating a vicious information cycle. It might also lead to the generation of new information pioneered product. This generative effect of meaningful and valued information is driving the information revolution. Another example of the information pioneered product is the self-driving autonomous car. A vehicle is capable of sensing its environment and navigating without human input. This requires the set of intelligent processes to be tailored, customized, modified, or replaced automatically to the optimum level to work on ever increasing the set of information about its environment while the car is in motion so that navigation and motion are optimum.

> **Note:** Information pioneered product is self-adapting, derives its value from the information which in turn generates more associated information and actionable decisions that led to refuel its engine or used to generate new information pioneered product.

1.3 ANALYTICS REVOLUTION

> "*Predict and act right at right time or perish.*"
> "*Prevdict right and act timely or perish.*"
>
> —Nitin Upadhyay

LO 4 *Understand the analytics revolution*

Industrial revolution happened in the 18th and 19th century. It lead to the change in the working culture of people involved in producing goods and products. Before the revolution, people had to spend tedious, long hours of hand labour even on simple objects (Lewis, 1992). It gradually progressed resulting into mechanization of machines; evolution of factories and industries; mass production of goods; and generation of power from primary steam and alternate sources.

Likewise industrial revolution, the analytical revolution has started in the 20th and 21st century. The dominant strategy for a key player in the market is to predict correctly and then act timely. Organizations are willing to monitor and track every aspect of data, material, process, and people to build models that could deliver them value which otherwise is not possible.

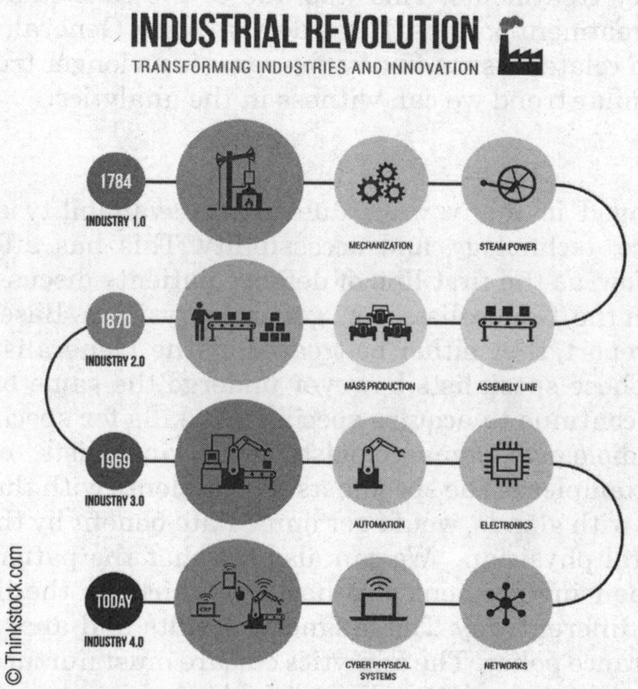

Fig. 1.4 Picture depicting industrial revolution

The industrial revolution transformed the artistic way of crafting and building products to modernized technologically enabled workloads, processes, and practices. This results in massive delivery and manufacturing of quality products. Nonetheless, we are witnessing the same type of revolution with the analytics. Industries are deploying their operational analytics models to predict defaults, failures, delays, quality, etc., and those are at scale, unimaginable a decade back. Analytics (models) must be operationalized to generate and deliver the value.

One of the key ingredients for the analytics revolution is the development of the analytics-driven culture. The others are the development of analytics model; followed by testing of the model; migration of model in a context; deployment of models; monitoring of models; tuning of models; optimizing the models. Making analytics operational does not remove any of the steps historically required to build an analytics process. Rather, it takes the process further.

> **Note:** The analytics revolution will empower organizations to automate decisions by incorporating operational analytics within business processes.

Analytics-driven Culture

Let us try to gaze the development of the medicinal treatments. Earlier, for everyone, a doctor was just a doctor. A doctor in the past could handle all kind of ailments and provide the necessary treatments. This was due to the constrained knowledge and poor availability of treatment options. These doctors were 'Generalists'. They could be visited for any health related issues. Today, the same is no longer true in the medicinal treatments and a similar trend we can witness in the analytics.

Why Specialists

The world has changed in many ways due to the availability of the resources—knowledge, literature, technology, and accessibility. This has affected the medical profession greatly. Now, as the first line of defence patients discuss their ailments or treatments plan with the 'Generalists', i.e., general physician. Based on the diagnosis or the result of the report, they either be treated by the 'Generalists' or further refer to the 'Specialists'. These specialists however undergo the same basic training as of generalists but also continue to acquire specialized skills for specific and subspecific medicine areas. Radiologists, gynaecologists, endocrinologists, orthopaedists, and much more are the examples of the specialists. The patients with the specific problems such as hormones or with glands, would get immediate benefit by the endocrinologists instead of any general physician. We can also see that the patients and doctors do not exist in silos. Their involvement also has given birth to the insurance industry and shaping it in a different way. The diagnosis results and analysis have a deeper impact on one's insurance policy. The analytics culture must nurture, both, generalists and specialists, like the one in the medicinal fields, and involvement of each can be decided upon the nature of problem in-hand or encountered. Analytic generalists can help organizations to locate opportunities, build a cohesive spectrum of skill set and capabilities, plan analytic strategies and manage the development of effective analytic processes. However, any specific problem can be referred to the specialist. The analytics specialists would undergo the same underlying mathematical and statistical educational and experiential foundation but incorporated specialized capabilities and skill set by learning specific areas of analytics. Thus, one can see the proliferation of analytic specialists in predictive models, deep learning, text analytics, graph/network analytics, and more.

> **Note:** No one would like to use a missile to kill a mosquito. Thus, the judicious involvement of general analytic team or special analytic team needs to be considered.

The organization must develop its analytic culture by developing generalist and specialists team. Different organizations need to have a different set of generalists and specialists; for example, optimization algorithm expertise is in high demand in manufacturing and logistics organizations as compared to other industries.

> **Note:** Each organization needs to build its team based on the demands it has. Do not hire specialists just because they exist. Incorporate the analytics as part of the corporate DNA.

Strategic Analytic Culture

Primarily, for an organization to build its analytics culture is to develop and build analytics team as a medical practice. What problems are you currently facing? What problem areas you would like to target? What analytics specialists do you need? How will they differentiate the existing capabilities of the team? How many generalists and multiple specialists are needed to create a power pack analytics culture to get the best answers? By appreciating the challenge and recognizing the need to look at your analytics organization in this different way, it will help you develop the analytic culture and adapt to today's new realities. Traditionally, every organization worked with the reactive and firefighting strategy. The moment they face the problems that moment onwards they began reacting to get the remedy of the problems. However, the result for such strategy ends with huge losses, delays, or even failures. In the analytic-driven culture, one must learn to prevent by predicting, as the reacting will not give a chance to prevent any more. The executive management of the organization must commit to building and sustaining the analytics culture. These people are responsible to set the analytics goals, hire people, and invest in technologies, people, and processes. Only enterprise-wide usage of analytics will push it to make it the part of the DNA of the corporate. Traditionally, organizations deal with the different category of reports varies from weekly, monthly, and ad-hoc formats, mostly helping them to take reactive decisions. Big data analytics changes the way the report is developed, projected, and displayed. Figure 1.5 shows the analytic maturity transformation that could be achieved by leveraging the analytical models and big data.

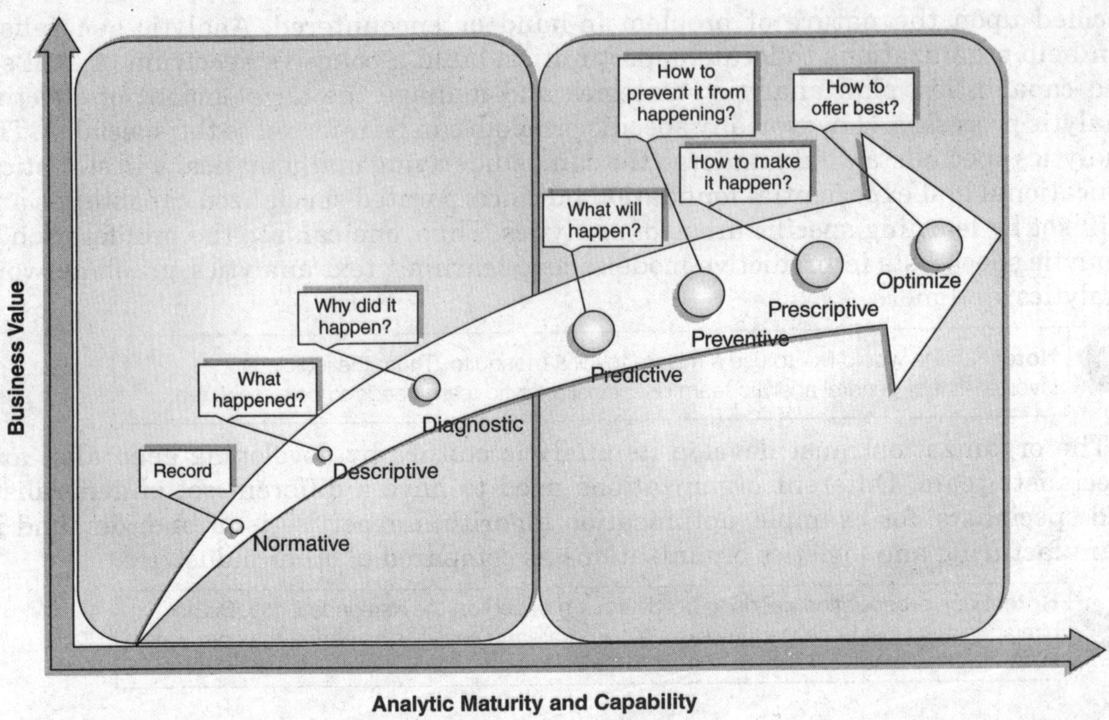

Fig. 1.5 Analytic maturity transformation

The journey to establish a sustainable analytics culture takes time, and one should embrace it as a marathon and not a sprint. Figure 1.6 illustrates that organization needs to think about building a strategic analytic culture as a phased and iterative journey.

- First, you must establish the critical and core processes, problems in context, enabling technologies, and the cultural and organizational changes required to move forward.
- In the integrate phase, you plan to introduce the analytic strategy and identify the projects to act on.
- In the deployment phase, the analytics solutions and models are deployed for the problems in context. This is being done after thorough testing and monitoring.
- In the optimize phase, data and analytics become an automated part of business processes. Executives can take action on results with a high degree of confidence because they know where the data and results are coming from.
- Once an optimized platform for automated, integrated analytics, and business processes are in place, it is time to innovate. Are there new data sources to add? New departments to bring on board? New business processes or service offerings to develop and test?
- In the propagation phase, the standardized analytics solutions and best practices for processes, problems, and context are widespread across the corporate DNA.

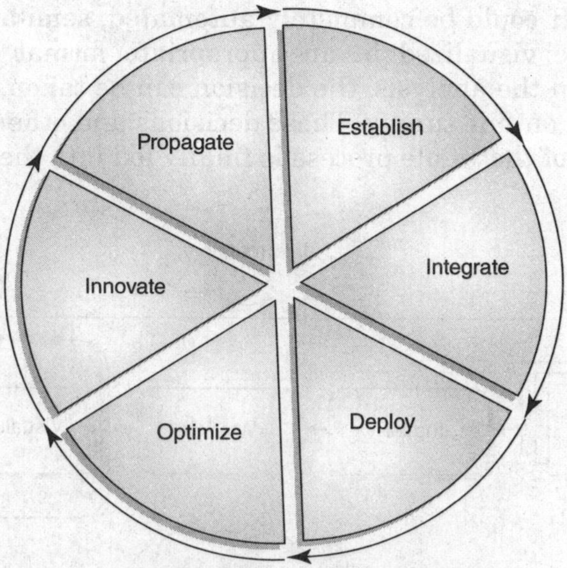

Fig. 1.6 Analytics culture cycle

The most likely result of the propagation phase is the need to return to the establish phase once it is determined that new technologies, goals, organizational, or cultural changes are needed.

1.4 BIG DATA MANAGEMENT ARCHITECTURE

> "*Architecture depends on its time. It is the crystallization of its inner structure, the slow unfolding of its form.*"
>
> —Ludwig Mies van der Rohe

LO 5 *Describe the big data management architecture*

One of the competing strategies for a successful Big Data company is to establish its Big data management architecture, information pioneered product pipeline (IPPP), and a value chain (IPPVC). IPPP reflects the pedagogical and mental model to understand the workflow of the information in IPP. The pipeline shown in Fig. 1.7 can be combined with other potential IPPPs or can work in isolation to deliver the meaningful and actionable decisions. In a typical analytical drive situation, various sources contribute the data. Data ingest comprises of the set of protocols, process, and rules to pull the relevant data from these sources for immediate use or to be stored in the distributed storage. After that, the raw set is converted to a compatible format by the wrangling processes. It could be completely automated, semi-automated, or manual. Later, the results are visualized in an appropriate format for the stakeholder's consumption. Based on the analysis, the decision can be taken, or further processing can be achieved based on fine tuning. These decisions and other relevant information that has emerged out of the whole process is finally fed into the IPPP.

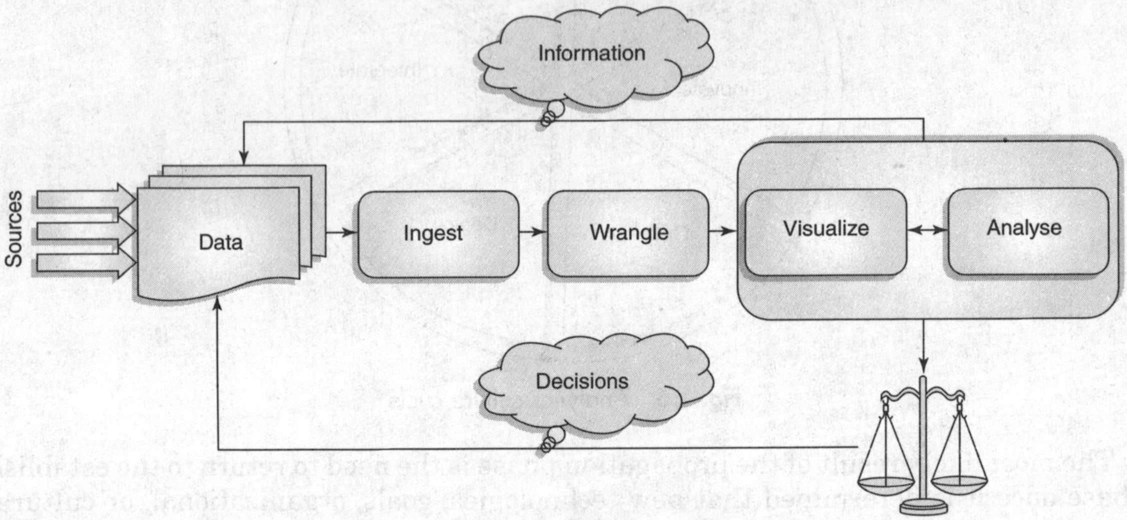

Fig. 1.7 Information pioneered product pipeline

Information Pioneered Product Value Chain

The information pioneered product value chain, shown in Fig. 1.8, recognizes the value activities—primary, secondary, and others required in the use of information to produce the actionable and valuable insights. The IPPVC set of primary activities refers to those activities, which help the organization in conceptualizing, designing, developing, marketing, testing, deploying, monitoring, and servicing the IPP. The secondary activities are required to support the primary activities in delivering the value to the stakeholders. These include storage, distribution, and processing. The set of others activities are not enterprise-wide applicable but could be utilized for specific contextual issues; for example, crowd innovation and crowdsourcing. Organization's infrastructure, policies, governance, management, and control mechanisms drive all the activities for successful execution and accomplishments.

Big Data-Big Way

By now, you must have got a perspective about the Big Data. Whether it is being utilized by the athlete to develop customized training regimes or by the company to derive targeted campaign for power savings, it should be converted to an insightful, valuable, and actionable decisions. We will try to focus now on what big data

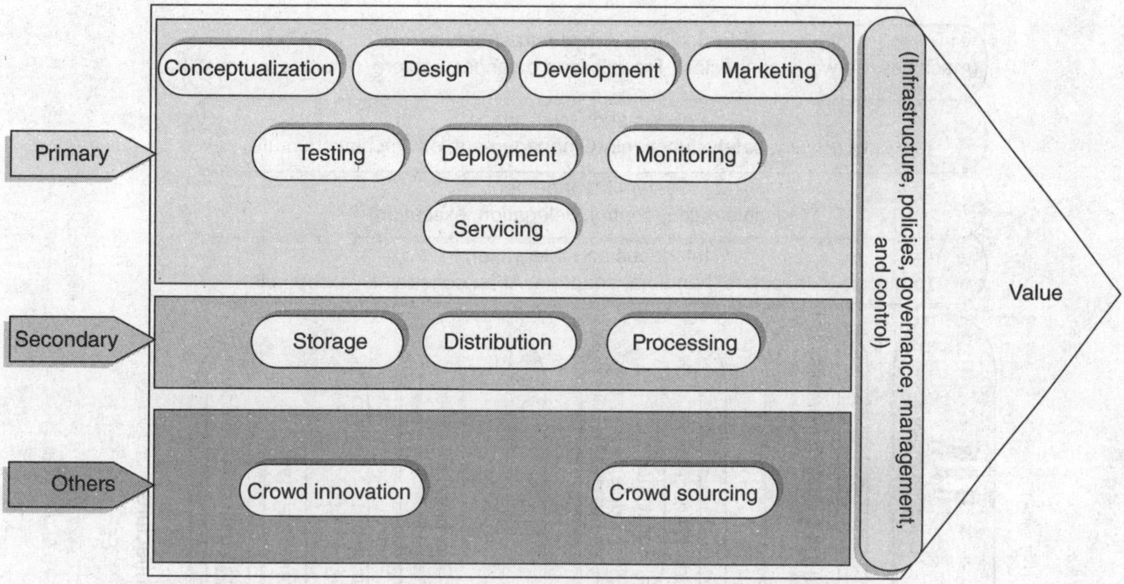

Fig. 1.8 Information pioneered product value chain

management means to us. To understand and work with the big data, one has to lay down the components of big data management architecture. Figure 1.9 shows the most typical components that are required to set up the fully functionally big data functional engine. The architecture is composed of two set of logical layers—horizontal and vertical layers.

Horizontal Layers

Horizontal layers comprise of four important layers:

1. **Sources:** This layer deals with the sources of data.
2. **Lookout:** In this layer, data is prepared for further processing.
3. **Analytics:** This layer is composed of two important parts: analytic engine and model management.
4. **Utilization:** In this layer, the result of the analytics layer is transformed for visualization, decision-making, and monitoring purpose.

Sources: This layer presents the entire data source required to solve the business problem. It is necessary for organizations to list and identify all the necessary sources of the data. It covers data sources such as structured, semi-structured, unstructured, geographical information, operational systems, data stores, internet of things; human generated content; data management system, legacy system, and aggregate data providers.

Lookout: This layer facilitates to load, convert, transform, and store the raw data to meaningful data for further processing.

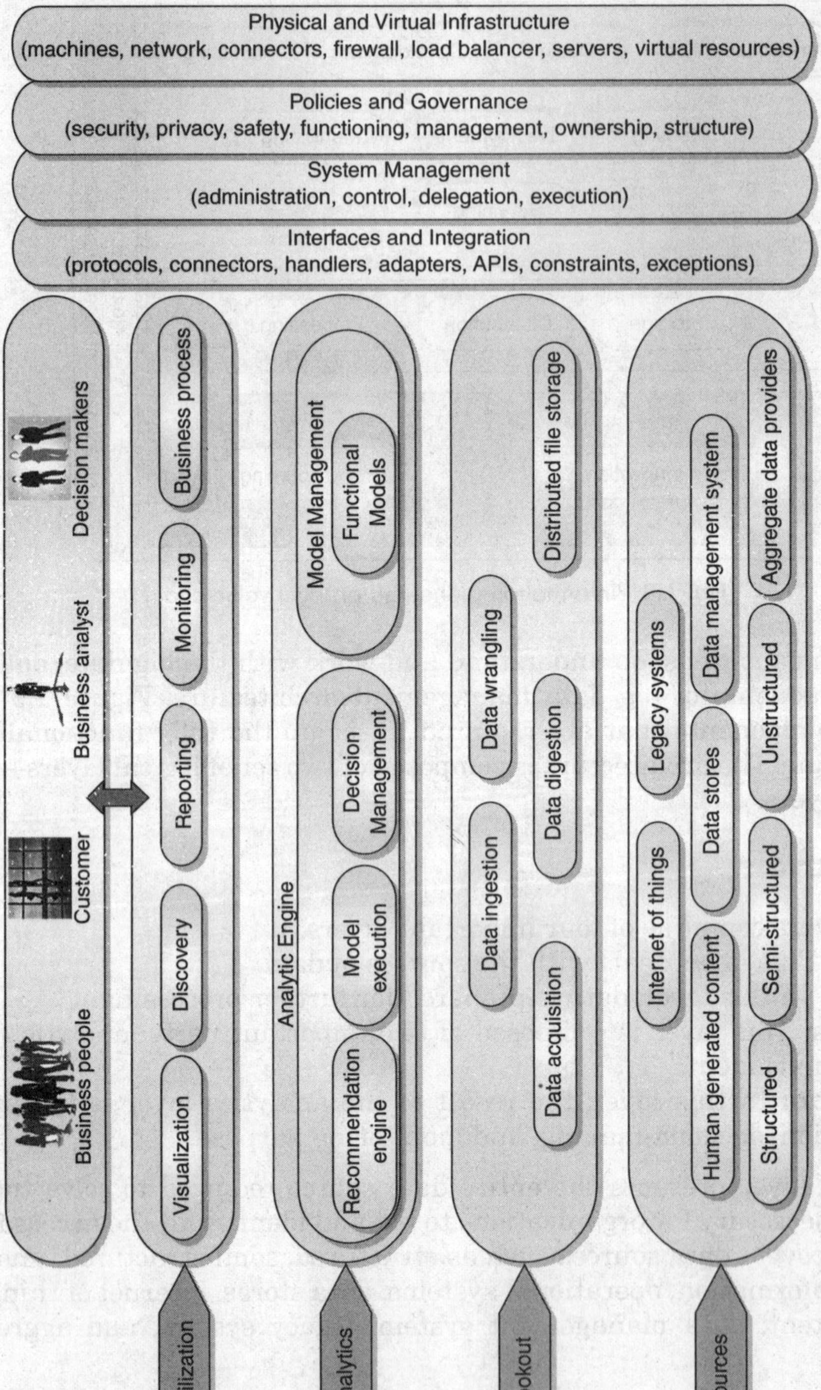

Fig. 1.9 Big Data Management Architecture

- ***Ingest*** To get the data into the data product that we are building or using
- ***Digest*** To convert the data into the correct format of usage
- ***Wrangle*** To select and transform data for further analysis
- ***Acquisition*** To gather data by keeping selective filters
- ***Distributed file storage*** To store data in distributed storage system (like HDFS)

Analytics: This layer facilitates the extraction of the actionable business insights. It is composed of two components—*analysis engine* and *model management*.

- ***Analysis engine*** It helps in processing and performing the analysis.
- ***Model management*** It manages various models such as statistical, machine learning, optimization, and simulation. It also contains processes to manage and control such models to achieve optimum efficiency and results.

Utilization: This layer consumes the actionable business insights from the analytics layer. Various applications are supported to present and display the appropriate value to various stakeholders. For example, CEO of a company would like to know the relevance of acquiring a new start-up to the company's asset portfolio. For that, he/she might have to understand the risk associated with it, and that can be understood by running the risk model for the prospective acquisition.

Vertical Layers

These layers refer to the set of layers that affect all the components of the logical horizontal layers.

1. Physical and virtual infrastructure
2. Policies and governance
3. System management
4. Interfaces and integration

Physical and virtual infrastructure: This layer acts as a supporting layer for the operation and scalability of the big data architecture. How one can develop and sustain without the availability of robust, reliable, and scalable physical and virtual infrastructure. Virtual infrastructure helps organizations to scale-in and scale-out on demand (on-premise cloud/off-premise cloud). The infrastructure must represent the different composition of the components to support parallel processing and distributed storage. This might include efficient management and usage of machines, network, connectors, firewall, load balancer, servers, and virtual resources. This layer should also support redundancy to provide timely availability of the resources. Your company can augment internal IT growth by leveraging the benefits of external cloud infrastructure.

Policies and governance: It refers to the set of rules, guidelines, and decisions to govern, control, manage, own, and disseminate processes, data, and information. Every company must elaborate the policies to protect sensitive and confidential data. The data that come from different sources, say Facebook data, might contain sensitive information about the identification of the user; it must be masked before you store, move, and process it without revealing such details. You must also adhere to the compliance and privacy policy of the data. For example, in a health industry where big data applications are used to maintain patient's demographics related to patient's need, training regimes, etc., should be made available to only those who have the authority to access such information, without compromising on the privacy of the patients. Various policies, rules, and guidelines must be developed for security, privacy, safety, functioning, management, ownership, and structure of data, processes, and organization.

System management: It deals with the management of various systems that pan across completely big data ecosystem for its effective functioning. Some of the key measures that organization needs to manage are as follows:

- logs coming from machines, applications, and people interaction to different systems and devices
- monitoring, tracking, and notifying resources
- key performance indices
- reporting and analytic solution
- development of models followed by testing, executing, deploying, and operationalizing it enterprise wide
- Service Level Agreements (SLAs) and Quality of Services (QoS)
- storage, scalability, capacity, and performance
- processes, systems, recovery, and remedies; management of clusters, virtual machines, and networks; and management of various policies.

Interfaces and integration: One needs data from various sources, and to do so various open application-programming interfaces are required. These APIs help to pull the data for further processing. For example, a social media company would be interested in understanding the sentiments of people on Twitter; and for that, it needs the 'tweets' for certain period. To fetch the 'tweets', it needs to use Twitter API which facilitates the company to pull all the relevant data, may be based on some hashtags. This layer facilitates other layers for the integration of data by providing relevant adapters, accelerators, connectors, APIs, and wrappers.

CASE STUDY: Smart Meter Smart Energy

Con Edison, a public company of New York, provides gas and electric power to the public. In the year 2015, it decides to deploy 4.7 million-unit smart meter to its entire jurisdiction with the planned overall $1.3 billion revenue. Smart meters are meant to gather and share more sophisticated data as compared to the traditional meters. It acts as a two-way communicator between the gas and electric central capacity/hub and the meter. Apart from measuring the

Fig. 1.10 Smart Meter

usage of gas and electric supply, it is capable of storing and sending the real-time usage data of the appliances in the house to which the smart meter is attached. Almost 1.5 billion data points are received daily at the central capacity for further processing. James Prettitore, director of technology services at Con Edison says, 'We're designing the system with advanced analytics in mind'. The performance of processing huge data with the central infrastructure results in output in the interval of 15 minutes or sometimes as short span of time such as five minutes. This means achieving the ingesting and processing around 10,416,667 data points per 15 minutes. Apart from using data point computation for the power usage billing, it also helps in

- identifying consumption patterns of the user regarding hourly usage. The consumption pattern identification of a consumer over a long period helps to deliver the right and the correct amount of power. It guides the consumers to use their calculators, to understand, to see how much energy their appliances use, thereby motivating them for saving money by simply making a few small choices throughout the day. It provides a calculator for lighting, programmable cooling, programmable heating, commercial energy, commercial lighting, and green usage.
- estimating the environment temperature for the consumption of power and energy.
- knowing and predicting the amount of power and energy for its consumers. This helps in strategizing the optimum economic balance in consuming the power and energy from the third party.

- categorizing the consumers so that targeted campaign for energy and power saving rebates and incentives could be executed. In one of the campaigns, they mentioned, 'We will pay you to temporarily reduce your electric usage. For every 100 kilowatts (kW) you reduce your usage of energy, you will be able to earn up to $18,000 a year. You can enrol either in 21 Hour Notifications, which ask you to reduce your usage 21 hours in advance, or in 2 Hour or fewer Notifications, which give you two hours of notice. Either way, by reducing your electric usage, you'll be helping maintain system reliability in your community.'

It can be seen that regardless of the huge amount of data and the computation required, the company is constrained by the fact that all the useful processing needs to be done within 15 minutes. This issue is not just about the multiple and huge data points rather the life-cycle of the insightful, valuable, and actionable decisions.

Questions

1. Which problem is big data helping to solve?

   Tip: Identify the use case scenarios for the gas and electric energy in the household. List down the requirements for the daily, weekly, monthly, quarterly, and yearly plan. Further, develop a list of challenges as consumers, producers, brokers, and regulators.

2. How is big data applicable in practice in gas and electric energy company?

   Tip: Map the use case scenarios of the electric and power energy with the business processes.

3. Which data is important for the power and energy company?

   Tip: Identify the context of data usage. Further, prioritize the use cases to gather the important type of data.

4. Which technology is being used to handle the power and energy data?

   Tip: Identity the primary, secondary, support, and other technological solutions.

5. What challenges does Con Edison need to overcome?

   Tip: Identify the journey of the stakeholders for electric and gas energy w.r.t. Con Edison. Further, map the journey with the milestones, goals, and setbacks.

6. Which patterns are effective for delivering gas and electricity power to the consumers?

   Tip: Identify the primary, secondary, support, and other use cases contributing to the underpinning assumption of 'Data and insight-driven decision' principle.

Reference

https://www.coned.com/en

SUMMARY

- Ours is a digital age generation that acts as a driving force towards the information revolution.
- The big data era is witnessing a big torrent of data flowing from the variety of sources.

- The data can be categorized into structured, semi-structured, and unstructured data.
- Any product that combines the capability of incorporating data and intelligent processes to generate meaningful and valued actionable decisions and associated information is considered as an information pioneered product.
- One of the key ingredients for the analytics revolution is the development of the analytics-driven culture.
- The analytics culture must nurture both 'Generalists' and 'Specialists'.
- The executive management of the organization must commit to building and sustaining the analytics culture.
- One of the competing strategies for a successful Big Data company is to establish its big data management architecture, information pioneered product pipeline, and a value chain.

EXERCISE

Review Questions

1. What is big data?

   Tip: Identify data around us and develop a taxonomy in terms of ownership, type, category, source, value, cost, time, effort, and issues.

2. Define dimensions of big data.

   Tip: Identify data around us and develop a taxonomy in terms of volume, velocity, variety, valence, value, and veracity.

3. Which important dimensions in big data are related to the following?
   — Social media
   — Finance
   — Agriculture
   — Automobile

   Tip: Identify use cases of each domain and related data usage. Develop a taxonomy in terms of dimensions—volume, variety, velocity, valence, value, and volume. Consider data generated based on the involvement—people-to-people, people-to-machine, machine-to-people, and machine-to-machine.

4. Explain the type of big data solutions for entertainment industry, journalism industry, automobile industry, and education industry.

   Tip: Identify use case interaction point for different domains. Further, develop interaction category in terms of software, hardware, and hybrid.

5. Give examples of information pioneered product in healthcare, finance, and mining industry.

   Tip: Identify use cases for information pioneered product for different domains—healthcare, finance, and mining industry. Perform the Google search for the important use case based product or services.

6. Explain the functioning of IPPP and IPPVC in healthcare, finance, and mining industry.

   Tip: Check the functioning of IPPP and IPPVC. Identify primary, secondary, support, and other use cases for different domains—healthcare, finance, and mining industry. Develop the IPPP and IPPVC.

7. 'New age journalism is different from the traditional journalism.' Justify the statement by citing and explaining different situations and examples in relation to big data technology and solutions.

   Tip: Check the development in the data and insight driven news contributing towards new age journalism.

8. What data are important for 'Smart home' solutions? Categorize the data into structured, semi-structured, and unstructured data.

   Tip: Check the functioning and use case for each of the 'Smart home' elements. Develop the category on the basis of data usage, data process, data results, and data metrics.

9. Do you think that elections nowadays are driven by data-based decisions? Explain the benefits and usage of big data solutions in deciding the fate of the candidate in the elections.

   Tip: Develop the 'election' information [big data] stakeholders, information product pipeline, and information product value chain. Describe the use cases that affect various categories of stakeholders and decisions.

10. How establishment of the big data architecture influences the corporates?

    Tip: Refer to the big data architecture and map each layer with the corporate's primary, secondary, support and other resources, and stakeholders. List down the use cases in each layer with respect to resources/stakeholders.

Exercise Case

The Fall of the Empire

One of the notably defaulter cases that has emerged in the recent past is of Mr Vijay Mallya. He owned Kingfisher Airlines, which was started in the year 2005 as the India's most premium domestic airlines. The airline under his ownership placed aggressive plane orders such as the Airbus A380 and bought low-fare carrier Air Deccan. However, plans backfired in the face of rising fuel costs, fierce competition and debt raised to fund its reckless expansion plans. In October 2012, workers reported of unpaid salaries; they decided to strike the work and protest for months. This resulted in the suspension of airlines' licence. Kingfisher owes $1billion to Indian banks, several hundred crores to airports, tax authorities, suppliers, and salaries of more than 3000 employees before airlines shut down.

A consortium of 17 banks led by the State Bank of India registered a case against Vijay Mallya for default of Rs. 9000 crores loan. It was notified to the judiciary that the loan was not paid to them since 2012. 'On March 8, 2016, the consortium of banks moved the Supreme Court to stop Mallya from leaving the country before repaying the loan.' However, before any action to be taken against him, he had already left the country on March 2.

Based on the complaint of the IDBI bank, the Central Bureau of Investigation (CBI) registered a case in the loan default case in July 2015. Further to the registered complaint, CBI court issued a non-bailable warrant against Mallya for the loan default case.

In one of the court hearings, the Attorney General (AG) said that 'Mallya has assets, both movable and immovable abroad, which are far in excess of the loans secured by him in the country. At this, the bench wanted to know how the banks granted him loan under such circumstances.' The AG specified that due to the presence of the fleet of aircraft for the Kingfisher Airlines as well as brand value and logo, the loans were given. In further clarifications, it was stated that, 'it is permissible to grant loans on intangible assets' when Justice Joseph sought clarifications for the banks about the grant of loans when 'pledged assets had only one-tenth or one-fifteenth of the value of loan'.

Questions

1. Is validating a loan applicant a data-driven decision?

   Tip: Identify usage of data, use cases, risk cases, and processes in validating a loan application.

2. What are the factors that are important for a bank to give loan to the applicant?

   Tip: List down few people in your friends and family network. Develop persona of people based on [an individual's] loan repayment capacity, earnings, savings, daily/weekly/monthly/quarterly/yearly expenditure, interest and hobbies, age, qualification, number of dependents, experiences, any open loans, livelihood, etc.

3. Why did banks give the loan to Kingfisher Airlines?

   Tip: List the factors for which the Kingfisher Airlines was known for in the market. Further, map each element with the loan liability and repayment capability.

4. Do you think that a loan to a potential defaulter like Mr Vijay Mallya, for Kingfisher Airline, could be avoided?

   Tip: Identify sources of data other than the company's data conveying its culture, growth [and fall], goals, contributions, sentiments, opinions, brand, etc. Further, develop use case scenarios for formal and informal database validation.

References

http://epaperbeta.timesofindia.com/Article.aspx?eid=31818&articlexml=Wind-up-Kingfisher-Airlines-says-HC-19112016004032 [accessed April 26, 2017];

http://www.financialexpress.com/industry/how-did-defaulter-vijay-mallya-get-loan-supreme-court/221736/ [accessed April 26, 2017];

http://www.livemint.com/Companies/smvfjlMWKkl5aX6RZo9MiK/The-cases-against-Vijay-Mallya-and-Kingfisher-Airlines.html [accessed April 26, 2017];

http://indianexpress.com/article/india/vijay-mallya-arrested-london-scotland-yard-cbi-extradition-pmla-loan-default-4618389/ [accessed April 26, 2017]

2 Big Data Ethics

> *"It is a capital mistake to theorize before one has data. Insensibly, one begins to twist the facts to suit theories, instead of theories to suit facts."*
>
> —Adventure I. A Scandal in Bohemia, p. 163

Learning Objectives

On completing this chapter, you will be able to:

- **LO 1** Understand the concept of ethical inquiry
- **LO 2** Describe the big data stakeholders
- **LO 3** Comprehend the big data industry
- **LO 4** Analyse the big data ethical elements
- **LO 5** Apply big data ethical framework
- **LO 6** Perform big data ethics test
- **LO 7** Execute big data audit

CASE STUDY: Humans as 'Social Subjects'

The plethora of social media platform made human life simple in terms of sharing views, opinions, photos, videos, feedback, and reviews. The technology helps people to build and create a social, virtual, and powerful network to connect with people and provide and get updates. However, what if we unknowingly become the 'subjects' of exploration on the lookout of data surge?

Facebook is a popular social media service launched in the year 2004. The registration to this service is easy. Anyone who is aged 13 or older can become a user of Facebook services. Based on the minimum age requirement, Facebook also has some variation in registering the users based on the local laws.

© Thinkstock.com

Fig. 2.1 People interacting on a social media platform

One can access the Facebook service through a variety of devices over the Internet and mobile networks. Once registered to the Facebook, a user is allowed to create his/her profile indicating his/her name, occupation, school attended, and so on. Each user can add other users as 'friends', post status updates, exchange messages, use chat services, share photos and digital videos and links, and use various other associated applications. They also receive notifications when others update their profile, status, or make posts. Users can create and join groups. These groups help users to share and discuss common topics, themes, and agendas.

As of March 31, 2017, Facebook has more than 1.94 billion active monthly users. This results in the generation of massive data. Facebook allows an individual user to set the privacy settings and who can see specific parts of their profile. It generates most of its revenue through advertising such as banner ads. Everyone can access user's name and profile picture at the Facebook site.

Facebook conducted a psychological experiment in the year 2011-2012 on the big data generated by the 7,00,000 people. The main aim of the experiment was to identify whether the company could alter the emotional state of its users—positive or negative. It was also designed in a way to assess whether increased positive or negative comments to the user's page (newsfeed) would affect how the user would update the page or make posts. On such massive data, Facebook applied an intelligent algorithm to filter content and perform the deep analysis. The experiment resulted in displaying that more negative comments generate more negative comments and vice versa. The findings of the experiment later published in the Proceedings of the National Academy of Sciences, USA. The company stated that the experiment was legitimate, as all users had to sign the terms and conditions, including consenting to '*internal operations*, *including troubleshooting*, *data analysis*, *testing*, *and research and service improvement*'.

However, the experiment backfired and Facebook received lots of criticism. In a blogpost on 2 October, 2014, Mike Schroepfer, Chief Technology Officer, said the company was 'unprepared' for the negative reactions it received when it published the findings of the psychological experiment. He also stated that in releasing the study, we failed to communicate clearly, why and how we did it. He also proposed guidelines on how to approach research at Facebook.

Questions

1. What services does Facebook provide to its users?

   Tip: Check the Facebook website for the kind of services that it is offering.

2. How can a user get the benefits by setting the privacy controls?

   Tip: List down the features or privacy controls by accessing Facebook's setting feature—website, mobile site, and application.

3. What challenges did Facebook face by performing the psychological experiment?

   Tip: Identify the use case scenarios of the psychological experiment and its impact on the associated stakeholders [more specifically, registered members/users].

4. What are the privacy and right implications on the social media platform? How does Facebook exercise them?

   Tip: Check the Facebook website and blogs to find out its guidelines to perform research. The company has guidelines on how to approach research at Facebook.

5. What could have been done in a different way to avoid backfire from the experiment?

   Tip: Find out the scenarios responsible for the backfiring. List down the points and the action plan to run the experiment successfully.

6. What ethical issues are raised due to the experiment?

   Tip: Refer to the chapter and list down the ethical dilemmas, issues, and concerns considering the stakeholders.

References

'Research at Facebook'. https://newsroom.fb.com/news/2014/10/research-at-facebook/ [accessed May 21, 2017];
'Information for Parents and Educators'. Facebook. [accessed online May 21, 2017];
'Company Info - Facebook Newsroom'. Facebook. [accessed online May 21, 2017];
'Search Privacy'. Facebook. [accessed online May 21, 2017];
Barton, Zoe (April 28, 2006). 'Facebook goes corporate'. ZDNet News. Archived from the original on May 26, 2008. Retrieved March 9, 2008.

> "*In God we trust. All others must bring data.*"
>
> —W. Edwards Deming

LO 1 *Understand the concept of ethical inquiry*

Ethical inquiry helps organizations to strengthen their philosophical thinking and inquiry. This inquiry, in turn, breaks the barriers for growth and success, thereby creating a sustainable and ethical culture.

We live in a mystical world where all are connected—inter-intra-societal and cultural in some way or the other. We release, exchange, reflect—energy, vibrations, wavelength, frequency, and more importantly emotions. Ethical inquiry, in relation to big data, will help the organizations to evolve big data technology and transform them into powerful, effective, and robust set of tools that can help us live better—ethically and sustainably. Big data ecosystem, as we have seen in Chapter 1, is transforming the society in which we live today. Big data is massive, and technology around us is expanding and evolving to create, connect, correlate, aggregate, store, pre-process, process and report. This wave can push us to consider its ethical nature including its implications such as societal, political, civil, and legal. We have to explore and develop the capability to engage ourselves in understanding situations. It will be only possible when we perform ethical inquiries in new ways and contexts.

2.1 BIG DATA STAKEHOLDERS

LO 2 *Describe the big data stakeholders*

People are optimistic about sharing their opinions, views, and feelings on social media platforms. They often compromise on their privacy to get features and services from the big data applications. In the hyper-connected society, the concept

> There exist five power zones each representing different stakeholder—**Collector, Utilizer, Generator, Regulator,** and **Broker.**

of power, which is more related to the dynamics of ethics, has been changing by the just mere inclusion of the networked systems. One might face a huge challenge in retaining one's own agency, i.e., knowledge and ability to act. The power of big data is shared among its stakeholders. Normally, there exist five power zones each representing different stakeholder—Collector, Utilizer, Generator, Regulator, and Broker, see Fig. 2.2.

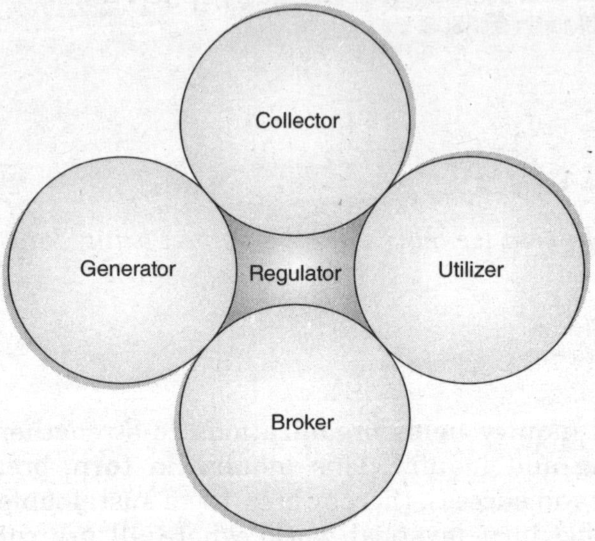

Fig. 2.2 Big data stakeholders

Big Data Collector

It determines *'what data needs to be collected'* and *'what data sources are needed to collect the data'*. It is also responsible for creating, using, and executing relevant policies to collect the data from the data sources. These data could be structured, semi-structured, or unstructured. The collector is also responsible for determining the lifetime of the data; for example, how long to store the data. The collector may or may not have a stake or any specific purpose for the collected data.

Big Data Utilizer

It is responsible for giving meaning and purpose to the collected data so that it can be used for a specific purpose. Utilizer can redefine the data set or mix it with the existing or other relevant data sets to achieve the competitive advantage. An insurance company might collaborate with a hospital for the patient data. In this way, the company can redesign or offer specific insurance schemes to the patients.

Fig. 2.3 Big data collector

Big Data Generator

A generator is any actor that contributes to the generation of data. This data could be generated by keeping informed the actor or otherwise. An actor knowingly or unknowingly participates in the contribution of the data. For example, Big Bazaar is a major retail store in India, which offers multiple brand products to its customers. It has several outlets across India in various cities. The customer gets very good offerings in the products with competitive pricing as well. Big Bazaar collects the customer data through customers' buying card. This card stores the transaction details of each customer who opts for the card. This huge set of data helps Big Bazaar to plan their inventory at various outlets and also helps in providing special discounts to the customers.

Big Data Regulator

It is responsible for setting the rules, directives, and guidelines that govern the data policy across the data jurisdiction. For example, the collector should not violate the rules established by the regulator to collect the consumers' data. Though the regulator's work is challenging and demanding, it is the need of the hour. Regulator needs to safeguard the policies and interest and regulate considering the state-of-the art technologies. A regulator may impart privacy policy on the data set but it also should not ignore the privacy on the aggregated set of data sets. For example, Cynthia Dwork clearly stated that 'regulators and businesses should not look at systems to protect privacy in isolation as when different data sets brought together or analysed over time, new privacy challenges may emerge.' Certainly, there is no harm in collecting the data about an individual like me in this situation—*'buying a loaf of bread'*. However, over a period, this data set starts reflecting the part of my profile; and in case if I stop buying a loaf of bread, then it can be concluded that I may have diabetes.

Big Data Broker

The one who knows everything about you and sells this information to the one who pays more to it is referred to as *broker*. According to Julie Brill, an ex-commissioner on the Federal Trade Commission views that brokers share just about everything; for example: 'It's what web pages we visit, where we're shopping, who we're interfacing with on social media—all of this information is available to be collected by entities that park themselves on various websites'. In the Newsweek article, Paul Boutin shares the secret world of selling the data by the brokers. He states that 'While many brokers claim, probably honestly, to only provide publicly available information that can be used to verify someone's identity or prevent fraud, there's a fast-growing market for what's called "consumer scores". Instead of a straight list of names, addresses, and other info, a consumer score is a computer-generated number that attempts to predict your likelihood to get sick or to pay off a debt.'

2.2 BIG DATA INDUSTRY

LO 3
Comprehend the big data industry

In his seminal research article in MIS Quarterly Executive, Martin proposes to analyse big data as the *'Big data industry'*. This perspective helps organizations and businesses to identify any systemic risks in current big data practices. It enables one to look its big data as a part of a system that includes other stakeholders of big data, processes, and norms to work with the data. We have discussed the information pioneered product value chain in Chapter 1. The information pioneered product value chain, as a big data industry, can be analysed both by the downstream distribution and use of big data as well as by the upstream sourcing, see Fig. 2.4.

In Fig. 2.4, the firm that is dealing with the big data can be any stakeholder amongst one of the big data stakeholders. In the downstream, this firm, as a big data industry, connects with the bidirectional flow of services and information with the other stakeholders. Similarly, it connects the other stakeholders in the upstream and exchanges the service and information in turn for the overall objective to generate the value.

Now, we will discuss the benefits and issues related to the downstream and upstream stakeholders and see how it affects the big data industry as a whole.

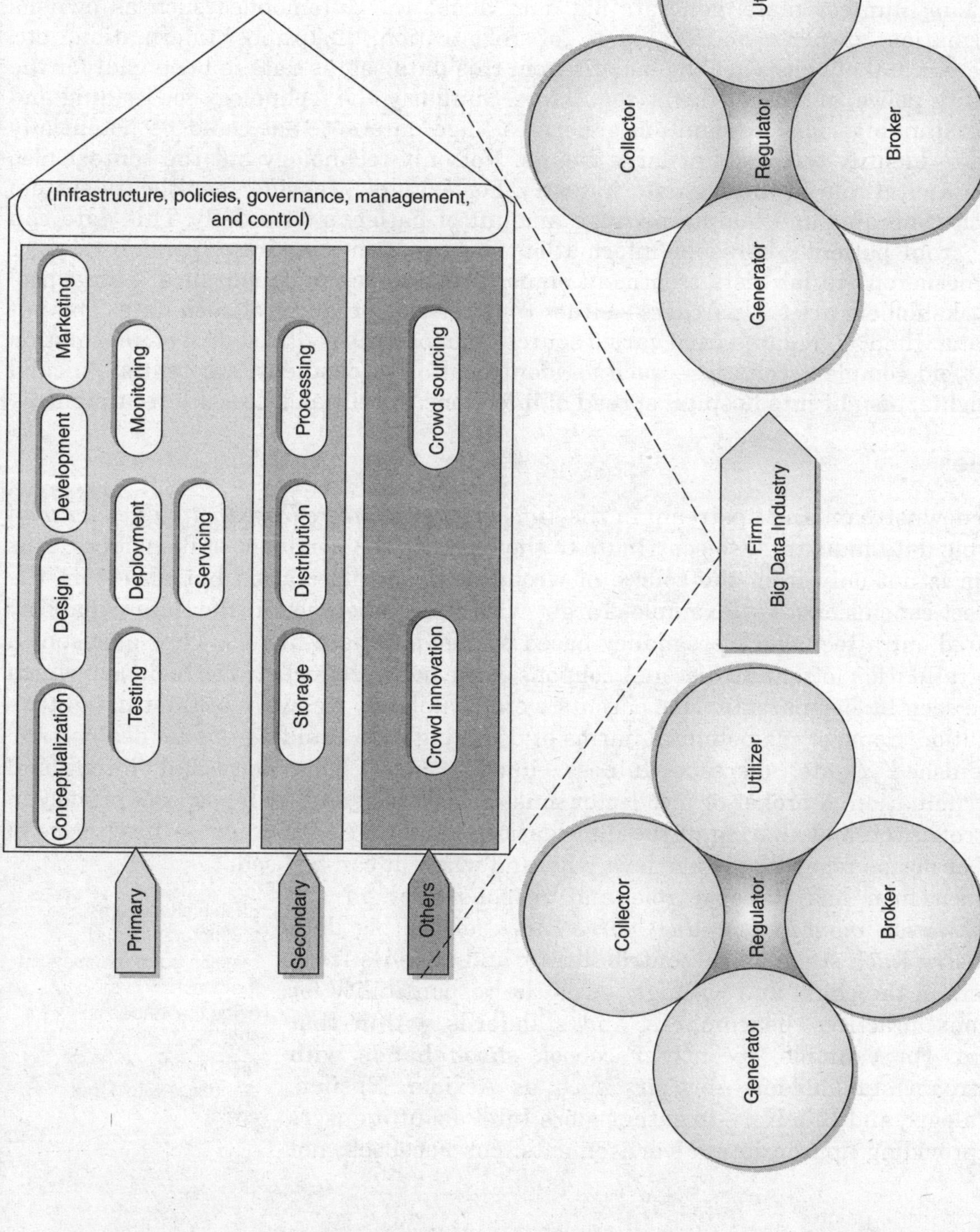

Fig. 2.4 Big data industry value chain

Benefits

The technology around the big data provides the customers and other prominent stakeholders variety of use cases. For example, the technology to read and manage licensing number plate, generate big data about the automobiles such as owner's information, owner's address, date of registration, insurance information, etc. Different stakeholders get the benefit from this data set, as data is beneficial for the Tollway, police, and other traffic regulators. Similarly, the technology for reading and understanding facial recognition generates huge data set that could be potentially used to identify terrorists at large events. Not only technology but the context also plays a vital role in the big data industry. For example, consider healthcare system which generates and maintains huge amount of patient's data daily. This data can vary from patient's personal information such as name, address, gender, disease, diagnosis reports, lab tests, treatment plans, drug dosages, and insurance. A large pool of stakeholders are the partners—either consumer or producer of such data. This set of data, when aggregated from varied sources, can become a vital source of information to unfold complex scenarios—such as identification of candidate's potential suicidal thoughts; insight into hospital spread of infections; potential successful treatments.

Issues

The downstream and upstream in the '*information pioneered product value chain*' of the big data industry also contribute to the harm to the pertinent stakeholders. This harm is not only from the source of wrong or false information but also from the correct conclusions. For example, Target with its competency in the data capability figured out a teenager's pregnancy based on her purchase history. They also sent a congratulation letter and discount coupons of the baby products to the teenager, which were seen by her parents. Her parents were completely unaware of their daughter's situation. Some of the potential harms of using big data could be—value destruction, diminished rights, disrespectfulness, unempathetic behaviour, and intentional discrimination. A broker or a collector must be assessed on how it respects privacy in the collection and sharing of the information. This information always has 'terms of use' or norms regarding when, how, why, and where it can be used.

Each firm has its own role and responsibility in the '*information pioneered product value chain*' of the big data industry. Each stakeholder contributes to, and benefits from, others in the chain and willingly owns the responsibility for actions, practices, benchmarks, and standards within that chain. For example, recently Facebook shook hands with upstream stakeholders—brokers such as Acxiom, Epsilon, Datalogix, and BlueKai—to gather more Intel about its users for providing appropriate advertisements. For Facebook, not

Each stakeholder contributes to, and benefits from, others in the chain and willingly owns the responsibility for actions, practices, benchmarks, and standards within that chain.

only they have to worry about their collection methods but also the methods used by the upstream for the collections of the user's data.

The firm, as a big data industry, needs to be little cautious about its presence and activities in the '*Big data industry value chain*'. The firm can easily monitor and control the ways, roles, and responsibilities of working with the big data inside its value chain but has little or no control over upstream and downstream sources. This is a major challenge and creates ethical dilemma. Figure 2.5 provides the 4-quadrant view for the ethical issues of the firm involved in the big data industry. Quadrant A presents the issues that a firm is involved with in its value chain when dealing with the data. On the other side, quadrant B represents upstream issues and quadrant D represents downstream issues. Quadrant C views some of the major issues when a firm is viewed as a part of a bigger system.

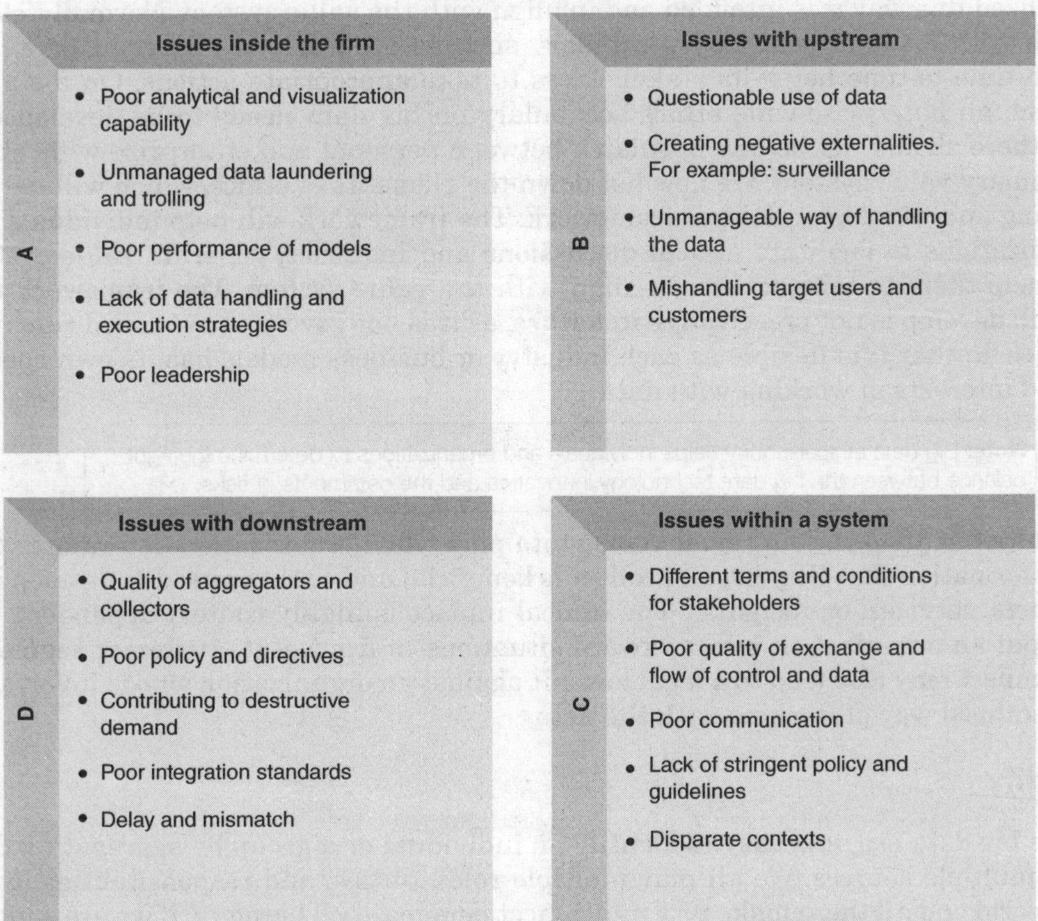

Fig. 2.5 Ethical Issues Quadrant for big data industry

> *"People must have righteous principles in the first, and then they will not fail to perform virtuous actions."*
>
> —Martin Luther

2.3 BIG DATA ETHICS ELEMENTS

LO 4 *Analyse the big data ethical elements*

Big data is ethically neutral as it does not provide any *'standardized'* value framework. However, individuals and organizations do have value systems; otherwise, we would not have witnessed the *'society'*. It is by only asking the ethical questions, which might put individuals and organizations in uncomfortable situations, we can ensure that big data is utilized in a way it is intended and in align with the value system. Normally, ethics comes with loads of polarized vocabulary such as good or bad and right or wrong, which time-to-time helps its stakeholders to take appropriate actions. On a similar ground, an enterprise-wide ethics vocabulary on big data needs to be developed so that there should not be any mismatch between personal and enterprise-wide ethics vocabulary value system. We now list down the elements of ethics, which will help us to bring and develop an ethical framework. The framework will help individuals and organizations to facilitate ethical discussions and inquiries, generate value system, and help them to take actions in align with the value system. The framework that we will develop is not prescriptive in nature, as it is not governed by stoned rules and policies. Rather it is flexible as each industry or business models has its own specific vested interests in working with data.

> **Note:** Big data ethical inquiry helps individuals and organizations to determine the right balance between the big data technology innovation and the detriments of risks.

Ethics has its own journey; it comes into play when organization determines that the information that they have or collect is beneficial and could be used to develop new products, services, or insights. The ethical impact is highly context-dependent and may put an organization into awkward situations in front of its customer segments. The impact may also lead to a legal lawsuit against an organization who is involved in an unethical way of working with the data.

Identity

In the big data era, it is easy to identify an individual or a group by aggregating data from multiple sources. We all play multiple roles, duties, and responsibilities in the real world and all these make us a multi-facet personality. Therefore, if we are a multi-facet personality, then we might also have a multi-valued ethical system. Mapping of such multi-facet physical personality to our virtual world needs deep and effective technological advancements. 'Identity' in a virtual world is surfacing and getting attention from all fields of studies and practice. 'What I buy online?', 'How I buy online', 'How often I buy online?' contributes to my digital trail and digital pattern and the data from disparate sources when combined my "identity" are revealed. How will our right to identity, our right to say, 'I am', fare in the big data era? With even the most basic access to a combination of big data pools such as phone records, surfing history, buying history, social networking posts, and others, 'I am' and 'I like' risk becoming 'you are' and 'you will like'. Every Google user is already influenced by big-data-fed feedback loops from Google's tailored search results, which risk producing individual and collective echo chambers of thought. In his article, *How Netflix Is Turning Viewers into Puppets*, Andrew Leonard explains how

> 'The companies that figure out how to generate intelligence from that data will know more about us than we know ourselves, and will be able to craft techniques that push us toward where they want us to go, rather than where we would go by ourselves if left to our own devices.' (Andrew, 2013)

Nevertheless, without developing any protections for big data identity now, no one can avoid the transformation of 'you are', 'you will like' to 'you cannot' and 'you will not'. The big data has a great power to use information in varied contexts such as—to nudge, to persuade, to influence, and even to restrict our identities.

Privacy

We keep discussing the power of big data now and then, but we also must look deep into its other factors such as privacy. In one of the sessions, the students of MBA were asked, 'How do you feel about compromising your privacy when you use digital services or applications like social media?' In addition, you will all be amazed to know the answer of the young generation and prospective managers. They mentioned, 'Exposing privacy, in turn, helps us to get better services; so, we have no issues'. Not only is the technology changing but also the people's mindset is changing. A funny cartoon that appeared in the New York Times specifying—*canines at the keyboard whose caption read*: *'On the Internet, nobody knows you are a dog'*. Though at that time it was so funny, now if we relook at it then we can have far more details about who is interacting. For example, considering the cartoon analogy, we now not only know that you are a dog but also what breed you are, your favourite snacks and whether you appeared on any dog show. Sometimes, people would like to keep their information private; then, in that case, a serious ethical question might arise: *'what right other people have to make it public?'* The mere creation of an artistic work provides its creator grant of extensive rights due to the presence of a strong creative act. Then, why not the creator of a data—for example, people by default—get such extensive rights naturally. Two important questions are important for ethical inquiry with regard to the privacy: is privacy similar in both offline and online mode?; what level of control do people have about their creation of 'data' and thereby themselves? Two decades back, we lived in anonymity; most of us do live but now with big data technology innovation it is changing. The goal of ethical inquiry here is to understand how to create a balance between innovation and risks inherent in that.

Our present and past could transform to the transparent frame to the intruders and hackers alike as we indulge ourselves in the cyber reality, which in turn to mirror our life in the virtual world (Beeger, 2013). The NSA files stated that Raytheon (a U.S. Defence contractor) developed the Rapid Information Overlay Technology (RIOT) software, which gathers freely accessible data from social networks and data associated with an IP address, etc. This helps in profiling the individuals (The Guardian, 2013).

Propensity

The movie *Minority Report* portrayed the vision of the future. The whole movie was all about predicting what people were likely to do and then they were incarcerated without an act committed. Though it looked terrifying, the future might not be that bad; but we can witness '*predictive policing*' in the cities like Los Angeles, where Big Data analytics point to certain streets, gangs or individuals, who are more likely to commit a crime, in order to have them subjected to extra surveillance (Perry et al., 2013). People will criticize if the police won't prevent the situation where a person is more likely to commit a murder. Such kind of problems fall under the political parameter. The society would expect that person to be incarcerated just like the dramatic incarceration in the movie. In another situation, if a Big Data reveals that a certain person living in certain neighbourhood (e.g., with no job, no money, no car, no family, etc.) has a likelihood of 96% to be involved in domestic violence, then social welfare organization can ask its social workers to control and monitor such kind of person. In situation like this, such act cannot be treated as imprisoning an individual. This might cause stigma to the family, friends, and neighbourhood. Furthermore, it also raises questions about the ethical role of those setting the intervention threshold and the data scientists developing the intelligent algorithms that calculate the chance based on certain variables available in the big data pool. One must understand the likely consequences of running the algorithms on the data set.

Ownership

We have seen the information pioneered values chain and stakeholders' involvement to generate the value. Since no single entity works with the data, data ownership is scattered and is more like non-exclusive and flexible ownership right in datasets. An individual can ask to override the economic interests, which we can understand by a notable case as follows:

> *The recent case of Google Spain and Google Inc v Agencia Espanola de Proteccion de Datos of Mario Costeja Gonzalez, decided by the Court of Justice of the European Union in May 2014, made it clear that an individual has the right to request the removal of information from an internet search engine which relates to that individual, and that the individual's right to data protection 'will override the economic interest' (i.e., the property right) 'of the operator of the search engine'.*

The article further explained that

> *'You might say there are competing economic interests in the same piece of personal information: the internet search engine has a right "in rem" (against the rest of the world) in connection with the investment it has made in the collection, arrangement, and accessibility of its Big Data. The individual, on the other hand, has a right "in personam" to require the "in rem" rightsholder to modify the contents of its Big Data insofar as the information relates to him. In addition, the in personam right will usually trump the in rem right. In these circumstances, it can be seen how tenuous the ownership rights of the Big Data rightsholder turn out to be. It is intriguing how little control businesses have over what can be their most prized asset. An illustration of this phenomenon was given when Facebook sought to change the rules it applied for the use of the personal information of its users last year. There was an outcry from its user base which threatened to leave the site en masse. In other words, Facebook faced the evaporation of its Big Data and, potentially, its very existence. In the face of this threat, Facebook took the only rational course open to it and retreated on the proposed change to its usage policy.'*

Source: https://www.taylorwessing.com/globaldatahub/article_big_data_ownership.html [accessed May 29, 2017]

Reputation

'*Who am I*' is not about our personal identity but also what people—specifically those who knew and frequently interacted with us—knew and thought about us. In the big data era, it is very difficult to control one's reputation by oneself as the data is not limited to the control of an individual. On an average, 500 million tweets are touched among various stakeholders and reputation of many are transformed by these tweets. Our old way of making, storing, and restoring reputation will not work in the digital era; rather a different thinking and management are needed. This also led us to develop ethical inquiry in building and maintaining reputations.

2.4 BIG DATA ETHICAL FRAMEWORK

LO 5
Apply big data ethical framework

We are now going to develop our 'big data ethical framework'. This framework, shown in Fig. 2.6, will help you and your organization to unfold ethical inquires, decision points, and ethical actions in align with the core value system to develop and manage products and services utilizing big data technologies. The framework provides you a set of tools to get very specific about your values in align with your specific context of interest. It provides you a starting step, a platform to perform ethical inquiries and take tactical actions.

> The ethical framework will help you and your organization to unfold ethical inquires, decision points, and ethical actions in align with the core value system to develop and manage products and services utilizing big data technologies.

Fig. 2.6 Ethical Framework

Inquiry

It helps individuals and organizations to discover and discuss their core values. A forum or a specific task team can look into attributing these factors. Once the factors attributing the big data ethics are identified, then those could be discussed at the leadership level followed by all organizational levels to get the consensus. There might be a situation where the concerned members of the task force need to perform the trade-offs. Once done with the trade-offs, a final consensus is sought among all. It results in generating ethical inquiry system that provides an understanding of *what our values are* and *not what we think they are*.

Analysis

At this phase, a specialized team has to review the current practices that are being followed for managing, controlling, and dealing with the big data and big data technologies. This team must understand the core value system of the organization and its purpose is to identify gaps, if any, by executing the reviews. The team can perform data-oriented audits to unfold any flaws and gaps in the current practices. A customization, modification, or alteration could be recommended in the current practices in align with the core values of the organization.

Delivery

In this phase, artefacts, documents, guidelines, and directives are formulated and delivered to the leadership team to deliberate and debate on the pathway to approach the value system. The team here really stresses upon the issues related to 'what is the current values system?' and 'whether the current practices are in align with the values system or not'. The goal here is to develop a roadmap covering principles and 'what an organization is going to do'.

Strategize

Each organization is different as it is affected by many factors in the context such as circumstances, culture, market, organization size, economic conditions, purpose, capabilities, and vast array of other factors. Thus, one size fits all does not make any sense and an organization needs to develop core strategies in align with its value system. Here, companies can also look at 'offensive' and 'defensive' strategies for establishing ethical practices and system. An 'offensive' strategy helps organization to pursue changes within to keep itself ahead in the competitive world; whereas, 'defensive' strategy makes an organization to develop its core set of data-oriented practices in align with the value system.

Action

In this step, the organization charters its action plan based on the strategies identified in the previous step. Four major action points need to be developed at this step: first, organizational alignments in action, business practices, individual behaviours on the values system, and anticipated outcomes. These action points help organization to detail out 'how one can achieve the value system'. It provides a way where an explicit ethical inquiry could transform the business in align with the value system.

Execution

This is the final step in the framework and the outcome of this step is again fed back to the first step (i.e., inquiry). In this step, the deployment and execution of the action plan are established. The best practices are transformed and benchmarks are developed in align with the value system. Nothing can persist forever; thus, the outcome of this needs to be propagated back to the inquiry step to make a cycle of a continuous innovation on building and establishing an ethical value system.

2.5 BIG DATA ETHICS TEST

LO 6
Perform big data ethics test

A more structured governance is needed to establish ethical value system. One must understand the purpose and intention of big data usage in the organization. It not only helps one to find out '*how best this resource can be used*' but also to identify any critical issues that may arise. Customers and stakeholders must be informed about their privacy rights and interests while collecting and using their data. In addition, it is better for the organization to keep abreast with the latest and sound methodical approaches for finding any risks and mitigating those as and when needed. They should explore the *'information pioneered product value chain'* to identify any weak link in the 'Big data industry'. The organization should not wait to take corrective mechanisms to resolve any damages; rather, it should generate the capability to perform preventive mechanisms to handle any situation before it becomes real.

One very important aspect of attaining ethical leadership is to perform routine audits, which will help the organization to develop the capability in the related field. More importantly, organizations must perform due diligence while using or acquiring third-parties data as these are subject to major risks. Organization must look into its upstream and downstream stakeholders to ensure that they also perform ethical standards and practices. We will now look at the ethical test, Table 2.1, that will help organizations, ethics, and compliance practitioners to find the status quo and help them to become ethical, compliant, sustainable, and competitive.

Table 2.1 Ethics test for organization

My organization uses big data.				
Strongly disagree	Disagree	Neutral	Agree	Strongly agree
My organization uses big data technologies.				
Strongly disagree	Disagree	Neutral	Agree	Strongly agree
My organization sends a privacy notice specifically mentioning 'how the data will be used' when we collect personal data.				
Strongly disagree	Disagree	Neutral	Agree	Strongly agree
My organization has an ethical policy on big data usage.				
Strongly disagree	Disagree	Neutral	Agree	Strongly agree
My organization has an ethical policy on big data technologies usage.				
Strongly disagree	Disagree	Neutral	Agree	Strongly agree
My organization assesses the risks linked to Big Data.				
Strongly disagree	Disagree	Neutral	Agree	Strongly agree
My organization assesses the risks linked to Big Data Technologies.				
Strongly disagree	Disagree	Neutral	Agree	Strongly agree
My organization has access to safeguard mechanisms to mitigate risks.				
Strongly disagree	Disagree	Neutral	Agree	Strongly agree
My organization has proper set of tools that manage risks.				
Strongly disagree	Disagree	Neutral	Agree	Strongly agree
My organization has proper timeline for mitigating risks.				
Strongly disagree	Disagree	Neutral	Agree	Strongly agree
My organization conducts proper due diligence when sharing or acquiring data from third parties.				
Strongly disagree	Disagree	Neutral	Agree	Strongly agree
My organization follows code of conduct in sharing and acquiring data in an information value chain.				
Strongly disagree	Disagree	Neutral	Agree	Strongly agree

*Total Score: ______

*The value of an individual question score varies from 1–5, where 5 denotes *strongly agree* and 1 denotes strongly *disagree*.

The total score of 60 means that your company has established its ethical value system and leading in the big data usage and technology innovation. The total score between 55 and 59 denotes that your company is following good values system and ethical practices when dealing with big data and big data technologies. The total score between 45 and 54 signifies that your company has a potential but lacks in strategic action plan towards establishing ethical value system. When your total score is between 34 and 44, then it means that you have just entered into the big data business and you need to create big data ecosystem, roadmap, and ethical and compliance value system. The total score between 25 and 33 denotes that your company is planning to enter into big data industry. Total score anything less than 24 signifies that your company need to understand big data ecosystems and utilize ethics framework to work and deal with the big data.

> **Note:** The ethical test will help organizations, ethics, and compliance practitioners to find the status quo and help them to become ethical, compliant, sustainable, and competitive.

2.6 BIG DATA AUDIT

LO 7 *Execute big data audit*

> One of the key aspects of evaluating organization's current practices of dealing with the data is to perform routine data practices audits.

One of the key aspects of evaluating organization's current practices of dealing with the data is to perform routine data practices audits. A specialized team having the understanding about organization's values system, data handling practices, benchmarks, and standards must work with all the stakeholders of the business. The team further must recommend the findings of their audit to the leadership on a routine basis so as to consider the execution of any suitable strategy in case of the need. The panel, shown in Fig. 2.7, describes select few audit questions that will help the auditors to unfold the ethical data practices status quo.

Now, we will see various tools and processes, which will help auditors to perform audits.

- **Process map:** It helps the team to find out how the data is used, acquired, integrated, processed, secured, and managed in products and services. It also lists the owner of the data and process clearly.
- **Security reviews:** It requires a whole gamut of expertise in the field as the breach of security to the sensitive data might result into legal suites and even to bankruptcy. The specialized team must develop security breach or attack scenarios to mitigate any data security breach.
- **Risk reviews:** The information pioneered product value chain and the big industry involves numerous stakeholders, which results in various risks. The team must generate risk scenarios and identify methodological approaches and tools to tackle or mitigate any risks.

Select Few Audit Questions

- Who has access to the data?
- What privilege rights are given to the individual who has the data access?
- Who owns the data?
- Who are the stakeholders of the data?
- Who owns the data-oriented process?
- Who outside your organization might be interested in accessing the data?
- Is your data trustworthy?
- What mechanisms are being used to identify data trustworthiness?
- What processes help to identify breach in trustworthiness?
- What data strategies are in place?
- What security measures are imposed on the data?
- What aggregation tools and processes are used?
- How to validate and verify the authenticity of the data?
- How are the data and processes managed, controlled, and owned?
- Where is your data stored, managed, and controlled?
- Where is the data moved and processed for analysis and visualization?

Fig. 2.7 Audit questions

- **Aggregation reviews:** The big data does not '*sit idle*'. It needs to be moved, aggregated, and processed for generating deep actionable insights. Thus, aggregation scenarios resulting any condition where customer and stakeholder information would actually be useful by aggregating previously disaggregated data sets must be identified. The team should also focus on ethical ways of '*data aggregation*'.
- **Facilitated workshop:** The team should routinely conduct and facilitate workshops to make every individual of the organization aware of '*what is ethical and what not*'.
- **One-to-One interview:** It is very specific and its purpose is to deal with individual's understanding of ethical data handling and data technologies capabilities.

CASE STUDY: Technology to Assist or to Intrude

The rise of a technological era is providing a lot of opportunities to people. Not only people are connected but also machines and other objects are connected. ABI research says, currently over 10 billion wirelessly connected devices are in use and it will go over and above 30 billion connected devices by 2020. The surge of 'Internet of Things (IoT)' provided a connected platform to more and more devices to the Internet; everything is connected —thermostat, dishwasher, toilet, front door, car, etc.

Fig. 2.8 Model of a Smart City

These smart devices make up the show as they themselves do most of the work by communicating the information with each other. VeraLite provides smart controller to manage 70 devices and controls over 750 smart products of all kinds. It also facilitates custom text and email alerts for any situation. Trustwave Holdings researchers found that VeraLite controller does not require any username or password by default to access the system. They also identified numerous ways to bypass the authentication.

A professor, Yoshi Kohno, of the University of Washington found many real vulnerabilities in smart connected devices. A toy having webcam could be turned on from anywhere. Another professor, Kamin Whitehouse, studied the smart buildings and observed that even the encrypted network traffic from the wireless devices are prone to hacking. Hackers could understand the network traffic pattern and by putting few assumptions, they could understand the human behaviour and what is happening inside the house. He stated that 'Once the house starts becoming fully connected, there's no reason to think that it won't become a target'.

People are getting interested in IoTs and the technology has touched Coates, Co-founder Product Club, in many ways as he has programmed sensor data to perform his own house's Twitter feed. It is interesting to know that his house tweets things like 'I just turned on the downstairs lights. It was getting a bit dark.' Or it might tweet 'Someone just activated the Sitting Room Sensor so I'm pretty sure someone's at home'.

It is of paramount importance to provide a high level of security to such connected devices. More secure device means more production time. The technology that is available to assist us can also intrude our privacy.

Questions

1. What are the challenges with the smart technology?

   Tip: Identify the use case scenarios for the smart technology. Further, map the use case with the smart objects, business processes, and stakeholders.

2. How is Internet of Things benefiting people?

   Tip: List down the problems and solutions based on the smart technology solutions to the different stakeholders.

3. Describe five scenarios where Internet of Things is used in practice.

   Tip: Perform the Google search and identify the five scenarios where Internet of Things is used in practice.

4. Do smart devices and IoT technology pose any ethical issues?

   Tip: Perform the ethical inquiry on the smart technology usage scenario.

5. Is technology a boon or bane?

   Tip: List down the [mis]use of the smart technology solutions considering its use case scenarios and stakeholders.

References

http://getvera.com/controllers/veralite/ [accessed May 25, 2017];
https://www.ifttt.com/ [accessed May 25, 2017];
https://www.technologyreview.com/s/517931/more-connected-homes-more-problems/ [accessed May 25, 2017];
http://www.abiresearch.com/press/more-than-30-billion-devices-will-wirelessly-conne [accessed May 25, 2017];
https://www.technologyreview.com/s/514941/home-tweet-home-a-house-with-its-own-voice-on-twitter/ [accessed May 25, 2017]

SUMMARY

- Ethical inquiry in relation to big data will help an organization to evolve big data technology and transform it into a powerful, effective, and robust set of tools that can help us live better—ethically and sustainably.
- There exist five power zones each representing different stakeholder—Collector, Utilizer, Broker, Generator, and Regulator.
- Each firm has its own role and responsibility in the 'information pioneered product value chain' of the big data industry.
- Ethical Issues Quadrant for Big Data Industry is prominent to understand issues related to—inside the firm, with the downstream, with upstream, and with the system.
- Big data is ethically neutral as it does not provide any 'standardized' value framework.

- An enterprise-wide ethics vocabulary on big data needs to be developed so that there should not be any mismatch between personal and enterprise-wide ethics vocabulary value system.
- In the big data era, it is easy to identify an individual or a group by aggregating data from multiple sources.
- The ethical framework will help individual and organization to unfold ethical inquires, decision points, and ethical actions in align with the core value system to develop and manage products and services utilizing big data technologies.
- A more structured governance is needed to establish ethical value system.
- Organizations must look into their upstream and downstream stakeholders to ensure that they also perform ethical standards and practices.
- One of the key aspects of evaluating organization's current practices of dealing with the data is to perform routine data practices audits.

EXERCISE

Review Questions

1. How will ethical inquiry benefit the organization?

   Tip: Frame the problem where you find yourselves helpless [considering ethical dilemma] in getting the right answer. Find out the way when ethical inquiry is helpful in solving the problem.

2. Describe ethical framework and match it with the current practice in your organization.

   Tip: Select [your] any organization and develop a different set of situations involving ethical dilemmas. Map the situations with the ethical framework and validate it with the practice in the organization. Prepare key stakeholders involvement and guideline.

3. What is the benefit of data audit?

   Tip: Find out the data stakeholders and the way they use the data. Develop few set of questions to check the validity, reliability, ownership, rights, privacy, safety, accessibility, authority, and quality of the data. List down the benefit use case scenarios.

4. Apply 4-quadrant ethical issues to your organization.

   Tip: Select a particular industry of your choice. Create a taxonomy of ethical issues based on 4-quadrant.

5. Describe with examples the stakeholders of the big data industry.

   Tip: Identify the information pioneered vlue chain and involvement of the stakeholders. List the stakeholders for entertainment, finance, mining, and health industry.

6. 'Big data is ethically neutral.' Justify the statement by providing suitable examples.

   Tip: Find out the ethical framework in [your] organization. Discuss the framework with your friend's/peer's organization framework and find out the similarity and dissimilarity.

Part II

Chapter 3: The Dawn of Data Centre Operating System

Chapter 4: Data Stock: Boon or Bane

Chapter 5: Hive and HBase: Win-Win Together

Chapter 6: Pig

Chapter 7: Data Lookout Readiness

The Dawn of Data Centre Operating System

3

> *"A function to each organ, and each organ to its own function, is the law of all organization."*
>
> —Herbert Spencer
> Social Statics: Or, The Conditions Essential to Human Happiness Specified, and the First of them Developed (1851), p. 274

Learning Objectives

On completing this chapter, you will be able to:

LO 1 Examine the data centre operating system

LO 2 Describe the Hadoop architecture, ecosystem, and offerings

LO 3 Assess Hadoop distribution elements, components, and features

LO 4 Design Hadoop cluster architecture

LO 5 Understand distributed computing MapReduce paradigm

CASE STUDY: NETFLIX—Watch What you WATCH

> "*Netflix has so thoroughly analysed viewer patterns that they now know what viewers enjoy and don't enjoy—before viewers even see the show.*"
>
> —Joe Kukura, February 2013

The entertainment industry has been transformed by the proliferation of handheld devices, ubiquitous technology, network infrastructure, and data. Netflix provides more than 125 million of hours of TV shows and movies per day, which also includes documentaries, original series, and featured films. It has grown up from DVD subscription service provider in the year 1999 to the world's largest leading internet television network.

Fig. 3.1 Large number of available TV shows and movies for viewers

As of now, it has 104 million members in 190 countries. Netflix has given a new face to big data technologies to govern, streamline, and drive the Internet media. It collects data from millions of subscribers covering metric of experience in an attempt to understand viewing habits and, thus, more specifically offers 'enjoyable entertainment' to all the customers.

Netflix launched the prize competition in the year 2006, offering $1 million, to get a solution on '*how their customers would rate a movie based on their previous ratings*'. They were looking for effective recommendation engine as they were having massive data. It announced the winner in the year 2009 and still the company is using and extending the same set of principles mentioned in the solution to improvise the recommendation engine. Netflix also provides to its customer base the feature of tagging a film. Initially, they paid the people to watch films and tag appropriately with the elements the movie contained. Based on the tags, people were recommended movies that had similarity to the specific tags and thus more probable choice for the customer. In fact, Netflix has defined around 80,000 micro-genres of the film based on viewership.

Netflix has transformed its business focus from distribution to the content creator for movies, studios, and other networks. It is putting all its efforts to understand 'quality of experience' of the customer base. The team at Netflix is constantly building and improvising various models for the massive data, which they collect, to understand '*how this affects customer behaviour*'. Based on the physical location of the data, they also position their content for optimal delivery and experience.

Management and processing of massive multidimensional data was not easy at Netflix. A specialized team was responsible to build, develop, and maintain huge infrastructure. The infrastructure comprised of typical five layers—Amazon Storage Service (S3) on cloud, Hadoop EMC cluster, Tools, Hadoop Platform as a Service, and Interactive Services.

Layer 1-Amazon Storage Service (S3): The S3 service is utilized to store any dataset that is worth retaining. It includes data from multiple sources and multiple dimensions. Billions of streaming events are captured every hour for Netflix enabled devices such as televisions, laptops, and mobile devices. For the intermediate processing and local storage, Hadoop distributed files system is used.

Layer 2-Hadoop EMR Cluster: At Netflix, the clusters were categorized based on the workload and services. For example, 500+ nodes query cluster is formed to be utilized by engineers, data scientists, and analysts to perform ad hoc queries; a production (or SLA) cluster executes extraction-transformation-load related jobs. All clusters have access to the same data but execute different workloads depending on the workload imitated by different stakeholders as per their requirements. They also have 'dev' category of clusters, which spun up as and when needed. The clusters are resized based on the peak time. For example, at night, the query cluster size is reduced and ETL cluster is increased; during night time, the query cluster is not pumped by large number of developer or user queries. Thus, the ETL jobs are scheduled and executed mostly at the night time. All the clusters are transient and in case of any failure, the identical size (potentially another availability zone, if needed) could simply be up within 10 minutes.

Layer 3-Tools: Various set of tools offered by Hadoop ecosystem are used by the Netflix developers. For example, Hive is used for ad hoc query and Pig is utilized to run ETL jobs. In case of complex algorithms, set of vanilla MapReduce programs are also used.

Layer 4-Hadoop Platform as a Service: At Netflix, team strives for innovation and they innovated on Amazon's Infrastructure as a service (IaaS) layer. Amazon's IaaS provides Hadoop services through EMR, which provides an API to provision and run Hadoop clusters. Building further level of abstraction, the team built Hadoop Platform as a Service (PaaS), '*Genie*', where without provisioning new Hadoop clusters and installing new clients related to Hadoop, Pig or HIVE, jobs related to query or productions clusters are executed.

Layer 5-Interactives services: Data pipelines are used to capture the massive and multidimensional data. Ursula is used a log data pipeline to capture every hour data from Netflix enabled devices such as televisions, mobiles, and laptops. For capturing multidimensional data, Cassandra supplied by Aegisthus data pipeline is being used. The layer also provides other useful Web based interfaces to submit multiple jobs for execution.

Netflix is looking forward to embrace Spark for streaming, machine learning, and analytics use case. They have lot of unstructured data that they captured in the form of audio and video file and the major challenge is to quantify all those to the 'enjoyable experience' metric. Some goals have already been achieved such as development of micro-genres but many are in the pipeline. In the near future, customers can expect to have personalized TV, where each one is empowered to schedule entertainment to consume, based on the preferences and choices.

Questions

1. What challenges are being faced by Netflix?

   Tip: Check the Netflix website for its service offerings. List down the usage pattern, segments, subscription, and quality of service measures.

2. Do you think that micro-genres provides any benefits on viewing predictions? Justify it by providing examples.

   Tip: List the important features/keywords/tags on which you will watch a particular entertainment video. Further, identify the benefits for the producers and the consumers. Map and scale it with the Netflix micro-genres.

3. Describe the high-level architecture of Netflix.

   Tip: Find out the components required for the Netflix product.

4. Is there any benefit of Hadoop PaaS over Amazon Hadoop IaaS?

   Tip: List down the benefits of IaaS and PaaS [check Netflix blogs].

5. What are the important parameters to predict the likelihood of the next show that viewer is going to watch?

   Tip: List down the scenarios based on the micro-genres where the use will have the high probability of watching the show/video.

6. How has Netflix quantified audio and video unstructured data for meaningful analysis?

   Tip: Identify the ways to accomplish meaningful analysis from the unstructured data. Develop metrics based on the micro-genres. Further, find out the data involved in developing the metrics.

References

Marr, Bernard. Big Data in Practice: How 45 Successful Companies Used Big Data Analytics to Deliver Extraordinary Results. Wiley; https://www.netflix.com/in/ [accessed July 27, 2017];

Sriram Krishnan and Eva Tse. Hadoop Platform as a Service in the Cloud https://medium.com/netflix-techblog/hadoop-platform-as-a-service-in-the-cloud-c23f35f965e7 [accessed July 28, 2017];
Dan Woods.Why Does Netflix Need a Hadoop Genie? https://www.forbes.com/sites/danwoods/2015/05/21/why-does-netflix-need-a-hadoop-genie/#43034e7622f1 [accessed July 28, 2017];
Big Data Lessons From Netflix. https://www.wired.com/insights/2014/03/big-data-lessons-netflix/ [accessed July 15, 2017];
Debapratim Purkayastha and Vijay Kumar Tangirala. 2013. netflix: leveraging big data to predict entertainment. www.thecasecentre.org/Netflix [accessed July 27, 2017]

> *"In pioneer days they used oxen for heavy pulling, and when one ox couldn't budge a log, they didn't try to grow a larger ox. We shouldn't be trying for bigger computers, but for more systems of computers."*
>
> —Rear Admiral Grace Hopper
> —In: Tom White, Hadoop: The Definitive Guide

3.1 DATA CENTRE OPERATING SYSTEM

LO 1 *Examine the data centre operating system*

To store and process massive data, one needs to manage complex infrastructure that facilitates management and processing of the data. Hadoop ecosystem provides various components by which management and processing of data becomes simple and easy. In fact, the immediate impact that is visible with the Hadoop ecosystem is the democratization of storage and computing resources and accessibility to larger pool of resources to the user communities. In this chapter, Hadoop as a data centre operating system is presented. The focus is to explore the capabilities and opportunities that Hadoop ecosystem provides. Distributed system and computation is not a new concept. It has been in the technological community for more than four decades. Before we see Hadoop ecosystem as an operating system, we will first understand the distributed storage and computation framework. This will enable us to work with the distributed algorithms, models, workflows, and jobs.

Distributed System

A distributed system defines a model where the components that reside on the networked computers communicate, act, and coordinate based on the messages that they exchanged. More specifically, some of the key characteristics of the distributed system are

- **Fault tolerance**: Failure of a component should not result into the failure of a system. Thus, system can go to a degradable performance (gracefully) stage but should not go off. Once the component recovers, it should be able to re-join the system to achieve the same level of performance before the failure.

- **Recoverability:** No system is ideal, but that does not mean a failure of a component or a system results into loss of data. Distributed system provides policy to handle such event and recover data in case of any failure.
- **Consistency:** The components perform multiple jobs towards the final goal of the workflow. Failure of one job should not affect the overall goal and performance of the workflow.
- **Transparency:** It deals with one unified system concept instead of multiple components. It address various levels of transparency such as
  - ***Access*** It hides the way in which data is represented and also how a resource is accessed.
  - ***Location*** The location such as physical (geographical location) and virtual (network address- several layers) of a resource, component, or a system is hidden from the user.
  - ***Relocation*** A resource can be moved to another location while it is being utilized for executing a particular job or task. This movement is hidden.
  - ***Concurrency*** A resource while being utilized by some workflow can also be shared across different jobs or tasks or even with other set of users without explicitly showcasing the process.
  - ***Replication*** A resource without revealing any information about the storage can be replicated in the distributed system.
  - ***Failure*** It hides the failure and recovery of resource. A user is completely unware of any failure and recovery process of a system or a component.
  - ***Migration*** Without providing any external information, movement of the resource can happen to perform the stipulated job.
  - ***Persistence*** The digital space of a resource whether it is in memory or a disk is hidden
  - ***Scaling*** The system automatically scales up and down to serve and execute the workflow request without revealing the whole process of scaling.

Hadoop Ecosystem and Stack

Hadoop was first developed by Doug Cutting and Mike Cafarella in the year 2005. The Hadoop project came into existence due to the critical requirement for the search engine at Yahoo. The architecture of the Hadoop is simple but profound. It is based on a very simple concept, '*instead of moving data to computation move computation to data*'. At a high level, Hadoop comprises of two major components: Hadoop distributed file system (HDFS) and resource and workload manager names as '*Yet Another Resource Negotiator*' (YARN). The application that runs on Hadoop gets its work done by distributing the processing in the clusters, close to the data. The processing in

Hadoop is achieved by MapReduce processing paradigm, which spans across multiple nodes in a cluster. The data is stored in the HDFS.

Foundational Concepts

Hadoop addresses characteristics of the distributed system and facilitates scalable computation in a distributed fashion. Understanding some foundational concepts is necessary before we move forward.

- A node is a commodity computer machine that can process and store data.
- A cluster in the Hadoop environment is a collection of nodes which provides the facility of computation and storage of data
- Hadoop cluster typically comprises of Master node and Slave nodes, where Master controls the storage and processing of the data but each slave is responsible to process the data. The processing is done near the data such that it results into low I/O costs.
- Data, when added to the cluster, is distributed immediately and replicated across the cluster nodes (depending on the replication policy).
- Data is stored into fixed size blocks (normally 128 KB) and each block is replicated to provide redundancy and data safety.
- A workflow is the collection of sequence of actions to be executed for the overall computation. A workflow typically comprises of multiple jobs in a cluster. Jobs are further broken into multiple tasks where each cluster node performs the task on a single block of assigned data.
- User of computation and data deals with the jobs that are written in the high-level language.
- Jobs are fault tolerant due to task redundancy scheme. Thus, in case of failure, the redundant jobs are executed.
- Each task should be independent of the other tasks and also nodes should not communicate while processing the data to avoid deadlock situation.

These concepts are important and made available at various Hadoop offerings, thereby ensuring the distributed system characteristics in driving the core architecture.

3.2 HADOOP ARCHITECTURE, ECOSYSTEM, AND OFFERINGS

LO 2 *Describe the Hadoop architecture, ecosystem, and offerings*

Here, we will cover the other open source components that typically have been deployed with the Hadoop. In fact, Hadoop is no longer limited to HDFS and MapReduce components and is better to be looked as an ecosystem where multiple open source components related projects with projects having similar or extended feature set and functionality are being considered for distributed computing and large scale processing. Apache foundation hosts most of these projects. Table 3.1 lists some of the popular projects.

Table 3.1 Apache Projects for Hadoop Ecosystem

Apache Project	*Details*
Ambari	It comprises of tools to administer Hadoop. It provides service to install, monitor, and maintain Hadoop cluster. Service to add and remove slave nodes are also included in the tool set.
Avro	It is a framework that supports efficient serialization to transform data into a compact binary format that could be transmitted or exchanged over the network.
Flume	It is a data flow service, which provides aggregation, collection, and movement of large volumes of log data into Hadoop.
HBase	It is a non-relational (NoSQL) database that uses HDFS for its underlying storage. With HBase, real-time read/write access can be achieved.
HCatalog	It is a service layer for Hadoop that helps user of different data processing tools to perform operations such as read/write into/from the cluster.
Hive	It is a distributed data warehouse built on top of Hadoop. It is utilized for data summarization, query, and analysis of data that is stored in HDFS. It provides a query language that is based on SQL (HiveQL).
Hue	It is an interface that facilitates administration of Hadoop with handy GUI tools for browsing files, issuing Hive and Pig queries, and developing Oozie workflows.
Mahout	It is a library that provides collection of machine learning statistical algorithms. These algorithms were implemented in MapReduce and can run natively on Hadoop.
Oozie	It is a workflow management tool to schedule and chain together Hadoop applications.
Pig	It is a platform to analyse very large data sets that runs on HDFS. It abstracts MapReduce programs by supporting an infrastructure layer consisting of a compiler to generate sequences of MapReduce equivalent programs. A language layer comprises of the query language named Pig Latin to perform tasks on the data.
Sqoop	It is a tool used to collect, aggregate, and move large amounts of data between relational databases and HDFS.
Zookeeper	It is a simple interface to the centralized coordination of services (such as naming, configuration, and synchronization) used by distributed applications.

Several different projects together are considered as part of Hadoop ecosystem, which can be deployed either as a single bundle or one by one as per the dependency. Hadoop as commercial distribution is also offered by different vendors and thus provides added features and functionality. Both Hadoop ecosystem and its commercial distributions continue to evolve, with new or improved technologies and tools emerging all the time. One can get Hadoop either from the Apache Software Foundation or from companies that offer their own Hadoop distributions. Figure 3.2 depicts the relationship among various Hadoop ecosystem projects:

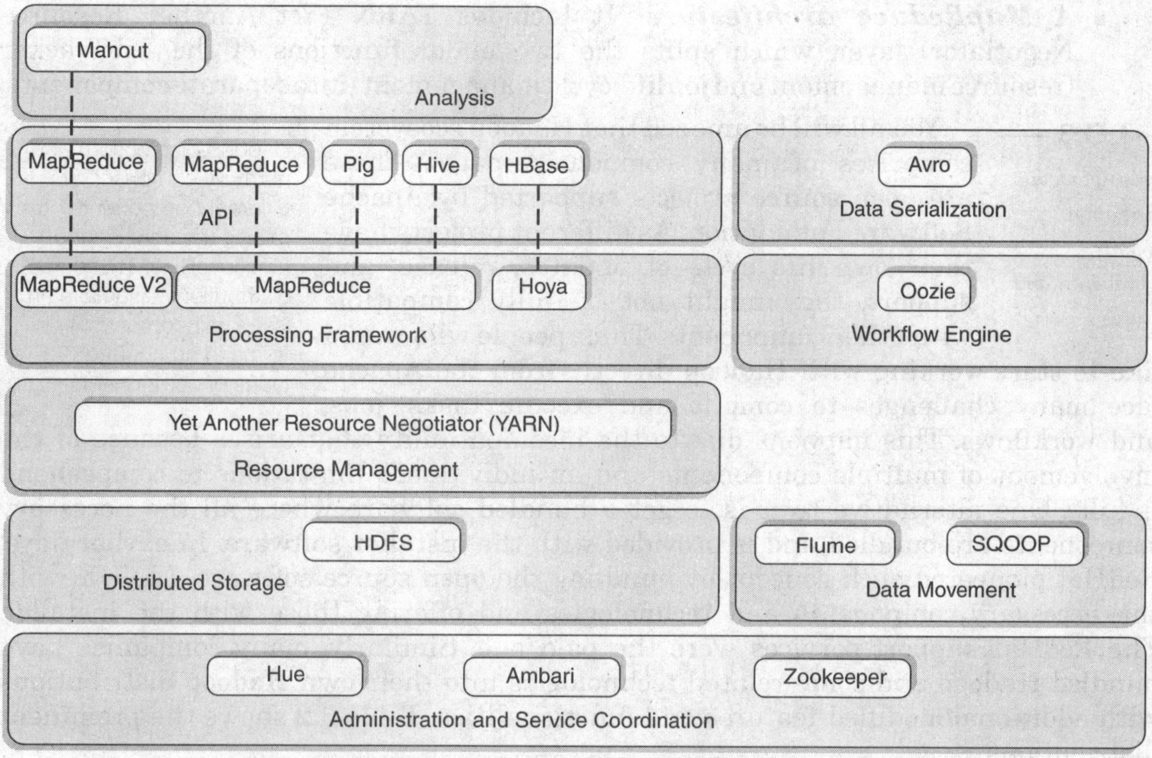

Fig. 3.2 Hadoop ecosystem components

> **Note:** Hadoop releases are supported by Apache Software Foundation. Thus, any commercial distribution of the product, which is in 'forked' form (represent modified or extended versions of original release), is not supported by the Apache Software Foundation.

Apache Hadoop's Two Important Release Series

Following are the two important release series of Apache Hadoop:

- **1.x:** In this series, version 1.2.1 is the most stable release of the Hadoop. Most of the production system still support version 1.2.1 even when the version 2.x became available. High availability of the Namenode was considered primarily by all the distributions of version 2.x.
- **2.x:** At the time of writing this book, this is the current version of Apache Hadoop (2.2.0), including the following features:
    - ***HDFS availability and scalability*** In 1.x series, the major limitation was that the NameNode was a single point of failure and in case of Namenode failure the other services immediately become inactive. In the series of 2.x, this limitation was overcome by including the concept of an active standby NameNode.

- ***A MapReduce architecture*** It includes YARN (Yet Another Resource Negotiator) layer, which splits the two major functions of the JobTracker (resource management and job life-cycle management) into separate components.

LO 3
Assess Hadoop distribution elements, components, and features

Hadoop distribution normally comprises of different components but retains the core Hadoop functionalities. These distributions also have an issue of incompatibility in terms of number and types of components.

You all will be amazed that Hadoop ecosystem comprises of many component parts. Those are open source projects supported by Apache Software Foundation. As different projects have their own life cycle of updates, release, and support, they might not be fully compatible with other components. Thus, people who would like to start working with Hadoop directly from the Apache face many challenges to compile and execute tasks, jobs, and workflows. This happens due to the incompatibility that arises because of the involvement of multiple components and an individual's limitations to comprehend it fully. One alternative to it is to get a bundled software where all the necessary components are bundled and is provided with the installer software. In earlier days, RedHat pioneered such concept by bundling the open source software, LINUX, with the necessary components and technologies and offering those with the installer. The RedHat support services were the paid one. Similarly, many companies have bundled Hadoop and some related technologies into their own Hadoop distributions with additional/modified features and functionalities. Table 3.2 shows the prominent distributions.

Table 3.2 Hadoop distribution

Company for Hadoop Distribution	*Description*
Cloudera (www.cloudera.com/)	It is a pioneer and market leader in providing competitive Hadoop distribution. Cloudera offers its flagship product—Cloudera Enterprise, which includes the Cloudera Distribution for Hadoop (CDH), an open-source-based distribution of Hadoop and its related projects as well as its proprietary Cloudera Manager. A technical support for all its distribution is also included. Cloudera also offers alpha and beta level code for the new Hadoop release.
EMC (www.gopivotal.com)	EMC offers Hadoop distribution, Pivotal HD, that natively integrates its massively parallel processing (MPP) database technology with Apache Hadoop. This integration gave advantage to EMC to offer a high-performance Hadoop distribution with true SQL processing for Hadoop.
Hortonworks (www.hortonworks.com)	Hortonworks offers Hortonworks Data Platform (HDP), which includes Hadoop as well as related tooling and projects. Of all the distribution vendors, Hortonworks is treated as the most committed to the open source movement. It has the largest number of committers and code contributors for the Hadoop ecosystem components. Unlike Cloudera, Hortonworks only offers production level release of the Hadoop distribution. One of the strength that lies with Hortonwork is to provide Hadoop distribution to the data management companies who do not have their own in-house Hadoop distributions.

(*Contd.*)

IBM (www.ibm.com/software/ data/ infosphere/ biginsights)	IBM Big Blue project improvised the base Hadoop stack and offers a range of Hadoop offerings such as the proprietary enhancements that are focused on various features and functionalities. The product offers standards-based SQL support, data security and governance, spreadsheet-style analysis for business users, text analytics, workload management, and the application development life cycle.
Intel (hadoop.intel.com)	Intel offers Hadoop distribution, Intel Distribution, which provides distributed processing and data management for enterprise applications that analyse big data. The product offer prime features such as improvised data security via encryption and decryption in HDFS, high performance with optimizations for Intel Xeon processors, Intel SSD storage, and Intel 10GbE networking; simple and strategic console to control, monitor, tune, and secure Hadoop distribution.
MapR (www.mapr.com)	MapR offers the converged data platform that combines operational and analytical workloads. MapR offers three distributions, M3, M5, and M7. Each distribution has different features and functionality to offer. The M3 Edition is free and available for unlimited production use; MapR M5 is an intermediate-level subscription software offering; and MapR M7 is a complete distribution for Apache Hadoop. MapR also provide improvements on the other Apache Projects such as HBase.

Though commercial distribution provides many benefits to the customers, such as no effort of assembling the components as the distribution comprise of a bundled product, it also poses many challenges. The prime challenge is '*how to select the best fit Hadoop distribution*'. In addition to open source software, vendors typically offer proprietary software, support, consulting services, and training. This is not easy as multiple criteria comes for the evaluation and selection of the best-fit product. Table 3.3 provides assessment report-cum-analysis to get quick insight.

Table 3.3 Hadoop Distribution Assessment Self Evaluation Report

How will Hadoop enable your business objective?
How can you use Hadoop to execute your business scenario?

(*Contd.*)

What business context do you want to address?
What type and dimensions of data will be stored and analysed?
Do you prefer to use proprietary components for achieving goals or utilize open source offerings?
Is the potential Hadoop infrastructure flexible enough for all your use cases?
Do you want to integrate any existing tools with Hadoop? If yes, what are those and can those be integrated with Hadoop? What is the effort required?
Is there any requirement of management tools? (Hadoop's core distribution doesn't include administrative tools.)
Will the potential Hadoop offering allow you to move to a different vendor product without any obstacle such as vendor-lock-in?
Do you require Hadoop distribution support and services?
Does the potential Hadoop consider your future needs?

The questions presented in the Table 3.3 are helpful to identify and assess the potential Hadoop distributions. Further, one could create a component and feature matrix for all the potential Hadoop distributions to understand which distribution best addresses the requirements around your specific business problems. Table 3.4 provides component list for three potential Hadoop distributions: Cloudera, Hortonworks, and MapR.

Table 3.4 Component matrix for Cloudera, Hartoworks, and MapR distributions

Component	*Cloudera [CDH 5.1.2]*	*Hortonworks [HDP 2.1.5]*	*MapR [MapR 4.01]*
File System	HDFS 2.3.0, FUSE-DFS	HDFS 2.4	MapR-FS, HttpFS
MapReduce	MapReduce 2.3	MapReduce 2.4	Propietary [MRv1, MRv2]
Non-relational DB	HBase 0.96, Apache Parquet 1.25 [columnar le]	HBase 0.98, Accumulo 1.5.1	HBase 0.98, Accumulo
Metadata	HCatalog 0.5	Services	Hive 0.12 Hive 0.12
Scripting Platform [data analysis platform]	Apache Pig 0.12 Apache Datafu 1.1	Pig 0.12.1	Apache Pig 0.12
Data Access & Query	Hive 0.12	Hive 0.13.1	Hive 0.12
Work-ow Scheduler	Apache Oozie 4.0	Apache Oozie 4.0	Apache Oozie 4.0.1
Cluster Coordination	Apache Zookeeper 3.4.5	Apache Zookeeper 3.4.5	Apache Zookeeper 3.4.5
Integration with RDBMS	Apache Sqoop 1.99, 1.44	Apache Sqoop 1.44	Apache Sqoop 1.99
Integration with Streaming/Log data	Apache Flume 1.4	Flume 1.4	Apache Flume 1.5
Machine Learning	Apache Mahout 0.8	Mahout 0.9	Apache Mahout 0.9, MLLib 1.0.2
Hadoop UI [data integration]	Cloudera Hue 3.5	Hue Talend Open Studio for Big data	Hadoop User experience [Hue] 3.5
Cloud Services	Apache Whirr 0.9	Whirr	Apache Whirr 0.8.1
Parallel Query Execution /Interactive SQL/BI	Cloudera Impala 1.3	Apache Tez 0.4.0	Tez 0.4, Impala 1.2.3 Drill 0.5
Full Text Search	Apache Solr 4.4 Cloudera Search 1.2		LucidWorks Search 2.6.1

(*Contd.*)

Non-MapReduce tasks	YARN 2.3.0	YARN 2.0.4	YARN 2.4.1
Administration	Cloudera manager	Apache Ambari 1.5.1	MapR Control System [MCS] – Heatmap, Job Metrics,
Installation	Cloudera manager	Apache Ambari 1.5.1	
Monitoring		Ganglia 3.5.7, Nagios 3.5.0	
Authorization	Apache Sentry 1.2		
Core Hadoop			2.4.1
Streaming			Spark Streaming 1.0.2
Others		Storm 0.9.1 Apache Falcon 0.5.0 [data management platform] Apache Knox 0.4.0 [REST API for Hadoop clusters] Apache Phoenix 4.0.0 [SQL Skin over HBase – JDBC driver]	Spark Streaming 1.0.2
Editions	Cloudera Express Cloudera Enterprise		Standard [M3], Enterprise [M5], Enterprise DB edition [M7]

Table 3.5 provides feature (requirement) list for three potential Hadoop distributions: Cloudera, Hortonworks, and MapR.

Table 3.5 Feature (requirement) list for three potential Hadoop distributions

Feature (Requirement)		*Cloudera*	*Hortonworks*	*MapR*
Performance and Scalability	Data Ingest	Batch	Batch	Batch and streaming writes
	Metadata Architecture	Centralized	Centralized	Distributed
	HBase performance	Latency Spikes	Latency Spikes	Consistent low latency
	NoSQL Applications	Mainly batch applications	Mainly batch applications	Batch and online/ real-time applications

(*Contd.*)

Dependability	High Availability	Single failure recovery	Single failure recovery	Self healing across multiple failures
	MapReduce HA	Restart jobs	Restart jobs	Continuous without restart
	Upgrading	Rolling upgrades	Rolling upgrades	Rolling upgrades
	Replication	Data	Data	Data + metadata
	Snapshots	Consistent only for closed files	Consistent only for closed files	Point-in-time consistency for all files and tables
	Disaster Recovery	File copy scheduling (BDR)	No	Mirroring
Manageability	Management Tools	Cloudera Manager	Ambari	MapR Control System
	Volume Support	No	No	Yes
	Heat map, Alarms, Alerts	Yes	Yes	Yes
	Integration with REST API	Yes	Yes	Yes
	Data and Job Placement Control	No	No	Yes
Data Access	File System Access	HDFS read-only NFS	HDFS read-only NFS	HDFS, read/write NFS (POSIX)
	File I/O	Append only	Append only	Read/Write
	Security; ACLs	Yes	Yes	Yes
	Wire-Level Authentication	Kerberos	Kerberos	Kerberos, Native

Choosing the latest distribution and release of the Hadoop from the official Apache will be beneficial if your purpose is to prototype and experiment. In case you are looking for a stable product for the production purpose, then your choice would be for the stable distribution and release, i.e., older version.

3.3 HADOOP CLUSTER ARCHITECTURE

LO 4 *Design Hadoop cluster architecture*

Hadoop is designed for distributed and large-scale processing deployed on a large cluster of networked computers. These clusters contain master nodes and slave nodes. Master node hosts service to control storage and processing of the data while slave node is responsible to store and process data. If you are considering working with Hadoop for the first time, you can deploy Hadoop on a single machine and still get all the benefits of Hadoop services. Otherwise, a fully deployed distribution of the Hadoop can be accessed as per the need. Hadoop provides the following two deployment modes:

Fig. 3.3 Cluster Architecture

- **Pseudo-distributed mode (single node):** A Hadoop distribution deployment where all the Hadoop services, including the master and slave node services, run on a single machine it is referred to as *pseudo-distributed node*. This kind of environment is best to quickly experiment and prototype the jobs, tasks, and workflows. Here, one need not worry about the cluster-centric services and management.
- **Fully distributed mode (a cluster of nodes):** A cluster-node Hadoop distribution deployment is referred to as running Hadoop master and slave services on a cluster of computers. This mode is more suitable for production and development clusters.

Hadoop at its core has two major components: *YARN* and *HDFS*. The original MapReduce layer is implemented on the top of YARN. YARN performs management of cluster resources. It allocates computational assets such as processing availability and memory on data nodes to applications for performing distributed computation. Figure 3.4 shows the typical architectural stack.

The prime principle of YARN and HDFS is to minimize the network traffic by performing computation such that computation is local to the data. Each time data is loaded into HDFS it is replicated to provide fault tolerance. Similarly, tasks are

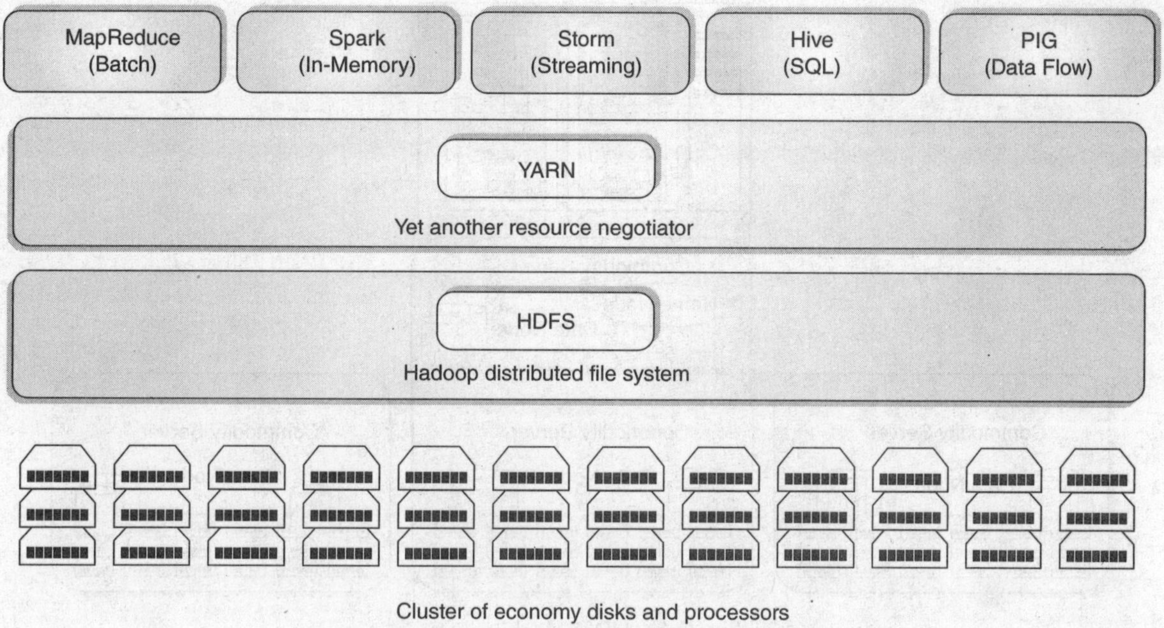

Fig. 3.4 Hadoop as YARN and HDFS

also fault tolerant, which are required for initiating the computation on data nodes. Together, HDFS and YARN as a platform facilitate management, control, and execution of big data applications. Moreover, the orchestration of HDFS and YARN acts like an operating system for big data.

Mostly, we have been discussing Hadoop deployment on a single node or cluster nodes. However, we have not yet discovered what is a cluster and what type of nodes are required to perform storage and computation. Hadoop collectively has HDFS and YARN that exposes set of APIs to developers and users without detailing out the low-level cluster administration. A set of networked machines that run HDFS and YARN is known as a *cluster*, and the individual machines are called *nodes*. A cluster can have a single node—for example, pseudo-mode deployment of Hadoop—or many thousands of nodes in case of fully-distributed deployment mode. All clusters have the capability to scale-out. Hadoop automatically identifies the presence and absence of nodes in a cluster and then control, manage, and execute the storage and processing. HDFS offers various set of services that provide capabilities for working with high volume and velocity data. The services include a 'NameNode' and multiple 'DataNodes'. Both YARN and HDFS are implemented by several daemon processes. NameNode keeps track of the physical location of the data and with the help of Resource manager and YARN; task is performed on the data. The typical architecture of Hadoop cluster comprising NameNode and DataNode is shown in Fig. 3.5.

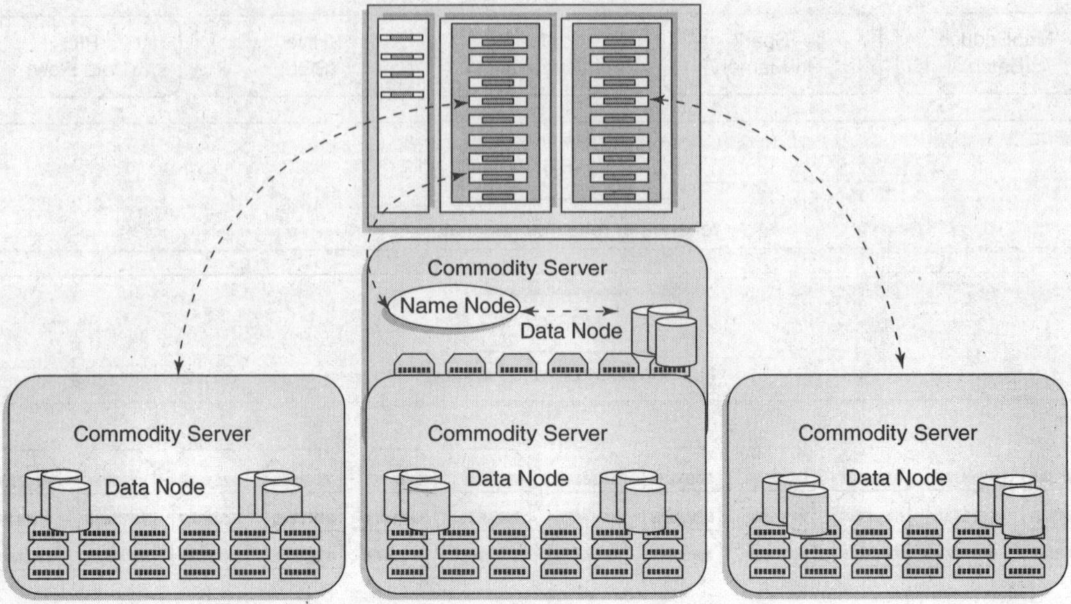

Fig. 3.5 HDFS Architecture

Two types of nodes manage the computation and storage in a Hadoop cluster.

Fig. 3.6 Depiction of a master and a worker

Master Node

It is the entry point to access the cluster. It runs coordinating services to manage, control, access, and drive the cluster. Without *master*, distributed storage and computation will not happen.

Worker Node

The cluster is built of worker nodes. Nodes of this type accept variety of tasks from the '*master*'—either to store or retrieve data or to execute any particular application. A distributed computation is achieved by parallelizing the computation of the tasks across worker nodes. Both HDFS and YARN have multiple master services responsible for coordinating worker services that run on each worker node. Worker nodes implement, both, HDFS and YARN worker services.

For HDFS, the master and worker services are as follows:

NameNodes
NameNodes maintain the namespace tree for HDFS—the directory tree of all files in the file system—and tracks the files across the cluster and a mapping of file blocks to DataNodes where the data is stored. NameNode acts as a single point of failure; thus, in the case of a high availability, cluster two NameNodes: *active* and *standby* are present. In a typical environment, a HDFS cluster primarily has single NameNode supported by a secondary NameNode. Thus, during the failure of a primary NameNode, standby NameNode takes up the responsibility. NameNode is also referred as the Master. HDFS breaks the large files into smaller chunks of data known as *blocks*. These blocks are stored at different DataNodes. NameNode tracks each block through the namespace and file metadata. Secondary NameNode performs housekeeping tasks and checkpointing on behalf of the NameNode.

Data nodes
Data nodes are resilient in nature, stores the data in a Hadoop cluster, and is the name of the daemon that manages the data. Within the HDFS cluster, data blocks are replicated across multiple data nodes and access is managed by the NameNode. For the optimal efficiency, the replication mechanism is designed when all the nodes of the cluster are collected into a rack. In fact, the NameNode uses a 'rack ID' to keep track of the data nodes in the cluster. DataNodes send 'heartbeat' messages to display connectivity and activeness between the Data Node and NameNode. In case of the absence of the 'heartbeat' message of any DataNode, the NameNode takes necessary action to activate the replicated tasks or workflows on any other DataNode. When the lost DataNode becomes active and sends the 'heartbeat' message to the NameNode, it also sends the list of blocks and the associated metadata. At a very high level, client application first makes a request to NameNode to access the data from the cluster. The NameNode then finds the blocks and the associated DataNode for the data being requested. The client then directly communicates to each of the DataNode for the data.

YARN has multiple master services and a worker service as follows:

ResourceManager (Master)
It is responsible for allocating and monitoring resources (e.g., physical assets such as memory and processor cores) for the cluster and make those available to applications.

ApplicationMaster (Master)
It is responsible for controlling and monitoring a particular application being run on the cluster as scheduled by the ResourceManager.

NodeManager (Worker)
It is responsible for managing, controlling, and executing various processing tasks on the nodes in a cluster. Not only this, it also monitors the health and status of each tasks. Each task requires a resource for its execution; thus, client must request set of resources from the *ResourceManager*, which assigns an application-specific *ApplicationMaster* for the duration of the job. While *ResourceManager* tracks the status of the nodes in a cluster, the *ApplicationMaster* tracks the execution of the job. Each individual *NodeManager* creates containers and executes tasks within them.

An example deployment of a small Hadoop cluster with six nodes—two masters and four workers—is shown in Fig. 3.7. In case of the large cluster, *NameNode* and Secondary *NameNode* reside in separate machines; thus, completion for resources never happen. There could be other set of services that might run in the cluster apart from the primary services.

3.4 DISTRIBUTED COMPUTING: MAPREDUCE

LO 5
Understand distributed computing MapReduce paradigm

MapReduce is a programmable paradigm model that supports the distributed computation of the data. In earlier version of Hadoop, MapReduce framework (pre-version 2) had a single master service called a *JobTracker* and several slave services called *TaskTrackers* (one per node in the cluster just to execute only MapReduce jobs). In this version, when a MapReduce job is submitted to the JobTracker, it is placed into a queue and gets executed based on the scheduled rules defined by the administrator. The assignment of the map and reduce tasks is accomplished by the TaskTracker. The limitation of this type of framework is that it is only restricted to MapReduce jobs. With Hadoop 2, YARN is introduced that not only executes the MapReduce jobs but also provides generic scheduling and resource management services to run other services.

MapReduce framework involves two phases: a *map phase* and a *reduce phase* to perform the distributed scalable computation on the cluster. The computation on the data involves data to be arranged in key-value pairs. A MapReduce job runs as follows:

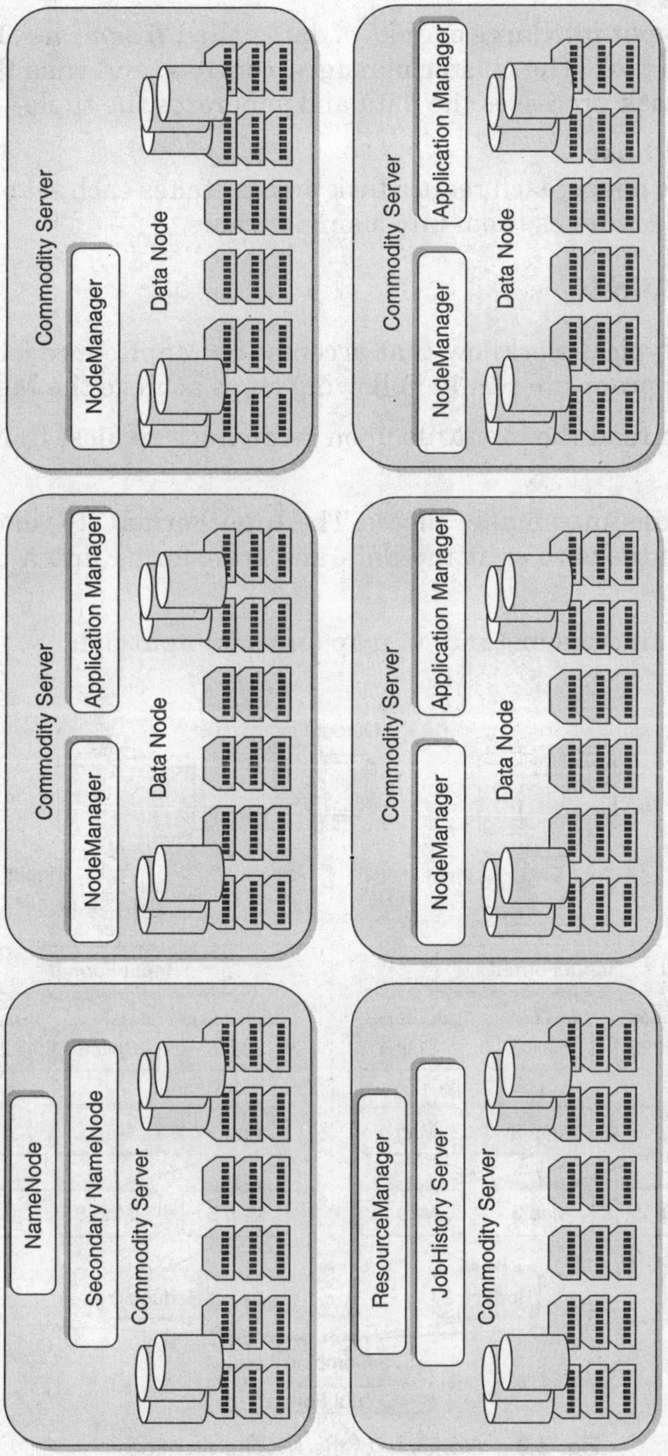

Fig. 3.7 Hadoop cluster with two master nodes and four workers nodes

Step 1: Map phase

The input data is split into large chunks of data called '*fragments*'. Each *fragment* is assigned to a map task. The cluster manages, controls, and runs these sets of map tasks. Each map task processes the data and generates the tuple—key-value pairs.

Step 2: Reduce Phase

During the Reduce phase, each reduce task process takes each set of values that has the same key and combines them into a single value.

MapReduce Workflow

Figure 3.8 shows a typical workflow that accepts the MapReduce job from the client and generates the appropriate result. Following steps achieve the MapReduce job:

Step1: Locate and read the input file upon receiving a request from a client for the MapReduce job.

Step 2: Split the file into smaller pieces. The InputFormat (IF) and Record Reader (RR) performs the tasks to split the data and transforms into a tuple—key/value pair.

Step 3: Assign distinctive instance of map for each input pair.

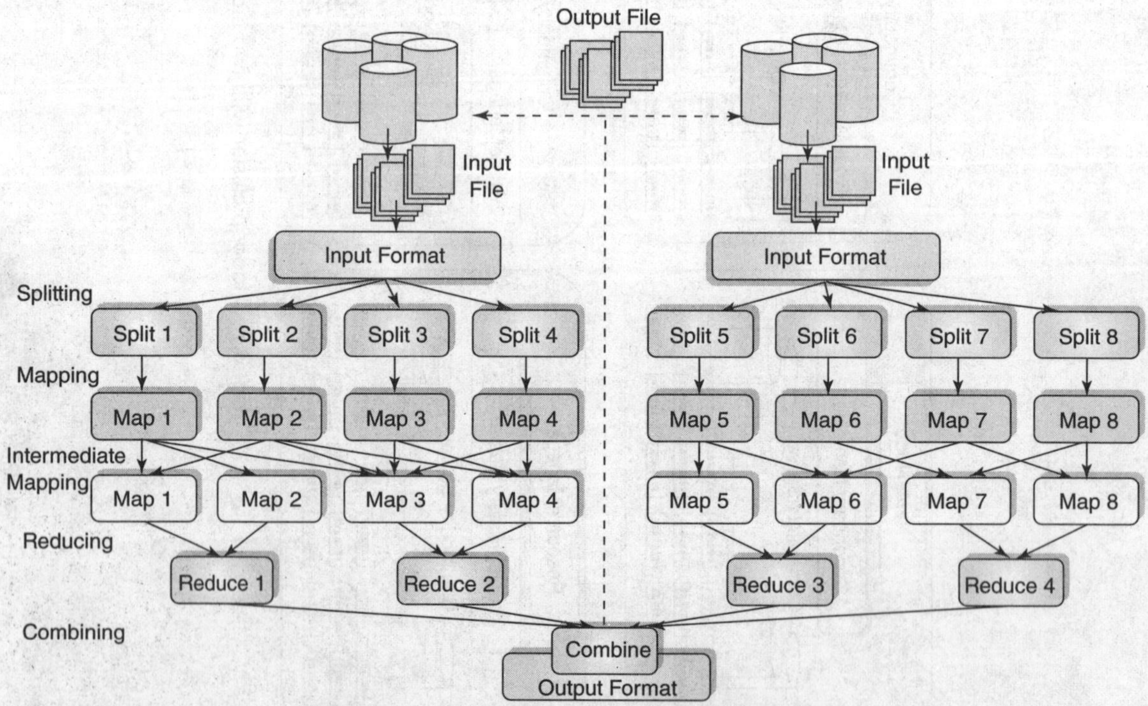

Fig. 3.8 Workflow of the MapReduce job

Step 4: Perform shuffling and a sort on the intermediate results (intermediate mapping) computed on different nodes generating the output pair.

Step 5: Assign the output pair to the Reduce job. Reduce job cannot begin until all map jobs are completed. The output of a Reduce job is also a tuple—key/value pair.

Step 6: Write the result into HDFS. The OutputFormat takes the tuple and organizes the output for writing to HDFS. The RecordWriter writes the formatted data to HDFS.

Illustrative Example

Let us understand the working of MapReduce by considering a text file containing the following text:

Clear River Ever

Blue Blue Ever

Clear Blue River

To obtain the word count of the text, we can execute the MapReduce workflow as shown in the Fig. 3.9.

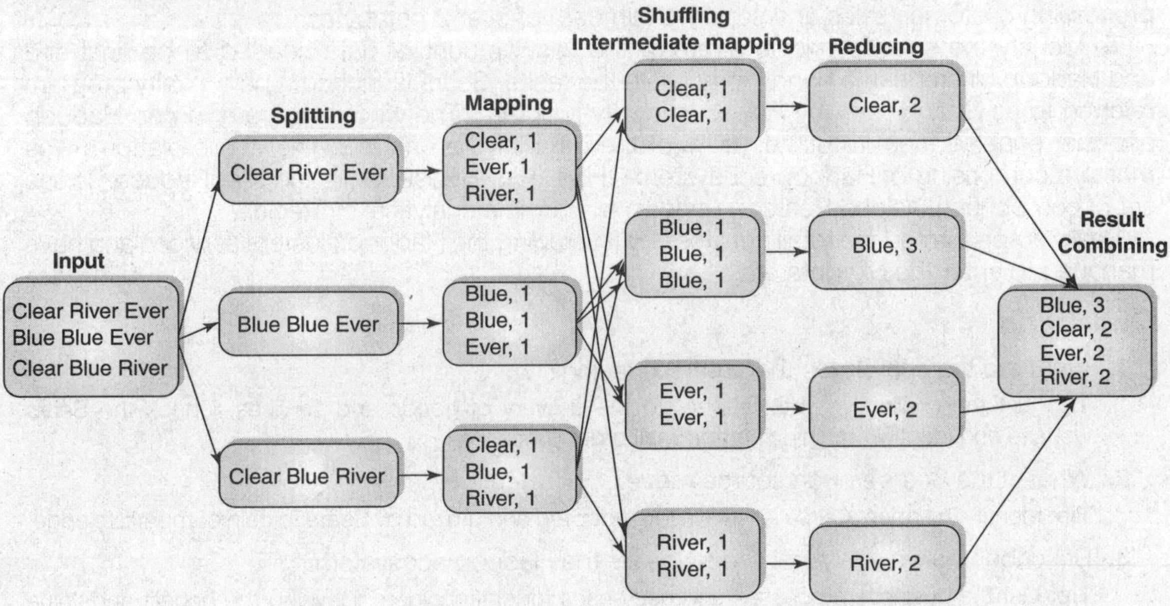

Fig. 3.9 Word count example of a MapReduce workflow

CASE STUDY: Sears Way of Embracing All-in Hadoop

Sears is a large retailer from the US. It was founded as a shipping and mail order company in the year 1893. Kmart acquired Sears in the year 2005 to maintain the business under Sears spectrum. In the competitive retail market, like other retailers, Sears was also facing challenges to deliver faster goods and services more specifically to get closer to the customers. In 2013, Kmart and Sears established around 798 stores and close to revenue of $21billion considered as the fourth largest department store in the US offering millions of products to the customers across the stores.

Data of more than 100 million customers were available with them. Their existing legacy BI systems, including mainframe applications, were slow and costly for performing complex ETL jobs and they were looking for quick answers to increasingly complex questions considering the reduction in the costs and resources. The company with the aggressive strategy of personalized marketing, to provide coupons, discounts, and offers to the individual customer, found that the existing technology and legacy systems are incapable to support the processing. Normally, analysis of such marketing campaigns for loyalty club members used to take six weeks.

Sears started working with the open source stack with Linux at the operating system and aware of the benefits and the strengths of the open source move. It's first move to experiment with the Hadoop began by running it in pseudo mode. Sears deployed its first set of cluster of 20 to 30 nodes in early 2010. In 2012, the cluster size increased to 300 nodes housing and processing customer, sales and supply chain data of over 2 petabytes.

To identify the specific pricing strategy, the vast amount of data needed to be analysed and Hadoop cluster came handy to achieve the tasks. Sears launched a new loyalty program referred to as *Shop your Way Rewards* loyalty program. The whole program run on Hadoop and that enabled them to utilize 100% of the data for the analysis. The whole platform was massive comprising of Hadoop ecosystem—Hive, Pig, HBase, Solr, and MapReduce. These set of components helped Sears to perform all possible analytical strategies.

Sears outperformed the retail business by leveraging the Hadoop clusters services and have managed to enter the Big data era.

Questions

1. What are the challenges that Sears is facing?

   Tip: List the challenges with respect to the delivery of goods and services. Check the Sears website and identify the shipping and mail order processes.

2. What is the Sears's open source move?

   Tip: Identify the open source infrastructure adopted and utilized by Sears to gain competitive edge.

3. Describe Sears's analytical scenarios for the Hadoop ecosystem.

   Tip: List the business processes and use cases for stakeholders. Develop the benefit and value metrics.

4. Why Sears wanted to capture personalized marketing?

   Tip: Check the vision and mission of the Sears on its website. List the Sears's competitors in the retail, shipping, and order industry for goods and services. Find out what Sears did to attain the leadership.

5. Is the big data technology like Hadoop ecosystem beneficial for Sears?

   Tip: Find out the gaps in addressing stakeholders and business cases concern/issue in providing the business value.

References

Sears Became a Real-Time Digital Enterprise Due to Big Data. https://datafloq.com/read/sears-real-time-digital-enterprise-big-data/265 [accessed July 2, 2017];
Why Sears Is Going All-In On Hadoop. https://www.informationweek.com/it-leadership/why-sears-is-going-all-in-on-hadoop/d/d-id/1107038?page_number=2 [accessed July 2, 2017];
Sears: Hadoop Data Hub. https://www.datameer.com/wp-content/uploads/2015/09/Sears_Hadoop_DataHub.pdf [accessed July 3, 2017]

SUMMARY

- Hadoop ecosystem provides various components by which management and processing of data becomes simple and easy.
- A distributed system defines a model where the components that reside on the networked computers communicate, act, and coordinate based on the messages that they exchanged.
- Hadoop addresses characteristics of the distributed system and facilitates scalable computation in a distributed fashion.
- Hadoop provides two deployment modes—Pseudo-distributed mode (single node) and Fully-distributed mode (a cluster of nodes).
- Hadoop at its core has two major components—YARN and HDFS.
- YARN performs management of cluster resources. It allocates computational assets such as processing availability and memory on data nodes for performing distributed computation.
- HDFS offers various set of services that provide capabilities for working with high volume and velocity data.
- Hadoop, collectively, has HDFS and YARN that exposes set of APIs to developers and users without detailing out the low-level cluster administration.
- MapReduce is a programmable paradigm model that supports the distributed computation of the data.

EXERCISE

Review Questions

1. Describe the Hadoop ecosystem.

   Tip: List the components of the ecosystem.

2. How HDFS and YARN orchestrate for the big data analytics?

   Tip: Check HDFS and YARN orchestration benefit for the Big data analytics.

3. Create a feature and component matrix for the Hadoop distribution for any start-up of your choice.

   Tip: Check feature and component matrix for the Hadoop distribution of any start-up of your choice.

4. Design a system considering deployment of a small Hadoop cluster with ten nodes, two master, and eight workers.

   Tip: Refer to the chapter and check an example deployment of a small Hadoop cluster with eight nodes, two master, and six workers. Develop a system considering deployment of a small Hadoop cluster with ten nodes, two-master, and eight workers.

5. Describe with examples the components of the Hadoop ecosystem.

   Tip: Refer to the chapter and check the Apache ecosystem component. Further, check the Apache open source project website—https://www.apache.org/.

6. 'Hadoop is the [big] data centre operating system.' Justify the statement by providing suitable examples.

   Tip: Identify the functioning of an operating system. Check the feature and functioning of key operating system. Map it with the feature and functionality of Hadoop.

Data Stock: Boon or Bane

4

> "The alchemists in their search for gold discovered many other things of greater value."
>
> —Arthur Schopenhauer, German Philosopher

Learning Objectives

On completing this chapter, you will be able to:

- **LO 1** Examine the database technology evolution
- **LO 2** Describe the types of database technology
- **LO 3** Summarize salient features of NoSQL
- **LO 4** Understand about transactions—OLTP, OLAP, and NoSQL
- **LO 5** Apply design guidelines for the transactions—OLTP, OLAP, and NoSQL

Massive data storage and processing capacity in the distributed fashion is the core functionality of the Hadoop. We will now look at the promising technologies of data storage and design principles that will enable readers to understand the benefits, challenges, and limitations of working with those technologies. As Hadoop ecosystem started getting its market share for distributed processing and storage, most of the early technologies that dealt with the data faced many challenges for their existence. Many vendors that offered relational database technologies had to leave the market. Some managed to strategize their offerings by putting feature of the product as '*dealing with structured data exclusively with relational database technologies*' and leaving unstructured data aside for the Hadoop. Thus, the vendors played smartly to address the customers about their data processing and storage needs—structured vs unstructured data. We need to understand the historical and operational differences between traditional and Hadoop technologies so that we will be in a position to leverage the Hadoop strengths with the existing and traditional technologies of data storage and processing.

4.1 BEGINNING OF THE DATA STOCK

LO 1 *Examine the database technology evolution*

'*Data stock*' specifies the way in which data is arranged, controlled, accessed, and managed by the software system and technologies. It was not clear when the first database system and model was formally conceived and implemented. However, when Charles Babbage invented the first complete Turing Machine, it was clear that computer would need some memory space to store and organize the data and a particular way of operating on data. It is interesting to understand when this '*memory space*' concept evolved to the database and what database does. A database is a collection of data in an organized fashion. Not all databases that hold the data in a particular way provide the functionality of management of data. For example, spreadsheets organize data into row and column format and provide operative functionality on that data but do not provide any particular management feature on the data. In database management system, '*management*' refers to the set of computer programs having specific instructions to manage the '*database*'.

> '*Data stock*' specifies the way in which data is arranged, controlled, accessed, and managed by the software system and technologies.

Thus, a database management system is responsible for and able to manage the data structure can provide access to data—store, retrieve, and operate in a correct and trustworthy fashion.

LO 2 *Describe the types of database technology*

Let us understand different phases of the evolution of database technologies. The first in the series cropped in the early 1960s. The term '*database*' first appeared in 1962 in the technical memo at Systems Development Corp. at California. In Fig. 4.1, we can see five different database technologies that mimic the whole evolution.

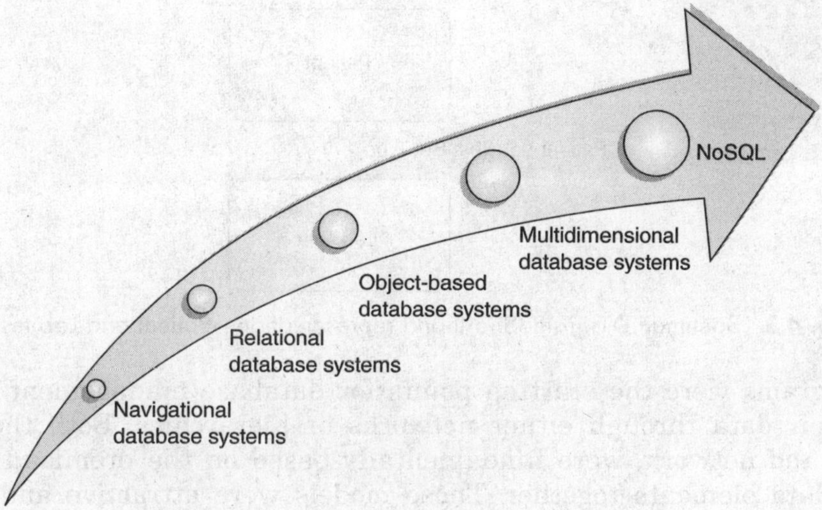

Fig. 4.1 Evolution of database technologies

Navigational Databases

Navigational databases are based on the design and model of a network of interrelated things proposed by Charles Bachman. The Bachman design typically provides the starting point for navigating the data that is connected to the network or graph like fashion. Figure 4.2 shows the representation of the patient and lab tests data set navigation, and Fig. 4.3 is the Bachman design of a data structure.

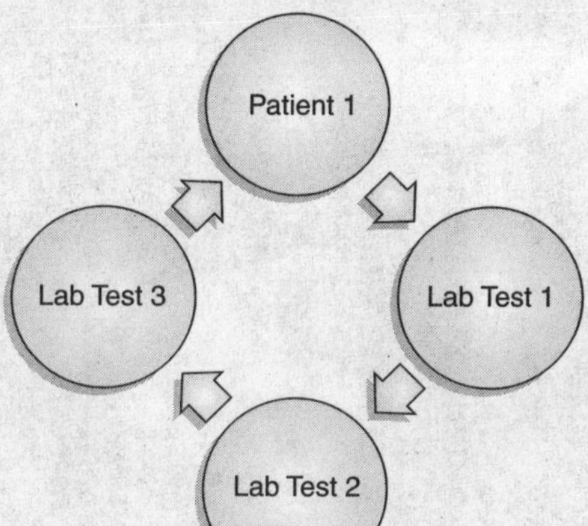

Fig. 4.2 Expanded Diagram (Patient and Lab tests)

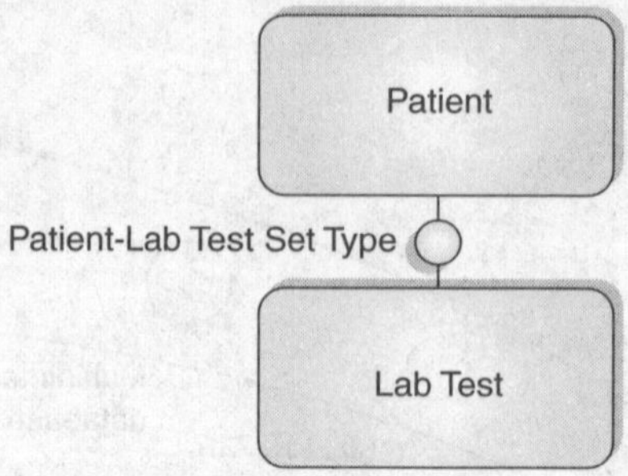

Fig. 4.3 Bachman Diagram (Shorthand representation—Patient and Lab tests)

These diagrams were the starting points for database management system that structure their data through either networks or hierarchies. Both the databases, hierarchical and network, were fundamentally based on the premise that pointers would link data elements together. These models were attractive and shaped the database industry and multiple products—IDMS, Cullinet, and IMS were developed and entered the market. IBM backed IMS navigational database and came under the classification of a hierarchical database. Navigational databases eventually set the path for future database technologies such as relational databases.

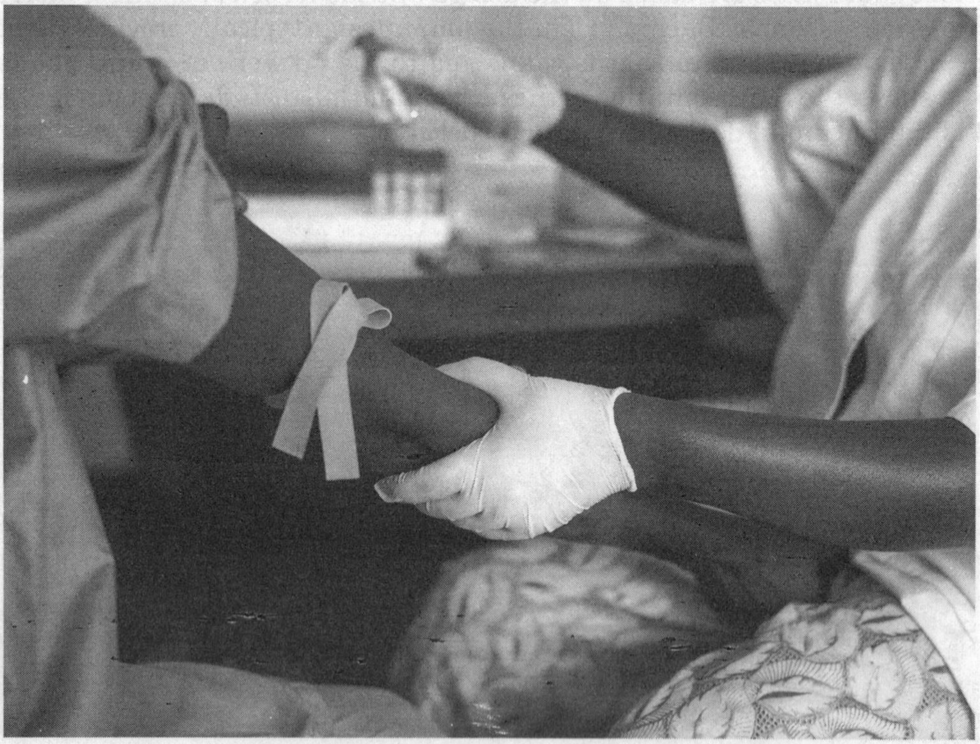

Fig. 4.4 Doctor conducting blood test on a patient

Relational Databases

Navigational database system had the limitations of working with the data. It did not provide the user a declarative language and relied on the necessary approach of finding the data. Thus, the access and working were limited to only those experts who could precisely mention the set of instructions for dealing with data. Edgar Codd, the researcher of IBM's San Jose, CA, presented series of papers on the relational model of the data. The model proposes an entirely different approach to structure the data. He proved that while adhering the implementation details of the navigational databases, the relational model can support intuitive declarative language to be working on the data. Several companies leverage the concept of the relational model to build relational database systems. In 1974, Chamberlain and others at IBM developed a high-level non-procedural language—structured language for managing data in relational database systems. Figure 4.5 shows the sample relational model.

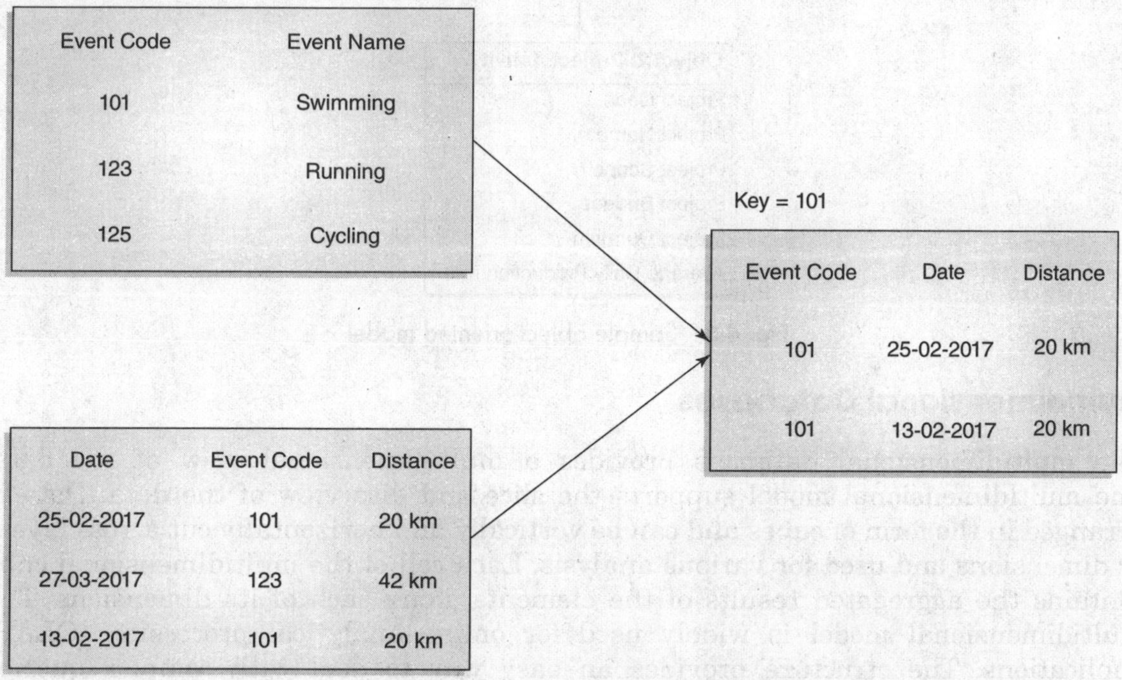

Fig. 4.5 Sample relational model

Object-oriented Databases

An object-oriented database represents the information in the form of objects. The term an 'object' came from the object-oriented paradigm. The object contains feature and the behaviour in an encapsulated way. The object data base technology provides an easy way to deal with complex data and perform operations by leveraging the relationships among the different objects by the pointers that are the links to establish relationships. The essential benefit that one can get working with objects is that it can be programmed with little procedural differences without affecting the entire system. Figure 4.6 shows a sample object-oriented database model.

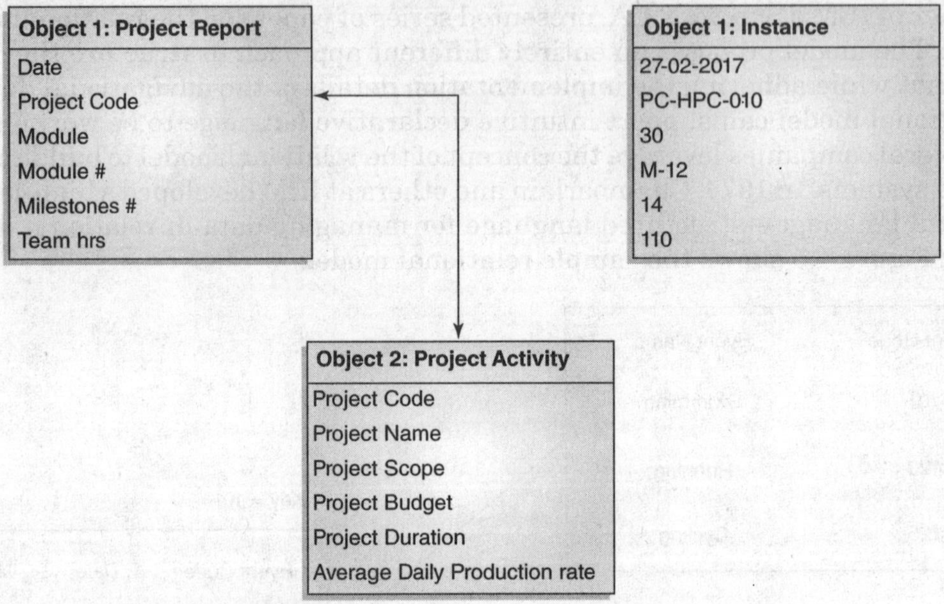

Fig. 4.6 Sample object-oriented model

Multidimensional Databases

The multidimensional database provides a multidimensional view of the data. The multidimensional model supports the slice and dice view of the data. Data is arranged in the form of cubes and can be vertically and horizontally cut across layers or dimensions and used for various analysis. Each cell of the multidimensional cube contains the aggregated results of the elements along each of its dimensions. The multidimensional model is widely used for online analytical processing (OLAP) applications. The structure provides an easy way to deal with complex queries efficiently. Figure 4.7 shows a sample multidimensional database model.

NoSQL Databases

LO 3 *Summarize salient features of NoSQL*

New databases came into existence with the new millennium and the explosion of Web content. It was not clear why it was referred to as NoSQL but somewhat it was clear that it was born out of frustration with relational systems. NoSQL initially subscribed to the notion 'Just Say No to SQL' but nowadays we treat it as 'Not Only SQL'.

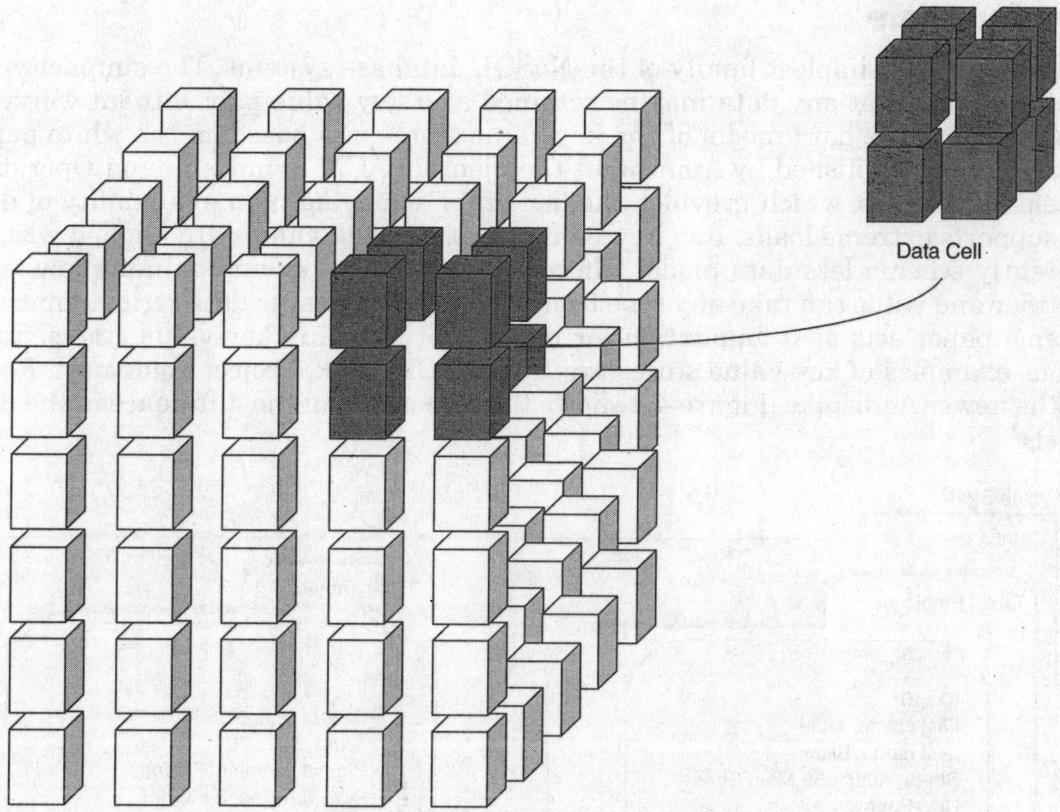

Fig. 4.7 Sample multidimensional model

One of the major drawbacks of the relational system is that it suffers at scale. For example, when the data grow in the form of tables or relations, then the queries to work on data turn into complex and inefficient computations. The relational schema also poses a very strict schema even we put our data, which is not feasible in the domains where *'one size works all'* schema approach is a failure. Though relational database seems to be a powerful tool to deal with the data with the relations, however, it fails to embrace some particular kinds of relations such as key-value pairs, or graphs and some usage patterns like extremely large-scale storage. Thus, it adds to the hardware and license cost forever increasingly [high] volume of data. NoSQL proposed efficient solutions to overcome the challenges posed by the relational systems. These NoSQL databases typically provide massive scalability by way of clustering and are often designed to enable high throughput and low latency.

The underlying philosophy of NoSQL is of *'task-oriented'* database management systems. Thus, depending upon the task at hand, NoSQL provides an appropriate solution to approach the task. We can see the following four categories of the NoSQL offerings based on their design and purpose.

> The underlying philosophy of NoSQL is of 'task-oriented' database management systems. Thus, depending upon the task at hand, NoSQL provides an appropriate solution to approach the task.

Key-value Store

It represents the simplest family of the NoSQL database systems. The simplicity lies within the fact that any data may be retained as a key-value pair without worrying of the schema. The data model of the key-value stores was based on the white paper, Dynamo paper published by Amazon at the biennial ACM Symposium on Operating Systems Principles, which provides the benefit of achieving high availability of data and supports extreme loads. In a key-value store, key and values are aligned with an inherently schema less data model where a row forms a key and value. A key is an identifier and value can take any type from an integer to a large data string. Amazon's Dynamo paper acts as a foundation for implementing many key-value stores. Some famous examples of key-value stores are DynamoDB, Riak, Project Voldemort, Redis, and the newer Aerospike. Figure 4.8 shows the screenshot of the difference in the data models.

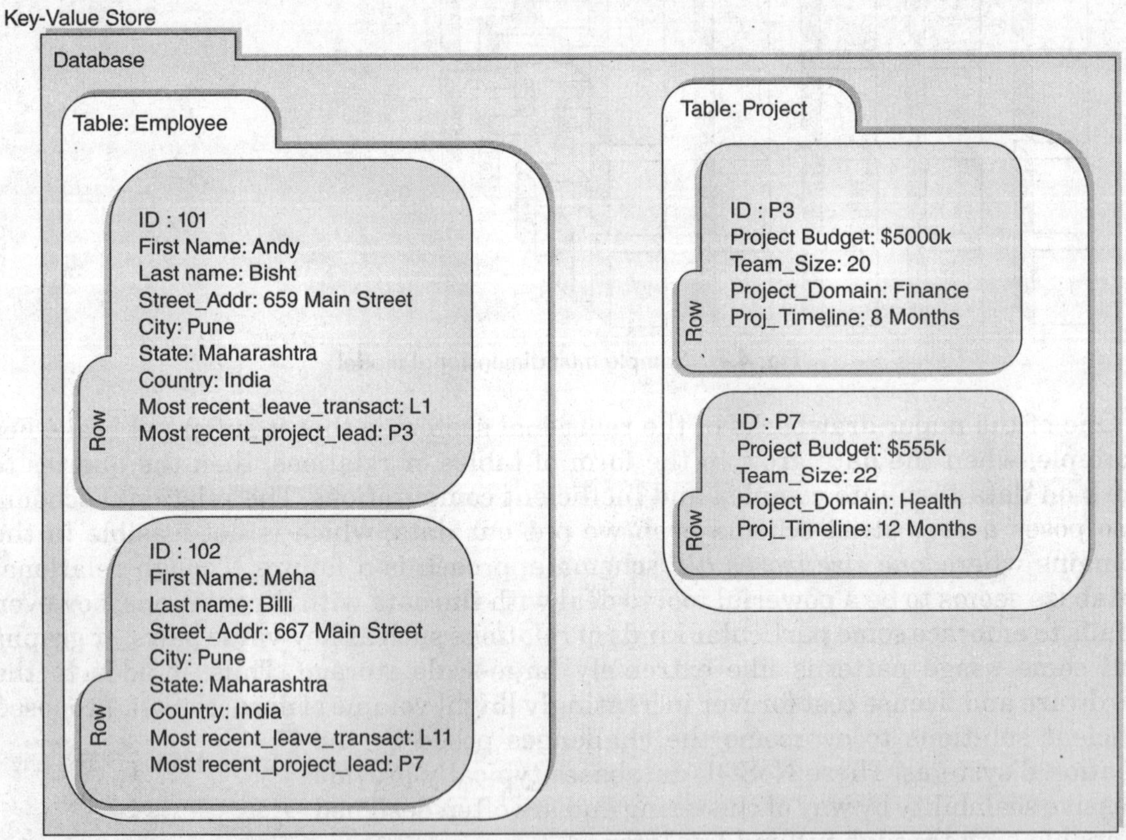

Fig. 4.8 Sample Key-Value Database

Column Family Store

It is another example of the task-oriented database solution, but the data model is a bit more complicated as compared to the key-value pair. This kind of database includes the sparsely populated table structure as column families. The column families are formed on grouping columns together. Google in its research paper presented 'BigTable' as a solution to the problem of efficiently storing and working with a sparse set of high-volume data. The article led open-source community to start many other projects in the similar directions, which gave birth to many open-source projects such as Apache Cassandra and HBase. In many cases, these systems are combined with batch-oriented systems that use Map/Reduce as the processing model for the advanced querying. Figure 4.9 shows a sample of column family database.

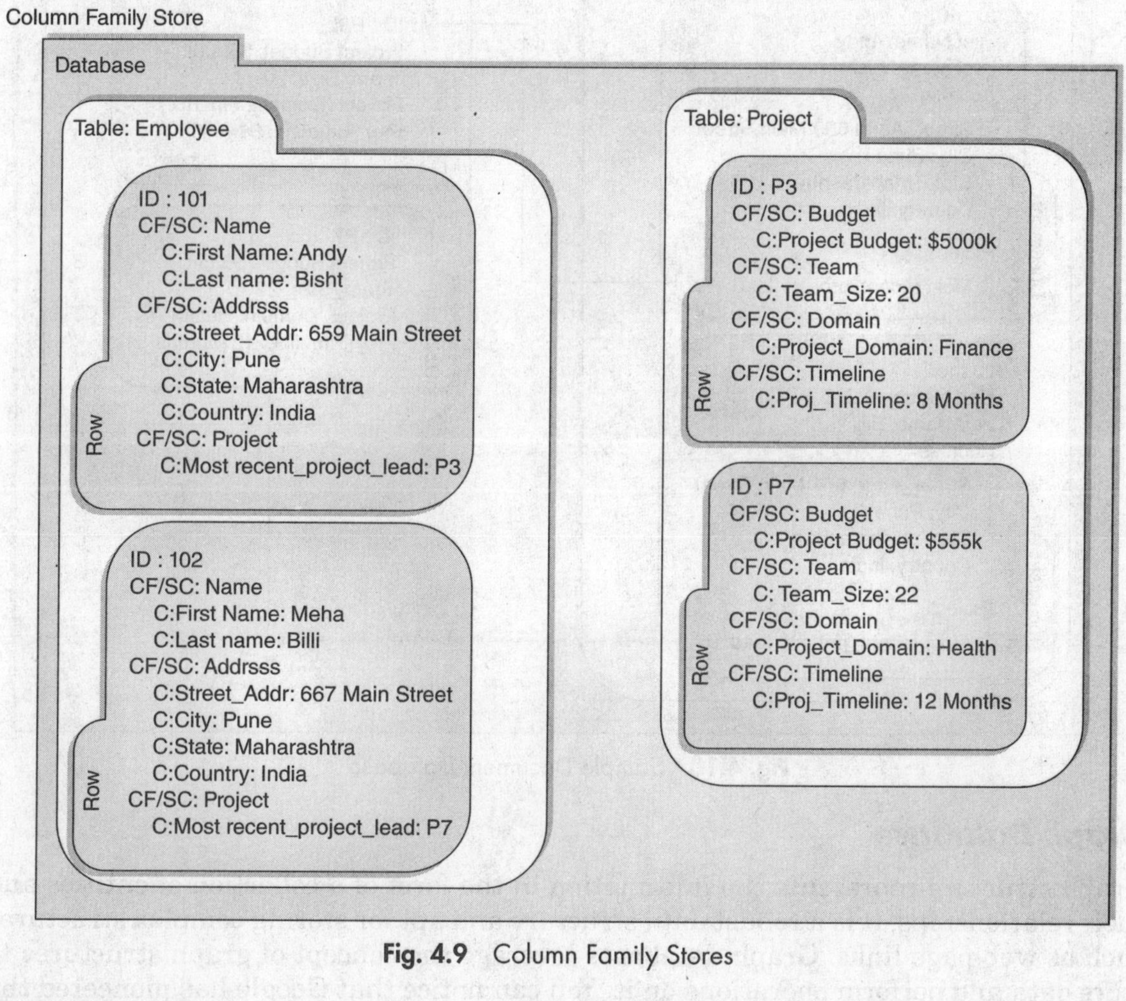

Fig. 4.9 Column Family Stores

Document Store

It represents one of the popular and well-known types of NoSQL, which stores the content such as Web content in the document category. It has a comprehensive set of offering that relies on a set of similarly encoded and formatted documents to improve efficiencies. Document represents a semi-structured unit of information. For example, a document can be XML, JSON, YAML, OpenOffice, and MS Office stored as schema less document. Some of the popular databases that support document store are MongoDB, Couchbase, MarkLogic, and Virtuoso. Figure 4.10 shows a sample Document database.

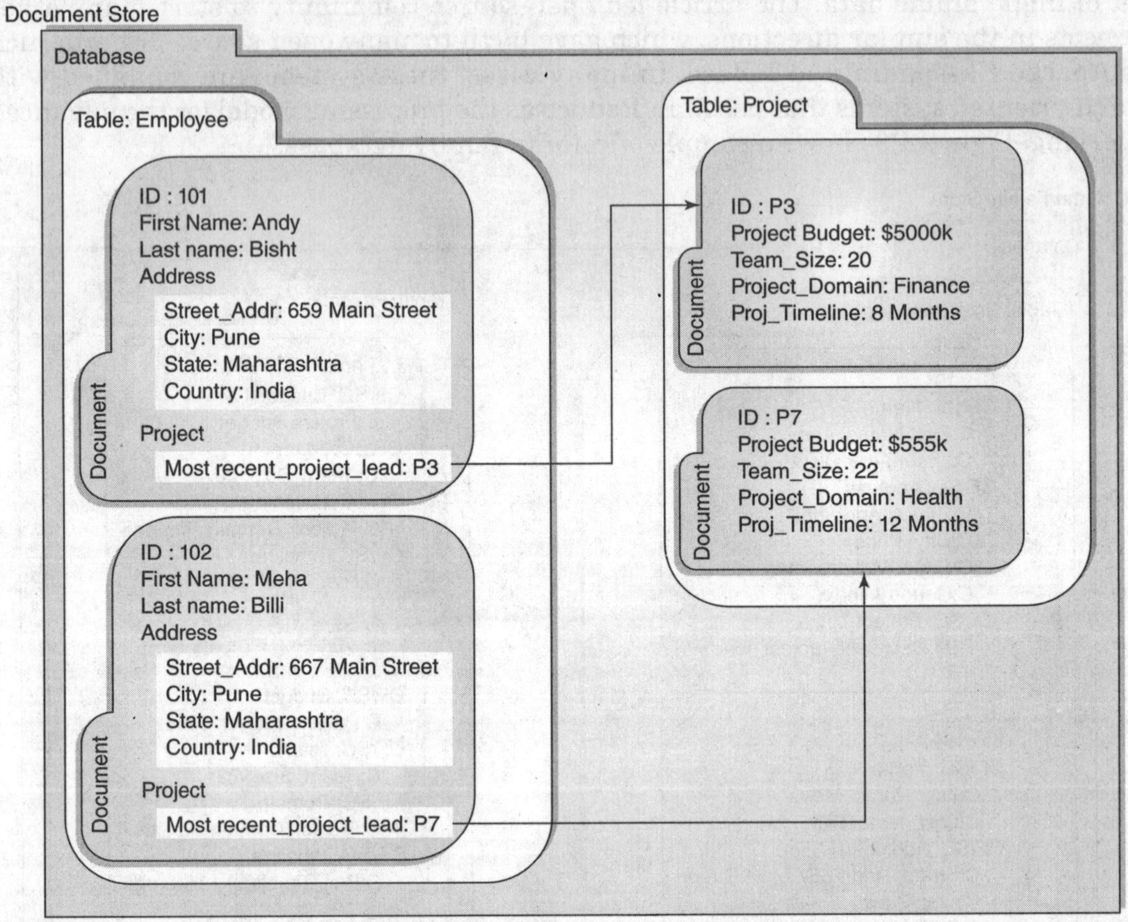

Fig. 4.10 Sample Document Database

Graph Database

Graph structure represents the information in the form of a collection of entities and their relationships. It is a robust data structure and apt for storing complex structures such as web page links. Graph databases leverage the concept of graph structures to store data and perform operations on it. You can notice that Google has pioneered the graph technology and invented a graph processing engine—Pregel, which is the driving force to power PageRank to provide efficient searches. In an open software ecosystem, the Apache project known as *Giraph* is being conceived based on the Pregel paper to process graph structures in HDFS. Some of the other popular graph databases are AllegroGraph, Dex, FlockDB, InfiniteGraph, OrientDB, and Sones. Figure 4.11 shows a sample Graph database model.

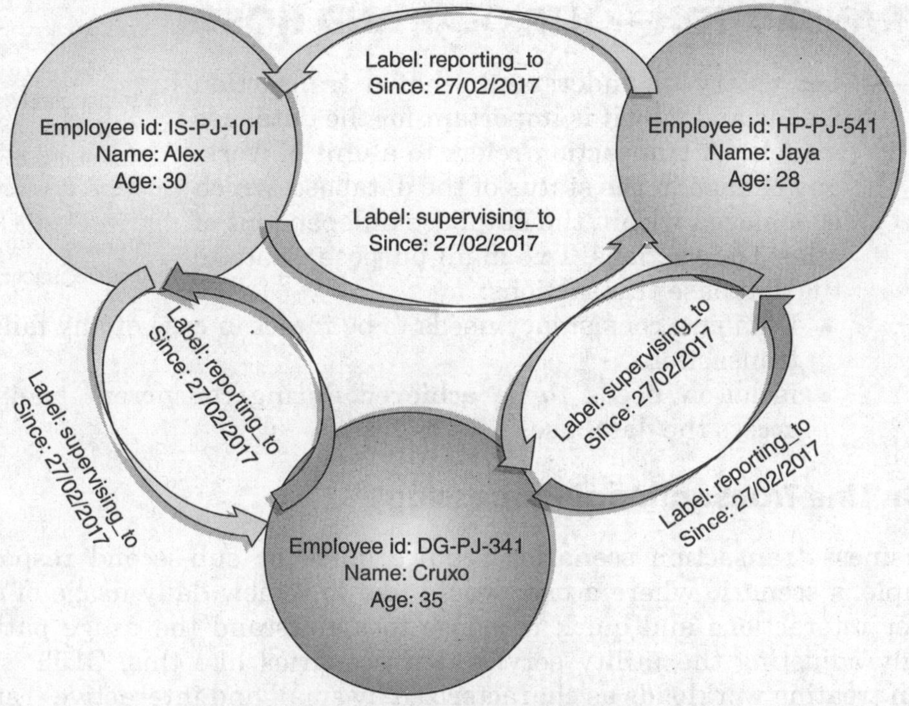

Fig. 4.11 A sample Graph database model

Table 4.1 summarizes the salient features of NoSQL.

Table 4.1 NoSQL data model features

Data model	*Performance*	*Scalability*	*Flexibility*	*Complexity*	*Functionality*
Key-Value Stores	High	High	High	Low	Variable (None)
Column Store	High	High	Moderate	Low	Minimal
Document Store	High	Variable (high)	High	Low	Variable (Low)
Graph Database	Variable	Variable	High	High	Defined by Graph theory

> *“The power must first of all be reasonable. You should ask of someone only what he is able to provide.”*
>
> —Antonie de Saint-Exupery, Le petit prince

4.2 TRANSACTION—OLTP, OLAP, AND NOSQL

LO 4 *Understand about transactions—OLTP, OLAP, and NoSQL*

Let us try to understand what a transaction means and why it is important for the database models. A transaction refers to a unit of work, any change in the status of the database, which is achieved within the database independent of other transactions. Two main purpose relate to the database transactions:

> A transaction refers to a unit of work, any change in the status of the database, which is achieved within the database independent of other transactions.

- Database consistency needs to be intact in case of any failure of the transactions.
- Isolation needs to be achieved during concurrent transaction to access the database.

OLTP (On Line Transactional Processing)

Many business transaction scenarios require quick or sub-second response time. For example, a scenario where a user would like to review daily usage of electricity needs user interactions and quick response to understand the usage patterns and accordingly adjusting the utility service. For scenarios like this, OLTP serves the purpose in treating workloads as characterized by small and interactive transactions. Such systems normally have concurrency mechanisms to achieve high efficiency in executing the transactions. A typical type of OLTP is the Batch OLTP, sometimes also

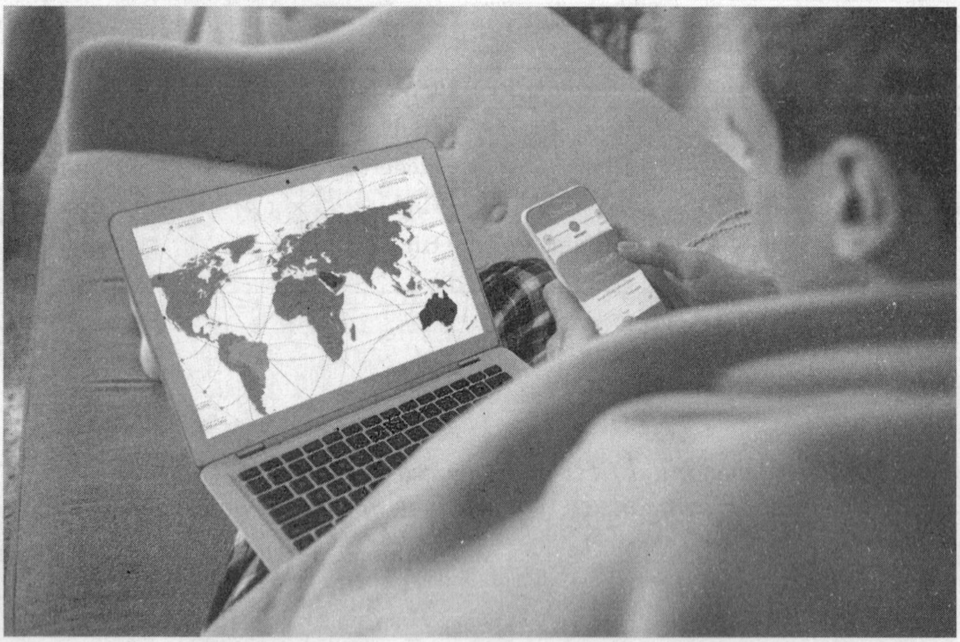

Fig. 4.12 Performing utility transactions

referred to as *Background* or *Asynchronous* OLTP, generally considers workloads in the batch format and characterized by the absence of user interaction. For example, check how you get your monthly utility bills. Utility applications process workloads in batches and typically do not require user interaction. One of the prime focus of OLTP systems is to achieve fast response query processing while maintaining the integrity in the multi-access environments.

OLAP (On Line Analytical Processing)

Business as a multi-facet activity requires multidimensional aspects to focus on, thereby achieving excellence and growth. OLAP helps in understanding the insights associated with the data by facilitating in performing complex high-level computations and data modelling. It also enables end-users to execute ad hoc analysis of the data in multiple dimensions. The multidimensional structure of the data is represented in the form of the cube covering dimensions and measures. Dimension represents an organized hierarchy of the levels to describe the data. One can perform various analysis on the dimension as it includes a similar set of members. For example, a sales dimension might include levels for Country, Region, State, and City. Thus, one can easily get the answers for the 'Sales by Country' or 'Sale by Region'. Similarly, a time dimension can have levels like 'year', 'Quarter', 'Month', and 'Day'. A measure is usually numeric and represents the summation of values in a cube.

LO 5
Apply design guidelines for the transactions—OLTP, OLAP, and NoSQL

The design and property of a transaction can be described as follows:

- ACID—Atomicity, Consistency, Isolation, and Durability
- BASE—Basically Available, Soft-state, Eventually consistent
- CAP—Consistency, Availability, and Partition Tolerance

ACID

ACID property of a transaction more or less is the benchmark for the relational databases. It describes the characteristics of the individual transaction. For a database transaction to be ACID compliant, it must adhere to

- **Atomicity:** Every transaction must adhere to its completeness. The transaction must completely succeed or fail. Partial completion is not allowed.
- **Consistency:** The status of the database at no point be invalid; thus, during the transaction, the database progresses from valid state to another state.
- **Isolation:** The database [client] transaction must execute in isolation to other [client] transaction.
- **Durability:** The result of the transaction must persist and available as per the valid status of the transaction.

An ACID-compliant transaction such as the transfer of funds between two accounts is broken into two transactions, which need to be tied together. In the first transaction, the withdrawal of the amount from one account is performed; and in the other transaction, the deposit of the amount takes place. In case of partial success, the partial operation is rollback resulting the balance in both the account to be valid.

CAP

You will be amazed to see that there is no concept of a transaction in the Hadoop, and NoSQL databases provide relaxation on ACID-properties to achieve flexibility, massive scalability, and performance. The CAP theorem proposed by Brewer suggest that the system has to choose any two properties among consistency, availability, and partition tolerance.

- **Consistency:** It refers to synchronization between different copies of the same piece of the data. Here, it reflects that every read of the data receives the most recent write or an error.
- **Availability:** It means the data is available all the time. It means that every request receives a non-error response with no guarantee of the recent write on the data.
- **Partition Tolerance:** It describes the way that the system operates despite any message being dropped by the network between the nodes.

Let us try to understand the CAP theorem with the help of an example. A company 'XYZ' has two data centres D1 and D2. Each data centre is running the database synchronized with each other. Thus, at no time, the data is inconsistent or in an invalid state. Now consider that at some point in time both the data centres lost the communication leading to the loss of synchronization; then we can see two options to work with the data centres [databases]:

- **Option 1 '*make system unavailable*':** Data centres D1 [and/or] D2 needs to stop processing further requests to avoid any inconsistency. It leads to the unavailability of the system as the client will not be able to modify the state of the databases.

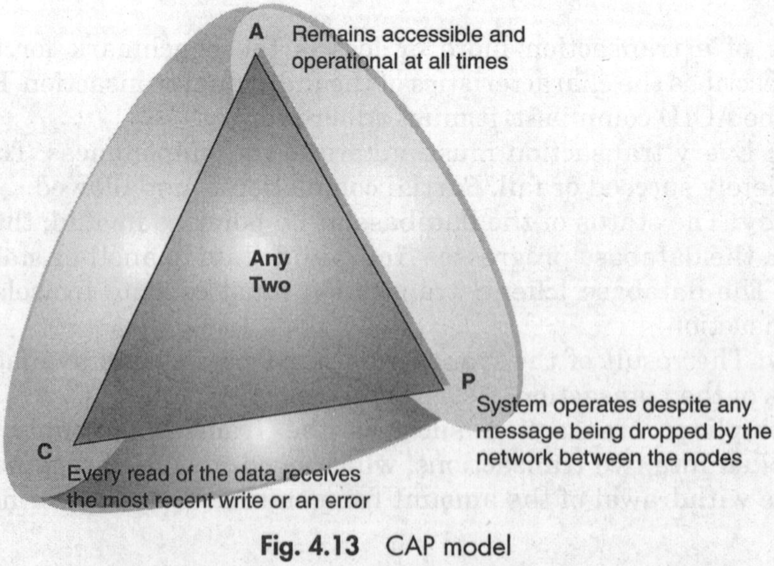

Fig. 4.13 CAP model

- **Option 2 *'make system available'*:** Data centres D1 [and/or] D2, both, are available independently but in isolation leaving aside the consistency. However, one can have access to the systems, but any updation in the database does not promise the consistency due to unavailability of the synchronization link.

The above example clearly states that in the case of the system partition, the connection and synchronization between different parts is absent—the system cannot have consistency and availability together. Figure 4.13 shows the CAP model.

BASE

We can notice that by applying CAP on the system partition, we have to choose between consistency and availability. A different approach to achieving consistency is desirable when choosing availability over consistency. The user application has to target achieving the consistency rather than the database itself. This approach is known as BASE (Basically Available, Soft state, Eventually consistent).

- **Basically Available:** It guarantees the availability of the systems for querying purpose to all the users.
- **Soft State:** It promises the change in the value that is stored in the system.
- **Eventually Consistent:** It represents the gradual progress of the system's state across all the nodes. Consider an example of the Hadoop; when the file is being written to the HDFS, the replicas of the data blocks are written gradually in the nodes after the original data. We can notice that for a short period before the replica of the data block is achieved, the system is in an inconsistent state.

Table 4.2 summarizes the features of ACID, CAP, and BASE.

Table 4.2 Features of ACID, CAP, and BASE

ACID	Atomicity	All or nothing of the N actions. Commit or Rollback
	Consistency	Transactions never observe or cause inconsistent data
	Isolation	Transactions are not aware of concurrent transactions
	Durability	Acknowledged transactions persist in all events
CAP	Consistency	Reflects that every read of the data receives the most recent write or an error
	Availability	Every request receives a non-error response with no guarantee of the recent write on the data
	Partition Tolerance	The system operates despite any message being dropped by the network between the nodes
BASE	Optimistic behaviour	Accept temporary database inconsistencies
	Basically Available	Availability by replication
	Soft state	It is the user's application's task to guarantee Consistency
	Eventually consistent	Weakly Consistent, the database will be consistent in the long run; 'stale' data is OK

Table 4.3 summarizes characteristics of the selected NoSQL databases.

Table 4.3 Summary table with characteristics of the selected NoSQL databases

		Aerospike	*Cassandra*	*Couchbase*	*CouchDB*	*HBase*	*MongoDB*	*Voldemort*
Category	Kay-value	√						√
	Column-store		√			√		
	Document-store			√	√		√	
	Graph							
CAP	CA							
	AP	√	√		√			√
	CP		√	√		√	√	
Consistency	Configurable	√	√			√	√	
	Eventual			√	√			
	Read-repair							√
Native partitioning		√	√	√		√	√	√
Partitioning scheme	Propriety	√						
	Hashing		√	√	√			√
	Range based					√		

SUMMARY

- Massive data storage and processing capacity in a distributed fashion is the core functionality of the Hadoop.
- 'Data stock' specifies the way in which data is arranged, controlled, accessed, and managed by the software system and technologies.
- A database is a collection of data in an organized fashion.
- In database management system, 'management' refers to the set of computer programs having specific instructions to manage the 'database'.
- Navigational databases are based on the design and model of a network of interrelated things.
- The multidimensional database provides a multidimensional view of the data.
- NoSQL databases typically provide massive scalability by way of clustering and are often designed to enable high throughput and low latency.

- The underlying philosophy of NoSQL is of 'task-oriented' database management systems. Thus, depending upon the task at hand, NoSQL provides an appropriate solution to approach the task.
- There are four categories of the NoSQL offerings based on their design and purpose—key-value store, column family store, document store, and graph store.
- In key-value store, any data may be retained as a key-value pair without worrying of the schema.
- Column databases include the sparsely populated table structure as column families.
- Document stores the content such as Web content in the document category.
- Graph databases leverage the concept of graph structures to store data and perform operations on it.
- A transaction refers to a unit of work, any change in the status of the database, which is achieved within the database independent of other transactions.
- One of the prime focus of OLTP systems is to achieve fast response query processing while maintaining the integrity in the multi-access environments.
- OLAP helps in understanding the insights associated with the data by facilitating in performing complex high-level computations and data modelling.
- ACID property describes the characteristics of the individual transaction.
- The CAP theorem suggests that the system has to choose any two properties among consistency, availability, and partition tolerance.
- Under BASE principle, user application has to target achieving the consistency rather than the database itself.

EXERCISE

Review Questions

1. Describe the evolution of database technologies.

   Tip: Perform Google search and check the evolution of database technologies.

2. What is the main difference between the relational and multidimensional database models?

   Tip: Develop the use case scenarios for relational and multidimensional database models. List down the challenges in managing and controlling models.

3. How NoSQL database model is helpful to the businesses of today? Explain with examples.

   Tip: Identify the information pioneered product and its value chain. List down the use case scenarios considering different data dimensions and map it with the [No]SQL solutions.

4. **Describe the categories of NoSQL database. Give suitable examples.**
   Tip: Perform a search on Google for more details about the examples.
5. **Describe transaction design principles in OLTP, OLAP, and NoSQL.**

Hive and HBase: Win-Win Together

5

"The men of experiment are like the ant; they only collect and use. But the bee...gathers its materials from the flowers of the garden and of the field, but transforms and digests it by a power of its own."

—Leonardo da Vinci

Learning Objectives

***On completing this chapter, you will be able to*:**

- **LO 1** Examine the Hive database model
- **LO 2** Describe Hive system architecture and components
- **LO 3** Perform HiveQL commands
- **LO 4** Examine the HBase database model
- **LO 5** Describe HBase shell and functionality
- **LO 6** Integrate Hive and HBase

CASE STUDY: Facebook—Unleashing the Power of Hive

The data infrastructure team at Facebook developed Hive. It is an open source peta-byte scale data-warehousing framework on top of the Hadoop.

Facebook has many products based on analytics, which utilize large data set analysis. These products range from simple reporting tool like Insights to a more advanced product like Lexicon. Each product has different functionality, but the underlying principle is to perform large-scale data analysis. Thus, the need to build flexible infrastructure to cater to the need of diversified applications and business cases is critical to Facebook.

Facebook data set grew from 15TB in 2007 to 2PB in size and increasing every single day by 15TB. The analysis was constrained with infrastructure setup and the timeline of the project. For example, some analytics jobs could take more than few days, which was undesirable. Thus, a new infrastructure to handle and operate on the large data was envisioned. Initially, Hadoop, a scalable and distributed processing platform, helped the Facebook to perform efficient and effective analysis; but because the jobs to be written in MapReduce-Java oriented, it was quite challenging to embrace the technology. Also, business users didn't have the access to the data stored in Hadoop. End users could not appreciate the technology as they had to write map/reduce programs even for a typical query. For example, it would be very challenging to write map/reduce programs for a trivial task such as count, average, etc. Facebook realized that most of their users already had a common skill—they knew SQL. Hadoop lacked the expressiveness of the familiar query language SQL.

The data infrastructure team at Facebook decided to extend the capability of the Hadoop by introducing the power of SQL to the unstructured data without compromising on the Hadoop feature of the flexibility and extensibility. Hive was developed to give access to data stored in Hadoop translating SQL-like statements into complex map-reduce jobs reading and processing data on a large distributed scale. Hive was conceptualized and available to the users as open source in August 2008. Since then many for their data processing needs are using it. Hive gets its way to for machine learning, analytics jobs, business intelligence, and many other business and scientific applications.

The evolution of Hive and its adoption for many business cases is a success story. Facebook is performing large-scale peta-byte analysis on thousands of computers. Hive is one intersection point for thousands of employees to run complex queries, which in turn execute thousands of MapReduce jobs every day and generate actionable insights.

Questions

1. What problem is big data helping to solve?

   Tip: Check the Facebook website for its service offerings. List the data sources and type of data involved in generating business value.

2. How is big data applicable in practice in Facebook?

   Tip: Describe the technology and [Big] data dimensions applicable to Facebook.

3. Which data is important?

   Tip: Describe the data usage scenarios.

4. Which technology is being used?

   Tip: Identify the technology used to store, manage, analyse, and query data.

5. What challenges does Facebook need to overcome?

   Tip: Identify the technology solution at Facebook. Further, map the use case requirement of the technology based on all of its stakeholders. Develop metrics to measure the success of the technology usage.

6. What patterns are effective for high-performance use cases?

   Tip: List the primary, secondary, support, and other key stakeholders and their usage of data contributing to the underpinning assumption of 'Data-driven-decision' principle.

References

Ashish T. Hive - A Petabyte Scale Data Warehouse using Hadoop. https://www.facebook.com/notes/facebook-engineering/hive-a-petabyte-scale-data-warehouse-using-hadoop/89508453919/ [accessed Sep 01, 2017];

UNCOVERING THE HIDDEN PATTERN's OF HIVE; FACEBOOK. http://www.edupristine.com/blog/facebook-hive-explained [accessed Sep 07, 2017];

Facebook, Hadoop, and Hive. http://www.dbms2.com/2009/05/11/facebook-hadoop-and-hive/ [accessed Sep 07, 2017];

Tom White. Hadoop and Hive at Facebook. Hadoop: The Definitive Guide. O'Reilly;

Wolfgang Lehner, Kai-Uwe Sattler. 2013. Web-Scale Data Management for the Cloud. Springer;

Vivek Kale. Big Data Computing: A Guide for Business and Technology Managers. CRC Press Taylor and Francis

> *"I live in a data landscape, which every single day of my life is enriching data."*
>
> —Daniel Day-Lewis

Organizations nowadays are inclined towards understanding their data and performing deeper analysis for actionable insights. The enterprise data warehouse (EDW) solutions that were based on multidimensional structure provide processing and analysis at scale. However, most of the EDWs solution utilize some form of relational database systems as the primary storage and query engine for the analysis. Such kind of solutions put a constraint on the data level most precisely at the schema level. Mostly, the efforts were in building design schema for the data and extract, transform, and load (ETL) operations. The ETL operations seem to be costly with long turnaround time, which does not provide efficiency in achieving useful analysis.

Not only this, but relational databases were also restricted to the structured data type leaving aside the storage and operational analysis for unstructured data. As Facebook took the lead on transforming its data infrastructure to extend the benefits of Hadoop (distributed processing and storage), a new open source peta-byte scale data warehousing framework was conceptualized and developed. In this chapter, we will cover aspects of Hadoop's most popular SQL-based querying engine, Hive and NoSQL database, and HBase.

5.1 HIVE—DATA MODEL

LO 1 *Examine the Hive database model*

The underlying data model of Hive relies on tables and partitions. A good partition scheme provides efficient pruning capability leading to efficient query processing and analysis. For example, if we are considering sales data of the products where the data is partitioned based on '*sale impressions*'. Then the partitioned data set has tables and partitions covering data as per the dates, days, quarter, month's, and year's impressions of the product sales. The partition data set is stored in directories in the HDFS. When one performs query on a particular date or a month for the processing and analysis, the other partitions are not considered. The partitioning scheme also provides benefit in managing the storage. For example, identifying the old archival data, which could be stored in the cheap storage and the relevant data could be partitioned and stored in high-level access storage. Considering our example of '*sale impressions*', the main data set is mapped to/warehouse/sales_impressions and each of the partitions based on the date stamp are mapped as warehouse/sale_impressions/ds=2017-08-25 (date stamp is a partitioning column; 2017-08-25 is the sample date). If a partitioning scheme considers multiple columns, then each column needs to be mapped internally with the level within the directory name space linking each column to the bucket of the files. These buckets can be hashed or random. Further, bucketing scheme to arrange the files helps in sampling the data and achieving fast processing and analysis. The fields or columns in the partitions and tables can be of primitive type—integers, doubles, floats, and strings or complex types—maps, lists, and structures. Hive also provides mechanisms to handle user defined types data.

5.2 SYSTEM ARCHITECTURE AND COMPONENTS

LO 2 *Describe Hive system architecture and components*

In this section, we will first understand the architecture and components of Hive and then will unleash the power of Hive for processing and analysis. Figure 5.1 provides the high-level architecture of Hive.

Primary Layers of Hive

There are two primary layers of Hive, which are described as follows.

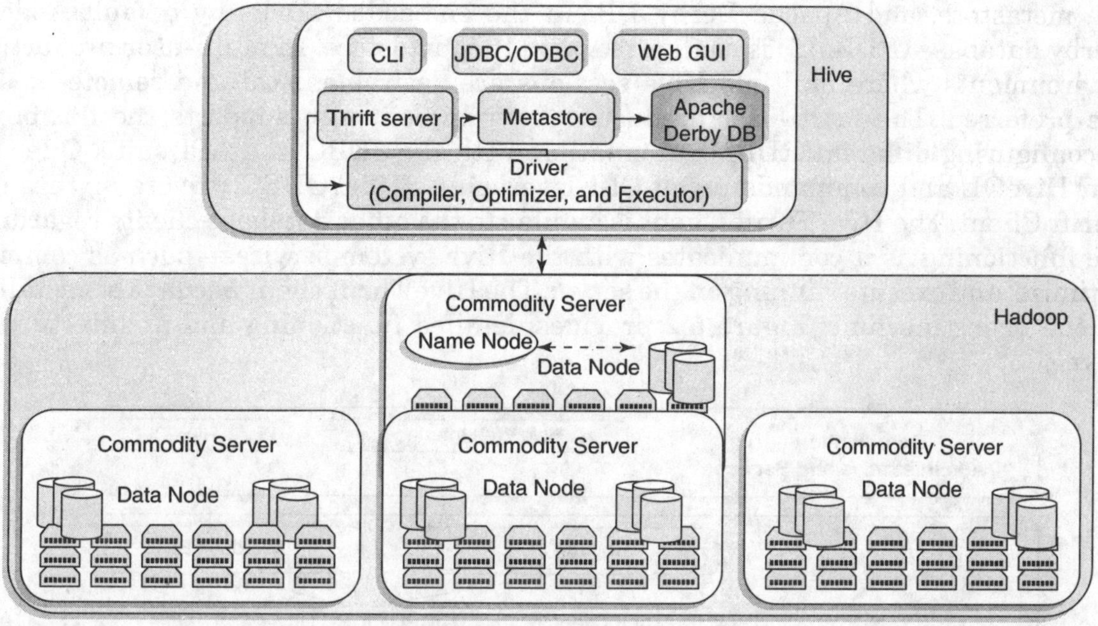

Fig. 5.1 System Architecture of Hive

Hadoop

It provides HDFS and MapReduce/Yarn as an underlying layer for the Hive to function. The Hive provides Hive Query Language (HQL) statements which are converted to the MapReduce codes and executed in the MapReduce paradigm. In case, the Hadoop 1 is utilized, then MapReduce codes are executed using MapReduce v1 (MRv1) infrastructure, i.e., jobTracker and TaskTracker are functional elements. For Hadoop 2, the MapReduce v2 (MRv2) and YARN are driving the elements.

Hive Elements

It comprises of Hive Driver, Metastore, Derby DB, Thrift Sever, Command Line Interface (CLI), Web Interface, and JDBC/ODBC connections. Hive driver converts the Hive queries to the MapReduce codes. For some cases, the Hive driver may also choose to execute the HiveQL statements and commands locally. The Hive Driver interacts with the metastore where the tables and partitions metadata and database are available. The Hive Thrift Server enables the access to Hive subsystem. People who prefer command interface to issue queries and administrative commands interact with Hive Command Line Interface (CLI); and those who prefer graphical way to approach, Hive provides them Graphical User Interface (Web interface).

Execution—HiveQL and Administrative Commands

—LO 3—
Perform HiveQL commands

Hive supports three different modes—embedded, local, and remote. The embedded mode supports single Hive session that means a single Java Virtual Machine (JVM) is running all the elements—Hive Driver, the metastore, and Apache Derby DB. In the embedded mode, by default Apache Derby database (RDBMS) is configured with the metastore. In multi-user production environments where multiple Hive sessions are desirable, local and remote modes are preferred. The multi-user production environment also supports the flexibility of configuring different RDBMS compatible with the JDBC and API suite. One can run HiveQL and commands using CLI leveraging JDBC/ODBC drivers or through Thrift Client. The Hive Thrift Client is similar to the other database clients regarding the functioning as it communicates with the Hive system services—such as compile, optimize, and execute running on the server. The Hive Thrift client needs to be installed on the user's machine. Figure 5.2 provides detailed functioning and architecture of Hive.

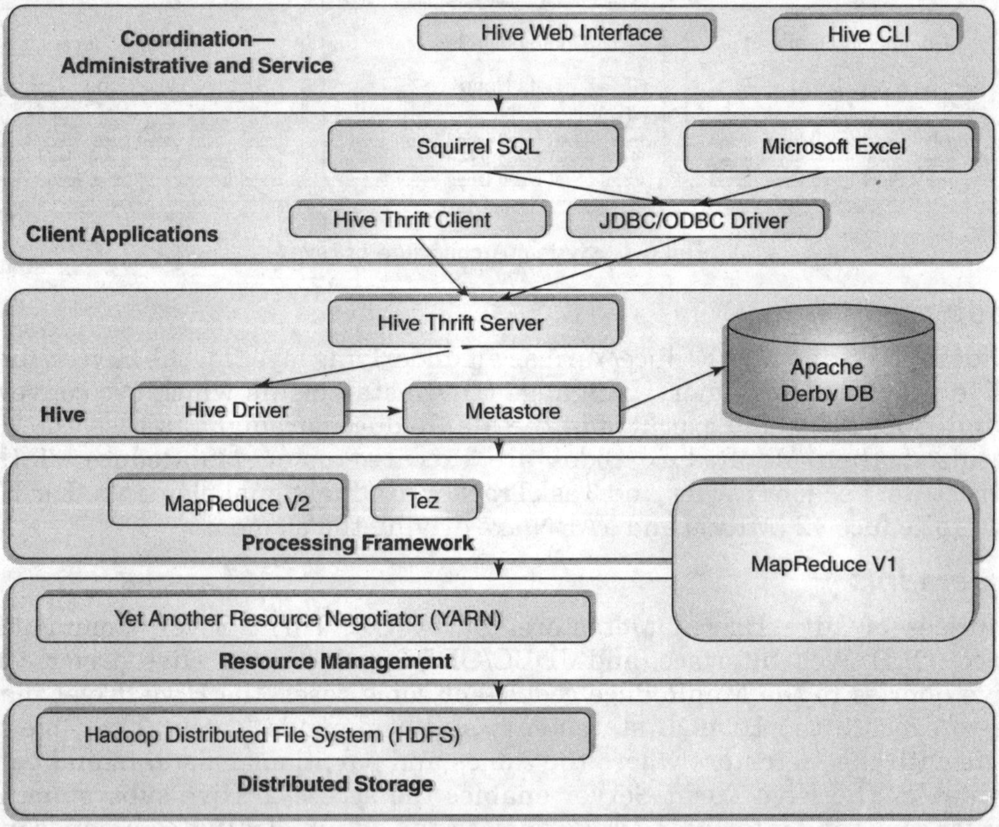

Fig. 5.2 Detailed functioning and architecture of Hive

Data Queries Control and Execution

Hive Query Language (HQL) looks similar to the other traditional database SQL language and, thus, who so ever has earlier worked with the SQL has an edge working with HiveQL. However, there exist several fundamental differences between

Fig. 5.3 Manager querying the subordinates

traditional SQL and HiveQl regarding functioning and overall service. Hive is based on Hadoop, which is intended for distributed storage and distributed processing targeting long sequential or batch scans. Thus, one can expect high latency time for getting the result of HiveQL (depending upon the complexity of the query). So, one cannot use Hive for fast response time applications. Hive is, predominantly, in the space of read-based solutions and, thus, not suitable for the transaction processing applications that require high write operations.

HiveQL supports many commonly used traditional SQL statements such as

- **Data definition statements:** These statements are used to define the structure in a database. For example, CREATE DATABASE/SCHEMA/TABLE.
- **Data manipulation statements:** These statements define the operation for the manipulation. For example, INSERT, UPDATE, LOAD, etc.
- **Data retrieval statements:** These statements define the operation for the retrieving the result. For example, SELECT.

Table 5.1 Different statements and their purpose

Item/purpose	*Command*	*Description*
Database	CREATE DATABASE|SCHEMA [IF NOT EXISTS] name_of_database;	To create a new database or schema. A database or schema with the name specified is created in case [IF NOT EXIST] clause is used. An error is shown in case the database is created with the same name as the existing database.
	SHOW DATABASES;	To show the existing set of databases
	DROP (DATABASE|SCHEMA) [IF EXISTS] name_of_database [RESTRICT|CASCADE];	To drop the database or schema. It has two options: RESTRICT or CASCADE. In the CASCADE clause, the respective tables are dropped before the whole database. In RESTRICT mode, the DROP command fails if the database is not empty.
	ALTER (DATABASE|SCHEMA) name_of_database SET OWNER [USER|ROLE] user_or_role;	To alter the database or schema with the specific ownership for user or role.
	USE name_of_database;	To work with the database having names as name_of_database.
Table	CREATE [TEMPORARY] [EXTERNAL] TABLE [IF NOT EXISTS] [name_of_database] name_of_table [(name_of_col type_of_data [COMMENT comment_of_col], ...)] [COMMENT comment_of_table] [ROW FORMAT format_of_row] [STORED AS format_of_file]	To create a table in the database. Many clauses are used with the CREATE TABLE statement. The row format fields are Line terminator, Collection Items, Map Keys, and Field Terminator. The file can be stored as 'TEXTFILE' or another compatible format (AVRO, SEQUENCEFILE, ORC, PARQUET, RCFILE. A comment can describe description about table or column as per the specific usage.
	ALTER TABLE name_of_table [RENAME TO new_name_of_table| ADD COLUMNS (col_spec[, col_spec ...])| DROP [COLUMN] name_of_column| CHANGE name_of_column new_name_of_column new_type_of_column|REPLACE COLUMNS (col_spec[, col_spec ...])]	To alter the table. Further, many different alteration can be achieved. For example, change of table name, column name, and column type. Also, Column can be added as well as dropped.
	DROP TABLE [IF EXISTS] name_of_table;	To drop the table. The table is dropped only when it exists otherwise an error is shown.
Retrieval	SELECT [ALL | DISTINCT] expression_for_selection, expression_for_selection, ... FROM reference_table_name [WHERE condition_constraint] [GROUP BY list_of_col] [HAVING condition_constraint] [CLUSTER BY list_of_col | [DISTRIBUTE BY col_list] [SORT BY list_of_col]] [LIMIT number];	To select a particular data set from the table based on certain conditions or constraints

Hive CLI (Command Line Interface) and HiveQL

Command line interface provides an interactive way to the user to deal with queries and administrative commands. The CLI comes handy when one would like to perform quick interactive query and command. Generally, few test queries need to be run before making it a production level suite, which is well handled by Hive. Hive's native installation has CLI to interact with Hive and run HiveQL statements. Now, we will explore how to use CLI and run few queries and commands. On successful installation of Hive, you can see the Hive prompt for the CLI as follows:

```
hive>
```

To check the current set of databases, following HiveQL is executed and the response is shown as follows:

```
hive> show tables;
OK
Time taken: 0.777 seconds
```

To show the databases list available in Hive, following HiveQL is executed:

```
hive> show databases;
OK
Time taken: 0.567 seconds
```

Let us consider an example of the typical educational university. A university 'EDU' has several departments, and each department has separate courses to offer to students. Some courses have the interdisciplinary approach of offering in sync with the goals to accomplish for learning. The university enrolls 50,000 students every year in various courses and one would like to perform analysis on the student data for the period of 2007–2017, i.e., 10 years. The records are humongous and spread over several data files. One such file is '*student.txt*' which contains records of students spread over five key fields: '*student id*', '*student name*', '*course name*', '*course id*', and '*student grade point average (gpa)*'. Therefore, the overall analysis will be on 5 million records. For simplicity, we look into the small sample of the file '*student.txt*' which is shown in Table 5.2:

Table 5.2 Sample record of the file 'student.txt'

EDU2007CS001	Meha Pujari	Big Data	BD501	4.0
EDU2007ME101	John Pinto	Public Speaking	PS401	3.7
EDU2008CE201	Rakhi Shakrma	Maths I	MT203	2.9
⋮	⋮	⋮		⋮
EDU2017CE201	Rishi Gohr	Big Data	BD501	3.9

We will create a '*college*' database; and then inside it, we will create '*student*' table.

```
hive> CREATE DATABASE COLLEGE;
OK
Time taken: 2.777 seconds
```

When the '*college*' database is created, the schema definition data is stored in the Hive Metastore. It happens whenever a new database is created in Hive. In case the database already exists, then Hive will throw an error. Now, to create '*student*' database inside the '*college*' database, we have first to make '*college*' database available as a working database and use it for the further purpose of analysis.

```
hive> USE DATABASE COLLEGE;
OK
Time taken: 0.667 seconds
```

Now, we have created our first database; the next thing is to create the layout of our data by creating the table. To create table '*student*', following HiveQL statement is executed:

```
hive> CREATE TABLE IF NOT EXISTS STUDENT (sid string,
>sname string, cname string, cid string, gpa double)
>comment 'student academic details'
>ROW FORMAT DELIMITED
>FIELDS TERMINTAED BY '\t'
>LINES TERMINTED BY '\n'
STORED AS TEXTFILE;
OK
Time taken: 2.777 seconds
```

We have added the 'IF NOT EXISTS' clause while creating the table. This is important as the table is created only when the table does not exist in Hive. Once the table is created, we can verify its definition by executing the following statement:

```
hive> DESCRIBE student;
OK
Time taken: 0.147 seconds
```

Now, if we want to see the table that we have just created, we need to execute the following statement:

```
hive> show tables;
OK
customers
student
Time taken: 0.645 seconds, Fetche: 2 row(s)
```

To perform analysis on the table, we must have data in it and to do so we need to fill the table with the appropriate data for the analysis. There are typically two ways by which we can place data on the table. First, by using 'INSERT' statement to insert each row into the table. It is cumbersome if you have large data set. Thus, we can use the another approach by which we can quickly place data in a batch fashion; it uses 'LOAD' statement to load the whole data into a table. You can load data either from your local file system or HDFS. Hive does not perform any data compliance verification nor does it support any transformation while loading the data into a table. It is the primary distinction as compared to the traditional databases where schema definition is the major constraint and enforced at the data design phase. Hive will return the result as Null if the case in it deals with the values of missing fields or type mismatch. The data load read operations are fast as no parsing, transformation, or verification is attempted. The 'INPATH' in the LOAD statement takes an argument to a path on the default file system, i.e., HDFS. However, for accessing the local system, we have to use 'LOCAL INPATH.' In case the OVERWRITE keyword is used, then the existing target data table is overwritten otherwise the new data is added to the target table.

Let us consider that the '*student.txt*' file is stored in a local file system, and the following statement is executed to load the file into Hive:

```
hive> LOAD DATA LOCAL INPATH '/home/user/student.txt'
> OVERWRITE INTO TABLE student;
OK
Time taken: 1.905 seconds
hive>
```

Partitioning of the data table provides benefits to the efficient search. For example, if one wants to search the details of the student for the year 2013, then the search is performed on the whole data set of the '*student*' table, in this case, 5 million records. The best way to optimize the such thing is to organize the data in the partitions. In this case, we can create a partition, the data set based on the '*year*' field of the '*student*' table. The following statement is executed to establish the partition:

```
hive> ALTER TABLE student
> ADD PARTITION (year='2013')
> location '/student/part2013';
OK
Time taken: 1.203 seconds
hive>
```

To perform good analysis on the data stored in tables and partitions, we have to understand built-in support of the operators and leveraging them for analysis. Hive has four built in operators—Relational, Arithmetic, Logical, and Complex Operators.

Relational Operators

These operators are used to provide the functionality of addressing the relational linking of the data. They are applied on operands to generate the result of the comparison. Table 5.3 highlights the description of the relational operators.

Table 5.3 Description of the relational operators

Operator	*Operand*	*Description*
A = B	all primitive types	The expression returns TRUE if the value of A is equivalent to B otherwise FALSE
A != B	all primitive types	The expression returns TRUE if the value of A is not equivalent to B otherwise FALSE
A < B	all primitive types	The expression returns TRUE if the value of A is less than B otherwise FALSE
A <= B	all primitive types	The expression returns TRUE if the value of A is less than or equal to B otherwise FALSE
A > B	all primitive types	The expression returns TRUE if the value of A is greater than B otherwise FALSE
A >= B	all primitive types	The expression returns TRUE if the value of A is greater than or equal to B otherwise FALSE
A IS NULL	all types	The expression returns TRUE if the value of A is NULL
A IS NOT NULL	all types	The expression returns TRUE if the value of A is not NULL
A LIKE B	Strings	The expression returns TRUE if the value (string pattern) of A is equivalent to B otherwise FALSE
A RLIKE B	Strings	The expression returns TRUE if the value (substring pattern) of A is equivalent to the regular expression of B otherwise FALSE

Arithmetic Operators

These operators are used to perform arithmetic operations on the operands. Each arithmetic expression results into number types. Table 5.4 shows the description of arithmetic operators.

Table 5.4 Description of the arithmetic operators

Operators	*Operand*	*Description*
A + B	all number types	The expression returns the value of addition of A's value and B's value
A – B	all number types	The expression returns the value of subtraction of B's value from A's value
A * B	all number types	The expression returns the value of multiplication of A's value and B's value
A / B	all number types	The expression returns the value of division of A's value by B's value

(*Contd.*)

A % B	all number types	The expression returns the value of remainder of A's value by B's value
A & B	all number types	The expression returns the bitwise AND value of A's value and B's value
A | B	all number types	The expression returns the bitwise OR value of A's value and B's value
A ^ B	all number types	The expression returns the bitwise XOR value of A's value and B's value
~A	all number types	The expression returns the bitwise NOT value of A's value

Logical Operators

The logical operators provide the functionality of logic regarding binary value TRUE or FALSE. Table 5.5 shows the description of the complex operators.

Table 5.5 Description of the logical operators

Operators	*Operands*	*Description*
A AND B	boolean	The expression returns TRUE if the value of A and B are TRUE otherwise FALSE
A && B	boolean	The expression returns TRUE if the value of A and B are TRUE otherwise FALSE
A OR B	boolean	The expression returns TRUE if either of the value of A and B is TRUE otherwise FALSE
A || B	boolean	The expression returns TRUE if either of the value of A and B is TRUE otherwise FALSE
NOT A	boolean	The expression returns TRUE if value of A is FALSE otherwise returns TRUE
!A	boolean	The expression returns TRUE if value of A is FALSE otherwise returns TRUE

Complex Operators

These operators support the complex operations by taking into account the complex type objects. Table 5.6 shows the description of the complex operators.

Table 5.6 Description of the complex operators

Operator	*Operand*	*Description*
A[n]	A represents the array and 'n' the index of the element and is of type int	The expression returns the value of index 'n' in the array A. The index of array begins from value 0.
M[key]	M is a Map<K, V> and key has type K	The expression returns the value of the key.
S.x	S is a struct	The expression returns the value of field 'x' of the structure 'S'

Data Analysis with Hive

Now, we have a good exposure on how we can create database, table, partition, define scheme, and load data set into the table. Let us understand some useful ways to perform analysis on the data by executing HiveQL queries.

To retrieve all student details in the '*student*' table, following statement is executed:

```
hive> SELECT * FROM student;
```

To retrieve all student details in the '*student*' table, where the year is 2013, following statement is executed:

```
hive> SELECT * FROM student WHERE year==2013;
```

To retrieve all student details in the '*student*' table where the year is 2013 and students gpa is more than 3.5, following statement is executed:

```
hive> SELECT * FROM student WHERE year==2013 AND gpa > 3.5;
```

To retrieve all student details, year wise count, in the '*student*' table group by the year where students gpa is more than 3.5, following statement is executed:

```
hive>  SELECT year, count(*) FROM student where gpa>3.5 GROUP BY year;
```

Hive also supports various aggregate and statistical functions to provide advanced functionality on the analysis. Table 5.7 shows the description of some of the useful aggregate functions. A full list of functions can be found at the link https://cwiki.apache.org (Hive operators and User Defined Functions (UDFs)).

Table 5.7 Useful built-in aggregate and statistical functions

Functions	*Description*
Count	to retrieve the number of rows
Sum	to add the value of a group or add the distinct values in a column
Average	to average the value of a group or average the distinct values in a column
Min	to retrieve the minimum value of a group or minimum value in a column
Max	to retrieve the maximum value of a group or maximum value in a column
Variance	to retrieve the variance value of a group or in a column (numeric)
Standard deviation	to retrieve the standard deviation value of a group or in a column (numeric)
Covariance	to retrieve the covariance of a pair of columns (numeric)

Hive provides quite a flexible way to work with data. However, the data should be in the form of structured table based format, and the computations should be in the form of batch-oriented OLAP queries fashion.

Extensibility and Writing Your Own Map/Reduce

Hive is quite flexible as it supports an extended framework to include computations, machine learning models, indexes of different types on data, and other appropriate applications. All such applications and meaningful constructs can be plugged into scripts in the SQL statements. HiveQL for the extensibility purpose supports special keywords—MAP, REDUCE, TRANSFORM, SORT BY, DISTRIBUTE BY, and CLUSTER BY to accomplish non-SQL related tasks.

5.3 HBASE

LO 4 *Examine the HBase database model*

In the first half of this chapter, we have explored the power of Hive and HiveQL for large-scale SQL-based analysis on the structured datasets. However, Hive utilizes popular data manipulation paradigm within Hadoop, the distributed storage (HDFS), and MapReduce in the batch-oriented fashion paradigm remains same. Figure 5.4 shows the interaction of HBase and HDFS.

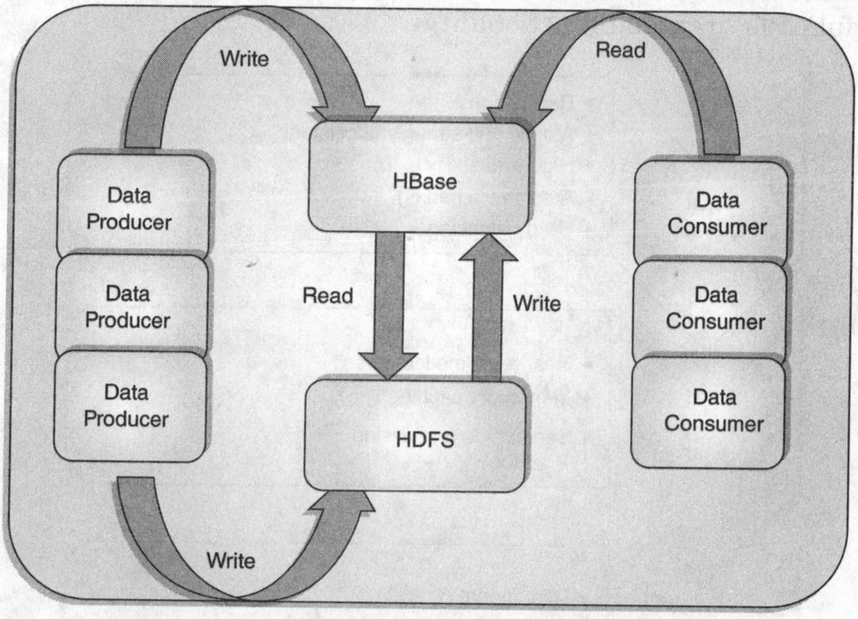

Fig. 5.4 HBase and HDFS

As opposed to the read only solutions, HBase provides the benefit of read/write solution to the extent that it can be used for real-time read/write access to large datasets. HBase can efficiently handle billion of rows and millions of columns. It also supports wide variety of data sources, structures, and schemas making it a popular choice for large-scale real-time applications. Not like Hadoop, which was developed with the primary purpose of write once and read many times, HBase is flexible and natively integrated with Hadoop to provide efficient read/write cycles. Following are the key characteristics of HBase, see Fig. 5.5:

Fault tolerant

- data replication to achieve fault tolerance in case of any failure as it is natively integrated with Hadoop
- consistent row-level operations and benefit of exercising atomic operations
- automatic failover to recover for high availability
- balancing of tables and sparse data effectively

Fast

- access to real-time read/write access and achieving fast lookups
- caching through in-memory fashion utilizing block cache and bloom filters
- processing at server side utilizing filters and co-processors
- low latency access to the rows

Usable

- supports wide array of use cases as the inherent data model is flexible
- easy-to-use metrics exports for optimization and usage
- Powerful APIs to extend functionality

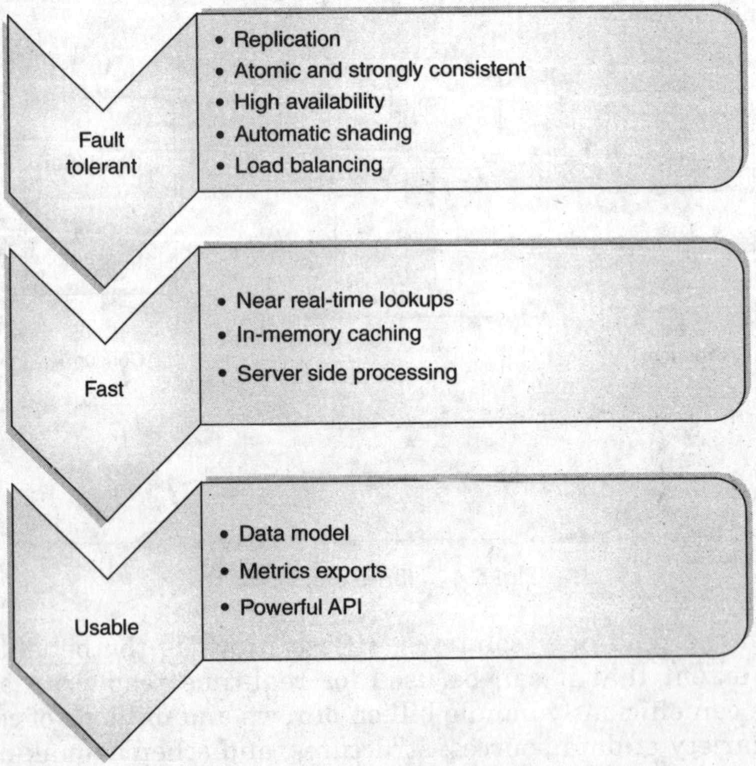

Fig. 5.5 HBase Characteristics

HBase is based on Google's Bigtable Architecture and is appropriate for

- low latency access
- strong consistency
- flexible data modelling achieving 'schema-less' feature

Storage Mechanisms

Though HBase sits on top of Hadoop and utilizes the flexibility of Hadoop, we need to understand the storage and processing mechanisms via which it addresses real-time write/read access to large data sets. HBase is a NoSQL database and belongs to the category of column family database. The large data tables in HBase are sorted by row to address the sparse issues. The schema of the table in the HBase is the key-value pairs, which defines the column families. Each column family can have multiple columns of interest of the data domain, and a table can have multiple column families. The values of each subsequent column are stored contiguously to achieve low latency lookups. The column cell value has a time associated with it.

The schema less data modelling is different from the traditional relational data modelling. The HBase consists of tables, and each table has rows. Each row has multiple column families where rows are identified by their unique *row key*. The *row key* is stored and recognized as a byte array and similar to the functionality of the primary keys in the traditional relational databases. Since *row key* is a byte array, any data such as strings, the binary representation of any object, serialized data structure, etc., can serve as a *row key.* The data lookup is attained by the key value pair.

In short, core elements of HBase table are described as follows, see Fig. 5.6:

- **Table:** It is a collection of rows.
- **Row:** It is a collection of column families.
- **Column family:** It is a collection of columns.
- **Column:** It is a collection of key values pairs.

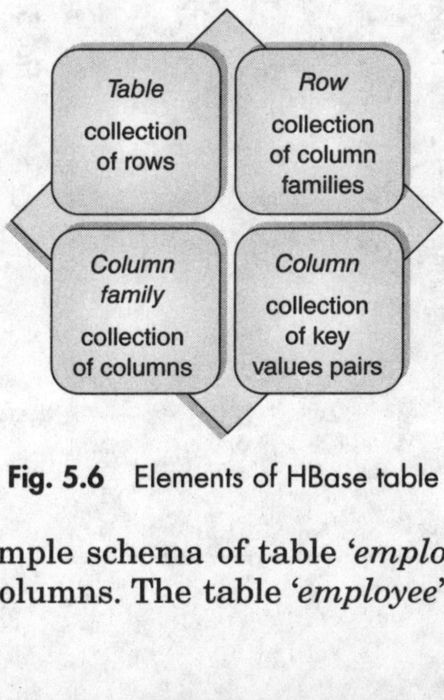

Fig. 5.6 Elements of HBase table

Figure 5.7 shows the example schema of table '*employee*' in HBase. Each column family has a related set of columns. The table '*employee*' shows two column families.

Row key	Personal Data				Project Data		
	ID	Name	Designation	Department	ID	Name	Duration
1	EPH101	Shreya Pathak	Project Manager	IT	PI105	ERP account extension	6 months
2	EPH509	Vikram Sara	Manager	Analytics	PI555	Predict sales model	8 months
3	EPH655	Benkim Chaterjee	General Manager	Software	PI509	Research ecosystem	12 months
.	.	.	.	.	.	.	.
.	.	.	.	.	.	.	.
50,00000	.	.	.	.	.	.	.

Fig. 5.7 Example schema of table 'employee' in HBase

Firstly, employee's personal details—name, id, designation, and department; and secondly, employee's project details—id, name, and duration. Each row in a table represents an employee and is accessed via a unique ID *row key*.

HBase Architecture

The architecture of HBase comprises of three core components: *master server*, *region server*, and *client library*. The master server is responsible for assigning regions to a region server. Each table is split into regions, and Zookeeper is also being used by the Mater server to accomplish such tasks. The description of each of the components of the architecture is given as follows, see Fig. 5.8:

Master server

- assigns regions to the region server
- utilizes Zookeeper services for the assignment of regions
- maintains the health of cluster and looks after load balancing
- attains schema changes and other metadata operations

Region server

- handles data related operations
- communicates with client to serve requests for the operations
- manages read/write requests for all the regions under it

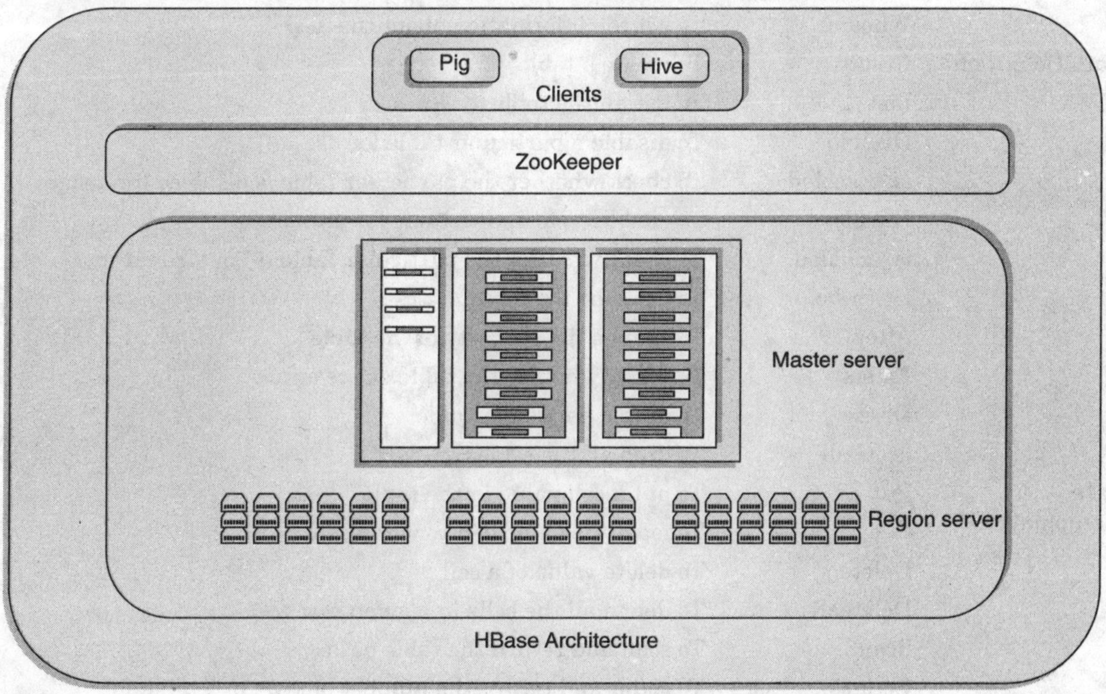

Fig. 5.8 HBase Architecture

- creates regions as per the region size threshold
- maintains the regions

Zookeeper

- provides multiple services such as coordination, configuration, synchronization, etc.
- provides communication channel between client and region servers
- tracks server failures and network partitions

HBase Shell and Functionality

LO 5 *Describe HBase shell and functionality*

In this section, we will understand the way in which we can interact with HBase. HBase installation provides HBase shell by which we can work with the large data sets stored in the HBase database. Table 5.8 shows relevant commands.

Table 5.8 Relevant commands

Item	*Command*	*Description*
General commands	Status	To check status of the HBase. For example: To get the details of numbers of active servers.
	Version	To check the versions of HBase being used
	table_help	To get help on table reference commands
	Whoami	To get the information about the user
Data Definition	Create	To create a table
	List	To list all the tables
	Disable	To disable a particular table for use
	is_disabled	To check whether the particular table is disabled for usage
	Enable	To enable a particular table for use
	is_enbaled	To check whether the particular table is enabled for usage
	Describe	To describe the table
	Alter	To change the property of the table
	Exists	To verify whether the table exists or not
	Drop	To drop a particular table
	drop_all	To drop all the tables
Data Manipulation	Put	To put a cell value in the table
	Get	To fetch the value of a row or a cell
	Delete	To delete value of a cell
	Deleteall	To delete all the cells in a given row
	Scan	To scan and return the table data
	Count	To count and return the number of rows in a table
	Truncate	To disable, drop, and recreate a particular table

You can work with HBase shell by invoking it from HBase. You will get the '*hbase*' prompt as follows:

```
hbase(main):001:0>
```

To create a table employee, you have to use the create command. The sample table creation is as follows:

```
hbase(main):001:0> create 'employee', 'personal data', 'professional data'
0 row(s) in 1.1300 seconds
=> Hbase::Table - employee
```

You can verify easily the newly created table as follows:

```
hbase(main):002:0> list
TABLE
employee
2 row(s) in 0.0340 seconds
```

To insert the rows into the '*employee*' table, we need to specify the name of the table and the value for the column family. This can be achieved by executing the '*put*' command as follows:

```
hbase(main):005:0> put 'empolyee','1','personal data:name','Shreya Pathak'
0 row(s) in 0.6600 seconds
hbase(main):006:0> put 'emp','1','personal data:Designation','Project Manager'
0 row(s) in 0.6600 seconds
hbase(main):007:0> put 'emp','1','personal data:Department','IT'
0 row(s) in 0.6600 seconds
hbase(main):008:0> put 'empolyee','1','project data:id','PI105'
0 row(s) in 0.6600 seconds
hbase(main):009:0> put 'empolyee','1','project data:name','ERP account extension'
0 row(s) in 0.6600 seconds
hbase(main):010:0> put 'empolyee','1','project data:Duration','6 months'
0 row(s) in 0.6600 seconds
```

Integrating Hive and HBase

LO 6 — *Integrate Hive and HBase*

The best way to get near real-time read/write analysis on large datasets utilizing the power of SQL and Hadoop flexible system is to integrate Hive and HBase. By integrating both the Hive and HBase, we can access HBase tables like native Hive tables and use HiveQL to perform the useful and complex analysis. Few steps are required to integrate the Hive and HBase together. There are two ways to achieve the integration. Firstly, by mapping existing

HBase table to Hive Table; and secondly, by creating new HBase table from Hive and performing analysis and other operations through HiveQL. Figure 5.9 shows the steps required to map existing HBase table to Hive table. Figure 5.9 shows the steps required to create new HBase table from Hive.

Mapping Existing HBase Table to Hive Table

To map the existing HBase table to Hive table, we need to use 'CREATE EXTERNAL TABLE'. Through this, the HBase table rows and column families can be accessed.

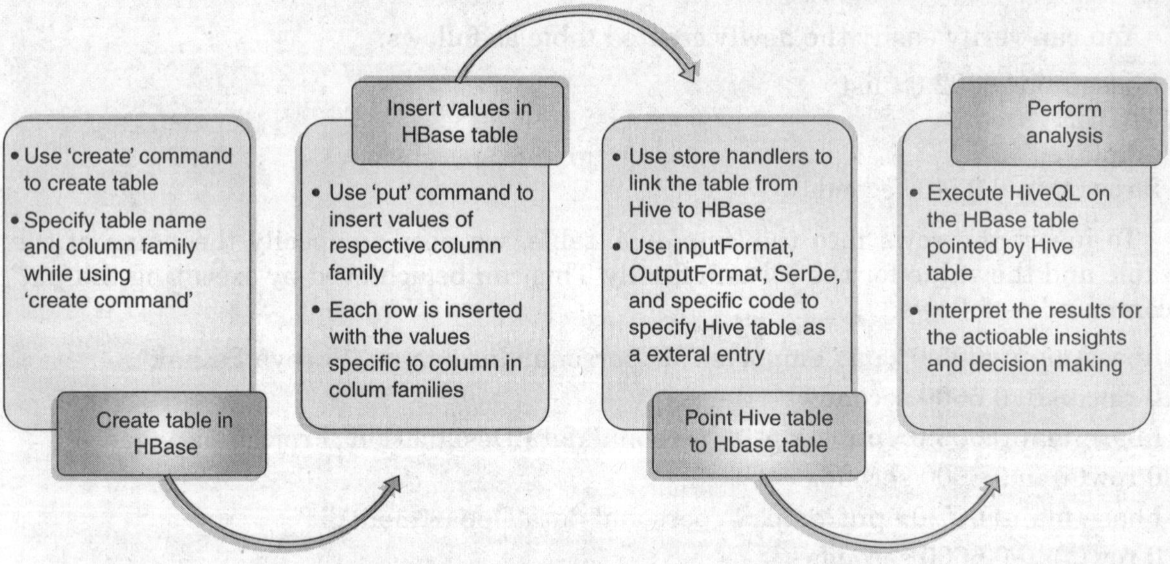

Fig. 5.9 Steps for mapping Hive and HBase Table

Let us create a corresponding Hive table, using HiveQL, for the '*employee*' table created in HBase. In the HiveQL statement, '*hbase.columns.mapping*' is required to validate against the existing HBase table's column families, but '*hbase.table.name*' is optional.

```
hive>create external table employee_hbase(id String, name string, designation
string, department string)
    >STORED BY 'org.apache.hadoop.hive.hbase.HBaseStorageHandler' with
serdeproperties
    >("hbase.columns.mapping"=":key,personal_data:id,personal_
data:name,personal_data:designation,
    >personal_data:department")
    >tblproperties("hbase.table.name"="employee");
OK
Time taken: 0.775 seconds
```

The above HiveQL statement maps the Hive table with the existing HBase '*employee*' table. It is better to have different tables for different column families. Later, HiveQL can be used to perform analysis and generate actionable insights. We need to specify the 'STORED BY' clause when we create the non-native Hive table using storage handler.

Creating HBase in Hive

In the other method of integration, we can create HBase table through Hive shell. The HiveQL statement, mentioned as follows, creates the HBase table '*employee_hbase*'. This table contains four columns in Hive—'*id*' of String type, '*name*' of String type, '*designation*' of String type, and '*department*' of String type. These are mapped to column family '*personal_data*' having four columns. In the Hive create table instruction, the parameter '*: key*' is mapped to the first column in Hive table; here '*:key*' is mapped to '*id*'.

```
hive>create table employee_hbase(id String, name string, designation string,
department string)
    >STORED BY 'org.apache.hadoop.hive.hbase.HBaseStorageHandler'  with
serdeproperties
    >("hbase.columns.mapping"=":key,personal_data:id,personal_
data:name,personal_data:designation,
    >personal_data:department")
    >tblproperties("hbase.table.name"="employee");
OK
Time taken: 1.905 seconds
```

Once the HBase table through Hive shell is created then the bulk data can be loaded into HBase table. This is achieved first by creating a temporary table '*emp_temp*' in Hive with the desired data and then transferring the table '*emp_temp*' to the HBase table. Below statement shows the functionality:

```
hive> create table emp_temp(id String, name string, designation string,
department string) row format delimited
    > fields terminated by '\t';
OK
Time taken: 15.905 seconds
hive> load data local inpath '/home/user/employee.txt' into table emp_temp;
OK
Time taken: 12.657 seconds
hive> insert overwrite table employee_hbase select * from emp_temp;
OK
Time taken: 13.543 seconds
```

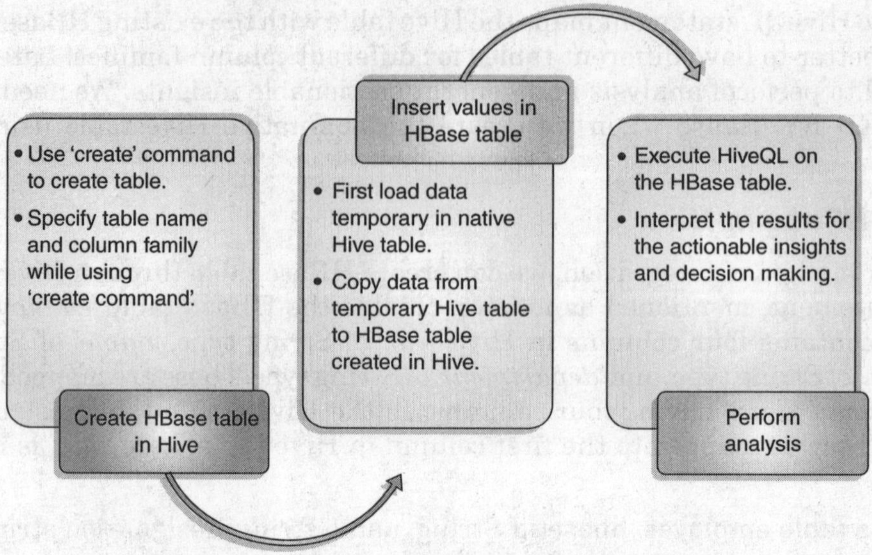

Fig. 5.10 Steps for creating HBase Table from Hive

SUMMARY

- The underlying data model of Hive relies on tables and partitions.
- Hive core elements comprise of Hive Driver, Metastore, Derby DB, Thrift Sever, Command Line Interface (CLI), Web Interface, and JDBC/ODBC connections.
- Hive supports three different modes—embedded, local, and remote.
- In the embedded mode, by default, Apache Derby database (RDBMS) is configured with the metastore.
- In multi-user production environments, where multiple Hive sessions are desirable, local and remote modes are preferred.
- Hive is based on Hadoop which is intended for distributed storage and distributed processing targeting long sequential or batch scans.
- One cannot use Hive for fast response time applications.
- Hive command line interface provides an interactive way to the user to deal with queries and administrative commands.
- Partitioning of the data table provides benefits to the efficient search.
- Hive also provides a lot of flexibility in supporting computations that may not completely fit the SQL processing model.
- HBase provides the benefit of read/write solution to the extent that it can be used for real-time read/write access to large datasets.
- HBase is flexible and natively integrated with Hadoop to provide efficient read/write cycles.

- HBase is a NoSQL database and belongs to the category of column family database.
- The architecture of HBase comprises of three core components: *master server*, *region server*, and *client library*.
- By integrating, both, the Hive and HBase, we can access HBase tables like native Hive tables and use HiveQL to perform the useful and complex analysis.

EXERCISE

Review Questions

1. Explain why the traditional ETL process is not well suited for modern data infrastructures.

   Tip: Detail out the traditional and modern way of working with data and map it with the old and modern technological solutions.
2. Describe the Hive data model and its benefits.
3. Describe the Architecture components of Hive. Briefly mention individual component functionality.
4. Given below is the data of the employees of a hypothetical company 'ABC Corps'.

Id	*Name*	*Age*	*Annual Salary (Rs in lakhs)*
EMPIT112	Meha Pujari	28	14.0
EMPIT221	John Pinto	27	13.7
EMPIT311	Rakhi Shakrma	29	12.9
EMPIT200	Kashi Hamara	27	13.7
EMPIT583	Rishi Aharwal	28	13.9
EMPIT113	Preeti Pujari	28	14.0
EMPIT202	Deepak	27	13.7
EMPIT333	Jamre Shakrma	29	12.9
EMPIT148	John koha	27	10.7
EMPIT588	Anjali Dixit	28	13.9
EMPIT102	Anike	28	14.0
EMPIT331	Prabhu Parth	27	11.7
EMPIT445	Vishnu	29	12.9
EMPIT554	Rakesh Kumar	28	14.0
EMPIT550	Wahida	27	12.7
EMPIT300	Abhishel Kumar	29	12.9
EMPIT009	Vicky	27	13.7

(*Contd.*)

EMPIT012	Rashmi panth	28	13.5
EMPIT700	Jeevan	28	14.0
EMPIT711	Sulekha	27	8.7
EMPIT766	Arabinda Kumar	29	8.9
EMPIT399	John Bajpayee	27	8.7
EMPIT789	Makdii Cachino	28	12.9

Write HiveQL for the following queries:

(a) Retrieve the details of the employees where annual salary is greater than 13.5 lakhs.

(b) What is the total salary that company is offering to the employees?

(c) Group the salary of the employees based on the similar age.

(d) Identify the mean of salary in each group.

Tip: Refer to the chapter for checking the syntax of HiveQL (For more details, check https://hive.apache.org/)

5. Describe the architecture and characteristics of HBase.

6. Explain the ways to integrate Hive and HBase.

Pig

6

> *"... the way we eat represents our most profound engagement with the natural world. Daily, our eating turns nature into culture, transforming the body of the world into our bodies and minds."*
>
> —Michael Pollan, The Omnivore's Dilemma: A Natural History of Four Meals

Learning Objectives

On completing this chapter, you will be able to:

LO 1 Describe the Pig Architecture
LO 2 Apply Pig Latin application flow
LO 3 Comprehend Pig Latin and execution environment
LO 4 Understand overview of Pig operator and its usage
LO 5 Define UDF scripting

CASE STUDY: *Batch.ly*—Flight Delay Impact Analysis

Aviation is a multibillion-dollar industry, and high performance is the utmost requirement. Different stakeholders of the industry due to flight delays incur a huge cost. Every year, almost 20% of flights schedule face a drift from the expected to the actual time of arrival. A study from the researchers at the University of California, Berkeley concluded that the annual cost of domestic flight delays of US carriers estimated to $32.9 billion.

Flight delay is not new and has become a very challenging problem for the airline industries. It is a huge risk for the airline industry regarding stake, brand, and business reputation. Not only airline business gets impacted by the flight delays but also the professional and personal life of passengers who get trapped into such flight delays. With ever increasing data and the development of the technology infrastructure, Batch.ly decided to develop a platform to perform the impact analysis on airline data set.

Fig. 6.1 Passenger waiting for the flight

The technology and resources that Batch.ly used to perform the impact analysis are as follows—Amazon EMR (Elastic MapReduce Cluster), Apache Pig, and 40GB TranStats Dataset. Amazon EMR is a Web service that uses Hadoop, to provide cost-effective and scalable processing on the vast amount of data through Amazon EC2 instances. The purpose of utilizing such set up of Amazon is to achieve cost-efficient processing with little or no IT overhead. The dataset was loaded into HDFS on EMR clusters, and the Pig Jobs were scheduled for different analysis. Pig is a data flow high-level scripting language used with Apache Hadoop, which enabled data workers to write complex data transformations for the impact analysis.

Batch.ly provides multiple features to spot the insights such as on-demand cost, savings, auto-scaling, etc. The company manages to attain high-performance impact analysis by achieving results per run—50 instances; 94.5% spot instance usage; 79% savings over on-demand AWS costs; No IT overhead.

Questions

1. What challenges does aviation industry face due to flight delays?

   Tip: List down the situations of aviation industry considering oil usage, buy-lease-rent of flights, operational and logistics aspects of flights, customer setbacks, brand, etc.

2. Who are the stakeholders that are impacted directly or indirectly due to flight delay?

   Tip: List down the primary, secondary, support, and other stakeholders of the [particular] flight and develop impact scenarios for each of them.

3. Describe the high-level architecture for delay impact analysis.

   Tip: Identify the key components involved in generating the insights [as documented in the case]. Perform Google search to check technology solutions that other aviation Industries [competitors] have deployed.

4. Is there any benefit of performing the impact analysis?

   Tip: List down the benefit scenarios of the concerned stakeholders.

References

http://news.berkeley.edu/2010/10/18/flight_delays/ [accessed July 27, 2017];
https://aws.amazon.com/emr/ [accessed July 27, 2017];
https://www.cmpute.io/case-studies.html [accessed July 27, 2017];
https://www.cmpute.io/files/Batchly-Pig-Flight-Analysis-Case-Study.pdf [accessed July 27, 2017];
https://pig.apache.org/[accessed July 27, 2017];
https://transtats.bts.gov/databases.asp?Mode_ID=1&Mode_Desc=Aviation&Subject_ID2=0 [accessed July 27, 2017]

> *"The goal is to turn data into information, and information into insight."*
>
> **—Carly Fiorina, former executive, President, and chair of Hewlett-Packard Co.**

Fig. 6.2 Multiple managers querying the data

One of the limitations of working with the Hadoop Distributed File System and MapReduce framework is that one has to rely on Java programs for map and reduce, mostly empowering developers to work with the framework. The big data has many stakeholders and, hence, having multiple ways of working with data is of utmost importance. Abstraction of such complex level of interaction and programming framework is the key to work with the Hadoop core components. Normally, people who are interested in understanding and exploring data for various use scenarios, but have limited capability of writing map-reduce programs, require a higher level of abstraction and interaction. However, there are declarative languages, like HiveQL, that are available to work with big data with the limitation on the set of operations to be performed on the data rather than how those operations are being performed. This kind of requirement gave birth to one of the product at Yahoo! known as *Pig*. Pig has best of both the worlds—a declarative language capability, i.e., SQL-like feature and a low-level procedural programming language that can develop MapReduce code. Thus, the key to working with the data is '*focus on what to do with the data rather than how to do*'. In the last quarter of 2007, Pig officially became the part of the Apache Software Project and included in most of the Hadoop distributions.

> **Note:** Pig programming language and a product itself got a name while relating it [programming language/product] with the Pig. Pigs eat everything that you throw at them. Likewise, Pig can work with all types of data—structured, semi-structured, and unstructured.

LO 1 — *Describe the Pig Architecture*

The Pig product is composed of two core components: *the language* and *the compiler*.

- **The Language [Pig Latin]:** It is a high-level language that provides syntax and semantics to achieve data processing and analysis.
- **The Compiler [Pig Latin]:** The Pig Latin code is converted to the executable code by the Pig Latin compiler. This executable code can be either an equivalent MapReduce program or a spawned process where pig code is run on a virtual Hadoop instance.

> **Note:** The sequence of MapReduce programs enables Pig programs to do data processing and analysis in parallel, leveraging Hadoop MapReduce and HDFS. Running the Pig job in the virtual Hadoop instance is a useful strategy for testing your Pig scripts.

Figure 6.3 depicts the relation of Pig with the Hadoop ecosystem. Regardless of the cluster mode, Pig programs can run on MapReduce v1 or MapReduce v2. Moreover, utilizing Tez API, the system can execute Pig scripts. It is better to use Apache Tez framework as it provides better and flexible way to run PIG scripts as compared to the MapReduce.

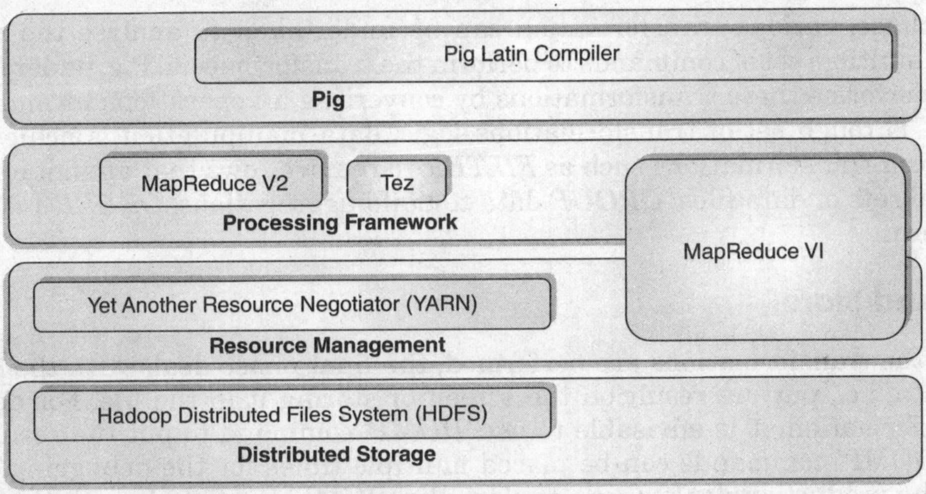

Fig. 6.3 Pig Architecture

6.1 PIG LATIN APPLICATION FLOW

LO 2 — *Apply Pig Latin application flow*

Pig is a data flow [procedural] language. It is easy to work with Pig language once we identify the flow of data and what transformation we need to perform on the data to achieve the overall analysis. The functioning and semantics of the Pig Latin language are different from other control flow languages where a set of control instructions are written to control the program flow. The control instruction can comprise of loops and control logic.

All kinds of data manipulation is achieved using Pig. Pig also supports user-defined function (UDF) through which code could be invoked in multiple programming languages [environment] Ruby, Python, and Java. One of the flexibility that Pig provides is embedding Pig scripts in other languages. You will not just use Pig to analyse data but also to build larger and more complex applications.

Let us look at the typical three phases, Fig. 6.4, involved in dealing with the data through Pig.

Load

The first phase is to get the data. This can easily be done by providing the data object path and data can be invoked. For a Pig program to access the data, the program must tell Pig which data file or files need to be loaded. '*LOAD*' command is used to load the data [file] and in case the '*LOAD*' command is pointing towards the directory, then all the files in that directory are loaded. Pig supports user-defined functions to load such files which are non-native to the Pig environment.

Transform

In this phase, various transformation can be undertaken to analyse the data. Pig provides multiple set of commands to perform the transformation. Pig, under the cover, smartly performs these transformations by converting all operations in '*mapper*' and '*reducer*'. Through set of transformations logic, data manipulation is achieved. One can perform transformations such as *FILTER* to remove rows that are not of interest, *JOIN* two sets of data files, *GROUP* data to build aggregations, *ORDER* results, and much more.

Dump and Store

Once all the transformations are performed, the final phase deals with the dumping of the data, i.e., putting result on the screen or storing it in the file. For debugging the transformation, it is advisable to use '*DUMP*' command to put the result on the screen. 'DUMP' commands can be placed multiple times for the debugging purpose. During the production/deployment, replace the '*DUMP*' commands with the '*STORE*' commands to store the result into the file.

Pig has become so much popular that it is being used by wide variety of people across the industry, research, academia, and in many projects. Pig is popular as it provides many benefits as follows:

- One can avoid complex MapReduce programs while working with Pig.
- Any prior knowledge of SQL helps in quick learning of Pig.
- By performing multi-query operations, one can write efficient code and get deeper insights.

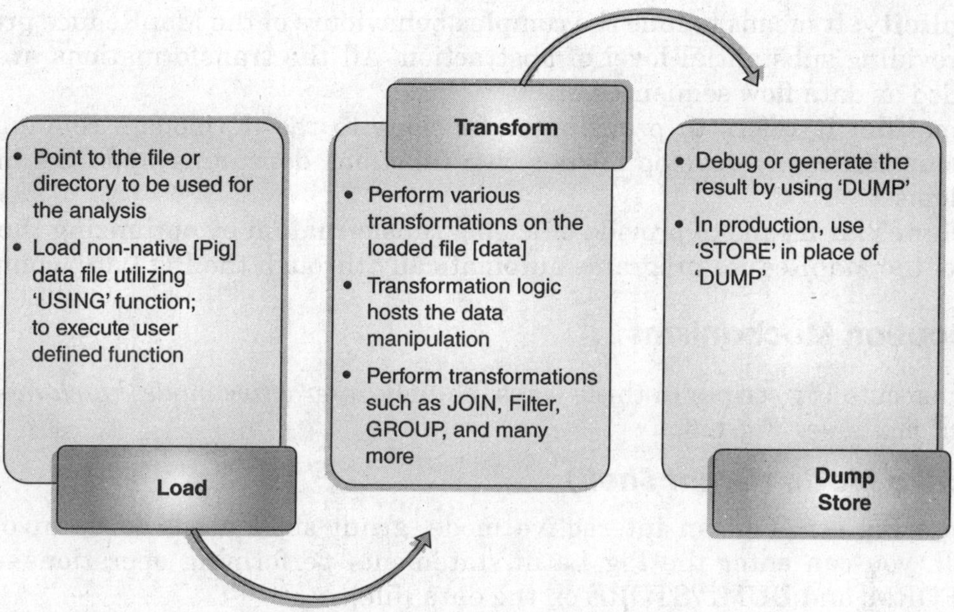

Figure 6.4 Three phases of Pig data flow

- Rich data sets such as Maps, Tuples, and Bags are powerful, which are not provided by MapReduce could be used in Pig.
- Multiple operations such as Filters, Ordering, and Joins to perform the transformation effectively.

6.2 PIG LATIN STATEMENTS AND EXECUTION ENVIRONMENT

LO 3 *Comprehend Pig Latin and execution environment*

Pig Latin is easy to understand, as it is in simple English with meaningful syntax. Each Pig Latin statement acts as an operator that takes an input (a '*relation*') and gives an output (a '*relation*'). This '*relation*' is a '*Bag*' of '*tuples*'. You can note that Pig relation is similar to the '*table*' in any other relational database. A '*tuple*' in the '*bag*' correspond to the '*row*' in a '*table*'. Unlike a table, a Pig relation does not put a constraint on the '*tuple*' to have all fields, and column field having same type of data. The processing of the '*tuples*' is un-ordered and parallelized and distributed. We will understand more in depth about '*relation*', '*bag*' and '*tuples*'.

Running of Pig Latin statements can be achieved via

- '*grunt*' shell or command line
- modes—'*MapReduce*' or '*local*'
- '*interactive*' or '*batch*'

The development team behind the Pig Latin followed three key design principles, which I call 'SeXY' (very easy to remember):

- **Simplicity:** It means to hide the complex behaviours of the MapReduce programs by providing substantial level of abstraction. All the transformations are easily encoded as data flow sequences.
- **eXtensible:** It refers to providing extensions to the developers community so that one can easily develop his/her own functions depending upon the business problems.
- **efficiencY:** It means to provide efficient transformation by optimizing the execution of the MapReduce programs automatically through the Pig Latin compiler.

Pig Execution Mechanisms

One can execute Pig scripts in three ways, namely, *interactive mode*, *batch mode*, and *embedded mode*, see Fig. 6.5.

Interactive Mode (Grunt Shell)

To execute Pig script in an interactive mode, grunt shell needs to be invoked. In this shell, you can enter the Pig Latin statements performing operations—LOAD, TRANSFORM, and DUMP/STORE on the data [file].

Batch Mode (Script)

A batch mode is useful when you would like to execute production level script and once for all '*Pig Latin statements*' for the data file. This can be accomplished by writing all Pig Latin statements in the file and saving the file with the extension '*.pig*'.

Embedded Mode (UDF)

By default, Pig has multiple functions to be performed on the data set, but Pig also provides extensibility in the terms that one can develop its own set of user-defined functions (UDF) in an external language such as Java, and use them in the pig script. By this, one can achieve powerful functionality.

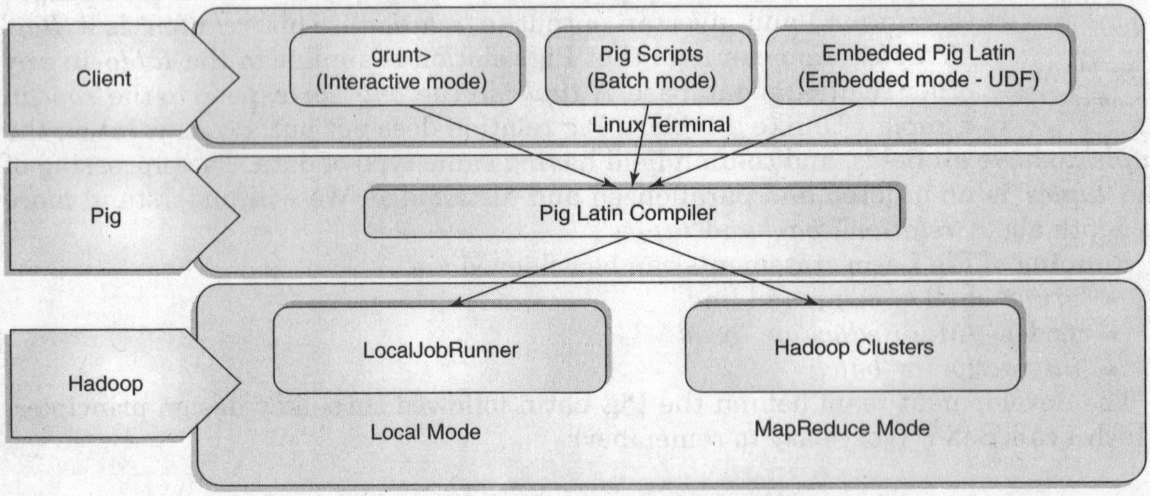

Fig. 6.5 Pig execution modes

Two basic modes are available with Pig for the overall execution.

- **Local mode:** In this mode, all the Pig scripts are run on a single machine, and there is no mandatory requirement of Hadoop MapReduce and HDFS. To perform testing, experimentation, and debugging, one can employ such kind of mode. For quick result on a smaller set of data, this mode seems to be more effective and efficient. To run PIG scripts in the local mode, you need to check the following statement:

```
pig -x local student.pig
```

> **Note:** Local mode doesn't require Hadoop. When you run in Local mode, the Pig program runs in the context of a local Java Virtual Machine, and data access is via the local file system of a single machine. Local mode is a local simulation of MapReduce in Hadoop's LocalJobRunner class.

- **MapReduce mode (also known as Hadoop mode):** In the Hadoop mode, Pig scripts are executed on the Hadoop cluster. The Pig Latin compiler transforms all the Pig Latin statements into the MapReduce workflow comprising of series of jobs, which later run on the Hadoop cluster. Hadoop mode is the default mode. To run the Pig script in the Hadoop mode, one can specify the following statement:

```
pig -x mapreduce student.pig
```

Let us go through our first Pig program—data flow sequence of statements, see Fig. 6.6.

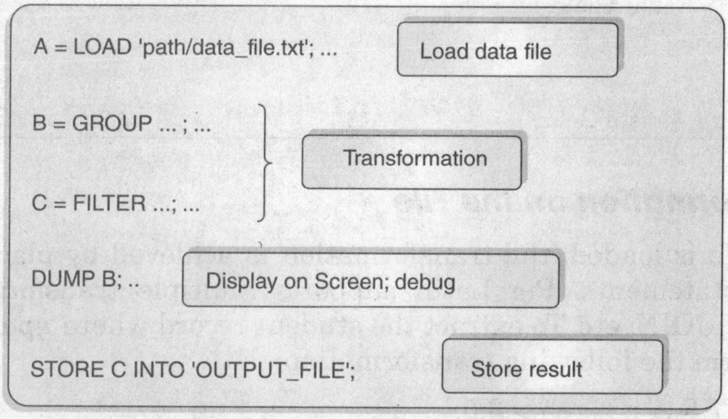

Fig. 6.6 Snippet—data flow sequence statements

The Pig Latin Program Statements begin by Reading of the Data from the HDFS

Pig has its data model by which it recognizes the input data. Loading of the input data file is achieved by using '*LOAD*' and '*USING*'. '*LOAD*' instructs the compiler to fetch the data file 'as given by the path details' to the session. '*USING*' is used to map the data file data type with the Pig, data model. We can further provide more information about the content of the data file. For example, we can use PigStorage(',') statement to consider comma-delimited file. Also, we can define the schema by specifying the name of each of the columns by putting '*AS*' after PigStorage(','). If you don't use an '*AS*' clause, you're telling the default LOAD function to expect a plain text file that is tab delimited. With no schema provided, the fields must be referenced by position because no name is defined. We can use a LOAD statement to load a file named 'student.csv' which is comma-delimited file and has three columns fields named as '*name*', '*age*', and '*gpa*' of type character array, integer, and floating point respectively.

```
grunt> A = LOAD 'student.csv' USING PigStorage(',') AS (id: chararray,
name:chararray, age:int, gpa:float);
```

Let us assume that an educational university 'EDU' enrolls 50,000 students every year in various courses and one would like to perform analysis on the student data for the period of 2007–2017, i.e., 10 years. The records are humongous and spread over several data files. One such file is '*student.csv*'. Therefore, the overall analysis will be on 5 million records. For simplicity, we look into the small sample of the file '*student.csv*' which is shown in Table 6.1:

Table 6.1 Sample record of the file student.csv

EDU2007CS001	Meha Pujari	18	4.0
EDU2007ME101	John Pinto	17	3.7
EDU2008CE201	Rakhi Shakrma	19	2.9
:	:	:	:
:	:	:	:
EDU2017CE201	Rishi Gohr	18	3.9

Perform Transformation on the File

Once the data file is loaded, the transformation is achieved by placing appropriate transformation statements. Pig Latin supports multiple transformation such as GROUP, FILTER, JOIN, etc. To extract the student record where '*gpa*' is greater than 3.5, we can perform the following transformation:

```
grunt> B = FILTER A BY gpa > 3.5;
```

Execute the Pig Latin Statements and Display/Store the Result

In an interactive mode, we can use the operator '*DUMP*', which means that the statements are executable immediately by invoking the MapReduce programs and the results are displayed on the screen.

```
grunt> DUMP B;
```

Here, the only sample of the output is shown:

```
(EDU2007ME101,John Pinto,17, 3.7)
: : : : : : : : : : : : : : : : : : : : : :
: : : : : : : : : : : : : : : : : : : : : :
(EDU2017CE201,Rishi Gohr,18, 3.9)
```

To store the result, one has to replace the operator '*DUMP*' with '*STORE*'.

```
grunt> STORE B INTO '/user/pigdata' ;
```

The result of the script is stored in the folder named '*pigdata*'. The '*pigdata*' now contains two files: _SUCCESS and part-r-00000. The file '*part-r-00000*' contains the output generated when the '*STORE*' statement is executed.

Typically, after performing all the transformations, we use the DUMP or STORE operators at the end.

—LO 4— *Understand overview of Pig operator and its usage*

In the context of a Hadoop environment, data access refers to load, store, and stream data; whereas, data transformation means the ability to group, join, combine, split, filter, and sort data. Table 6.2 gives an overview of the operators associated with each operation.

Table 6.2 Overview of Pig operator and its usage

Operator	*Description*
Loading and Storing	
LOAD	To read data from the file present in the system—local/HDFS
STORE	To write data to file system—local/HDFS
Filtering	
FILTER	To apply predicate and remove records that do not meet the condition
DISTINCT	To remove duplicate rows from a relation
FOREACH, GENERATE	Typically, works in the fields, i.e., columns. Apply an expression to each record and output one or more records.
STREAM	Through external binary, send all the records. Normally, to transform a relation using an external program.
Grouping and Joining	
JOIN	To join two or more relations based on certain conditions
COGROUP	To group the data in two or more relations based on certain conditions
GROUP	To group the data in a single relation based on certain conditions
CROSS	To create the cross product of two or more relations based on certain conditions
Sorting	
ORDER	To arrange a relation, based on the key, in a sorted order on one or more fields (ascending or descending)
LIMIT	To get a subset of tuples from a relation

(Contd.)

Combining and Splitting	
UNION	To combine two or more relations into a single relation
SPLIT	To split a single relation into two or more relations (bags) based on the predicate
Diagnostic Operators	
DUMP	To print and display the contents of a relation on the console
DESCRIBE	To map and describe the schema of a relation
EXPLAIN	To view the logical, physical, or MapReduce execution plans to compute a relation
ILLUSTRATE	To depict and view the step-by-step execution of a series of statements

6.3 PIG DATA TYPES

The Pig data model represents the composition of the Pig data types. The data model of the data file that you wish to load from the storage is defined when you provide the LOAD statement. The Pig understands the data model by looking at the syntax of the Pig Latin statement and the types of data types used in the statement. For example, one can enforce a particular schema of data model while loading the data file. Pig data model by its set of fundamental structure can handle most of the data structure. Typically, it has two categories of data types— *scalar* and *complex*. The scalar data type contains a single value as '*Atom*'. For example, name of a person. The Atom can be represented by typical scalar value data type such as int, float, chararray, long, double, bytearray, etc. The complex types contain other types such as *Tuple*, *Bag*, and *Map* types.

Tuple

A tuple is a record that comprises of a sequence of fields. Here, each field can depict a particular type, allowing to have values of varied type—int, chararray, and float. Think of a tuple as a row in a table.

For example, a sample tuple in the file '*student.csv*' is shown as follows:

```
(EDU2007ME101,John Pinto,17, 3.7)
```

Bag

A collection of the non-unique tuple in a relation refers to the '*bag*'. Thus, by notion your data, '*bag*' schema is flexible—the collection of the tuple has a flexibility in holding tuples that can have an arbitrary number of fields and each field can be of any type. The bag is more flexible than the table in other relational databases.

Map

A map represents the collection of key-value pairs. In the (key, value) pair, the value contains any 'type of' data, but the key must be of type '*chararray*' and needs to be unique.

Figure 6.7 offers some examples of Tuple, Bag, and Map data types as well.

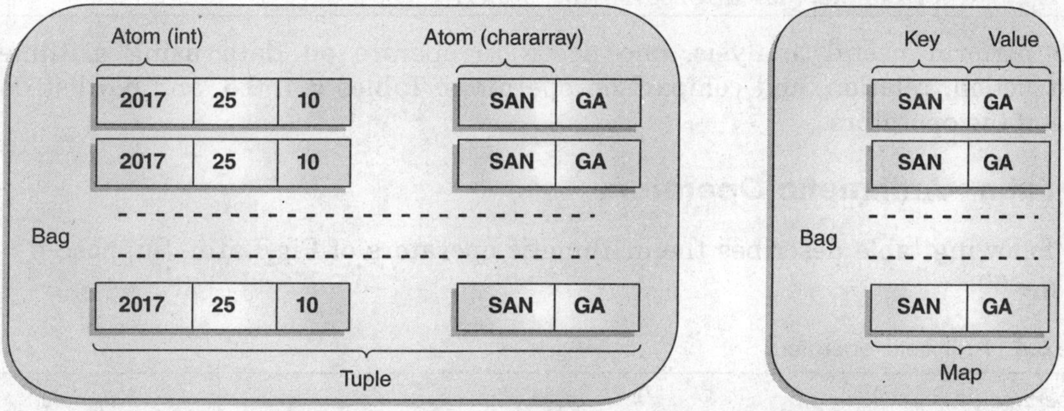

Fig. 6.7 Sample Pig data types—scalar and complex

The following table describes the Pig Latin data types.

Table 6.3 Pig Latin data types

Data Type	*Description and Example*
Int	a signed 32-bit integer **Example:** 25
Long	a signed 64-bit integer **Example:** 35L
Float	a signed 32-bit floating point **Example:** 3.95F
Double	a 64-bit floating point **Example:** 4.5
chararray	a character array (string) in Unicode UTF-8 format **Example:** 'Pig'
Bytearray	a Byte array (blob)
Boolean	a Boolean value **Example:** true/false
DateTime	a date-time **Example:** 2017-02-02T00:00:00.000+00:00
biginteger	a Java BigInteger **Example:** 70809080808
bigdecimal	a Java BigDecimal **Example:** 154.3257684932645

Tuple	an ordered set of fields **Example:** (EDU2007ME101,John Pinto,17, 3.7)
Bag	a collection of tuples **Example:** {(EDU2007ME101,John Pinto,17, 3.7), (EDU2017CE201,Rishi Gohr,18, 3.9)}
Map	a set of key-value pairs. **Example:** ['id# EDU2007ME101, 'age'#17]

To perform useful analysis, one needs to operate on data using arithmetic, construction, relation, and comparison operators. Tables 6.4, 6.5, and 6.6 list down some of the operators.

Pig Latin—Arithmetic Operators

The following table describes the arithmetic operators of Pig Latin. Suppose p = 20 and q = 60.

Table 6.4 Arithmetic operators

Operator	*Description*	*Example* *p=20, q=60*
+	**Addition**—The expression returns the value of addition of p's value and q's value.	p + q will give 80
–	**Subtraction**—The expression returns the value of subtraction of p's value from q's value.	p – q will give –40
*	**Multiplication**—The expression returns the value of multiplication of p's value and q's value.	p * q will give 1200
/	**Division**—The expression returns the value of division of p's value by q's value.	p / q will give 2
%	**Modulus**—The expression returns the value of remainder of p's value by q's value.	q % p will give 0
? :	**Bincond**—Evaluates the Boolean operators. It has three operands as shown below. variable **x** = (expression) ? **value1** *if true* : **value2** *if false*.	q = (p == 1)? 20: 60; if p=1 the value of q is 20. if p!=1 the value of q is 60.
CASE WHEN THEN ELSE END	**Case**—The case operator is equivalent to the nested bincond operator.	CASE f2 % 2 WHEN 0 THEN 'TRUE' WHEN 1 THEN 'FALSE' END

Pig Latin—Comparison Operators

The following table describes the comparison operators of Pig Latin. Suppose a=5 and b=6.

Table 6.5 Comparison operators

Operator	*Description*	*Example a=5, b=6*
==	**Equal**—The expression returns TRUE if the value of 'a' is equivalent to 'b' otherwise FALSE.	(a = b) is not true
!=	**Not Equal**—The expression returns TRUE if the value of 'a' is not equivalent to 'b' otherwise FALSE.	(a != b) is true
>	**Greater than**—The expression returns TRUE if the value of 'a' is greater than 'b' otherwise FALSE.	(a > b) is not true.
<	**Less than**—The expression returns TRUE if the value of 'a is less than 'b' otherwise FALSE.	(a < b) is true.
>=	**Greater than or equal to**—The expression returns TRUE if the value of 'a' is greater than or equal to 'b' otherwise FALSE.	(a >= b) is not true.
<=	**Less than or equal to**—The expression returns TRUE if the value of 'a' is less than or equal to 'b' otherwise FALSE.	(a <= b) is true
matches	**Pattern matching**—tests right-hand side constant with the string on the left-hand side and checks whether it matches.	f1 matches '.*hadoop.*'

Pig Latin—Type Construction Operators

The following table shows the Pig Latin Type construction operators.

Table 6.6 Construction operators

Operator	*Description*	*Example*
( )	A tuple can be constructed using this operator.	(EDU2007ME101,John Pinto,17, 3.7)
{ }	A bag can be constructed using this operator.	{(EDU2007ME101,John Pinto,17, 3.7), (EDU2017CE201,Rishi Gohr,18, 3.9)}
[ ]	A map can be constructed using this operator.	['id# EDU2007ME101, 'age'#17]

Note: By default, when you specify the pig command without any parameters, it starts the Grunt shell in Hadoop mode. If you want to start the Grunt shell in the local mode, just add the –x local flag to the command. For example: pig -x local

6.4 UDF SCRIPTING WITH PIG LATIN

LO 5
Define UDF scripting

Pig is by design an extensible scripting framework, which can be extended through user-defined functions (UDFs). As Hadoop ecosystem is continuously growing and evolving, Pig design's extensibility provides rich functionality. One can write UDFs as per the requirement in multiple languages such as Java, Python, and JavaScript. Three types of user-defined functions can be created while working with Java, which are as follows:

- **Filter Functions:** These functions describe the filtering operation (condition) for the input as provided by the Pig value and return the Boolean value as the output.
- **Eval Functions:** The Eval functions accept a Pig value as input and return a Pig result which is to be included in the instruction 'FOREACH-GENERATE' statements.
- **Algebraic Functions:** These functions work on inner bags in FOREACH-GENERATE statements.

Apart from UDFs, integration of Pig can also happen in the existing applications by embedding Pig in an application designed in host languages such as Java, Python, and JavaScript. Thus, one can overcome the limitations of Pig in a variety of ways such as introducing the flexibility by the involvement of control statements.

> **Note:** One needs to be cautious of embedding Pig in other control flow languages. For example, if a Pig statement is embedded in a loop, then it triggers the MapReduce jobs every time the loop iterates.

SUMMARY

- Pig has best of both the worlds—a declarative language capability, i.e., SQL-like feature and a low-level procedural programming language that can develop MapReduce code.
- The Pig product is composed of two core components: the language and the compiler.
- Pig is a data flow [procedural] language.
- It is easy to work with Pig language once we identify the flow of data and what transformation we need to perform on the data to achieve the overall analysis.
- Each Pig Latin statement acts as an operator that takes an input (a 'relation') and gives an output (a 'relation').
- The development team behind the Pig Latin followed three key design principles—'SeXY' [Simplicity, eXtensibility, and efficiencY].
- One can execute Pig scripts in three ways, namely, interactive mode, batch mode, and embedded mode.
- Two basic modes are available with Pig for the overall execution—Local mode and MapReduce mode.
- Pig is by design an extensible scripting framework, which can be extended though user-defined functions (UDFs).

EXERCISE

Review Questions

1. Describe the two modes of working with Pig. Give examples in each case to use the specific modes.
2. Explain the process of analysing data through Pig.
3. Find the scalar and complex data type for the sample data of the employee of the hypothetical company 'ABC Corps' given below:

Id	*Name*	*Age*	*Annual Salary (Rs in lakhs)*
EMPIT112	Meha Pujari	28	14.0
EMPIT221	John Pinto	27	13.7
EMPIT311	Rakhi Shakrma	29	12.9
EMPIT200	Kashi Hamara	27	13.7
EMPIT583	Rishi Aharwal	28	13.9
EMPIT113	Preeti Pujari	28	14.0
EMPIT202	Deepak	27	13.7
EMPIT333	Jamre Shakrma	29	12.9
EMPIT148	John koha	27	10.7
EMPIT588	Anjali Dixit	28	13.9
EMPIT102	Anike	28	14.0
EMPIT331	Prabhu Parth	27	11.7
EMPIT445	Vishnu	29	12.9
EMPIT554	Rakesh Kumar	28	14.0
EMPIT550	Wahida	27	12.7
EMPIT300	Abhishel Kumar	29	12.9
EMPIT009	Vicky	27	13.7
EMPIT012	Rashmi panth	28	13.5
EMPIT700	Jeevan	28	14.0
EMPIT711	Sulekha	27	8.7
EMPIT766	Arabinda Kumar	29	8.9
EMPIT399	John Bajpayee	27	8.7
EMPIT789	Makdii Cachino	28	12.9

4. Write Pig script in an interactive mode for the following queries:
   (a) Find out the tuples where annual salary is greater than 13.5 lakhs.
   (b) Store the result in to a folder as '*employee*' in the HDFS.
   (c) What is the total salary that company is offering to the employees?
   (d) Group the salary of the employees based on the similar age.
   (e) Identify the mean of salary in each group.
   (f) Perform the increment of the salary w.r.t. the mean of the group salary. Each employee's salary is multiplied by the mean and the result is added as the increment of the salary for each employee. Store the result in the folder named '*Increment*' in HDFS.

   Tip: Refer to the chapter to check the syntax for Pig script (For more details, check https://pig.apache.org/)
5. Explain the utility of the User Defined Function by providing suitable examples.

   Tip: Refer to the chapter and check the User Defined Function. For more details, check https://pig.apache.org/

Data Lookout Readiness

7

"*The reason why we have never found measure of wealth. We never sought it.*"

—George S. Clason, The Richest Man in Babylon

Learning Objectives

***On completing this chapter, you will be able to*:**

- **LO 1** Examine the data lookout elements
- **LO 2** Describe data ingestion
- **LO 3** Comprehend Sqoop and Flume
- **LO 4** Analyse jobs in Sqoop and Flume
- **LO 5** Execute Sqoop workflow
- **LO 6** Perform Flume topology design

One of the specialties of Hadoop is that it can take data from multiple sources and of varied types. It is a significant feature of Hadoop to make it so attractive that businesses have started considering Hadoop to store and process data. In this chapter, we are going to understand the principles behind data lookout readiness and the way in which it can be accomplished in Hadoop. In Chapter 1, we have covered the big data architecture and discussed the importance of lookout layer briefly. Data lookout facilitates to load, convert, transform, and store the raw data to meaningful data for further processing. It supports

- getting the data into the data product that we are building or using.
- converting the data into the correct format of usage.
- selecting and transforming data for further analysis.
- gathering data by keeping selective filters.
- storing data in the distributed storage system (like HDFS)

LO 1
Examine the data lookout elements

Figure 7.1 shows the data lookout elements.

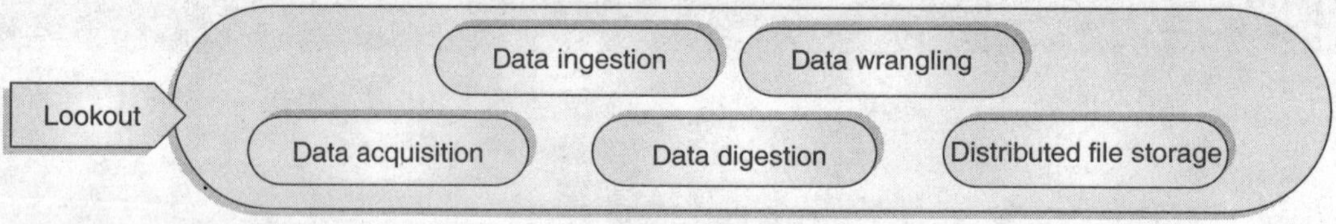

Fig. 7.1 Data lookout elements

The lookout layer depends upon the sources layer (Fig. 1.9, Chapter 1). The sources layer presents the entire data source required to solve the business problem. It is necessary for organizations to list and identify all the significant sources of data. It covers data sources such as structured, semi-structured, unstructured, geographical information, operational systems, data stores, Internet of things; human generated content; data management system, legacy system, and aggregate data providers.

> The sources layer presents the entire data source required to solve the business problem.

The process of getting or obtaining data for immediate use or to store the data in the database for further usage is referred as the *data ingestion*. There are various ways by which data can be ingested and most commonly categorized into two forms—*batch mode* and *real-time streaming mode*. It is challenging for an organization when they have multiple sources and various format of data to store and process to get a competitive advantage. Moreover, vendors that offer software solutions also have a restriction to software and hardware environments. A proper strategy to ingest data by leveraging the software and hardware solutions provide an edge in the competitive market.

> "*In every action, we must look beyond the action at our past, present and future state, and at others whom it affects, and see the relations of all these things.*"
>
> —Blaise Pascal, The Thoughts of Blaise Pascal

7.1 DATA LOOKOUT

© Thinkstock.com

Fig. 7.2 Manager asking for data of different types

LO 2 *Describe data ingestion*

Data ingestion brings data into the data processing system. It includes a wide variety of tasks to be accomplished to prepare data for processing. To solve a business problem, the primary concern for most of the businesses is '*what data is available*' and '*what other data is needed*'. Many enterprise solutions provide large data sets but have limited exposure to the business use cases and, thus, unable to exploit the data. Even though the data is available in full or part for the usage, several other issues such as rights and permissions to access and working with the data make it more challenging. To make the situation worst, organizations due to lack of synergy between various departments keep overlapping data having inconsistent schemas. Organizations too have issues with other external sources of big, social, and open data. The cost of integrating and preprocessing of data is inevitable, and one has to identify the value of the data that can contribute towards solving the business problem. Four dimension principle—**E**xtent, **C**omplex, **O**ccurrence, and **E**xpectancy (**ECOE**)—helps the organization to identify the value of the data before investing in the infrastructure and resources for the data lookout. Figure 7.4 describes the value identification of data based on four-dimension value principle.

The cost of integration and preprocessing of data is inevitable, and one has to identify the value of the data that can contribute towards solving the business problem. Four dimension principle—**E**xtent, **C**omplex, **O**ccurrence, and **E**xpectancy (**ECOE**)—helps the organization to identify the value of the data before investing in the infrastructure and resources for the data lookout.

Extent

The data in full or part must cover the variance of the business problem. For example, an organization, located near the airport, is seeking to understand the ear problem of its employees and a leading indicator is a sound factor; the *extent* can be insufficient if there is no data for aircraft sound, say, level of sound in decibels. Checking the data variance and the distribution of the data to cover the problem is promising for the organization to understand the scope of the data.

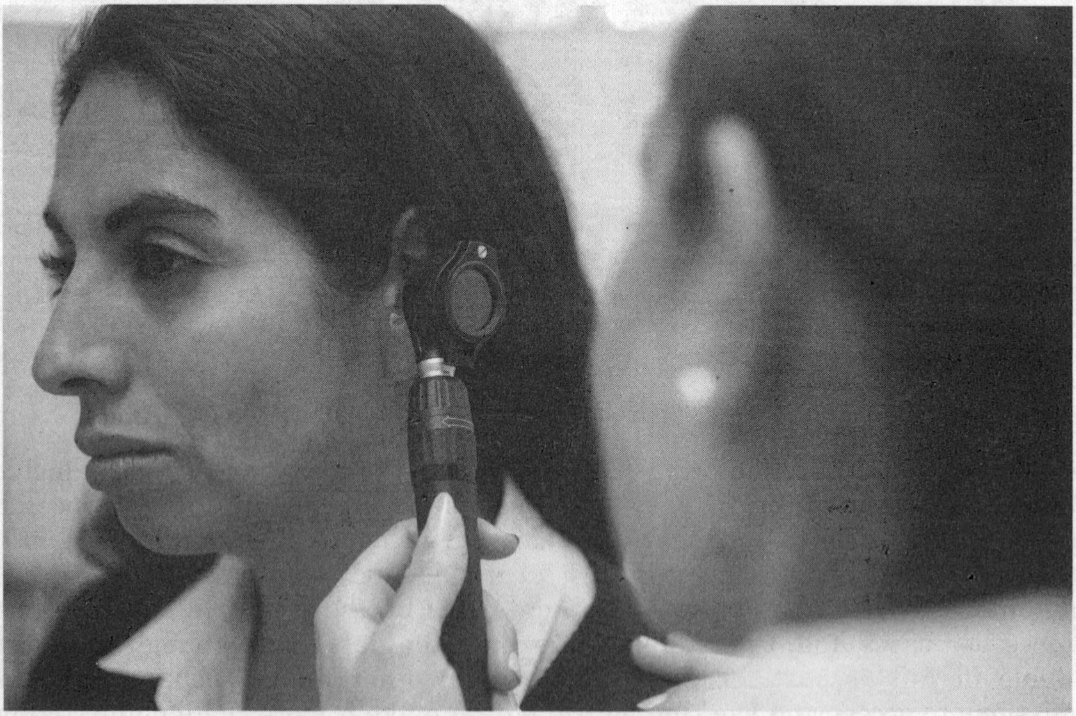

Fig. 7.3 Doctor checking the ear (hearing sound) problem

Complex

The data in full or part must cover the complexity of the business problem. For example, to understand the phenomena of sales that occur due to Christmas that falls on Tuesday in a leap year needs detailed historical data to select the right sample size. Checking for the presence and significance of data to cover the problem provides benefit to the organization to understand the complex phenomena.

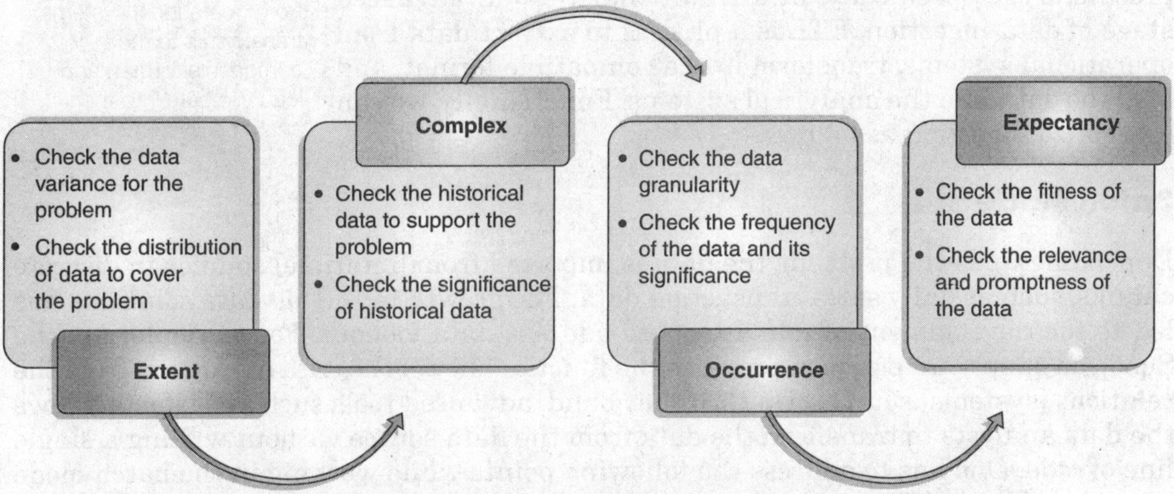

Fig. 7.4 Value identification of data based on ECOE principle

Occurrence

The data in full or part must cover the frequency of events or data points of the business problem. For example, monthly sales data is reasonable enough to describe the seasonality effect of the product sales; but in the absence of event occurrence coverage, the data set is not capable of providing details of the product or sales resulting to favourable profit on a particular day. Checking the data granularity, its frequency, and significance help an organization to unfold the hidden treasure.

Expectancy

The data in full or part must cover the immediate action towards the business problem. For example, an organization seeking immediate action on the social media trolling for their products must have current real-time streaming data. In case immediate action is not required, then investing in real-time processing infrastructure is not necessary. Checking the fitness of the data, relevance, and promptness of the data will help the organization to plan their investment in data infrastructure.

The process of acquiring, ingesting, wrangling, and digesting data comes in wide fashion depending on multiple sources and data formats, schemas, constraints, filters, volumes, and update frequencies. There are other factors which are important to consider addressing reliability and complexity of the process. For example, the source of the data (database, events, logs, Web services, and files), the protocol used for data transport, and data semantics for the incoming data (append, replace, and modify). The popular extract-transform-load (ETL) is a particular case of the lookout process, more specifically, in a traditional way an advanced stage of data ingestion. ETL is a process to extract data from operational systems, transform it to a compatible format, and load the data into the analytical systems. Functionally, we can categorize ingestion as follows.

The popular extract-transform-load (ETL) is a particular case of the lookout process, more specifically, in a traditional way an advanced stage of data ingestion. ETL is a process to extract data from operational systems, transform it to the compatible format, and load the data into the analytical systems.

Batch Mode

Depending upon the problem, the data is imported from [multiple] sources in discrete chunks, such as daily sales transaction data. The growth in the big data solutions has led to the development of many tools to address data lookout. For example, Apache Sqoop an open source project provides the functionality of the data extraction from the relations [systems] sources. On the other hand, advanced tools such as Trifacta allows the data analysts to transform the data from the data source without writing a single line of code. One has to address the following points while working in the batch mode of getting data (see Fig. 7.5):

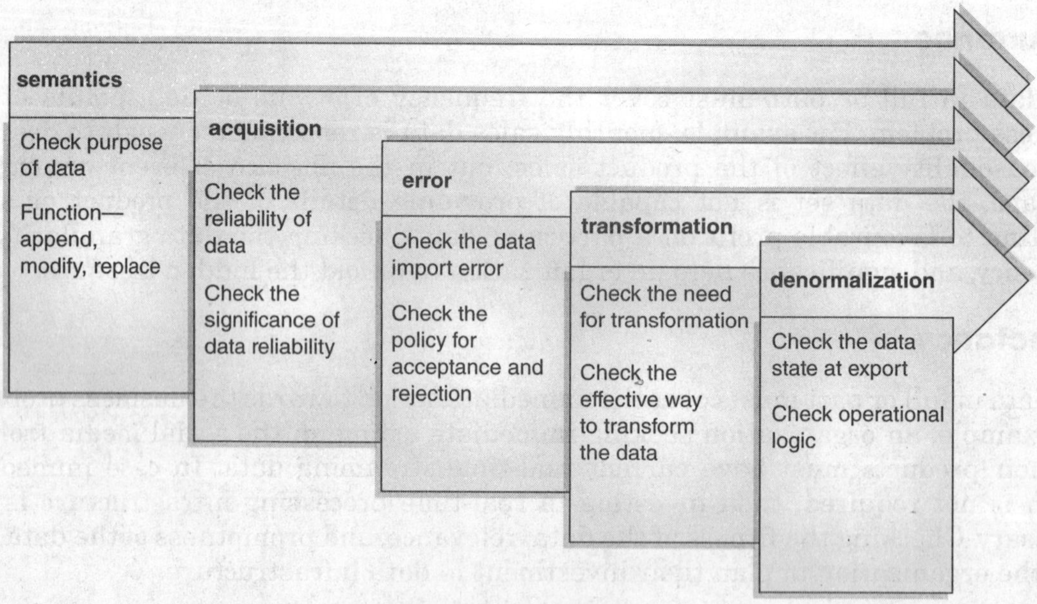

Fig. 7.5 Batch mode

- **Data semantics:** The data that is incoming must be checked for what purpose it is going to be used. For example, whether the incoming data will append, replace, or modify the existing data or it is just the collection of data having different states or time stamps.
- **Data acquisition:** It refers to identifying the way in which data can be imported reliably. Reliable data is critical for the efficient analysis.
- **Data error:** Policy for accepting, retaining, and rejecting the data or batch data needs to be formed. For example, while importing data in a batch mode, a batch rejection policy for the injection might be enforced when the batch threshold value of the error is more than 50%.
- **Transformation:** It means identifying the way to transform the data before it is available for data analysis. The data that is not transformed appropriately leads to long analysis cycle or poor analysis.
- **Denormalization:** While importing data from relational systems, one has to deal with normalized data, which is meant for the operational purpose. But, while importing large-scale [relational] data, denormalization at export place constraints on the processing environment to understand the operational logic.

Streaming Mode

© Thinkstock.com

Fig. 7.6 Streaming on-demand

Many business use cases need action on the current state or transitions of the systems, which require a continuous stream of data. For example, in financial trading, real-time streaming is required to abreast of the latest [time stamp] value of the stock. The analytical model also provides effective result in that case. Popular frameworks such as Apache Storm, Apache Flume, and Apache Kafka provide streaming data support. Apache Flume is less process oriented as compared to Apache Storm, which provides scalable, fault-tolerant distributed real-time computation. The most popular use case of Apache Flume is to ingest log [files] data into stores such as HBase, HDFS, etc. Apache Kafka is a newer framework, is a distributed streaming platform, and is used to build real-time data pipelines and applications. One has to address the following points while working in the streaming mode of getting data (see Fig. 7.7):

- **Capacity:** It is better to have a scalable system to address the ever-increasing volume of streaming data. The system check to capture, store, and process large data set is vital for streaming processing.
- **Reliability:** Mostly, real-time streaming processing requires fault-tolerant framework and, thus, a proper check and policy for achieving fault tolerant must be in place.
- **Context:** Though real-time streaming, data is available but the usage of those for business cases and application is of utmost importance. Identification of use cases and applications is vital to harness the capability of streaming data.

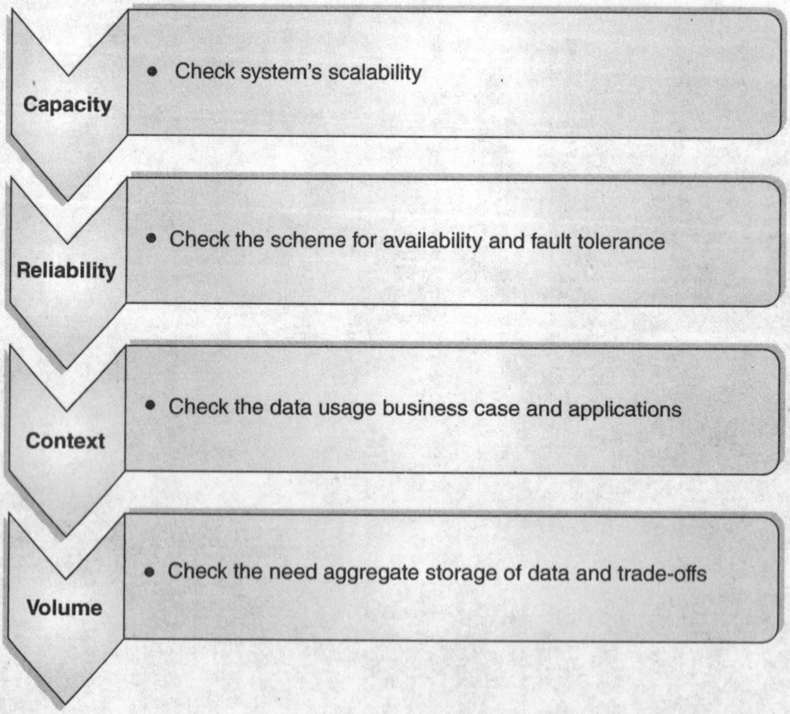

Fig. 7.7 Streaming mode

- **Volume:** It may be important for few business cases to store the aggregate data and, thus, one needs to understand the trade-offs between storing streaming and aggregate data.

Now, we will explore two popular options for data lookout: Apache Sqoop (Batch Mode) and Apache Flume (Streaming mode) functionality.

7.2 SQOOP—SQL FOR HADOOP

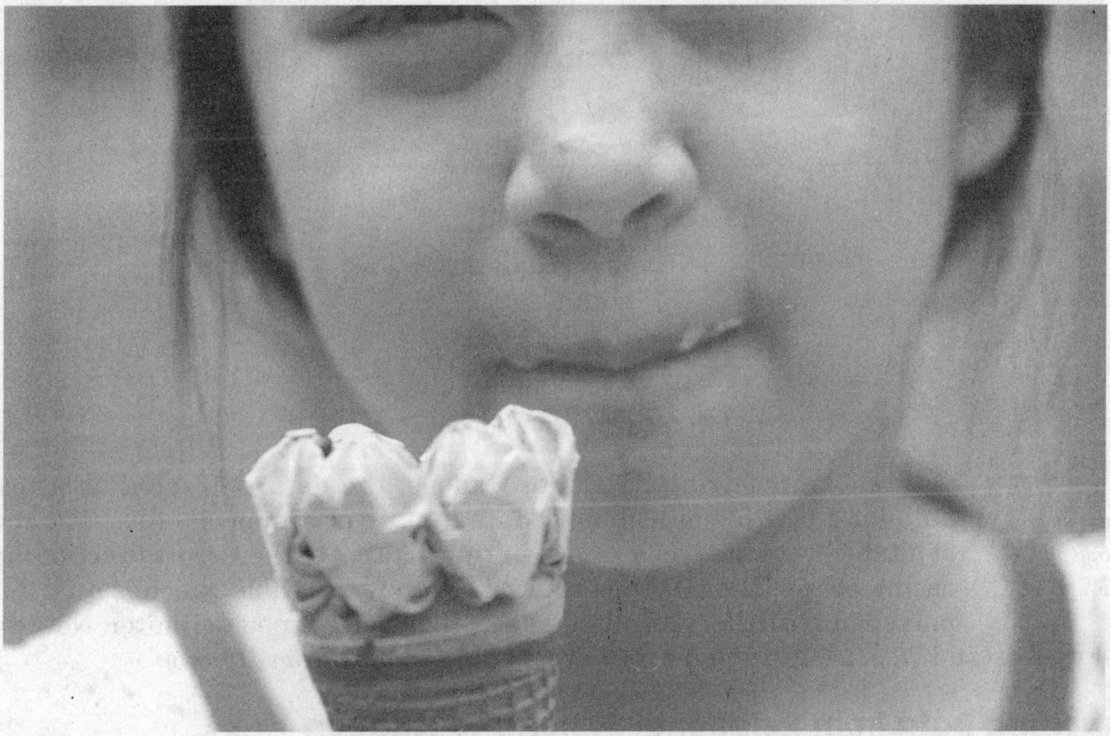

Fig. 7.8 'Sqoop' of an ice cream

LO 3 *Comprehend Sqoop and Flume*

Sqoop, '*SQL for Hadoop*', is primarily the best tool for data import and export from/to relational systems. It is created by Cloudera and recognized as one of the prime Apache open-source projects. The Sqoop is designed for efficiently transferring data from relational systems such as MySQL or Oracle to Hadoop data store including HDFS, HBase, and Hive. It uses MapReduce to provide the functionality of data import and export. The best way of working with Sqoop is that it does not change the status of production data while transferring it into and from Hadoop. Figure 7.9 shows the workflow of Sqoop for import and export of data.

> Sqoop, '*SQL for Hadoop*', is primarily the best tool for data import and export from/to relational systems. The Sqoop is designed for efficiently transferring data from relational systems such as MySQL or Oracle to Hadoop data store including HDFS, HBase, and Hive. It uses MapReduce to provide the functionality of data import and export.

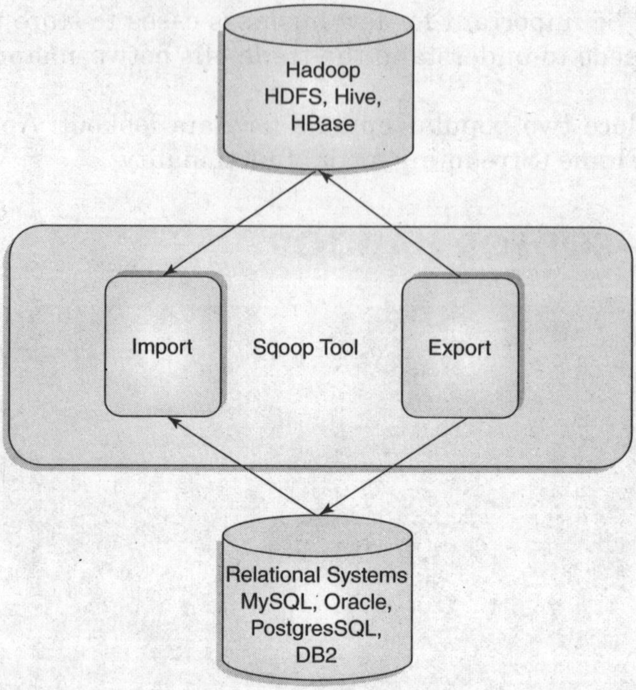

Fig. 7.9 Workflow of Sqoop

LO 4 *Analyse jobs in Sqoop and Flume*

While transferring data into Hadoop, the data is treated as a text data for a text file or as binary data in Avro or sequential files. The row of a table is treated as a record in the HDFS. On the export functioning, each record of the HDFS is treated as a row of a table which is read and parsed and further delimited as per the user-defined delimiter. Now, we will understand '*how we can import and export data to and from Hadoop*'.

Importing Data from Relational Systems to Hadoop

It is necessary to use '*import tool*' to import the data from relation systems such as MySQL, Oracle, DB2, etc., Following [generic] command, with appropriate parameters, needs to be run on Hadoop to import the data:

```
$ sqoop import (generic-args) (import-args)
$ sqoop-import (generic-args) (import-args)
```

Consider you have a sales data for your product portfolio. All the data is stored in the form of tables in MySQL database. Assume that the MySQL resides on the same host as your Hadoop/Sqoop services. Further, there are four tables—sales_electronic, sales_fashion, sales_furniture, and sales_general; these tables cover aspects of sales of different products that fall in different categories—electronic, furniture, fashion, and general items. All these tables come under the database '*sales*' in a MySQL database.

For each table, the attributes '*product id*', '*product name*', '*product specification*', '*product cost*', and '*product category*' reflect unique identification number, name, specification, cost, and category aspects, respectively.

Following command is run to import the *sales_electronic* table. Likewise, another table can be imported.

```
$ sqoop import \
--connect jdbc:mysql://localhost/sales \
--username root \
--table sales_electronic --m 1
```

Upon successful executing the import command, you can verify the table and its content by running the following command:

```
$ $HADOOP_HOME/bin/hadoop fs -cat /sales_electronic/part-m-*
```

By default, the files that are imported to HDFS are saved as comma-separated files in the directory with the name as that of the table name (that is imported). We can also mention the target directory where the imported data is to be stored. Following command stores the imported '*sales_electronic*' to the '*sales_details*' directory:

```
$ sqoop import \
--connect jdbc:mysql://localhost/sales \
--username root \
--table sales_electronic --m 1
--target-dir /sales_details
```

Further, we can also put the conditional clause before we import the data depending upon the analysis that we want to perform on the imported data set. The following statement upon running imports the subset of '*sales_electonic*' data where the cost of each of the product is more than or equal to Rs.28000.

```
$ sqoop import \
--connect jdbc:mysql://localhost/sales \
--username root \
--table sales_electronic --m 1\
--where cost > = 28000 \
--target-dir /sales_details
```

To import all the tables from the relational systems, we have to ensure that all the tables have primary keys and then the following command comes handy in importing all the tables.

```
$ sqoop import-all-tables \
--connect jdbc:mysql://localhost/sales \
--username root
```

By executing the above command, all the tables namely sales_electronic, sales_fashion, sales_furniture, and sales_general are imported to the HDFS.

Exporting Data to Relational Systems from Hadoop

LO 5
Execute Sqoop workflow

The export tool is necessary to export the desired data from Hadoop to relational systems. To import '*sales_electronic*' table from Hadoop, we have to first create the table and its schema in MySQL (assuming we are exporting data to MySQL). Following command creates the table in MySQL:

```
$ mysql
mysql> USE Sales;
mysql> CREATE TABLE sales_electronic(
 pid INT NOT NULL PRIMARY KEY,
 pname VARCHAR(20),
 pspec VARCHAR(20),
 pcost DOUBLE,
 pcatg VARCHAR(10));
```

Once the table is created in MySQL, we can run the export table command to export the data table to MySQL database.

```
$ sqoop export \
--connect jdbc:mysql://localhost/sales \
--username root \
--table employee \
--export-dir /sales_details/sales_electronic
```

For easy use, we can also create the Sqoop jobs and execute them as and when needed. To create the Sqoop job, we have to use the 'Sqoop job' statement. Once we create the Sqoop, we can verify, inspect, and execute the Sqoop job. For example, to create the Sqoop job for the '*import*' task, we have to run the following statements:

```
$ sqoop job --create my_import_job \
--import \
--connect jdbc:mysql://localhost/sales \
--username root \
--table sales_electronic --m 1
```

To retrieve the job list in Sqoop, you need to run the following command:

```
$ sqoop job --list
```

It will show the available user defined jobs as follows:

```
Available jobs:
 my_import_job
```

To get the details of your job, you need to inspect and verify it by executing the following command:

```
$ sqoop job –show my_import_job
```

Following sample output is shown when we run the above inspect command:

```
Job: my_import_job
 Tool: import Options:
 ----------------------------
 direct.import = true
 codegen.input.delimiters.record = 0
 hdfs.append.dir = false
 sales.table = sales_electronic
 ...
 incremental.last.value = 8996
 ...
```

The incremental value specifies that the import mode is incremental, i.e., append mode where import is done on the updated rows from relational systems to HDFS. The value '8996' signifies that there are total 8996 rows in the table '*sales_electronic*'. To execute the Sqoop job, simply run the following command:

```
$ sqoop job --exec my_import_job
```

It is easy to work with Sqoop to import and export data to and from Hadoop. You can just create your jobs for easy processing and usage of Sqoop.

7.3 FLUME

LO 3 *Comprehend Sqoop and Flume*

Flume provides the functionality of placing a high volume of streaming data to Hadoop. It is best used for those business cases where a high volume of streaming data is needed for further analysis. The data is written '*as-is*' to the Hadoop, and no particular batch application is written to collect and store the data into Hadoop or any other Hadoop's data sink options such as Hive, HBase, etc. Flume has flexible, scalable, fault-tolerant, and distributed architecture. Flume's high-level architecture is easy to use, adapt, and extend as it is built on a streamlined codebase. The project does not lead to a risk of data loss due to high fault tolerant topologies. Flume reduces the overall downtime as it supports dynamic reconfiguration. Thus, the need to restart Flume repeatedly is not required. The Flume architecture, as shown in Fig. 7.10, has following components:

> Flume provides the functionality of placing a high volume of streaming data to Hadoop. It is best used for those business cases where a high volume of streaming data is needed for further analysis. The data is written '*as-is*' to the Hadoop, and no particular batch application is written to collect and store the data into Hadoop or any other Hadoop's data sink options such as Hive, HBase, etc.

- **Event:** It refers to unit data that is transferred through Flume. For example, it could be a single log entry or a single tweet.
- **Source:** It is an entity that provides data to the Flume. It can be active (producing the data) or can be passive (wait for the data to be given to the Flume).

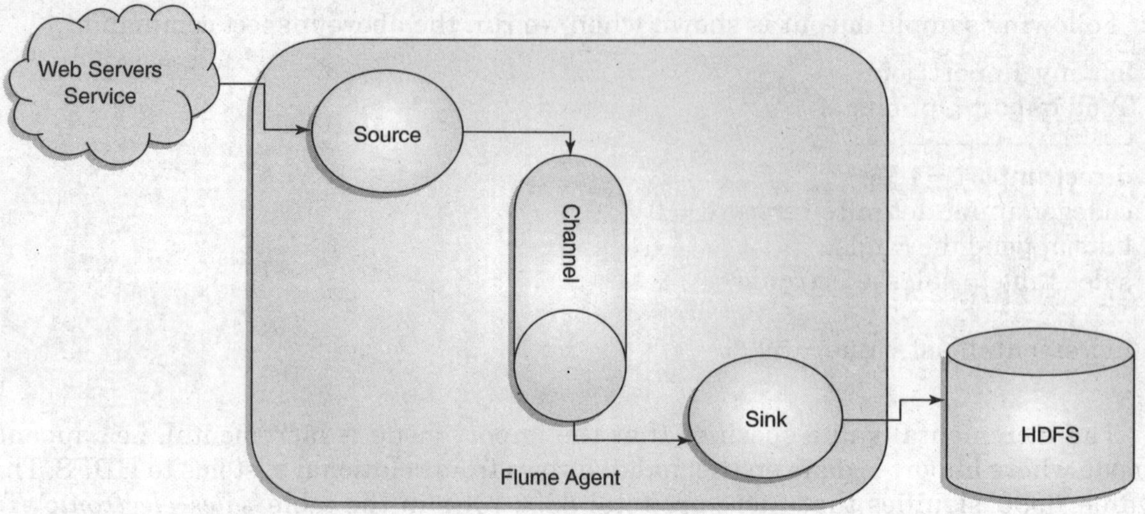

Fig. 7.10 Flume architecture

- **Sink:** It is an entity that places the data to the target. For example, an HDFS sink delivers the event data to the HDFS.
- **Channel:** It is an entity that bridges the source and the sink, where source sends the data through the bridge and sinks receives all the data from the bridge.
- **Agent:** It is an independent daemon process running physical Java virtual machine for Flume. It comprises of sources, sinks, and channels.
- **Client:** It is an entity that produces and transmits the data to the agent's source.

Flume is adaptable and can be configured to support multiple agents, i.e., multiple sources, channels, and sinks. For example, we can have event data from several sources; and before it is stored in HDFS, it can be consolidated. Figure 7.11 shows the whole process of multiple agent data flow. The architecture supports multi-hop flow model, where an event can travel to multiple agents before it actually reaches the destination. We can categorize the multi-hop model into two broad ways.

Multi-hop Fan-out Flow

In this model, the data flows from one source to multiple channels before reaching the destination. It supports the following two modes:

- **Fan-out Replication:** Data is replicated to all the channels involved in transmitting the data.
- **Fan-out Multiplexing:** Data is transmitted to the selected channels.

Multi-hop Fan-in Flow

In this model, data is received from multiple sources and the Fan-in source acts as a common point where various functions take place to update/modify/transform/process the incoming data.

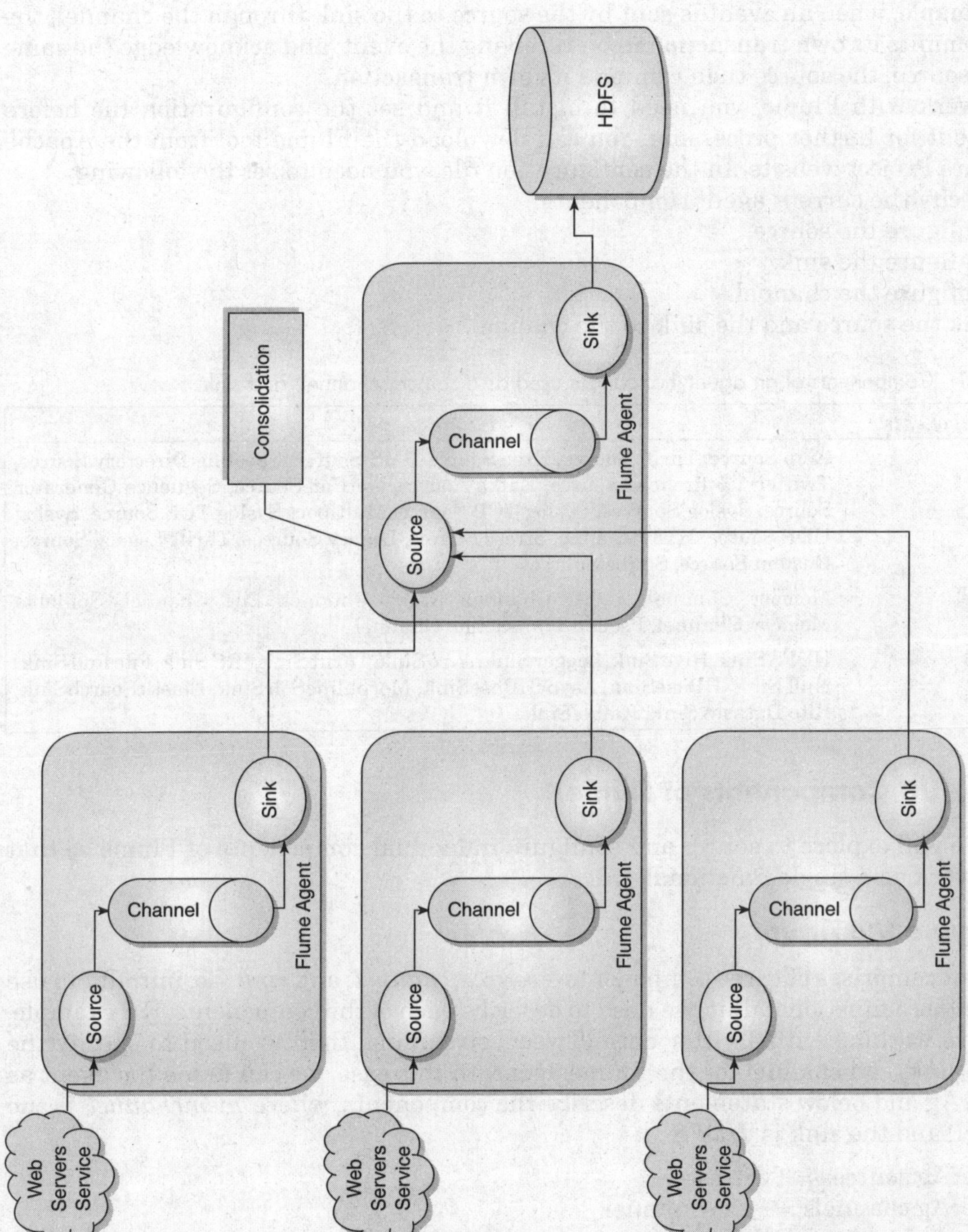

Fig. 7.11 Multiple agent data flow

Flume handles the event failure by transmitting two signals for every transaction. For example, when an event is sent by the source to the sink through the channel, the sink commits its own transaction upon receiving the event; and acknowledge the same to the source; the source then commits its own transaction.

To work with Flume, you need to install it and set the configuration file before you use it for further processing. You can download the Flume tool from the Apache Software Project website. In the configuration file, you need to set the following:

- Specify the current agent components.
- Configure the source.
- Configure the sink.
- Configure the channel.
- Link the source and the sink to the channel.

Table 7.1 Components of an agent that can be used as a source, channel, and sink

Components	*Flume support*
Source	Avro Source, Thrift Source, Exec Source, JMS Source, Spooling Directory Source, Twitter 1% firehose Source, Kafka Source, NetCat Source, Sequence Generator Source, Syslog Sources, Syslog TCP Source, Multiport Syslog TCP Source, Syslog UDP Source, HTTP Source, Stress Source, Legacy Sources, Thrift Legacy Source, Custom Source, Scribe Source
Channel	Memory Channel, JDBC Channel, Kafka Channel, File Channel, Spillable Memory Channel, Pseudo Transaction Channel
Sink	HDFS Sink, Hive Sink, Logger Sink, Avro Sink, Thrift Sink, IRC Sink, File Roll Sink, Null Sink, HBaseSink, AsyncHBaseSink, MorphlineSolrSink, ElasticSearchSink, Kite Dataset Sink, Kafka Sink

Setting Up Components of Flume

Now, we will explore to set up and configure individual components of Flume so that it can work as a single functional unit.

Configure the Agent

An agent comprises of three components—*source*, *channel*, and *sink*. So, initially, to use an agent as a functional unit, we need to describe each of the components. For example, if we are working with Twitter data (Tweet) streaming, then we need to specify the source, sink, and channel for the Flume agent. In this case, we can name the agent as TwitterAg and below statements describe the components, where '*memchannel*' is the channel, and the sink is '*HDFS*'.

```
TwitterAg.sources = Twitter
TwitterAg.channels = MemChannel
TwitterAg.sinks = HDFS
```

Configure the Source

In this step, we have to specify the properties of the sources involved. In the single agent data flow, we need to specify only one source; but for multiple agents data flow, multiple sources need to be described. For example, to configure the Twitter source we need to provide properties such as consumer key, consumer secret key, access token key, and access token secret key. All these keys are generated by the Twitter when you wish to create your Twitter application. With these keys, actually you are agreeing with Twitter to access the data (Tweets). The following property values need to be mentioned to configure the properties:

```
TwitterAg.sources.Twitter.type = Twitter (type name)
TwitterAg.sources.Twitter.consumerKey = "_Place_you_key_"
TwitterAg.sources.Twitter.consumerSecret = "_Place_you_key_"
TwitterAg.sources.Twitter.accessToken =  "_Place_you_key_"
TwitterAg.sources.Twitter.accessTokenSecret = "_Place_you_key_"
```

Configure the Sink

In this step, we have to describe the properties of the sinks involved. In the single agent data flow, we need to specify only one sink; but for multiple agents data flow, multiple sinks need to be described. Consider that the sink is '*HDFS*' sink to store the Twitter data (Tweets) to HDFS. The following property values need to be mentioned to configure the properties:

```
TwitterAg.sinks.HDFS.type = hdfs (type name)
TwitterAg.sinks.HDFS.hdfs.path = "_Place_you_directory_name_here_"
```

Configure the Channel

In this step, we have to describe the properties of the channels involved. In the single agent data flow, we need to describe only one channel; but for multiple agent data flow, multiple channels need to be described. The following property values need to be mentioned to configure the properties:

```
TwitterAg.channels.MemChannel.type = memory (type name)
```

Link to Source and the Channel

Now, we have to connect, both, the source and the sink together with the channel so that source can initiate sending the event data and sink can drain the channel (by fetching data from the channel and placing data to the target store). The following property values need to be mentioned to configure the properties:

```
TwitterAg.sources.Twitter.channels = MemChannel
TwitterAg.sinks.HDFS.channels = MemChannel
```

Finally, we are ready with the configured Flume agent. We have to start the Flume agent to achieve the desired functionality. Following statement needs to be mentioned to start the Flume agent.

```
$ bin/flume-ng agent --conf ./conf/ -f conf/twitter.conf
Dflume.root.logger=DEBUG,console -n TwitterAg
```

The following table shows the description of the elements of the Flume start statement.

Table 7.2 Description of Flume start statement elements

Element	*Description*
Agent	to initiate the Flume agent
--conf ,-c<conf>	to use configuration file in the conf directory
-f<file>	to specify a config file path, if missing
--name, -n <name>	to provide name of a Twitter agent
-D property =value	to set a Java system property value

7.4 DESIGNING FLUME TOPOLOGY

LO 6 *Perform Flume topology design*

We have explored the flexibility and adaptability of Flume deployment. It varies from single agent data flow to multiple agent data flow including multiple hops. Thus, proper consideration needs to be given while designing the topology for the given scenario subjected to the [business] problem. Following points are important to explore before you deploy your Flume topology:

- *Is it a good fit?*
  Flume is best utilized for streaming data and not for data that need to be loaded in bulk or batch. Check '*what kind of data is required for the problem—streaming or batch?*" before you plugin to Flume.
- *Is flow reliable?*
  Data flow is important as its loss leads to poor or inefficient analysis. Thus, one needs to understand the type of channels being utilized—durable vs non-durable. In durable channels (disk or storage based), the data persists even during failure or downtime. In addition, does the channel have the capacity to take the sufficient workload? For example, the buffering capacity can affect the other incoming flow in case buffer threshold is achieved. Further, understanding and preparing for adequate number of replicated flows across the channels to achieve the fault-tolerant behaviour is of utmost importance. Check failure of each component (full

or part) of the Flume and prepare mitigation strategy along the line to get the full or desirable functionality.

- *Is the capacity—hardware and networking—sufficient?*
  You need to understand the maximum throughput of your topology, i.e., the maximum events and bytes per second need to be handled at any given time. It helps in deciding on the capacity and number of each node to support the full behaviour.

SUMMARY

- Data lookout facilitates to load, convert, transform, and store the raw data to meaningful data for further processing.
- The lookout layer depends upon the sources layer.
- The process of getting or obtaining data for immediate use or to store the data in the database for further usage is referred to as the data ingestion.
- Data can be ingested into two forms—batch mode and real-time streaming mode.
- To solve a business problem, the primary concern for most of the businesses is '*what data is available?*' and '*what other data is needed?*'
- Four dimension principle—**E**xtent, **C**omplex, **O**ccurrence, and **E**xpectancy (**ECOE**)—helps the organization to identify the value of the data before investing in the infrastructure and resources for the data lookout.
- The process of acquiring, ingesting, wrangling, and digesting data comes in wide fashion depending on multiple sources and data formats, schemas, constraints, filters, volumes, and update frequencies.
- The popular extract-transform-load (ETL) is a particular case of the lookout process, more specifically, in a traditional way an advanced stage of data ingestion.
- ETL is a process to extract data from operational systems, transform it to the compatible format, and load the data into the analytical systems.
- Sqoop is primarily the best tool for data import and export from/to relational systems.
- Flume provides the functionality of placing a high volume of streaming data to Hadoop.
- Flume reduces the overall downtime as it supports dynamic reconfiguration. Thus, the need to restart Flume repeatedly is not required.
- The Flume architecture supports multi-hop flow model, where an event can travel to multiple agents before it reaches the destination.

EXERCISE

Review Questions

1. Explain the benefits of data lookout and the way to approach it.

   Tip: Identify the information pioneered product pipeline, its value chain, and big data architecture. List down the way of working with the data.

2. Describe the scenarios with suitable examples to use Flume and Sqoop.

   Tip: Develop scenarios of collecting [and/or] ingesting data from varied sources.

3. Explain with examples the usage of multi-hop Flume topology.

4. How the Four dimension principle—**E**xtent, **C**omplex, **O**ccurrence, and **E**xpectancy (**ECOE**)—will help the following industries?
   - Aviation
   - Oil
   - FMCG (Fast Moving Consumer Goods)
   - Hospitality
   - Tourism
   - Health
   - Education

   Tip: Four dimension principle—**E**xtent, **C**omplex, **O**ccurrence, and **E**xpectancy (**ECOE**)—helps the organization to identify the value of the data before investing in the infrastructure and resources for the data lookout. Identify **ECOE** for each of the industries--Aviation, Oil, FMCG (Fast Moving Consumer Goods), Hospitality, Tourism, Health, and Education. Identify the business scenarios in each of the sector/domain.

5. Explain the data flow through proper schematics to perform streaming processing using Flume.

   Tip: Refer to the chapter to understand the data flow through proper schematics to perform streaming processing using Flume. For further details check *https://flume.apache.org/*.

Part III

Foundation of 'R': Hands-on

8

Learning Objectives

***On completing this chapter, you will be able to*:**

- **LO 1** Examine the 'R' environment
- **LO 2** Describe installation and usage of 'Packages'
- **LO 3** Understand fundamentals of data analysis
- **LO 4** Perform data visualization

8.1 R SWIFT

LO 1
Examine the 'R' environment

The language of data science and statistics 'R' has surpassed over three million global active users. It has more than 6 thousand add-on packages providing the varied functionality of interest, is free, open source, powerful, and extensible. In this chapter, we will have our first hands-on experience to unleash the power of 'R' for analytics and visualization. During the 1990s, the 'R' language was first conceptualized and developed by the two colleagues, R. Ross Ihaka and Robert Gentleman, at the University of Auckland, New Zealand. The 'R' language was based on the 'S' language, a commercial programming language for statistics.

8.2 FIRST STEP TO 'R'

To download 'R' you need to access <r-project.org>, and various downloadable versions of 'R' are available that could run on Windows, MAC, and LINUX. As of writing of this book, the 3.4.1 is the stable version of 'R' available for download. The best way to work with 'R' language is to install free R Integrated development environment 'RStudio'. You may get better features such as auto completion, debugging, syntax highlighting, multi-pane workspace, and much more. Figure 8.1 shows the sample RStudio multi-pane workspace. From multi-pane workspace, you can manage, monitor, and control - commands, scripts, command history, visual charts, etc. The description of a four-pane workspace is mentioned as follows:

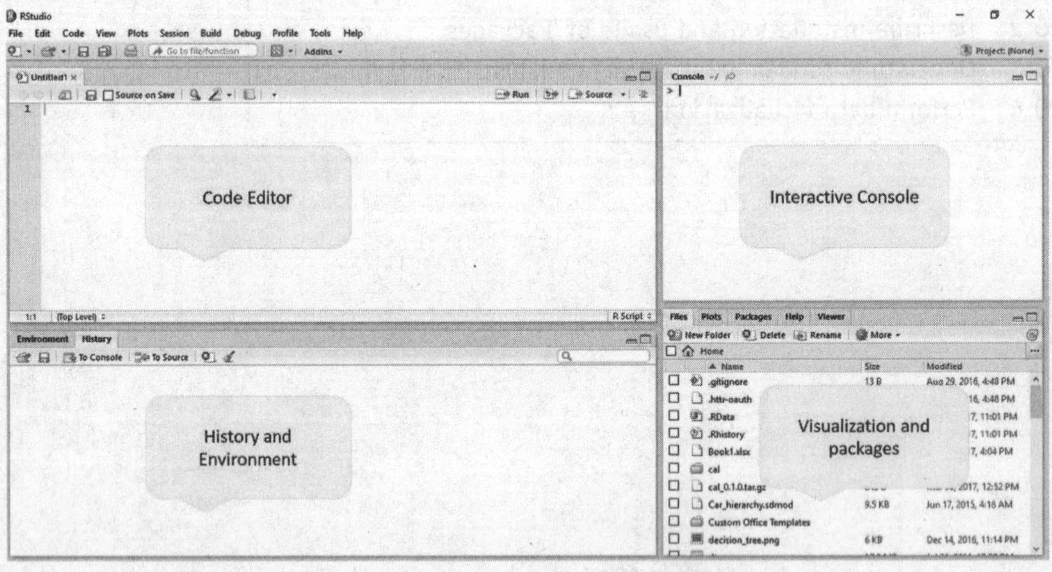

Fig. 8.1 RStudio multi-pane workspace

This text incorporates RStudio product screenshots.
RStudio is a free and open-source integrated development environment (IDE) for R. This text incorporates RStudio screenshots for educational purpose.

- **Code Editor:** In this pane, you will be mostly writing your scripts. Each script has 'R' syntax instructions to work with aspects of data such as importing/exporting of data, manipulating and transforming data, visualizing data and performing analytics, etc.
- **Interactive Console:** This pane provides the flexibility of writing single 'R' instructions. It comes handy when you would like to quickly know the output of single 'R' instructions before you finish writing big scripts and then executing it at once.
- **History and environment:** In this pane, you will get the list of objects that you have created in the 'R' session; and by managing the **history** tab, you can transfer 'R' instructions (one or all) to either *Code editor* or *interactive console*.
- **Visualization and packages:** In this pane, aspects of visualization, namely, plot, previous plots, exporting plots, etc., can be monitored and viewed. You may also track the installed and available packages for 'R'.

Shortcuts for RStudio

- **Tab:** It acts as an autocompletion function. While writing 'R' instructions, you can use 'tab' to check the probable file names or functions and choose the one that you need either by pressing 'enter' key or by 'tab' key.
- **CTRL + UP arrow key:** It shows the history of all the commands/instructions that you have typed (and executed) so far in your current 'R' session in an *interactive console* mode and then you can select any one for the execution.
- **CTRL + Enter key:** It transfers the selected line—single or multiple—from the *Code editor* and then executes the selected instructions.

Working with 'R and RStudio'

You need to first set the working directory for your 'R' jobs. It can be accomplished by executing the following 'R' instruction:

```
setwd("D:/RDirectory/RProjects")
```

> **Note:** You need to put the forward slash '/' no matter whether you are working with Windows or any other OS. You can also access the 'Set Working Directory' under 'Session' menu to select and set the current working directory.

In addition, to check whether the directory is set or not, you can execute the following 'R' instruction:

```
getwd()
## [1] "D:/Cengage_Book/R"
```

8.3 INSTALLING AND USING PACKAGES

LO 2
Describe installation and usage of 'Packages'

You may wish to utilize the powerful functionality of 'R' by accessing its add-on packages available through CRAN, the *Comprehensive R Archive Network*. For example, to install the package 'ISLR', you need to execute the following 'R' instruction:

```
install.packages("ISLR")
```

Note: You can also access 'Install Packages' under 'Tools' menu item to install any package.

You can easily put the comment by putting the symbol # to make your 'R' instructions readable and understandable.

Once you install the package, you need to load it in the current active 'R' session and to do this following 'R' instructions need to be executed:

```
library("ISLR") #Loading package in the current session
## Warning: Package 'ISLR' was built under R version 3.3.3
```

You can update and remove the package by executing the following 'R' instructions:

```
update.packages("ISLR")
remove.packages("ISLR")
```

Getting HELP!!!

You can easily get help to explore and understand any function in R. Don't worry if you are new to the function, we will explore it in later sections. To get help for function *mean*( ), we can execute the following 'R' instruction.

```
?mean # '? mark' followed by the function name
## starting httpd help server ...
## done
```

8.4 WORKING WITH DATA

Once you have configured and set your working environment, it's time to work with data. Let us first understand 'R' supported data types and objects. You can type your data in interactive *console*. However, when you actually working with large data set you would want the data set to be accessed via files—availabe on local computer or on Web. There exist several ways by which you can access the data into 'R' session, which are discussed as follows.

Built-in Data

'R', by default, provides sample data to perform some test analysis. You can get the details of existing data set by the following 'R' instruction:

```
data()
```

You will get the list of pre-loaded data set. In case, you would like to see the data values you have to select the data set first and then look inside the data items. One of the data set is '*mtcars*', which provides the data about various automobile models that come from *Motor Trends*. You can execute the following 'R' instruction to get the entire data set on the console:

Table 8.1 mtcars data

##		mpg	cyl	disp	hp	drat	wt	qsec	vs	am	gear	carb
##	Mazda RX4	21.0	6	160.0	110	3.90	2.620	16.46	0	1	4	4
##	Mazda RX4 Wag	21.0	6	160.0	110	3.90	2.875	17.02	0	1	4	4
##	Datsun 710	22.8	4	108.0	93	3.85	2.320	18.61	1	1	4	1
##	Hornet 4 Drive	21.4	6	258.0	110	3.08	3.215	19.44	1	0	3	1
##	Hornet Sportabout	18.7	8	360.0	175	3.15	3.440	17.02	0	0	3	2
##	Valiant	18.1	6	225.0	105	2.76	3.460	20.22	1	0	3	1
##	Duster 360	14.3	8	360.0	245	3.21	3.570	15.84	0	0	3	4
##	Merc 240D	24.4	4	146.7	62	3.69	3.190	20.00	1	0	4	2
##	Merc 230	22.8	4	140.8	95	3.92	3.150	22.90	1	0	4	2
##	Merc 280	19.2	6	167.6	123	3.92	3.440	18.30	1	0	4	4
##	Merc 280C	17.8	6	167.6	123	3.92	3.440	18.90	1	0	4	4
##	Merc 450SE	16.4	8	275.8	180	3.07	4.070	17.40	0	0	3	3
##	Merc 450SL	17.3	8	275.8	180	3.07	3.730	17.60	0	0	3	3
##	Merc 450SLC	15.2	8	275.8	180	3.07	3.780	18.00	0	0	3	3
##	Cadillac Fleetwood	10.4	8	472.0	205	2.93	5.250	17.98	0	0	3	4
##	Lincoln Continental	10.4	8	460.0	215	3.00	5.424	17.82	0	0	3	4
##	Chrysler Imperial	14.7	8	440.0	230	3.23	5.345	17.42	0	0	3	4
##	Fiat 128	32.4	4	78.7	66	4.08	2.200	19.47	1	1	4	1
##	Honda Civic	30.4	4	75.7	52	4.93	1.615	18.52	1	1	4	2
##	Toyota Corolla	33.9	4	71.1	65	4.22	1.835	19.90	1	1	4	1
##	Toyota Corona	21.5	4	120.1	97	3.70	2.465	20.01	1	0	3	1
##	Dodge Challenger	15.5	8	318.0	150	2.76	3.520	16.87	0	0	3	2
##	AMC Javelin	15.2	8	304.0	150	3.15	3.435	17.30	0	0	3	2
##	Camaro Z28	13.3	8	350.0	245	3.73	3.840	15.41	0	0	3	4
##	Pontiac Firebird	19.2	8	400.0	175	3.08	3.845	17.05	0	0	3	2
##	Fiat X1-9	27.3	4	79.0	66	4.08	1.935	18.90	1	1	4	1
##	Porsche 914-2	26.0	4	120.3	91	4.43	2.140	16.70	0	1	5	2
##	Lotus Europa	30.4	4	95.1	113	3.77	1.513	16.90	1	1	5	2
##	Ford Pantera L	15.8	8	351.0	264	4.22	3.170	14.50	0	1	5	4
##	Ferrari Dino	19.7	6	145.0	175	3.62	2.770	15.50	0	1	5	6
##	Maserati Bora	15.0	8	301.0	335	3.54	3.570	14.60	0	1	5	8
##	Volvo 142E	21.4	4	121.0	109	4.11	2.780	18.60	1	1	4	2

Existing Local Data

'R' provides various functions to read data that is avaialbe in different formats. For example, to read the 'comma-separated files', you need to import '.csv' file in your current working session and this can be achieved by executing the following 'R' instruction:

```
myData <- read.csv("firstfile.csv")
```

> **Note:** '<-' is 'R' assignment operator. Here, the data file 'firstfile.csv' is loaded into the 'R' session and is assigned to the variable 'myData', which is 'R' data frame, i.e., table of data, similar to a spreadsheet or a database table. You may later access the data set with 'myData'.

To access the entire data set, you can execute the following:

```
print(myData, row.names = FALSE)
##    No  Review
##     1     101
##     2     102
##     3     103
##     4     104
##     5     105
##     6     106
##     7     107
##     8     108
##     9     109
```

The function *'read.csv'* assumes that there exist a header for each of the column of the data set and placed at row 1. In case the data does not contain any header, you can directly import the file by putting 'header' parameter of 'read.csv' as FALSE. By default, 'R' will put some temporary name to the column header, which you can change later on.

```
#myData <- read.csv("firstfile.csv, header=FALSE")
myData
##      No  Review
## 1    1   101
## 2    2   102
## 3    3   103
## 4    4   104
## 5    5   105
## 6    6   106
## 7    7   107
## 8    8   108
## 9    9   109
```

It may happen that your data might have separate delimiter other than 'comma'. For example, file can also be delimited by 'tab'. In that case, 'R' provides generic function to read such data file.

```
myData <- read.table("firstfile.txt", header=TRUE, sep = "\t") # tab
delimited file
myData
```

Note: You can include separator information in the 'read.table' function to mention the delimiter for the data items. In this case, it is tab delimited, so you need to mention - sep(" ").

Data Values

'R' has its roots in statistics. Thus, any non-numeric data as character strings that comes to 'R' is treated as a statistical factor, but you may not wish to treat them as categories or group them together. You can avoid such situation by passing '*stringsAsFactor = FALSE*' to the '*read.table*' function. Alternatively, you can also use RStudio's import dataset command mentioned in the *History and environment* pane.

Copying Data in the Clipboard

In this way of importing the data, you need to copy the data to the Windows clipboard and then place the value of the parameter 'file' of '*read.table*' function as 'clipboard'.

```
#myData <- read.table(file = "clipboard", header=TRUE, sep = "\t") # tab
delimited file
#myData
```

To read data from other formats such as SPSS, SAS, Stata, and various relational databases, 'R' provides appropriate packages. Some packages come handy to import data from different database systems. For example, RPostgresSQL, RMySQL, RMogo, ESQLite, and RODBC are dedicated packages.

Importing Remote Data

In some cases, you may wish to import data from your Google spreadsheet to your current 'R' session. Instead of first downloading it to your local computer and then accessing/importing it with either '*read.csv*' or '*read.table*' function, you can publish the data and use it through '*read.csv*' function.

You need to be cautious about publishing the data as the data will be available to public access (only if one knows the precise URL to access the data). From Google sheet 'File' tab, you need to select File> Publish on the Web option. Further, select the sheet of data and then click 'Start publishing'. You will get the option where you can get the URL of the published data and can include in *read.csv* function as follows:

myWebData <- read.csv("URL address of published data")

You can remove any variable from the memory which is no longer needed by using the *rm(variable name)* function. To remove variable *myData* you can mention as follows:

rm(myData)

Persist Data and Commands

At times, you want to persist the data and commands for further analysis. It can be achieved by writing 'R' script and saving data into the file. You can save the 'R' instructions by saving the file with '.R' extension. You can also save your entire workspace by executing the following:

```
save.image()
```

The above statement will store the whole workspace with the file having the extension '.RData' which can be further retrieved as per the need and you will get the actual workspace.

An individual 'R' object such as variable 'myData' can be saved on your local computer by executing the following:

```
#save(myData, file="newData.rda") # saving the myData object in the file named "newData.rda""
```

In addition, to reload the file, you need to execute

```
#load(newData.rda) #loading the new data file
```

8.5 FUNDAMENTAL DATA ANALYSIS

LO 3 *Understand fundamentals of data analysis*

'R' supports several basic and rich data types. Some data types are obvious to understand and use but others need attention before we use them in 'R' to extract its full potential. Following are the data types that frequently appear in 'R': * *Numeric* It is a default data type in 'R' and represents any decimal values. We can check the data type of any value by using the function *class*. Following code shows the usage of numeric data type value:

```
nu_data_dec <- 25.25 #assigning a decimal value
nu_data_dec # printing the value of nu_data

## [1] 25.25
nu_data_int <- 10 #assigning an integer value
nu_data_int  # printing the value of nu_data_int

## [1] 10
class(nu_data_dec)

## [1] "numeric"
class(nu_data_int)

## [1] "numeric"
```

You can notice that numeric data consider both decimal and integer data values.

Integer

It is the most common data type used across different programming paradigms. To create integer variable in 'R', we need to invoke '*as.integer*' function and any value can be checked for its integer validity by using function '*is.integer*'. Following code shows the usage:

```
nu_data_int1 <- 25 #assigning an integer value
nu_data_int1 # printing the value of nu_data_int1
## [1] 25
nu_data_int2 <- as.integer(25) #assigning an integer value
nu_data_int2  # printing the value of nu_data_int2
## [1] 25
class(nu_data_int1)
## [1] "numeric"
class(nu_data_int2)
## [1] "integer"
```

Simple Sum using simple objects

Sum of two numbers

```
num1 <- 5
num2 <- 7
num3 <- num1 + num2
num3 # displays the sum of two numbers
## [1] 12
```

Complex Data Type

'R' defines complex data type by including the usage of an imaginary value '*i*'.

```
nu_data_complex <- 25 + 10i #assigning a complex value
nu_data_complex # printing the value of nu_data_complex
## [1] 25+10i
class(nu_data_complex) # print the class of nu_data_complex
## [1] "complex"
```

Logical Data Type

It is used to compare values of two variables. It is the most common data type used accross many situations. For example, before you import data item, you can perform a logical check on the compatibility of the data. Following code shows the usage of logical data type:

```
nu_data_log1 <- 25 #assigning a decimal value
nu_data_log2 <- 30 # assigning a decimal value

result <- nu_data_log1> nu_data_log2 # storing the output of the
comparison into result

result

## [1] FALSE
```

The value of result is 'FALSE' which is very evident as the value of 'nu_data_log1 is less than the value of nu_data_log2.

Character

In 'R', the string values are represented by the character data type. Likewise integer conversion, we can also convert objects into character type, and is achieved by the following code:

```
nu_data_char <- as.character(25)  #assigning a character value
nu_data_char # printing the character value

## [1] "25"

class(nu_data_char) # checking the type of the nu_data_char

## [1] "character"
```

Two different string values can be concatenated with the help of '*paste*' function and are shown in the following code:

```
nu_data_char1 <- "Hello" #assigning a string value
nu_data_char2 <- "World !" # assigning a string value

result <- paste(nu_data_char1, nu_data_char2) # storing the output of
the paste into result

result

## [1] "Hello World !"
```

We can also use the 'C' programming functionality of '*sprintf*' function in 'R', which is shown in the following code:

```
sprintf("%s is happy with %d piece of brownies", "Brownie", 2)
## [1] "Brownie is happy with 2 piece of brownies"
```

We can perform string manipulation by utilizing basic functions and by invoking advanced string manipulation packages. Some basic functions such as extraction of a sub-string or replacement of the characters is shown in the following code:

```
sprintf("To extract the substring from the %dth and %dth position, we have to execute substr()", 5, 10)

## [1] "To extract the substring from the 5th and 10th position, we have to execute substr()"

substr("The world is not funny but the mind is!!!", 5, 10)

## [1] "world"
```

In the above code, the sub-string that is extracted is 'world'. In case, if you want to replace the first occurrence of the word 'funny' with the word 'sad', then '*sub*' function needs to be executed as follows:

```
sprintf("To replace first occurrence of the word %s with the word %s, we have to execute sub()", "funny", "sad")

## [1] "To replace first occurrence of the word funny with the word sad, we have to execute sub()"

sub("funny", "sad", "The world is not funny but the mind is!!!")

## [1] "The world is not sad but the mind is!!!"
```

To check other basic string manipulations, you can run the *?help(sub)* instruction.

Vector

It is a collection of elements of same data type. We can create a vector by using the '*C*()', where 'C' represents collection. Few examples of vectors are as follows:

```
nu_vec_char <- c("Hello", "World", "!") # assigning vector of strings
nu_vec_num <- c(1,2,3,4,5) # assigning vector of decimals

nu_vec_char #printing the value of nu_vec_char

## [1] "Hello" "World" "!"

nu_vec_num  #printing the value of nu_vec_num

## [1] 1 2 3 4 5

length(nu_vec_char) #printing the length of nu_vec_char

## [1] 3

length(nu_vec_num) #printing the length of nu_vec_num

## [1] 5
```

Vector Manipulation

We can manipulate a vector in many ways. Following are a few examples of *Vector concatenation*. Two or more than two vectors of same type can be concatenated using the function *C*() as follows:

```
nu_vec_char1 <- c("Hello") # assigning vector of strings
nu_vec_char2 <- c("World")  # assigning vector of strings

result <- c(nu_vec_char1, nu_vec_char2) #concatenation of value of
nu_vec_char1 and nu_vec_char2
result  #printing the concatenation of value of nu_vec_char1 and
nu_vec_char2

## [1] "Hello" "World"
```

Vector Arithmetic

We can perform various arithmetic operations such as addition, multiplication, division, subtraction, etc., on Vector—*Vector index*. It represents the collection of elements of same type. For example, the members of a vector could be a collection of all days in a week or dates in a month. Thus, the arithmetic operations that are performed on a vector depends on the type of data. Normally, the operations are performed member-by-member. For example, the arithmetic operations for the two vectors nu_vec_1 and nu_vec_2 results into the following:

```
nu_vec_1 <- c(1,2,3,4,5)  # assigning vector of numbers
nu_vec_2 <- c(6,7,8,9,10)  # assigning vector of numbers

nu_vec_1 # showing the vector members

## [1] 1 2 3 4 5

nu_vec_2 # showing the vector members

## [1] 6  7  8  9 10

result <- nu_vec_1 + nu_vec_2 # performing the addition operation on
both the vectors

result # showing the output of the addition operation

## [1] 7 9 11 13 15

nu_vect_1 <- nu_vec_1 * 5
nu_vect_2 <- nu_vec_2 * 5

nu_vect_1 # showing the newly created vector members

## [1] 5 10 15 20 25

nu_vect_2 # showing the newly created vector members

## [1] 30 35 40 45 50
```

```
result <- nu_vec_1 + nu_vec_2 # performing the addition operation on
both the vectors

result  #showing the output of the addition operation

## [1] 7 9 11 13 15
```

We might encounter vectors of different length and in those cases the operation is performed considering the shorter length value over the longer length value as follows:

```
nu_vec_1 <- c(1,2,3) # assigning vector of numbers
nu_vec_2 <- c(6,7,8,9,10,11)  # assigning vector of numbers

nu_vec_1 # showing the vector members

## [1] 1 2 3

nu_vec_2 # showing the vector members

## [1] 6  7  8  9 10 11

result <- nu_vec_1 + nu_vec_2 # performing the addition operation on
both the vectors

result # showing the output of the addition operation over the different
length vectors

## [1] 7  9 11 10 12 14
```

Once the vector is created, its value can be accessed through the index, which is defined in the square bracket. The first element of the vector is indexed at '1' and thus to access the value at 'third place' index, we have to invoke the index '3'. A negative index will strip the value placed on the index while returning the overall result. For example, passing '–3' index to the vector means that except the value stored at index '3' all values are considered. In addition, in case of the out-of-range index, a missing value is reported via 'NA' symbol.

```
nu_vec_1 <- c(6,7,8,9,10,11)  # assigning vector of numbers

nu_vect_1 # showing the vector members

## [1]  5 10 15 20 25

nu_vec_1[2] # showing the vector member placed at index '2'

## [1] 7

nu_vec_1[3] # showing the vector member placed at index '3'
## [1] 8

nu_vec_1[-2] # showing the vector members except value placed at index '2'

## [1]  6  8  9 10 11

nu_vec_1[-3] # showing the vector members except value placed at index '3'
```

```
## [1]  6  7  9 10 11

nu_vec_1[7]

## [1] NA
```

Various other operations can be performed utilizing vector index. For example, multiple vector members can also be extracted and wherever required range of vector members in terms of the indices are considered for any further operations.

```
nu_vec_1 <- c(6,7,8,9,10,11)  # assigning vector of numbers

nu_vect_1 # showing the vector members

## [1]  5 10 15 20 25

nu_vec_1[c(1,2,5)] # showing the vector member placed at index '1', '2', and '5'

## [1]  6  7 10

nu_vec_1[3:6] # showing the vector member placed between index '3' and index '6'; all inclusive
## [1]  8  9 10 11
```

We can also assign names to vector members. For example, following vector represents the collection of unnamed strings.

```
nu_vec_unnamed <- c("Big Data", "Text Book", "400") # assigning vector of strings

names(nu_vec_unnamed) <- c("Book Name", "Book Category", "Book Price")

nu_vec_unnamed
##       Book Name Book Category    Book Price
##     "Big Data"    "Text Book"         "400"

nu_vec_unnamed[3] # retrieving index '3' value and associating member name

## Book Price
##      "400"
```

Matrix

It is collection of 2-dimensional set of data elements. Consider collection of 'vectors' as matrix. You may create a matrix by using the function '*matrix*( )' as follows:

```
nu_matrix <- matrix(c(1,2,3,4,5,6), nrow=2, ncol = 3, byrow = TRUE) # the data elements are stored row-wise

nu_matrix
```

```
##      [,1] [,2] [,3]
## [1,]    1    2    3
## [2,]    4    5    6
```

```
nu_matrix <- matrix(c(1,2,3,4,5,6), nrow=2, ncol = 3, byrow = FALSE) #
the data elements are stored column-wise

nu_matrix

##      [,1] [,2] [,3]
## [1,]    1    3    5
## [2,]    2    4    6
```

To access an element at the mth row and nth column of the matrix '*P*', you have to use the expression P[m, n]. Some basic operations are mentioned as follows:

```
nu_matrix <- matrix(c(1,2,3,4,5,6), nrow=2, ncol = 3, byrow = TRUE)
# the data elements are stored row-wise

nu_matrix

##      [,1] [,2] [,3]
## [1,]    1    2    3
## [2,]    4    5    6

nu_matrix[2,2] # fetch the data element value at 2nd row and 2nd column

## [1] 5

nu_matrix[2,] # fetch all the data elements at 2nd row

## [1] 4 5 6

nu_matrix[,3] # fetch all the data elements at 3rd column

## [1] 3 6

nu_matrix[,] # fetch all the data elements

##      [,1] [,2] [,3]
## [1,]    1    2    3
## [2,]    4    5    6
```

We can transpose the matrix by applying the transpose function 'T()' on the matrix as follows:

```
nu_matrix <- matrix(c(1,2,3,4,5,6), nrow=2, ncol = 3, byrow = TRUE)
# the data elements are stored row-wise

nu_matrix

##      [,1] [,2] [,3]
## [1,]    1    2    3
## [2,]    4    5    6
```

```
trans_matrix <- t(nu_matrix)

trans_matrix

##      [,1] [,2]
## [1,]    1    4
## [2,]    2    5
## [3,]    3    6
```

Note: The columns of two matrices can be combined only when both the matrices have same number of rows.

To combine a new column, we can use '*cbind*( )', and by using '*rowbind*( )' a new row can be combined as follows:

```
nu_matrix_1 <- matrix(c(1,2,3,4,5,6), nrow=2, ncol = 3, byrow = TRUE) #
the data elements are stored row-wise

nu_matrix_1

##      [,1] [,2] [,3]
## [1,]    1    2    3
## [2,]    4    5    6

nu_matrix_2 <- matrix(c(11,22,33,44,55,66), nrow=2, ncol = 3, byrow =
TRUE) # the data elements are stored row-wise

nu_matrix_2

##      [,1] [,2] [,3]
## [1,]   11   22   33
## [2,]   44   55   66

comb_matrix <- cbind(nu_matrix_1, nu_matrix_2)

comb_matrix

##      [,1] [,2] [,3] [,4] [,5] [,6]
## [1,]    1    2    3   11   22   33
## [2,]    4    5    6   44   55   66

nu_matrix_1 <- matrix(c(1,2,3,4,5,6), nrow=2, ncol = 3, byrow = FALSE) #
the data elements are stored row-wise

nu_matrix_1

##      [,1] [,2] [,3]
## [1,]    1    3    5
## [2,]    2    4    6

nu_matrix_2 <- matrix(c(11,22,33,44,55,66), nrow=2, ncol = 3, byrow =
FALSE) # the data elements are stored row-wise
```

```
nu_matrix_2

##      [,1] [,2] [,3]
## [1,]   11   33   55
## [2,]   22   44   66

comb_matrix <- rbind(nu_matrix_1, nu_matrix_2)

comb_matrix

##      [,1] [,2] [,3]
## [1,]    1    3    5
## [2,]    2    4    6
## [3,]   11   33   55
## [4,]   22   44   66
```

List

It represents the generic vector and is a collection of elements of different types. For example, the following variable *nu_list* is a list containing copies of three vectors—number vector, charatcer vector, and logic vector. To reference the list members directly, you have to use double brackets.

```
nu_vec_num <- c(6,7,8,9,10,11)  # assigning vector of numbers
nu_vec_num # showing the vector members

## [1]  6  7  8  9 10 11

nu_vec_str <- c("Big Data", "Text Book", "400")  # assigning vector of
strings/characters
nu_vec_str # showing the vector members

## [1] "Big Data"  "Text Book" "400"

nu_vect_log <- c(TRUE, TRUE, FALSE, TRUE, FALSE)  # assigning vector of
logic values
nu_vect_log # showing the vector members

## [1]  TRUE  TRUE FALSE  TRUE FALSE

nu_list <- c(nu_vec_num,nu_vec_str,nu_vect_log)
nu_list

##  [1] "6"      "7"         "8"         "9"      "10"
##  [6] "11"     "Big Data"  "Text Book" "400"    "TRUE"
## [11] "TRUE"   "FALSE"     "TRUE"      "FALSE"

nu_list[c(2,4)] # fetch 2nd and 4th members of nu_list

## [1] "7" "9"

nu_list[c(7,11)] # fetch 7th and 11th members of nu_list

## [1] "Big Data" "TRUE"
```

```
nu_list[[2]] #fetch 2nd member of nu_list
## [1] "7"
nu_list[[10]] #fetch 2nd member of nu_list
## [1] "TRUE"
```

Data Frame

It is used to store data tables and represent the list of vectors of equal length. Following statements create a data frame by using the function '*data.frame*()' on three equal different type but sized vectors. The most common way to access the data frame members is by using the *$* symbol.

```
nu_vec_num <- c(6,7,8)  # assigning vector of numbers
nu_vec_num # showing the vector members

## [1] 6 7 8

nu_vec_str <- c("Big Data", "Text Book", "400") # assigning vector of strings/characters
nu_vec_str # showing the vector members

## [1] "Big Data"  "Text Book" "400"

nu_vect_log <- c(TRUE, TRUE, FALSE)  # assigning vector of logic values
nu_vect_log # showing the vector members

## [1]  TRUE  TRUE FALSE

nu_df <- data.frame(nu_vec_num,nu_vec_str,nu_vect_log) # creating a data frame

nu_df # showing members of the data frame

##   nu_vec_num nu_vec_str nu_vect_log
## 1          6   Big Data        TRUE
## 2          7  Text Book        TRUE
## 3          8        400       FALSE

nu_df$nu_vec_num[1:3] # fetch first member and its data elements from 1st to 3rd position

## [1] 6 7 8

nu_df$nu_vec_str[1:3] # fetch second member and its data elements from 1st to 3rd position

## [1] Big Data  Text Book 400
## Levels: 400 Big Data Text Book
```

8.6 BASIC DATA ANALYSIS

Perhaps, you would like to understand and explore the data first before you perform some deep analysis. More likely, your data is arranged and stored in a vector format or a data frame. We are going to cover some basic but useful commands that come handy when you would like to work to understand the data objects.

Assume that you have imported your data object and stored in a variable named '*myDataObject*". To look at the first few rows of the data object, we can use *head*() function and pass the data object '*myDataObject*" to the function. By default, we can view the details of 6 rows. To view the details of more rows, we can pass another parameter to the function, i.e., number of rows (first few rows). Below statements show the variation of *the head*() over the *myDataObject*. To see the last few rows of the *myDataObject*, we can use the *tail*() function. The *tail*() is useful when you would like to understand the behaviours of an external data. For example, whether anything got jumbled or any foot note is unnoticed.

```
myDataObject <- mtcars  # assigning data frame mtcars "default" data

head(myDataObject) # fetch column header and first 6 rows

##                    mpg cyl disp  hp drat    wt  qsec vs am gear carb
## Mazda RX4         21.0   6  160 110 3.90 2.620 16.46  0  1    4    4
## Mazda RX4 Wag     21.0   6  160 110 3.90 2.875 17.02  0  1    4    4
## Datsun 710        22.8   4  108  93 3.85 2.320 18.61  1  1    4    1
## Hornet 4 Drive    21.4   6  258 110 3.08 3.215 19.44  1  0    3    1
## Hornet Sportabout 18.7   8  360 175 3.15 3.440 17.02  0  0    3    2
## Valiant           18.1   6  225 105 2.76 3.460 20.22  1  0    3    1

head(myDataObject, n=11) # fetch column header and first 11 rows

##                    mpg cyl  disp  hp drat    wt  qsec vs am gear carb
## Mazda RX4         21.0   6 160.0 110 3.90 2.620 16.46  0  1    4    4
## Mazda RX4 Wag     21.0   6 160.0 110 3.90 2.875 17.02  0  1    4    4
## Datsun 710        22.8   4 108.0  93 3.85 2.320 18.61  1  1    4    1
## Hornet 4 Drive    21.4   6 258.0 110 3.08 3.215 19.44  1  0    3    1
## Hornet Sportabout 18.7   8 360.0 175 3.15 3.440 17.02  0  0    3    2
## Valiant           18.1   6 225.0 105 2.76 3.460 20.22  1  0    3    1
## Duster 360        14.3   8 360.0 245 3.21 3.570 15.84  0  0    3    4
## Merc 240D         24.4   4 146.7  62 3.69 3.190 20.00  1  0    4    2
## Merc 230          22.8   4 140.8  95 3.92 3.150 22.90  1  0    4    2
## Merc 280          19.2   6 167.6 123 3.92 3.440 18.30  1  0    4    4
## Merc 280C         17.8   6 167.6 123 3.92 3.440 18.90  1  0    4    4

head(myDataObject, 12) # fetch column header and first 12 rows

##                    mpg cyl  disp  hp drat    wt  qsec vs am gear carb
## Mazda RX4         21.0   6 160.0 110 3.90 2.620 16.46  0  1    4    4
## Mazda RX4 Wag     21.0   6 160.0 110 3.90 2.875 17.02  0  1    4    4
## Datsun 710        22.8   4 108.0  93 3.85 2.320 18.61  1  1    4    1
```

```
## Hornet 4 Drive       21.4   6 258.0 110 3.08 3.215 19.44  1  0   3   1
## Hornet Sportabout 18.7   8 360.0 175 3.15 3.440 17.02  0  0   3   2
## Valiant              18.1   6 225.0 105 2.76 3.460 20.22  1  0   3   1
## Duster 360           14.3   8 360.0 245 3.21 3.570 15.84  0  0   3   4
## Merc 240D            24.4   4 146.7  62 3.69 3.190 20.00  1  0   4   2
## Merc 230             22.8   4 140.8  95 3.92 3.150 22.90  1  0   4   2
## Merc 280             19.2   6 167.6 123 3.92 3.440 18.30  1  0   4   4
## Merc 280C            17.8   6 167.6 123 3.92 3.440 18.90  1  0   4   4
## Merc 450SE           16.4   8 275.8 180 3.07 4.070 17.40  0  0   3   3
```

```
tail(myDataObject) # fetch column header and last 6 rows
##                 mpg cyl  disp  hp drat    wt qsec vs am gear carb
## Porsche 914-2  26.0   4 120.3  91 4.43 2.140 16.7  0  1    5    2
## Lotus Europa   30.4   4  95.1 113 3.77 1.513 16.9  1  1    5    2
## Ford Pantera L 15.8   8 351.0 264 4.22 3.170 14.5  0  1    5    4
## Ferrari Dino   19.7   6 145.0 175 3.62 2.770 15.5  0  1    5    6
## Maserati Bora  15.0   8 301.0 335 3.54 3.570 14.6  0  1    5    8
## Volvo 142E     21.4   4 121.0 109 4.11 2.780 18.6  1  1    4    2
```

```
tail(myDataObject, n=11) # fetch column header and last 11 rows
##                    mpg cyl  disp  hp drat    wt  qsec vs am gear carb
## Dodge Challenger  15.5   8 318.0 150 2.76 3.520 16.87  0  0    3    2
## AMC Javelin       15.2   8 304.0 150 3.15 3.435 17.30  0  0    3    2
## Camaro Z28        13.3   8 350.0 245 3.73 3.840 15.41  0  0    3    4
## Pontiac Firebird  19.2   8 400.0 175 3.08 3.845 17.05  0  0    3    2
## Fiat X1-9         27.3   4  79.0  66 4.08 1.935 18.90  1  1    4    1
## Porsche 914-2     26.0   4 120.3  91 4.43 2.140 16.70  0  1    5    2
## Lotus Europa      30.4   4  95.1 113 3.77 1.513 16.90  1  1    5    2
## Ford Pantera L    15.8   8 351.0 264 4.22 3.170 14.50  0  1    5    4
## Ferrari Dino      19.7   6 145.0 175 3.62 2.770 15.50  0  1    5    6
## Maserati Bora     15.0   8 301.0 335 3.54 3.570 14.60  0  1    5    8
## Volvo 142E        21.4   4 121.0 109 4.11 2.780 18.60  1  1    4    2
```

```
tail(myDataObject, 12) # fetch column header and last 12 rows
##                    mpg cyl  disp  hp drat    wt  qsec vs am gear carb
## Toyota Corona     21.5   4 120.1  97 3.70 2.465 20.01  1  0    3    1
## Dodge Challenger  15.5   8 318.0 150 2.76 3.520 16.87  0  0    3    2
## AMC Javelin       15.2   8 304.0 150 3.15 3.435 17.30  0  0    3    2
## Camaro Z28        13.3   8 350.0 245 3.73 3.840 15.41  0  0    3    4
## Pontiac Firebird  19.2   8 400.0 175 3.08 3.845 17.05  0  0    3    2
## Fiat X1-9         27.3   4  79.0  66 4.08 1.935 18.90  1  1    4    1
## Porsche 914-2     26.0   4 120.3  91 4.43 2.140 16.70  0  1    5    2
## Lotus Europa      30.4   4  95.1 113 3.77 1.513 16.90  1  1    5    2
## Ford Pantera L    15.8   8 351.0 264 4.22 3.170 14.50  0  1    5    4
## Ferrari Dino      19.7   6 145.0 175 3.62 2.770 15.50  0  1    5    6
## Maserati Bora     15.0   8 301.0 335 3.54 3.570 14.60  0  1    5    8
## Volvo 142E        21.4   4 121.0 109 4.11 2.780 18.60  1  1    4    2
```

We can also check the details about the structure of the object such as type of the object, number of rows and columns, data type of each column, and first few entries of each column. This can be achieved by using the '*str*()' function and passing it the data object. To just check the column names of the data object, you have to use the *colnames*() function. Similarly, you can fetch the row names by using the function *rownames*(). To extract a few basic statistical summary of the data, namely, mean, median, minimum value, maximum value, and quartile range (for number data type); and number of each factor in the column (for the factor data type), we can use the *summary*() function. For further analysis, you can install package '*psych*' and use *describe*() function. It will help to find out various other statistical measures such as standard deviation, mean absolute deviation, skew (data distribution is symmetrical or not) and kurtosis (sharp or flatter peak near the mean).

```
myDataObject <- mtcars  # assigning data frame mtcars "default" data

str(myDataObject) # fetch the structure details of the data object

## 'data.frame':     32 obs. of  11 variables:
##  $ mpg : num  21 21 22.8 21.4 18.7 18.1 14.3 24.4 22.8 19.2 ...
##  $ cyl : num  6 6 4 6 8 6 8 4 4 6 ...
##  $ disp: num  160 160 108 258 360 ...
##  $ hp  : num  110 110 93 110 175 105 245 62 95 123 ...
##  $ drat: num  3.9 3.9 3.85 3.08 3.15 2.76 3.21 3.69 3.92 3.92 ...
##  $ wt  : num  2.62 2.88 2.32 3.21 3.44 ...
##  $ qsec: num  16.5 17 18.6 19.4 17 ...
##  $ vs  : num  0 0 1 1 0 1 0 1 1 1 ...
##  $ am  : num  1 1 1 0 0 0 0 0 0 0 ...
##  $ gear: num  4 4 4 3 3 3 3 4 4 4 ...
##  $ carb: num  4 4 1 1 2 1 4 2 2 4...

colnames(myDataObject) #fetching the column names

##  [1] "mpg"  "cyl"  "disp" "hp"   "drat" "wt"   "qsec" "vs"  "am"  "gear"
## [11] "carb"

rownames(myDataObject) #fetching the row names

##  [1] "Mazda RX4"           "Mazda RX4 Wag"       "Datsun 710"
##  [4] "Hornet 4 Drive"      "Hornet Sportabout"   "Valiant"
##  [7] "Duster 360"          "Merc 240D"           "Merc 230"
## [10] "Merc 280"            "Merc 280C"           "Merc 450SE"
## [13] "Merc 450SL"          "Merc 450SLC"         "Cadillac Fleetwood"
## [16] "Lincoln Continental" "Chrysler Imperial"   "Fiat 128"
## [19] "Honda Civic"         "Toyota Corolla"      "Toyota Corona"
## [22] "Dodge Challenger"    "AMC Javelin"         "Camaro Z28"
## [25] "Pontiac Firebird"    "Fiat X1-9"           "Porsche 914-2"
## [28] "Lotus Europa"        "Ford Pantera L"      "Ferrari Dino"
## [31] "Maserati Bora"       "Volvo 142E"
```

```
summary(myDataObject) # fetching the summary
##      mpg             cyl             disp             hp       
##  Min.   :10.40   Min.   :4.000   Min.   : 71.1   Min.   : 52.0  
##  1st Qu.:15.43   1st Qu.:4.000   1st Qu.:120.8   1st Qu.: 96.5  
##  Median :19.20   Median :6.000   Median :196.3   Median :123.0  
##  Mean   :20.09   Mean   :6.188   Mean   :230.7   Mean   :146.7  
##  3rd Qu.:22.80   3rd Qu.:8.000   3rd Qu.:326.0   3rd Qu.:180.0  
##  Max.   :33.90   Max.   :8.000   Max.   :472.0   Max.   :335.0  
##      drat             wt             qsec             vs        
##  Min.   :2.760   Min.   :1.513   Min.   :14.50   Min.   :0.0000  
##  1st Qu.:3.080   1st Qu.:2.581   1st Qu.:16.89   1st Qu.:0.0000  
##  Median :3.695   Median :3.325   Median :17.71   Median :0.0000  
##  Mean   :3.597   Mean   :3.217   Mean   :17.85   Mean   :0.4375  
##  3rd Qu.:3.920   3rd Qu.:3.610   3rd Qu.:18.90   3rd Qu.:1.0000  
##  Max.   :4.930   Max.   :5.424   Max.   :22.90   Max.   :1.0000  
##        am              gear            carb      
##  Min.   :0.0000   Min.   :3.000   Min.   :1.000  
##  1st Qu.:0.0000   1st Qu.:3.000   1st Qu.:2.000  
##  Median :0.0000   Median :4.000   Median :2.000  
##  Mean   :0.4062   Mean   :3.688   Mean   :2.812  
##  3rd Qu.:1.0000   3rd Qu.:4.000   3rd Qu.:4.000  
##  Max.   :1.0000   Max.   :5.000   Max.   :8.000  
```

'*R*' supports many sophisticated functions to perform more detailed analysis such as probability distribution, correlations, significance tests, regressions, ANOVA (analysis of variance between groups), and many more.

> **Note:** You might face the problem while executing some functions on the data set that contain some *missing values*. For example, *mean()* returns NA even when only one value is missing (NA) in the data set. Either you have to perform *imputation*, or you can ignore rows having missing values by passing the parameter *na.rm = TRUE* to avoid any problem.

Subsetting Data

By now, you have explored the basic features and functionality of '*R*'. We will not be using functions over the complete data set; rather depending upon the problem, we might have to use the function on particular row set or column set. For example, we can use *cor*( ) to check the correlation among 3 columns out of 25 columns of the data set. '*R*' provides slicing and subsetting feature by which we can work on the part of our data set effectively. To subset data set, you need to use bracket notation on the data set. For example, *myDataObject* contains 11 columns, and you would like to view the details of only 3 columns, say, from column 4 to column 6. This can be accomplished by using the name of the data object followed by the bracket notation [rows, columns], i.e., *myDataObject[,4:6]* will fetch all rows for the contiguous columns 4, 5, and 6 only. You can also fetch the multiple non-contiguous columns by using *c*() function. For example, *myDataObject[,c(2,4,6)]* will fetch all rows of columns 2, 4, and 6 only.

```
myDataObject <- mtcars  # assigning data frame mtcars "default" data
myDataObject[,4:6] # fetch all rows for the contiguous columns 4, 5, and
6 only
##                      hp drat    wt
## Mazda RX4           110 3.90 2.620
## Mazda RX4 Wag       110 3.90 2.875
## Datsun 710           93 3.85 2.320
## Hornet 4 Drive      110 3.08 3.215
## Hornet Sportabout   175 3.15 3.440
## Valiant             105 2.76 3.460
## Duster 360          245 3.21 3.570
## Merc 240D            62 3.69 3.190
## Merc 230             95 3.92 3.150
## Merc 280            123 3.92 3.440
## Merc 280C           123 3.92 3.440
## Merc 450SE          180 3.07 4.070
## Merc 450SL          180 3.07 3.730
## Merc 450SLC         180 3.07 3.780
## Cadillac Fleetwood  205 2.93 5.250
## Lincoln Continental 215 3.00 5.424
## Chrysler Imperial   230 3.23 5.345
## Fiat 128             66 4.08 2.200
## Honda Civic          52 4.93 1.615
## Toyota Corolla       65 4.22 1.835
## Toyota Corona        97 3.70 2.465
## Dodge Challenger    150 2.76 3.520
## AMC Javelin         150 3.15 3.435
## Camaro Z28          245 3.73 3.840
## Pontiac Firebird    175 3.08 3.845
## Fiat X1-9            66 4.08 1.935
## Porsche 914-2        91 4.43 2.140
## Lotus Europa        113 3.77 1.513
## Ford Pantera L      264 4.22 3.170
## Ferrari Dino        175 3.62 2.770
## Maserati Bora       335 3.54 3.570
## Volvo 142E          109 4.11 2.780
myDataObject[,c(1,4,6)] # fetch the multiple non-contiguous columns 1,
4, and 6 only
##                      mpg  hp    wt
## Mazda RX4           21.0 110 2.620
## Mazda RX4 Wag       21.0 110 2.875
## Datsun 710          22.8  93 2.320
## Hornet 4 Drive      21.4 110 3.215
## Hornet Sportabout   18.7 175 3.440
```

```
## Valiant             18.1 105 3.460
## Duster 360          14.3 245 3.570
## Merc 240D           24.4  62 3.190
## Merc 230            22.8  95 3.150
## Merc 280            19.2 123 3.440
## Merc 280C           17.8 123 3.440
## Merc 450SE          16.4 180 4.070
## Merc 450SL          17.3 180 3.730
## Merc 450SLC         15.2 180 3.780
## Cadillac Fleetwood  10.4 205 5.250
## Lincoln Continental 10.4 215 5.424
## Chrysler Imperial   14.7 230 5.345
## Fiat 128            32.4  66 2.200
## Honda Civic         30.4  52 1.615
## Toyota Corolla      33.9  65 1.835
## Toyota Corona       21.5  97 2.465
## Dodge Challenger    15.5 150 3.520
## AMC Javelin         15.2 150 3.435
## Camaro Z28          13.3 245 3.840
## Pontiac Firebird    19.2 175 3.845
## Fiat X1-9           27.3  66 1.935
## Porsche 914-2       26.0  91 2.140
## Lotus Europa        30.4 113 1.513
## Ford Pantera L      15.8 264 3.170
## Ferrari Dino        19.7 175 2.770
## Maserati Bora       15.0 335 3.570
## Volvo 142E          21.4 109 2.780
```

```
myDataObject[,c(1,4:6)] # fetch the multiple contiguous and non-
contiguous columns 1, 4, 5, and 6 only
```

```
##                     mpg  hp drat    wt
## Mazda RX4           21.0 110 3.90 2.620
## Mazda RX4 Wag       21.0 110 3.90 2.875
## Datsun 710          22.8  93 3.85 2.320
## Hornet 4 Drive      21.4 110 3.08 3.215
## Hornet Sportabout   18.7 175 3.15 3.440
## Valiant             18.1 105 2.76 3.460
## Duster 360          14.3 245 3.21 3.570
## Merc 240D           24.4  62 3.69 3.190
## Merc 230            22.8  95 3.92 3.150
## Merc 280            19.2 123 3.92 3.440
## Merc 280C           17.8 123 3.92 3.440
## Merc 450SE          16.4 180 3.07 4.070
## Merc 450SL          17.3 180 3.07 3.730
## Merc 450SLC         15.2 180 3.07 3.780
## Cadillac Fleetwood  10.4 205 2.93 5.250
```

```
## Lincoln Continental 10.4 215 3.00 5.424
## Chrysler Imperial   14.7 230 3.23 5.345
## Fiat 128            32.4  66 4.08 2.200
## Honda Civic         30.4  52 4.93 1.615
## Toyota Corolla      33.9  65 4.22 1.835
## Toyota Corona       21.5  97 3.70 2.465
## Dodge Challenger    15.5 150 2.76 3.520
## AMC Javelin         15.2 150 3.15 3.435
## Camaro Z28          13.3 245 3.73 3.840
## Pontiac Firebird    19.2 175 3.08 3.845
## Fiat X1-9           27.3  66 4.08 1.935
## Porsche 914-2       26.0  91 4.43 2.140
## Lotus Europa        30.4 113 3.77 1.513
## Ford Pantera L      15.8 264 4.22 3.170
## Ferrari Dino        19.7 175 3.62 2.770
## Maserati Bora       15.0 335 3.54 3.570
## Volvo 142E          21.4 109 4.11 2.780
```

It is possible to select the data items based on '*data characteristics*'. For example, *myDataObject$mpg>19* does not list up all the rows where the '*mpg*' value is greater than 19; rather, it results into a vector showing whether each row matches the condition (TRUE or FALSE). To get the value of all the rows matching the conditon, the result is then fed to the data object. For example, *myDataObject[myDataObject$mpg>19,]* lists all the rows where the '*mpg*' value is greater than 19.

```
myDataObject <- mtcars  # assigning dataframe mtcars "default" data

myDataObject$mpg>19 # fetch vector showing whether each row matches the condition (TRUE or FALSE)

##  [1]  TRUE  TRUE TRUE  TRUE FALSE FALSE FALSE  TRUE  TRUE  TRUE FALSE
## [12] FALSE FALSE FALSE FALSE FALSE FALSE TRUE  TRUE  TRUE  TRUE FALSE
## [23] FALSE FALSE  TRUE  TRUE  TRUE  TRUE FALSE  TRUE FALSE  TRUE

myDataObject[myDataObject$mpg>19,] # fetch all the rows where the "*mpg*" value is greater than 19

##                  mpg cyl  disp  hp drat    wt  qsec vs am gear carb
## Mazda RX4       21.0   6 160.0 110 3.90 2.620 16.46  0  1    4    4
## Mazda RX4 Wag   21.0   6 160.0 110 3.90 2.875 17.02  0  1    4    4
## Datsun 710      22.8   4 108.0  93 3.85 2.320 18.61  1  1    4    1
## Hornet 4 Drive  21.4   6 258.0 110 3.08 3.215 19.44  1  0    3    1
## Merc 240D       24.4   4 146.7  62 3.69 3.190 20.00  1  0    4    2
## Merc 230        22.8   4 140.8  95 3.92 3.150 22.90  1  0    4    2
## Merc 280        19.2   6 167.6 123 3.92 3.440 18.30  1  0    4    4
## Fiat 128        32.4   4  78.7  66 4.08 2.200 19.47  1  1    4    1
## Honda Civic     30.4   4  75.7  52 4.93 1.615 18.52  1  1    4    2
## Toyota Corolla  33.9   4  71.1  65 4.22 1.835 19.90  1  1    4    1
## Toyota Corona   21.5   4 120.1  97 3.70 2.465 20.01  1  0    3    1
```

```
## Pontiac Firebird 19.2   8 400.0 175 3.08 3.845 17.05  0  0   3  2
## Fiat X1-9         27.3   4  79.0  66 4.08 1.935 18.90  1  1   4  1
## Porsche 914-2     26.0   4 120.3  91 4.43 2.140 16.70  0  1   5  2
## Lotus Europa      30.4   4  95.1 113 3.77 1.513 16.90  1  1   5  2
## Ferrari Dino      19.7   6 145.0 175 3.62 2.770 15.50  0  1   5  6
## Volvo 142E        21.4   4 121.0 109 4.11 2.780 18.60  1  1   4  2
```

8.7 EASY DATA VISUALIZATION

LO 4 *Perform data visualization*

R provides in-built graphics functions and supports advanced graphics libraries to help us to develop impactful and efficient visualization on the data set. We will explore basic and few advanced graphic and visualization tactics. In subsequent chapters, we will explore more advanced visualization concepts.

Scatter Plot

It is a fundamental plot that displays values for typically two variables using Cartesian coordinates for the data set. You can use '*R*' in-built function *plot*( ) and pass it two parameters. For example, to display, Fig. 8.2, the value of *myDataObject* engine displacement (on the x-axis) and miles per gallon (on the y-axis), we can run the following commands.

```
myDataObject <- mtcars  # assigning data frame mtcars "default" data
plot(myDataObject$disp, myDataObject$mpg)
```

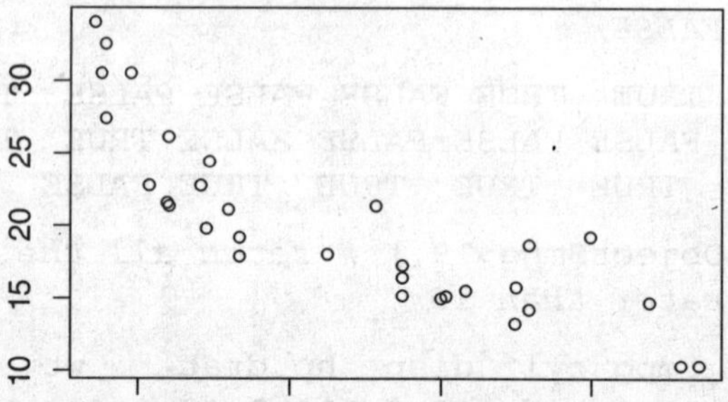

Fig. 8.2 Default display for engine displacement (on the x-axis) and miles per gallon (on the y-axis)

By default, '*R*' does not provide a much valuable feature in the plot. But, it supports the add-in customization. For example, we can label the axes, set the limits, edit the main title, change the color, etc. Some commands are shown below to generate the Fig. 8.3:

```
myDataObject <- mtcars  # assigning dataframe mtcars "default" data
plot(myDataObject$disp, myDataObject$mpg, xlab="Engine displacement",
ylab="miles per gallon", main="miles per gallon vs engine displacement")
```

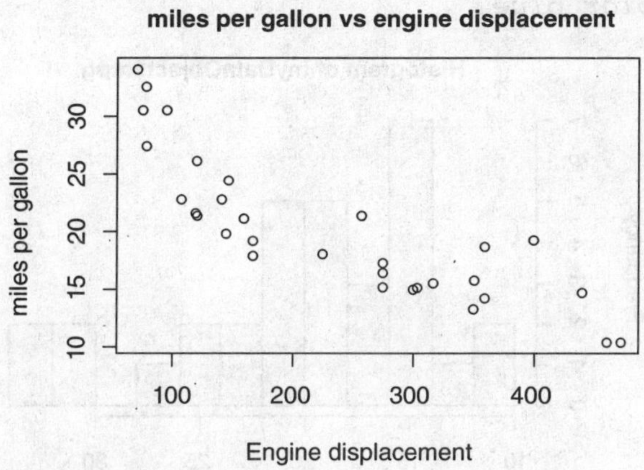

Fig. 8.3 Customized display for engine displacement (on the x-axis) and miles per gallon (on the y-axis)

Histogram

The histogram on the data set can be created easily by using the function *hist*( ) and passing it the numeric parameter. Further, features such as '*freq*' (to plot probability densities when the value is FALSE) and '*breaks*' (to plot the number of bins) can be used. To check the histogram, Fig. 8.4, of "*miles per gallon*", following command is executed:

```
myDataObject <- mtcars  # assigning dataframe mtcars "default" data
hist(myDataObject$mpg) #histogram on column mpg
```

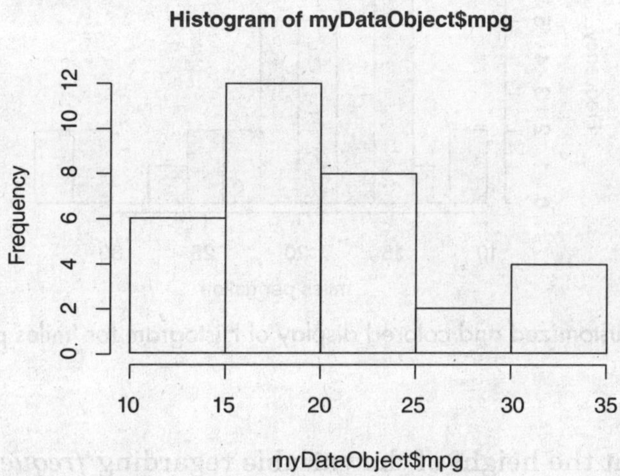

Fig. 8.4 Default display of Histogram for 'miles per gallon'

We can generate colored display, Fig. 8.5, of the histogram by running the following command:

```
hist(myDataObject$mpg, breaks =12, col = "blue") # histogram on column mpg, 10 bins and color blue
```

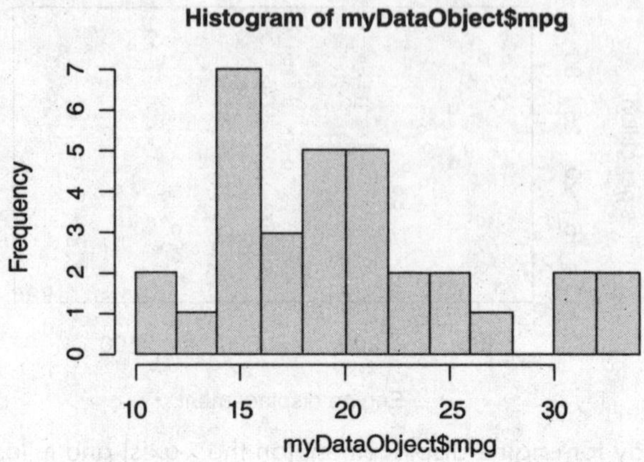

Fig. 8.5 Colored display of Histogram for 'miles per gallon'

```
hist(myDataObject$mpg, breaks =12, col = "blue", xlab = "miles per gallon", main = "Histogram for mpg") #histogram on column mpg, 10 bins and color blue, main title
```

We can generate the customized and colored display, Fig. 8.6, of the histogram by running the following command:

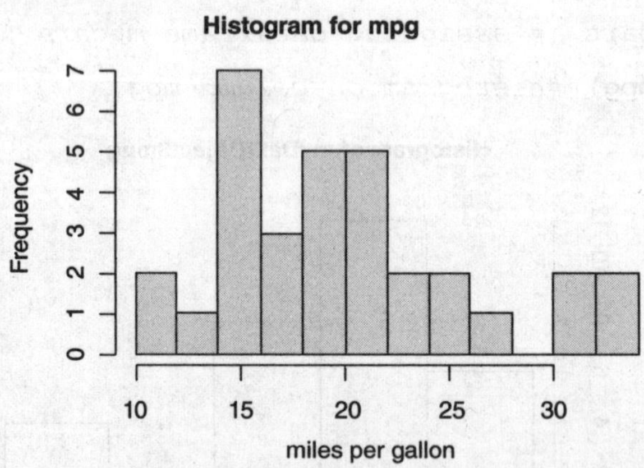

Fig. 8.6 Customized and colored display of Histogram for 'miles per gallon'

Bar plot

It is used to represent the height of the variable regarding '*frequency*'. You can create the bar plot by using the '*barplot( )*'function. We can input either a vector to determine the heights of bars or a matrix to this function. The parameter matrix has distinct uses;

for example, when the option beside=FALSE, then each column height is represented with the bar, contributing to the formation of stacked 'sub-bars'. While when the option beside=TRUE, then all column values are juxtaposed rather than stacked. You can label the bars by including the option names.arg=(character vector). Also, The option horiz=TRUE can be used to create the horizontal barplot. Sample bar plot for 'mtcars' data set is shown in Fig. 8.7.

```
myDataObject <- mtcars  # assigning data frame mtcars "default" data

gearcounts <- table(myDataObject$gear)
barplot(gearcounts, main="Gear distribution in cars", xlab="number of gears")
```

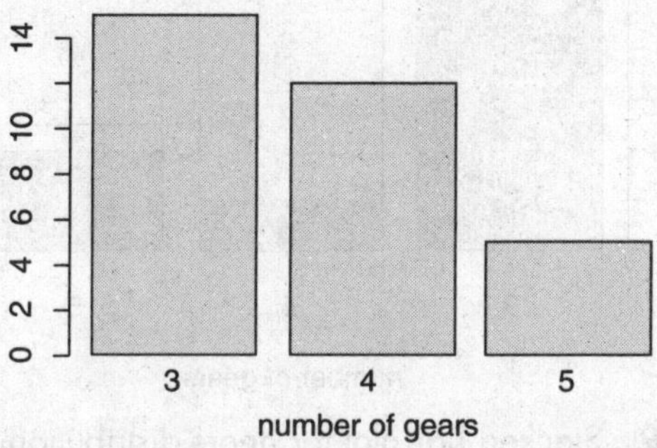

Fig. 8.7 Bar plot for gears distribution in car

Figure 8.8 shows bars with added labels for the '*myDataObject*' variable '*gear*' which is created by the following command:

```
myDataObject <- mtcars  # assigning data frame mtcars "default" data

gearcounts <- table(myDataObject$gear)
barplot(gearcounts, main="Gear distribution in cars", horiz=TRUE, names.arg=c("Three Gears", "Four Gears", "Five Gears"))
```

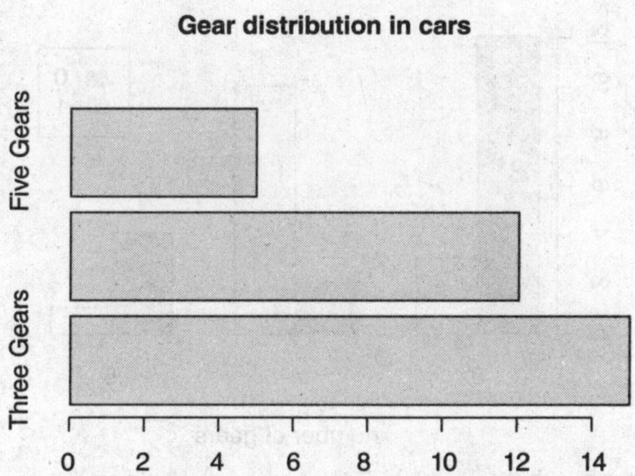

Fig. 8.8 Bar plot with added labels for gears distribution in car

You can create the stacked bar plot, Fig. 8.9, as follows:

```
myDataObject <- mtcars  # assigning data frame mtcars "default" data
gearcounts <- table(myDataObject$vs, myDataObject$gear)
barplot(gearcounts, main="Gears and VS distribution in cars",
xlab="number of gears", col=c("darkblue","red"), legend =
rownames(gearcounts))
```

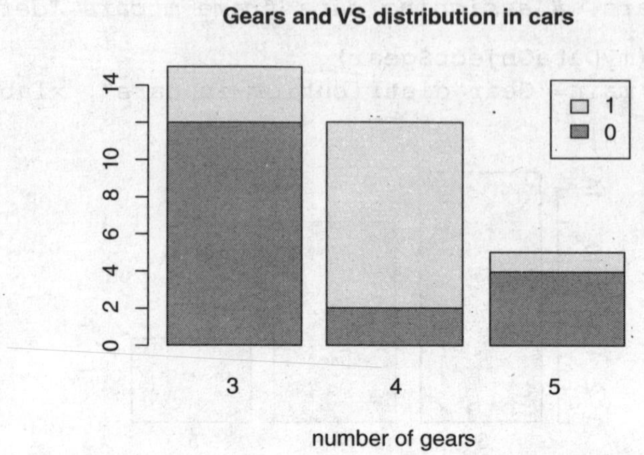

Fig. 8.9 Stacked bar plot for gears distribution in car

Easily, you can create the grouped bar plots, Fig. 8.10, as follows:

```
myDataObject <- mtcars  # assigning data frame mtcars "default" data

gearcounts <- table(mtcars$vs, mtcars$gear)
barplot(gearcounts, main="Gears and VS distribution in cars",
xlab="number of gears", col=c("darkblue","red"), legend =
rownames(gearcounts), beside=TRUE)
```

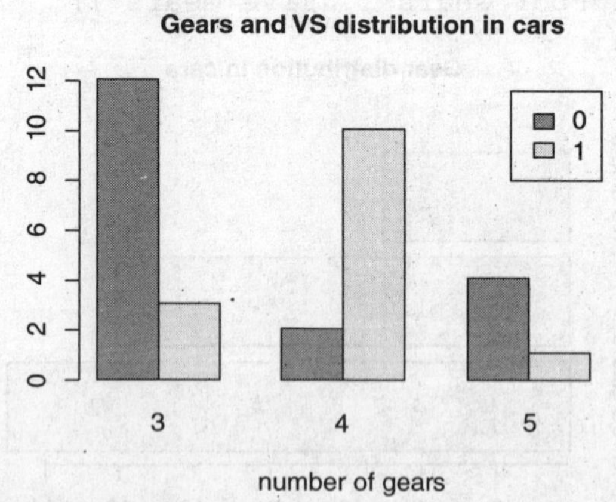

Fig. 8.10 Grouped bar plot for gears distribution in car

Kernel Density Plot

To view the distribution of the variable more efficiently, *the density*( ) function can be used. For example, to explore the distribution of the '*miles per gallon*' variable, we can plot the density, Fig. 8.11, as follows:

```
myDataObject <- mtcars  # assigning data frame mtcars "default" data

den <- density(myDataObject$mpg) # fetch the column mpg
plot(den, main="density of miles per gallon")
```

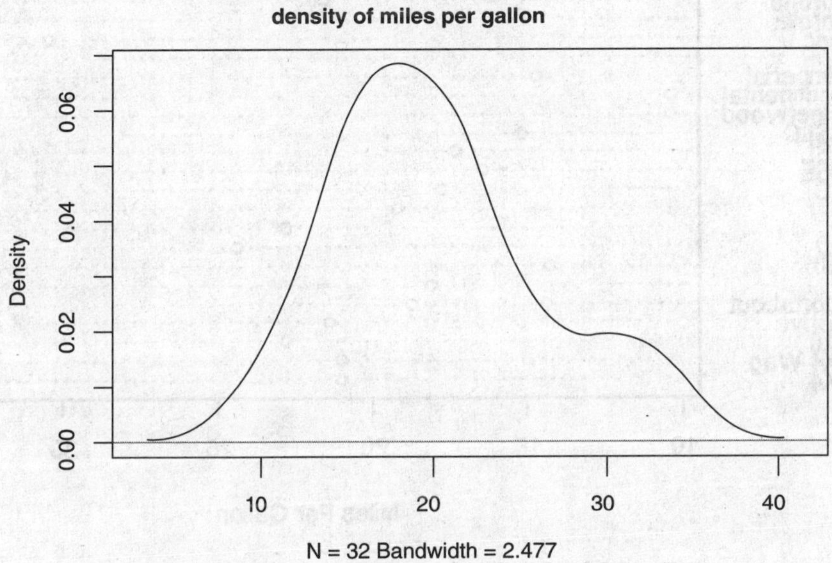

Fig. 8.11 Density plot for miles per gallon in car

Dot Plots

These plots are useful to provide much more detailed information about the variable that is being displayed. You can simply use '*dot chart*( )' function and pass it a numeric vector and labels (vector for each point). For example, we can label the '*mpg*' by row names and get more detailed information, Fig. 8.12, as follows:

```
myDataObject <- mtcars  # assigning data frame mtcars "default" data

dotchart(myDataObject$mpg,labels=row.names(myDataObject),cex=.7,main="Mi
lage per gallon for Car Models",
   xlab="Miles Per Gallon")
```

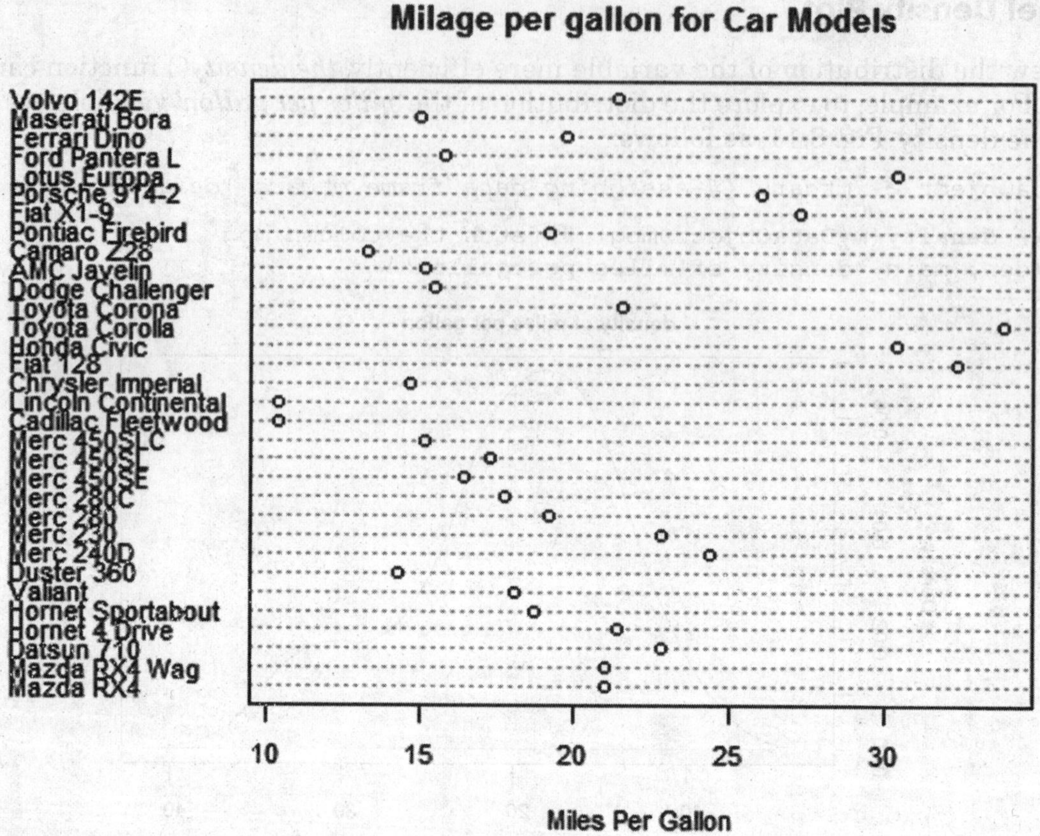

Fig. 8.12 Dot plot for miles per gallon in car

BoxPlot

It provides a graphical view of the typical statistical measures that are useful to understand the data set. The measures such as median, quartiles, maximum, and minimum of the data variables can be seen by using the function '*boxplot*()', Fig. 8.13, as follows:

```
myDataObject <- mtcars  # assigning data frame mtcars "default" data
boxplot(myDataObject, main="Mileage per gallon for Car Models",
xlab="Miles Per Gallon")
```

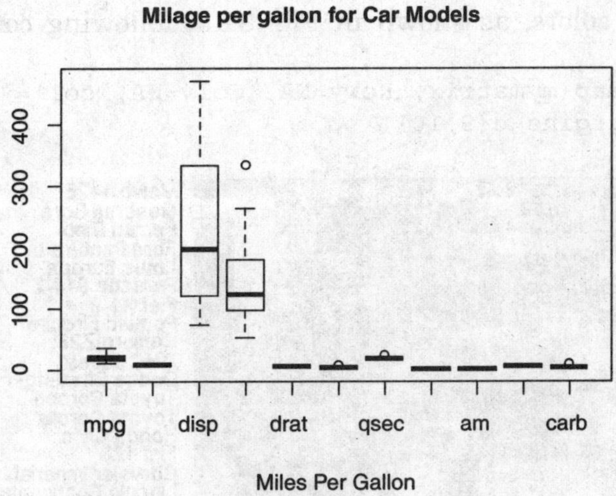

Fig. 8.13 Box plot for miles per gallon in car

Heatmap

It represents the data values in the graphical color format. The data values need to be arranged in the matrix format. The color shade is proportional to the value of the data that help in differentiating the different level of data values. The following code shows the heatmap, Fig. 8.14, for the '*R*' in-built data set '*mtcars*'.

```
myDataObject <- mtcars  # assigning data frame mtcars "default" data

mymatrix <- data.matrix(myDataObject)
myheatmap <- heatmap(mymatrix, Rowv=NA, Colv=NA, col = cm.colors(256),
scale="column", margins=c(5,10))
```

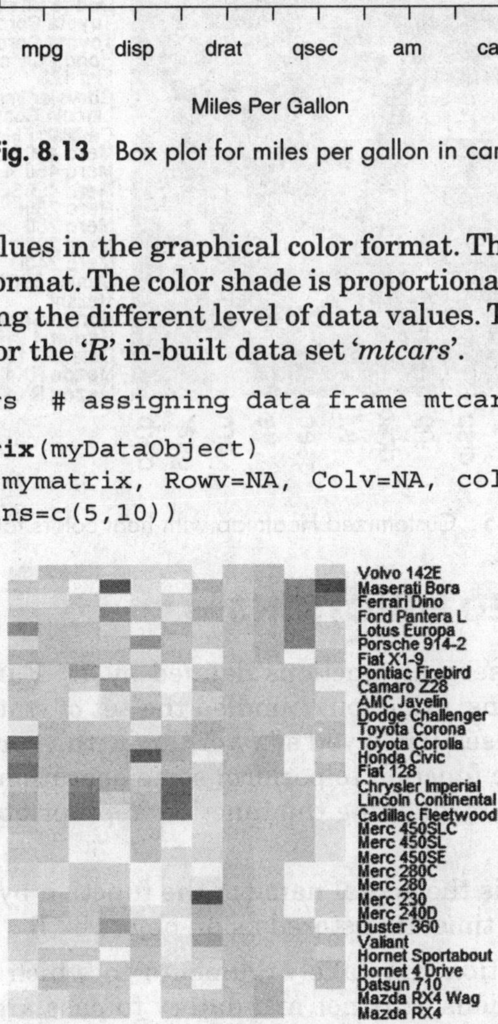

Fig. 8.14 Heatmap for mtcars data set for gears distribution in car

To customize the colors, as shown in Fig. 8.15, following command needs to be executed:

```
myheatmap <- heatmap(mymatrix, Rowv=NA, Colv=NA, col = heat.colors(256),
scale="column", margins=c(5,10))
```

Fig. 8.15 Customized Heatmap with heat colors for mtcars

8.8 USER-DEFINED FUNCTIONS

Till now, we have used several functions defined by 'R'. Further, different packages provide different functions. Functions bundled the set of statements to perform some specific tasks. In some cases, when you are working with your own data set, you would like to have your specific function to perform some operations on the data. In 'R', you can define your function by defining the function appropriately. A function definition has four different parts:

- **Function name:** It is the actual name of the function by which a function can be invoked any point in time. It is stored as an object in 'R'.
- **Arguments:** A function can take arguments to which you can pass values to perform some operations. It is not mandatory to pass arguments to the function. It all depends on what specific task you want to perform the function. Also, you can set some arguments with default values. So, in case if you are not passing the

values to those parameters (having default values), the default values will be used for further processing.

- **Function body:** It defines the set of statements to perform a specific task.
- **Return value:** It is the last expression to be evaluated in the function body. It specifies what needs to be returned after the function execution is complete.

Given below is a function that computes the average of a given sequence.

```
## defining function "avgseq": it generates the mean of the sequence
between value of a and value of b
avgseq <- function(a,b) {
  result <- mean(a:b)
  return(result)
}

## invoking function "avgseq"

avgseq(5,10) # generating the mean of the sequence between value of a
and value of b

## [1] 7.5
```

SUMMARY

- The best way to work with 'R' language is to install free R Integrated development environment 'RStudio'.
- CRAN, the Comprehensive R Archive Network provides powerful packages for analysis.
- 'R' by default provides sample data to perform some test analysis.
- 'R' provides various functions to read data that are available in different formats.
- 'R' provides valuable function 'str()' to understand the structure of the object such as type of the object, number of rows and columns, data type of each column, and first few entries of each column.
- 'R' provides slicing and subsetting feature to work on the part of data set effectively.
- 'R' provides in-built graphics functions and supports advanced graphics libraries to develop impactful and efficient visualization on the data set.

EXERCISE

Review Questions

1. Explore the 'Sunspot.year' in-built data set in 'R'. The dataset is collection of annual observed sunspot numbers recorded between the period 1700 and 1988.

Perform the following tasks:
  (a) Convert the data set into a data frame.
  (b) Check the first few and last few rows.
  (c) Confirm whether the data set is containing any negative number
  (d) Verify the boundary values for the years.
  (e) Identify the maximum number of sunspots in any year.
  (f) Compute the total years that have data of observed five or fewer sunspots.
  (g) Generate the summary of the data set.
  (h) Add new column in the data set covering total number of sunspots observed during the study period.

2. Explore the 'airquality' in-built data set in 'R'. The dataset is collection of measurements of daily air quality during May to September 1973 in New York. Perform the following tasks:
  (a) Check the first few and last few rows.
  (b) Check the mean value of the data set. Is there any discrepancy? Explain and handle it accordingly.
  (c) Confirm whether the data set is containing any negative number
  (d) Generate the summary of the data set.
  (e) Identify the mean ozone value (in ppb)for the data set.
3. Design a function in 'R' to perform the temperature conversion from ^{0}F to ^{0}C as per the below formula:

   C = 5/9 * (F–32)

   where C = temperature in degree Celsius and F = temperature in degree Fahrenheit
4. Plot a Scatter graph for the 'airquality' in-built data set in 'R' depicting relationship between ozone and temperature. Customize the graph to include more valuable information such as axis labels, main title, and colors.
5. Generate the Heatmap for the 'airquality' in-built data set in 'R'. How can you make it more readable and valuable?

9 Supervised Learning

> *"I think every film is made better by having smart music supervision that's really in tune with the spirit of the visual content."*
>
> —John Legend

Learning Objectives

On completing this chapter, you will be able to:

- **LO 1** Understand supervised and semi-supervised learning
- **LO 2** Describe linear regression and its performance measures
- **LO 3** Perform cross validation
- **LO 4** Describe classification and its performance measures
- **LO 5** Comprehend classification trees and random forest

LO 1
Understand supervised and semi-supervised learning

One of the core foundation of evolution is to learn, behave, and act through experience and observation. The whole human race, as a 'learner', has evolved and continues to do so to experience and observe unseen '*world*' and '*environment*'. Machines like a computer, in early days, were programmed to perform computational tasks only. The early 1990s witnessed the introduction of a discipline named Machine Learning (ML), as a special branch of artificial intelligence (AI), which impacted the functioning of the computing machines to perform some actions on new, unseen examples/tasks after getting exposed to the learning data set. Machine learning depicts the science behind the whole 'learning-acting' phenomenon for the computing machines. Through ML computing, machines could act without being explicitly programmed based on the 'learning'. We can notice the proliferation of the ML discipline to the development of self-driving cars, natural language processing, practical speech recognition, effective Web search, smart assistant, and a vastly improved understanding of the human genome. Most of the time, we use ML in various ways that it has become so pervasive that we don't know that we are using it. Most of the researchers have a strong belief that through ML one can make progress towards achieving the human-level AI. Broadly, ML tasks are classified into two categories—*Supervised Learning* and *Unsupervised Learning*. A blended hybrid learning 'semi-supervised' is also considered for some specific tasks. In the supervised learning, the goal is to map the input data set to the output data set through the learning algorithm by generating the set of appropriate rules. The assumption is that both the sets—'input' and 'output' data sets— are available. While in unsupervised learning, the output data set is not provided to the learning algorithm and only input data set is being used to generate the patterns, rules, and insights. In the semi-supervised learning, the learning algorithm is provided with the partial data set—input and output. The goal of the learning algorithm is to generate rules, patterns, and insights where the output data set is unavailable and then use the complete output set, all together, like a supervised learning.

In this chapter, we will first understand the regression technique to predict the numerical outcomes of the unseen observations. The regression technique is different from the classification technique that we will study in depth that targets to predict the discrete outcome. Though the ever-increasing data has posed a challenge to the organization to interpret it timely and wisely, it also offers an opportunity to understand some of the very challenging questions which otherwise were very difficult to answer. For example, businesses are now interested in understanding '*how many units of their products will be sold?*' or '*what would be the appropriate price of the product that the customer would like to pay?*' The prime goal is to understand the data—'*how it is going to affect the outcome*'. Two types of thinking mindset are important to attempt such challenging questions—firstly, to model to understand the data generation process and thereby explore the relationships among the data; and secondly, to model to predict the outcome of interest accurately. We have covered the first thinking mindset in the early chapters of the book where we discussed the data, data types, dimensions, relationships, tools, and techniques to explore and describe the relationships among the data. We will now focus our understanding on the other thinking mindset. You will learn to use 'regression' to achieve the second thinking mindset.

9.1 LINEAR REGRESSION TECHNIQUE

LO 2 *Describe linear regression and its performance measures*

Regression helps to model numerical relationship within data. The regression models help to predict the value of the unseen data based on the training data. In Fig. 9.1, variable 'y' is the dependent variable, and its output is dependent on the value of variable 'x'. The variable 'x' is known as a *predictor*. The life expectancy, salary could be denoted by the variable 'y', and a predictor such as 'age' or 'education' could be used as predictors. The linear regression helps to fit the straight line in the data to represent the best possible relationship within the data, see Fig. 9.2.

Fig. 9.1 Dependent and independent variable space

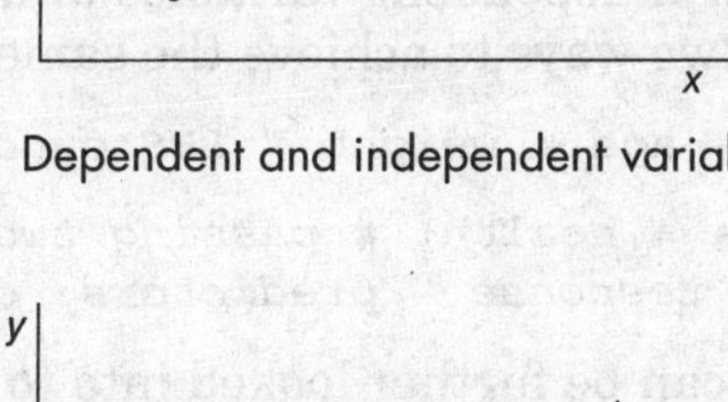

Fig. 9.2 Linear regression line

One of the fundamental assumptions of the linear regression technique is that the expected outcome value is the sum of the weighted inputs. Also, the change in the value of the predicted outcome is linearly related to the change in the inputs. The expression in eq. (1) shows the relationship between the dependent and independent variables.

$$y = \beta_0 + \beta_1 x_1 + \beta_2 x_2 + \ldots \quad \text{eq. (1)}$$

where,

- the response variable 'y' is linearly related to each predictor 'x_i'.
- each predictor 'x_i' contributes additively to response 'y'.
- each β_i is the coefficient related to each predictor with the exception to the first coefficient which assumes the absence of any predictor.

In 'R', we can perform the linear regression by utilizing the function '*lm*'. A formula can be developed for an easy execution of the linear regression technique. The L.H.S. (Left Hand Side) represents the outcome to be predicted, and the R.H.S. (Right Hand Side) represents the set of the predictors. The string can be converted to the formula by passing the string representing the expression of a linear technique to the function '*as.formula*'. Below snippet in 'R' shows an easy way to create formulas.

```
frmla <- blood_pressure ~ age + weight # LHS outcome and RHS: Inputs
frmla <- salary ~ education + experience # LHS outcome and RHS: Inputs

frmla <- as.formula("blood_pressure ~ age + weight") # Converting string
to the formula
frmla <- as.formula("salary ~ education + experience") # Converting
string to the formula
```

To perform the linear regression, we can pass two parameters of interest to the function '*lm*'—dependent and independent variables and the data set. For example, the following snippet shows two ways to achieve the same.

```
frmla <- blood_pressure ~ age + weight # LHS outcome and RHS: Inputs

lmmodel <- lm(frmla, data = health) # passing two parameters - formula
showing the relationship response ~ predictors; data set = Health
```

The model, say, '*lmmodel*', can be further looked into to understand the coefficients for the expression that could predict the expected outcome of interest. Let us consider a sample of a data set depicting a fascinating problem of '*measuring the temperature of the environment through the chirping of the cricket*'. The data set 'Cricktchrp' contains two variables—'*chirps_per_sec*' detailing the number of chirps made by the cricket per sec and temperature depicting the temperature at respecting intervals of the '*chirps_per_sec*' record. Below snippet shows the development of the robust model for predicting the temperature at the particular level of '*chirps_per_sec*'.

```
frmla <- temperature ~ chirps_per_sec # LHS outcome and RHS: Inputs
cricktchrp <- readRDS("cricktchrp.rds")

chirp_model <- lm(frmla, data = cricktchrp) # passing two parameters
- formula showing the relationship response ~ predictors; data set =
Health
```

Fig. 9.3 Count cricket chirping to measure temperature

Here, we developed the model '*chirp_model*' and the structure of the model can be seen by invoking it directly in 'R' by its name as follows:

```
chirp_model # describing details about coefficients and response

##
## Call:
## lm(formula = frmla, data = cricktchrp)
##
## Coefficients:
##    (Intercept)  chirps_per_sec
##         25.232           3.291
```

The intercept represents the 'β_0' when all the inputs are assumed to be zero. The other variable is the weights for the weighted sum of the inputs. In the example, the weight of the variable '*chirps_per_sec*' is 3.291. This weight simply signifies two things—first, the weight is positive and, thus, the increase in the value of the input variable increases the value of the outcome of interest positively; secondly, for every unit change in the '*chirps_per_sec*', there is at least more than 3 units change in the value of the temperature. Detailed model diagnostic can be obtained by invoking the function '*summary*' on the model that includes values, standard errors, and other diagnostics as follows.

```
summary(chirp_model)  # describing detail diagnostics about
coefficients, response, and predictors
##
## Call:
## lm(formula = frmla, data = cricktchrp)
##
## Residuals:
##     Min      1Q Median      3Q     Max
## -6.515 -1.971  0.490  2.807  5.001
##
## Coefficients:
##                 Estimate Std. Error t value Pr(>|t|)
## (Intercept)      25.2323    10.0601   2.508 0.026183 *
## chirps_per_sec    3.2911     0.6012   5.475 0.000107 ***
## ---
## Signif. codes:  0 '***' 0.001 '**' 0.01 '*' 0.05 '.' 0.1 ' ' 1
##
## Residual standard error: 3.829 on 13 degrees of freedom
## Multiple R-squared:  0.6975, Adjusted R-squared:  0.6742
## F-statistic: 29.97 on 1 and 13 DF,  p-value: 0.0001067
```

Prediction

It is easy to perform predictions on the data set after developing the model. We can use the function '*predict*' to predict the outcome of interest. The function, by default, returns training data predictions.

The expected outcome can further be checked via a plot with the actual predictions as shown in Fig. 9.4:

```
# load the ggplot2 package
library(ggplot2)

# Make a plot to compare predictions to actual (prediction on x-axis)

cricktchrp$prediction <-  predict(chirp_model) # predict the outcome of
interest

plot <- ggplot(cricktchrp, aes(x = prediction, y = temperature)) +
  geom_point() +
  geom_abline(color = "red", linetype = "dashed")

plot
```

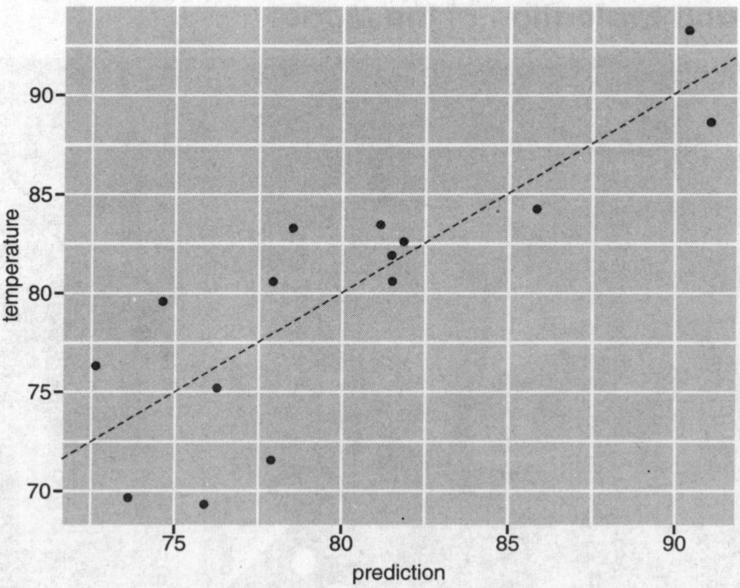

Fig. 9.4 Regression of outcome of interest on the 'Cricktchrp' data set

We can perform prediction for any unseen data and then check the variations. For example, the value of '*chirps_per_sec* = 16.6' can be shown in the snippet as follows.

```
new datapoint <- data.frame(chirps_per_sec = 16.6)
newdatapoint$prediction <- predict(lmmodel, newdata = newdatapoint)

newdatapoint

##   chirps_per_sec prediction
## 1           16.6   79.86447
```

The model predicts that for the value of '*chirps_per_sec*' the temperature should rise to 80 degrees. The aim of the accurate prediction lies on the fitting of the model on the data set.

It is to be noted that from the prediction perspective multi-variate linear regression behaves much as simple (single-variable) linear regression does. Linear regression models are concise, easy to fit and apply to the data set. The limitations of the models are such that they cannot represent the relationship which is non-linear and complex additive. One major shortcoming of the linear regression model is that it is incapable to filter out the collinearity. The collinearity depicts the partial relationship between the independent variables and causes for coefficients to have large values and contributes to the instability of the model.

Performance and Evaluation of the Model

Fig. 9.5 Assigning ratings

One of the critical and mandatory phase of developing the models is to assess the performance and evaluate the models. To do so, we need to define the performance measure for our models depending upon the context of their usage. In some cases, the performance is the measurement of the accuracy; for example, to provide a particular disease treatment, the doctor must be presented with the accurate information about the presence and level of the disease in a patient. So, in this case, the model must predict the accurate positive and negative cases and, thus, accuracy is a good performance measure. In other scenarios, computational time is often critical while considering data set in a batch mode or real-time streaming mode. Further, the model needs to perform well for different tasks—regression, classification, and clustering, etc. We will cover the performance and evaluation of the regression and classification models in this chapter, and in the next chapter we will cover these criteria for clustering models.

The linear regression model can be evaluated easily. Consider the prediction plotted by two different models, as shown in Fig. 9.6. We can easily see that the first model, Fig. 9.6 (a), fits the data and there is much more scattered distribution of the data above and below the prediction line. Thus, the first model provides effective and better predictions of the outcome of interest as compared to the second model.

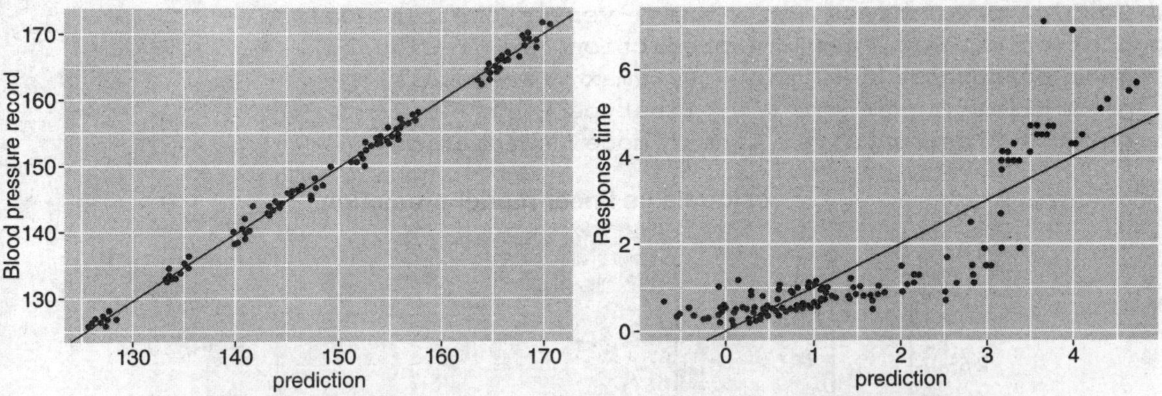

(a) A well-fit model (b) A poorly-fit model

Fig. 9.6 Model—well vs poorly fit

The second model also represents that there might be the case that important variables are not considered or there is some set of level of errors that is causing poor coverage of complex relationship. One way to check the difference between the actual and predicted value is to look at the residual plot. The residual plot represents the difference between the outcome of the predictions and the actual predictions, see Fig. 9.7.

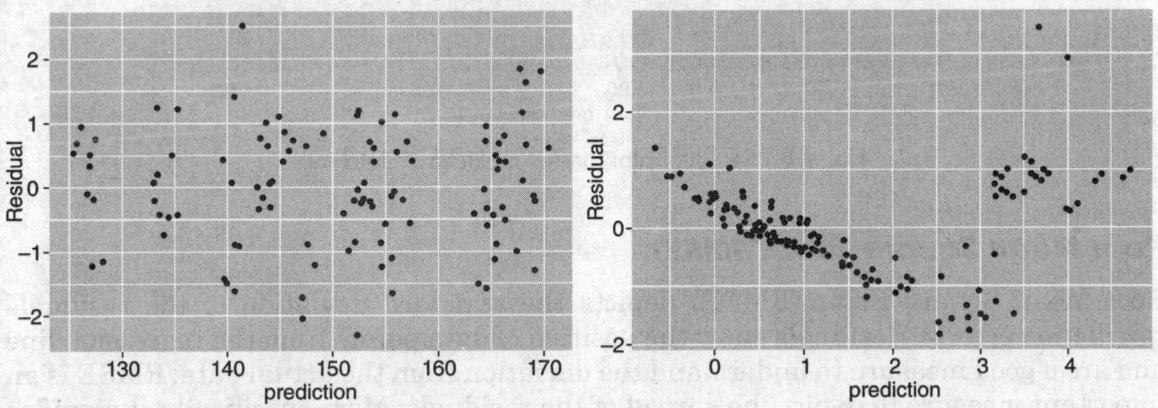

(a) A well-fit model (b) A poorly-fit model

Fig. 9.7 Residual Plot Model—well vs poorly fit

We can quickly compute the residual of the prediction for the '*cricktchrp*' data set as follows, and the resultant residual plot is shown in Fig. 9.8.

```
# residuals
# Calculate residuals
cricktchrp$residuals <- cricktchrp$temperature - cricktchrp$prediction
```

```
# To plot predictions (on x-axis) versus the residuals
ggplot(cricktchrp, aes(x = prediction, y = residuals)) +
  geom_pointrange(aes(ymin = 0, ymax = residuals)) +
  geom_hline(yintercept = 0, linetype = 3) +
  ggtitle("residuals vs. linear model prediction")
```

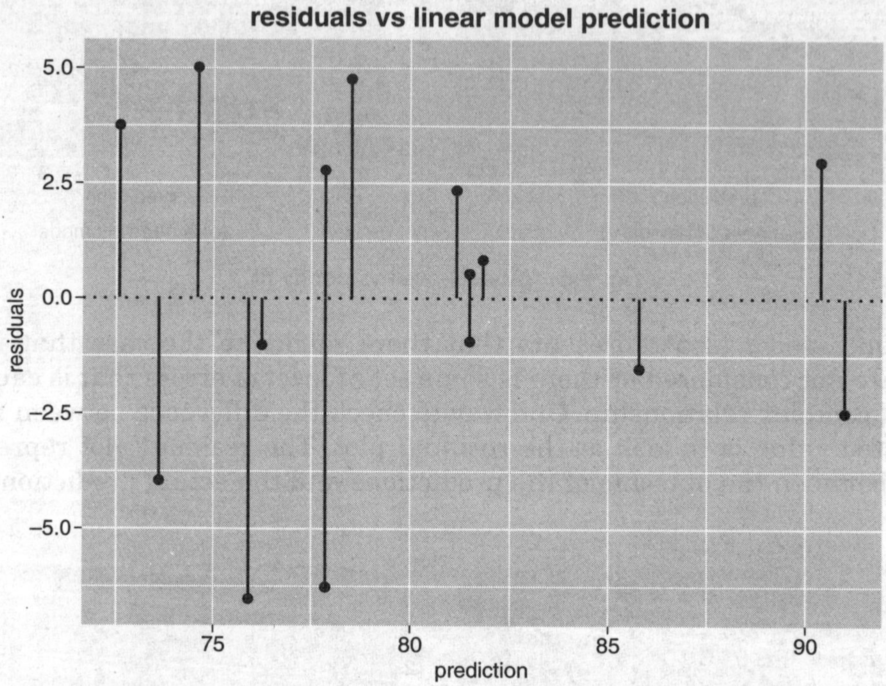

Fig. 9.8 Residual plot for the 'crcktchirp' data set

Root Mean Square Error (RMSE)

Root Mean Square Error (RMSE) depicts the standard deviation of the residuals (prediction errors). Residuals show the position of data points from the regression line and are a good measure to understand the deviation from the actual data. RMSE is an important measure to depict the spread of the residuals. More specifically, it signifies the best fit line where all the data is concentrated. RMSE is the typical prediction error of the model on the data set and can be represented by the expression eq. (2). The algorithms to model the predictions minimize the error value of the RMSE considering minimizing the distance between estimates and the regression line. By reducing the RMSE value, one can attain the model effectiveness.

$$\text{RMSE} = \sqrt{(pred - obser)^2} \qquad \text{eq. (2)}$$

where,

- *pred* refers to the prediction value
- *obser* indicates the true outcome
- (*pred* – *obser*) represents the error or residuals vector
- $\overline{(pred - obser)^2}$ refers to $(pred - obser)^2$

R-Squared (R^2) Method

This method identifies the fitness of the model over a given data set. Its value ranges between 0 and 1. The value near to 1 signifies that the model fits well and value close to 0 signifies that the model is more towards guessing the average value. The R^2 sometimes refers to the variance explained by the model as it includes the total sum of squares (variance of the data).

Consider '*obser*' refers to the true outcome, '*p*' is the prediction from the model, and '*res=y–p*' are the residuals of the predictions. Then the total sum of squares 't_{ssq}' (total variance) of the data, see eq. (3), is calculated as follows.

$$t_{ssq} = \Sigma(y - \bar{y})^2 \qquad \text{eq. (3)}$$

where, $\bar{y}$ is the mean value of y.

The residual sum of squared errors of the model, r_{ssq} in eq. (4), is given by

$$r_{ssq} = \Sigma \text{res}^2 \qquad \text{eq. (4)}$$

R^2 (R-Squared), the 'variance explained' by the model, see eq. (5), is calculated as

$$R^2 = 1 - \frac{r_{ssq}}{t_{ssq}} \qquad \text{eq. (5)}$$

Model Performance—Training and Test Set

One of the fundamental characteristics of supervised learning is to predict the unseen observation based on the '*learning*'. To train the model to understand the data set, we divide the data set into two main parts—*training set* and *test set*. The model is built on the training set, and then it is tested on the '*test*' data set for its prediction power and performance. Training set and test set, both, are disjoint data sets and do not contain any common observations. It is to be noted that the concept of *training* and *test* data is applicable only to supervised learning. In unsupervised learning, the data set is not labelled; thus, there is no question of splitting the data set into training and test data set.

One of the critical tasks is to decide on '*what comprises the training and test data*'. Rule of thumb is to have a training set with larger number of data instances [70%–75% of the whole data set], and the distribution of the samples should be normal and random. Figure 9.9 shows the typical way of achieving the predictive power.

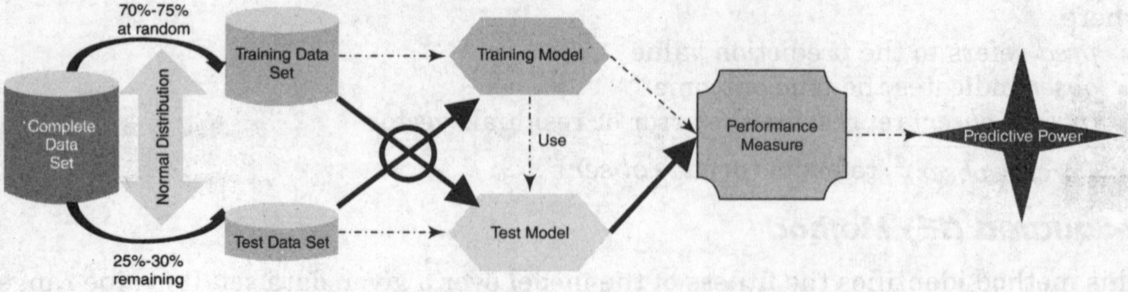

Fig. 9.9 Performance—Training and Test

Performing Cross-validation

LO 3 — *Perform cross validation*

A sampling of the data set can affect the performance of the model. Thus, we can use a method named '*Cross-validation*' to avoid such biases of '*sampling*' and achieve a robust model. The idea of cross-validation is simple: sample the data set multiple times with different partitions and then apply the model on each of the sample data set having different partitions. The result of all models is then aggregated to form a robust measure. In the *n*-fold cross-validation test, data set is folded over data set '*n*' times and each test set is $1/n$ the size of total data set. The 4-fold cross-validation is shown in Fig. 9.10.

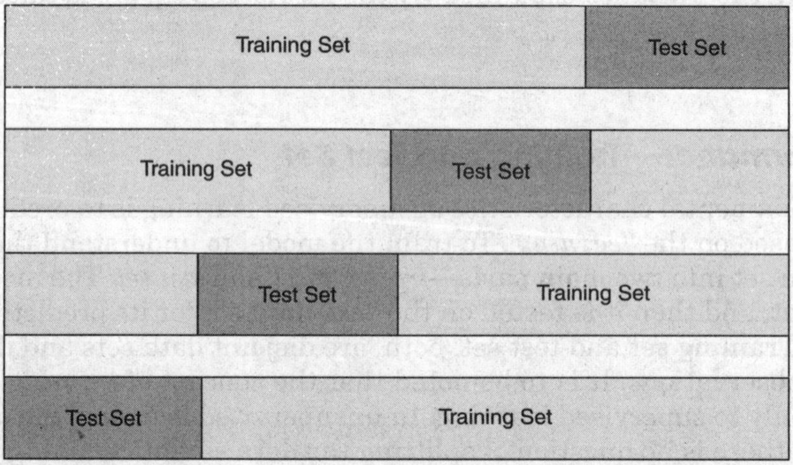

Fig. 9.10 4-fold Cross-validation

In an n-fold cross-validation, we need to split the data into n-subsets. Let us consider that our data set is divided into the three subsets 'A', 'B', and 'C'. In the cross-validation process, we simply chose the different data sets to make, train, and test the models. For example, in Fig. 9.11 subsets A and B can be used to develop and train the model and then applied on subset C for the test. Similarly, subsets B and C can be used to develop and train the model and then applied on subset A for the test. Likewise, subsets A and C can be used to develop and train the model and then applied on subset B for the test. One thing we must notice that none of these models provide the outcome of interest on its training data, but all the predictions are based on the test data set. Thus, RMSE and R^2 values generated will give unbiased results and a good point to evaluate the models.

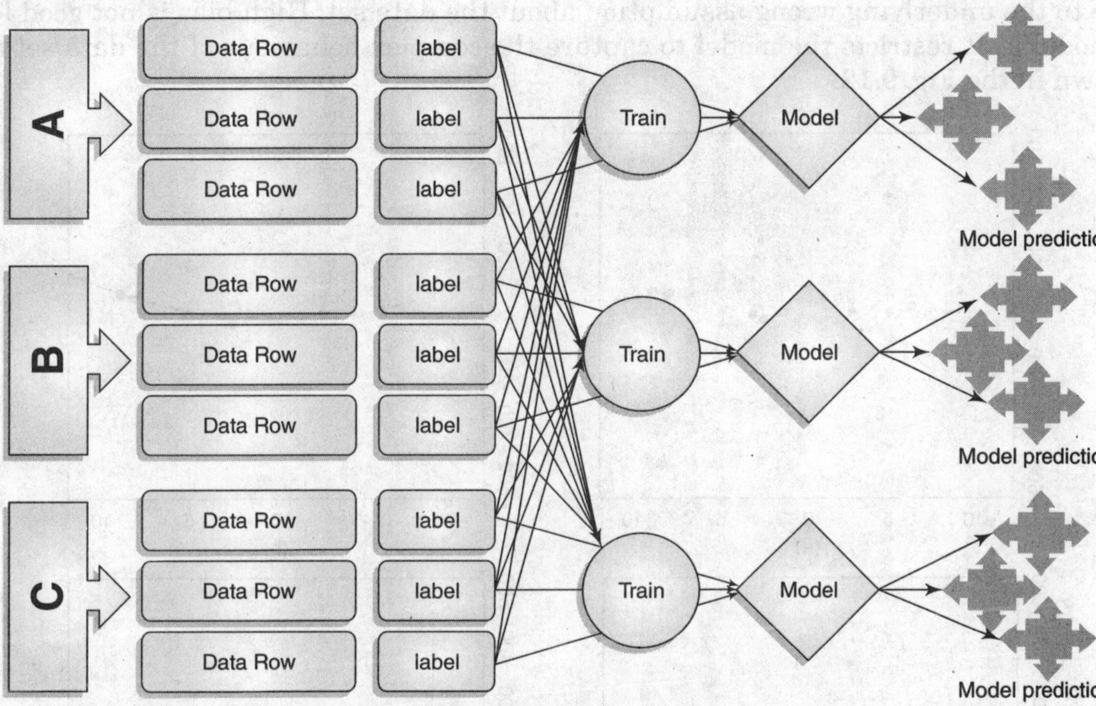

Fig. 9.11 Cross-validation process

We can perform cross-validation in 'R' by utilizing function '*kWayCrossValidation*' of the package '*vtreat*'. In this function, we can pass the number of rows of the training set and the number of folds for generating the predictions.

Bias and Variance

As we have seen that the performance of the prediction model is significantly affected by the sampling and distribution of the data set, we also need to understand the type of the prediction error generated by the prediction model. The prediction error is comprised of two parts, which are as follows.

- **Reducible error:** It refers to the difference in the gap between well-defined fit and the poor-fit model. The reducible error is split into two error types—error due to bias and error due to variance.
- **Irreducible error:** It refers to the noise that is present in the data and is unavoidable. It also shows the irregulation in the data.

Bias

It is developed due to wrong assumptions by the model about the prediction w.r.t the true values. Assume that the data is *'quadratic'* in nature (Fig. 9.12 (b)) and you have applied a *'linear regression'* on the set (Fig. 9.12 (c)). Further, due to the involvement of the *'linear regression'* technique, the error in the prediction performance is high due to the underlying wrong assumption about the data set. High bias is not good for a model as it restricts the model to capture the complex behaviour of the data set as shown in the Fig. 9.12.

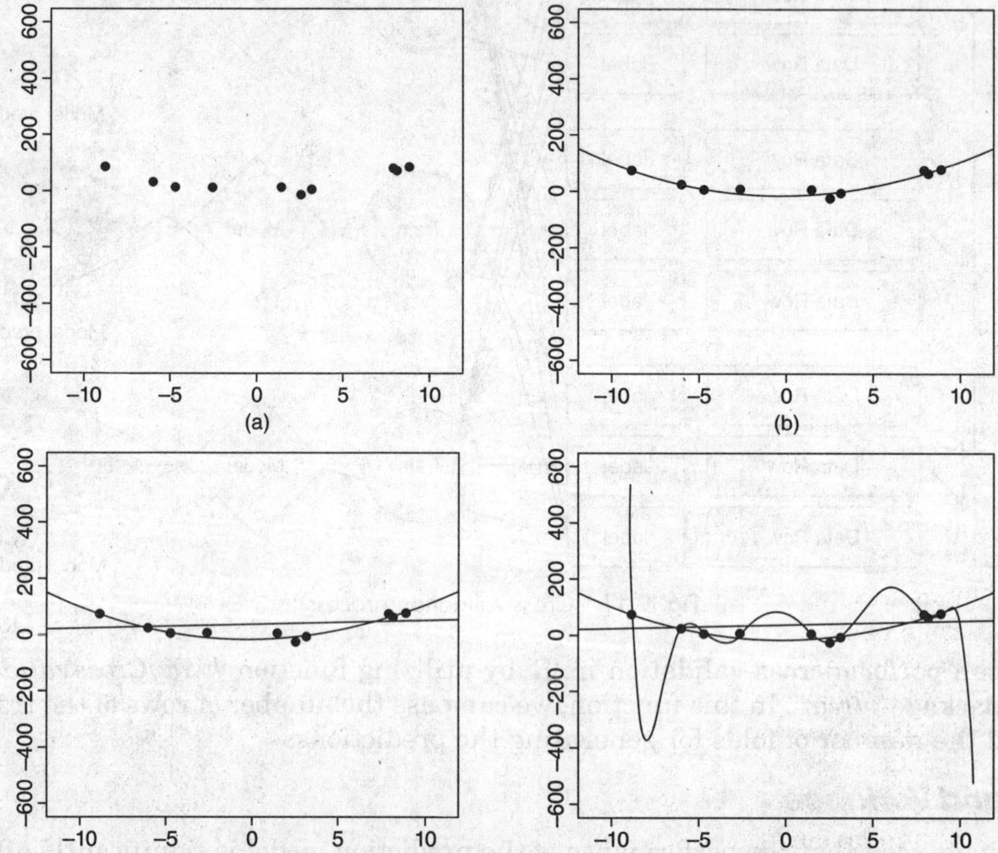

Fig. 9.12 Bias and Variance

Variance

This error is caused due to the sampling of the data set (training). Assume that you are fitting the data set with the *'polynomial distribution'* curve for the data set shown in Fig. 9.12 (d) which now covers the whole data points. Though the *'polynomial distribution'* covers the whole data set points, it has a severe limitation—as of deviating from the complete coverage to the poor coverage of the distribution when there is a slight change in the data point, say, due to the sampling. In this case, the whole curve needs to undergo a change, and thus it causes a *variance* error. High variance model behaves poorly in predicting the test data set.

Bias–Variance trade-offs

It is to be noted that with the high variance the fitting of the curve to the training set results into '*overfitting*'. Overfitting indicates that the model is perfect to describe the training set but poorly performs in describing the test data set resulting in very specific and restricted model. While '*underfitting*' of the model, due to high bias, is restricted to capture the complex behaviour of the data set and, thus, poorly describes the data set (test) resulting into a very general model. Figure 9.13 shows the bias–variance trade-offs.

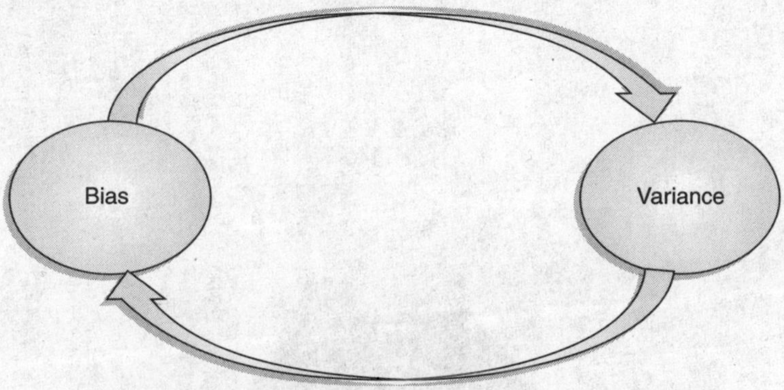

Fig. 9.13 Paradox Bias and Variance

9.2 CLASSIFICATION

—LO 4— *Describe classification and its performance measures*

Classification defines the category of the problem where the concept needs to be learned. One of the most common and interesting techniques to achieve supervised learning is based on the classification. The data set is trained, tested, and result is finally assigned to bins as per the 'Class' labels. Four major techniques, namely, K-Nearest Neighbours (KNN), Naïve Bayes, Logistic Regression, and Classification trees are most often used to perform exploration, visualization, and analysis over the data. These techniques help in developing insights into actions. Let us take an example of 'Driverless car', which must observe the object through the camera and other sensors and generate insight to act on it. One action could be to classify the 'Road sign type'. Whether the direction for a particular way is towards 'left' or 'right' or to act on a 'sign post' which is showing the information of the limit of the driving speed to be 'Speed Limit 30 Km/hrs', see Fig. 9.14. Such kind of learning is accomplished when the machine, in this case, 'Driverless car', learns based on the past behaviour, gets trained and tested on the training and test data; and gets validated on the action been taken. The whole process is a continuous process of learning, but comes under the spectrum of supervised learning and most specifically, classification problem. In case, the car learned about 'signs post' based on the past data set and a new unseen 'sign post' that comes under the category or look alike as close as one of the objects 'sign post' in the existing (past) data set, then the car will act accordingly. So, if the unseen sign post looks similar to 'Stop' sign post, then the car will stop.

Fig. 9.14 Stop sign post

A data set for the traffic signals can be developed based on the intensity of the level of the colors involved to form the traffic signal captured in the 4 × 4 grid as shown in Fig. 9.15. The data set further be tested on the different traffic signs.

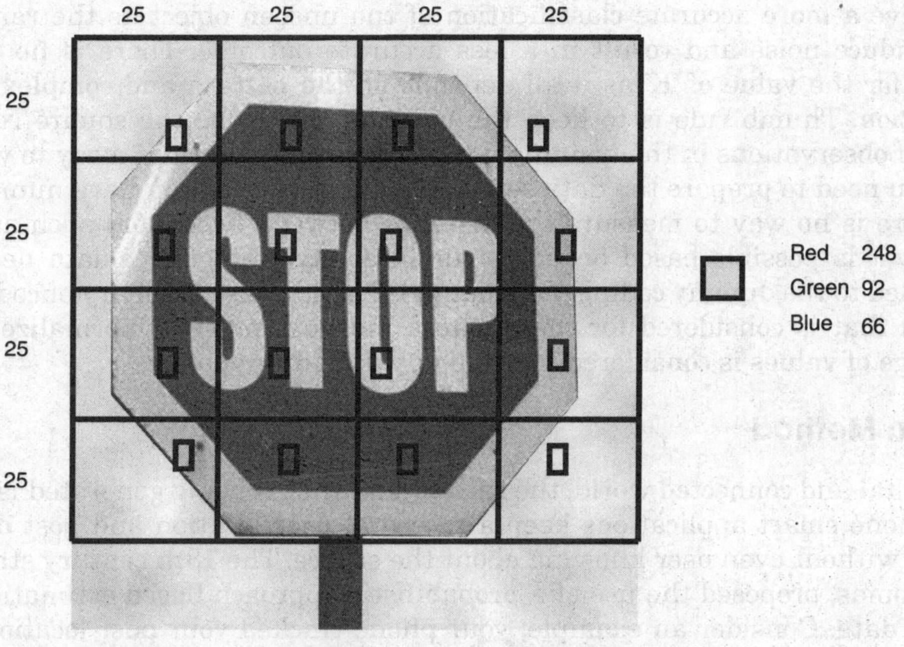

Fig. 9.15 Grid—traffic signal

It is easy to understand the functionality of the autonomous 'driverless' car to recognize the traffic signal and then act accordingly. We will now understand some essential classification techniques—nearest neighbour, bayesian method, logistic regression, and decision tree.

K-Nearest Neighbours (KNN)

In this technique, the objects are classified based on the distance of the objects. The distances are not the physical distance, rather the distance in the space. For example, the 'sign post' has different properties such as color combination, pictures, size, etc; thus, all these properties can be arranged in a feature space, and similarity of the objects can be measured based on the feature space distances. There are various distance measures—Euclidean, Manhattan, etc., to measure the distance between objects as specified in the form of coordinates in the space. The KNN classify an 'unlabelled' object based on 'K' number of nearest labels.

You need to download the 'class' package so that the appropriate KNN technique can be used for further analysis. It specifies the KNN function that accepts three parameters—training data set, test data set, and training labels. The default value of 'K' is 1 to classify the object based on the single similar property. The value of 'K' has a substantial impact on the performance of the overall classification. The object is matched to the 'K' nearest neighbour and then based on the 'K' nearest results; a voting is achieved to minimise the classification error of the unseen object. In case of a tie, the winner is decided based on the random results. It does not mean that bigger

'K' will give a more accurate classification of the unseen object as the randomness of data induce noise and result in a less accurate outcome. There is no universal standard for the value of 'K' as it all depends on the pattern and complexity of the classification. Thumb rule is to keep the value of the 'K' as the square root of the number of observations in the training data. Before jumping right away to work with 'KNN', you need to prepare the data set. 'KNN' assumes that you have numeric data. Thus, there is no way to measure the distance between two colors such as 'Red' or 'Blue' but it is possible based on its colour intensity. Categorical data needs to be transformed to the dummy coding; for example, 0 or 1 in case of binary encoding. Also, each data that is considered for the distance measure must be normalized so that same range of values is considered to avoid any data discrepancy.

Bayesian Method

In the digital and connected world, the rate of data that is being generated is massive. Mobile phone smart applications keep a record of user location and post offers and discounts without even user knowing about the source. The 18th century statistician, Bayes Thomas, proposed the use of a probabilistic approach based estimation on the historical data. Consider an example; your phone tracked your past locations where you have been through such as workplace (25 times), restaurant (3 times), clinic (2 times), and store (10 times). Thus, the probability of visiting work is around 62.5% and the probability of visiting clinic is just 5%, which is computed as follows.

The probability of *A* is denoted as *P*(*A*).

$$P(workplace) = 25 / 40 = 62.5\%$$

$$P(clinic) = 2 / 40 = 5.0\%$$

In this case, the most probable future event is visiting the workplace. So, one can identify the probability of an event by estimating from the historical data. You can note that the information is not complete and is partial, leading to the poor estimate. It is so as the application is just tracking where a person was and has not recorded the aspect of time and date of user location. When events occur together, they have the joint probability and result in stronger estimates. Venn diagram comes handy to depict such kind of joint events and joint probability.

The joint event caters to the information that the user has a higher probability of working in the afternoon as compared to the evening. The joint probability of events *A* and *B* is denoted as *P*(*A* and *B*).

P(workplace and evening) = 1%

P(workplace and afternoon) = 20%

There could be dependent and independent events, where in the independent event, neither of the joint events are predictive of each other nor can influence as well. But the dependent events are predictive and influential in nature. Conditional probability depicts the way in which one event depends on another, i.e., how one event is getting influenced by another event and, thus, have a strong root in the prediction of the dependent events.

The conditional probability of events A and B is denoted as $P(A \mid B)$

$$P(A \mid B) = P(A \text{ and } B) / P(B)$$

$$P(workplace \mid evening) = 1 / 25 = 4\%$$

$$P(workplace \mid afternoon) = 20 / 25 = 80\%$$

The conditional probability depicts that there is 80% probability that given the event probability of afternoon the user might be in the workplace as compared to just the 4% probability of a user to be in the workplace in the evening.

The Naïve based algorithm uses the conditional probability of the event to generate the outcome of the event. The whole technique is simple and can be attained in 'R' by utilizing the package '*naivebayes*'.

Logistic Regression

A different set of problem that we face in our everyday life is to make choices. For example, for a bank loan application, the bank manager would be interested in finding out the predictability of the loan applicant as a potential risk applicant. Such kind of models deal with the placing of outcome in the categories. Here, in this case, the category could be '*no risk-prone*', '*weak risk-prone*', '*moderate risk-prone*', and '*high risk-prone*'. Based on the categories of the loan application outcome, the bank manager can decide whether to pass the loan application and also what type and duration of loan need to be approved. Suck kind of models perform fitment of the curve to the numerical data to predict the binary outcome. These models are known as *logical regression models*. The logistic regression models are useful when instead of a whole range of numerical outcome one is interested in the binary or categorical outcome. Thus, for the binary outcome problem, the plot represents the binary outcome regarding 0 or 1, see Fig. 9.16. Here, value 0 or 1 can be linked to any business goal such as 'loan defaulter'

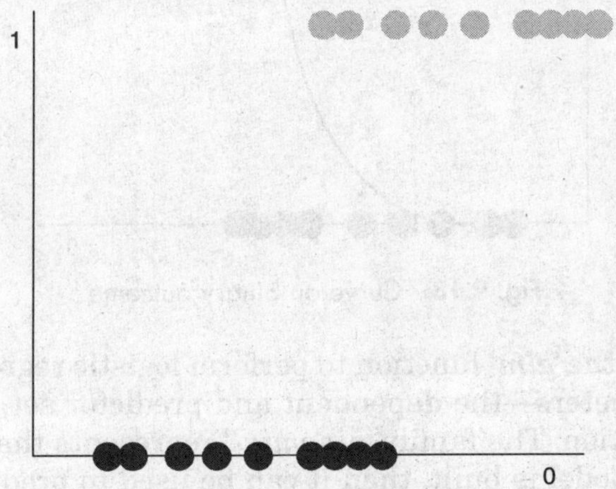

Fig. 9.16 Binary outcome

or 'no loan defaulter'. Figure 9.17 does not fit the linear line over the data set; thus, results into a poor performance prediction as for some values of the variable 'X' the model predicts values less than 1 which is not needed. Our goal is to fit the data best, and, in this case, we can choose the curve line instead of the linear line which is depicted in Fig. 9.18. The curve line is developed based on the logistic function by which the output value of an input data set is generated that falls between 0 and 1. It works like probability; thus, higher the probability towards 1, higher the fitness of the output value to 1.

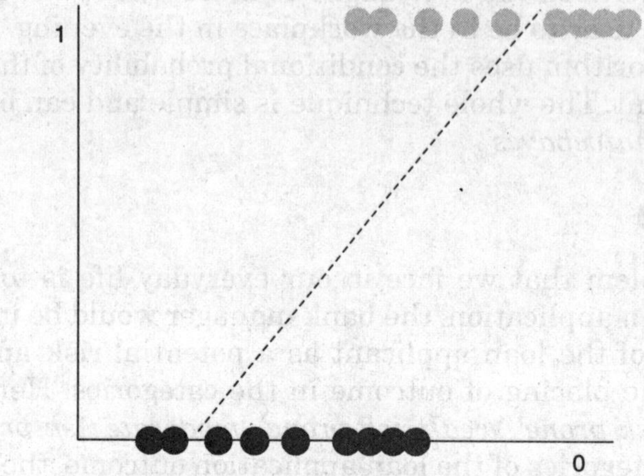

Fig. 9.17 Regression on binary outcome

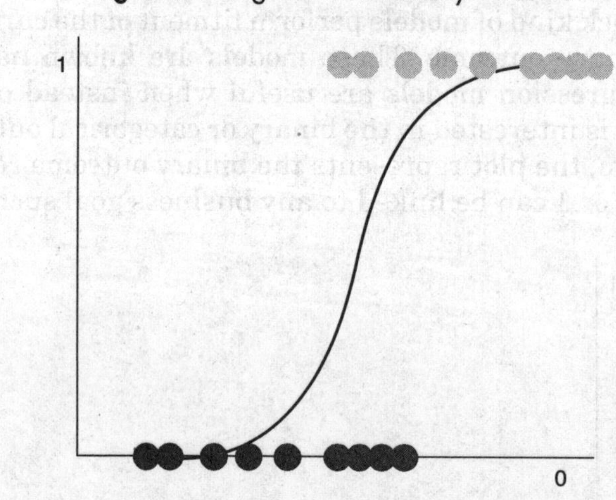

Fig. 9.18 Curve on binary outcome

In 'R', we can utilize the '*glm*' function to perform logistic regression on the data set. It accepts three parameters—the dependent and predictor set, the data set, and the family of the classification. The family '*binomial*' represents that model is the logistic regression. Once the model is built, then it can be used to predict the outcome of the data set by using the function '*predict*'. Here, it accepts three parameters—the model, the test data set, and the type of result. The value of the type as 'response' generates the predicted probabilities which are easy to understand. These, probabilities can be fed into the '*ifelse*' function to generate the outcome of the interest. For example, any probability value higher than 0.5 is treated as outcome value 1. Figure 9.19 shows that the threshold values can be adjusted depending upon the business problem.

```
frmla <- y ~ x1 + x2 + x3 # LHS outcome and RHS: Inputs

lg_model <- glm(frmla, data = my_dataset, data = "binomial" ) #passing
three parameters - formula showing the relationship response ~
predictors; data set = my_dataset and family =  binomial to represent
logistic regression
pred <- perdict(lg_model, data = my_dataset, type = "response" )
```

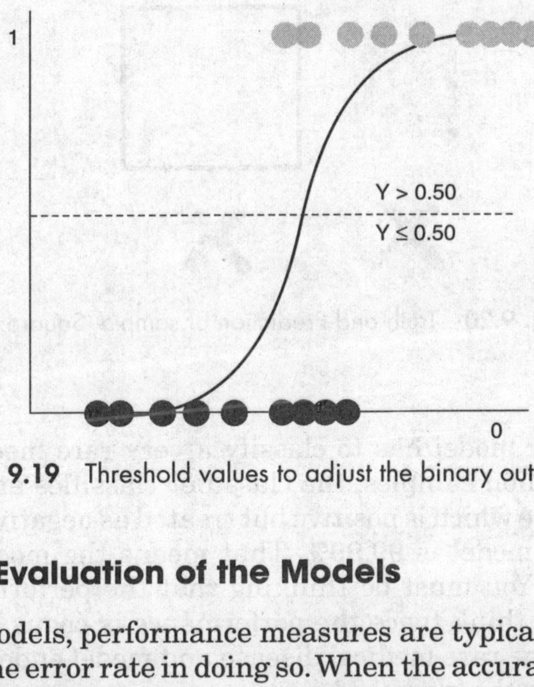

Fig. 9.19 Threshold values to adjust the binary outcome

Performance and Evaluation of the Models

In the classification models, performance measures are typically linked with accuracy of the prediction and the error rate in doing so. When the accuracy rate in predicting the outcome of interest goes high, then the error rate goes down. Accuracy is the measure of classifying correct instances over the total number of instances. The accuracy and the error rate are depicted in eq. (6) and eq. (7), respectively.

$$\text{Accuracy} = \frac{\text{correct classified instances}}{\text{total number of classified instances}} \qquad \text{eq. (6)}$$

The error rate is given by

$$\text{Error} = 1 - \text{Accuracy} \qquad \text{eq. (7)}$$

Consider that you have a data set of 5 squares with a 2-feature set representing 'size' as 'small/big' and 'border' as 'dashed/bold' and a label set 'space' as 'filled/empty'. The accuracy of the model as shown in Fig. 9.20 is 60% as out of 5 samples 3 squares are classified correctly, i.e., 3/5, and two are classified wrongly. Though accuracy is a good measure of showcasing the performance of the model, it has limited coverage and, thus, we have to look for some robust measures.

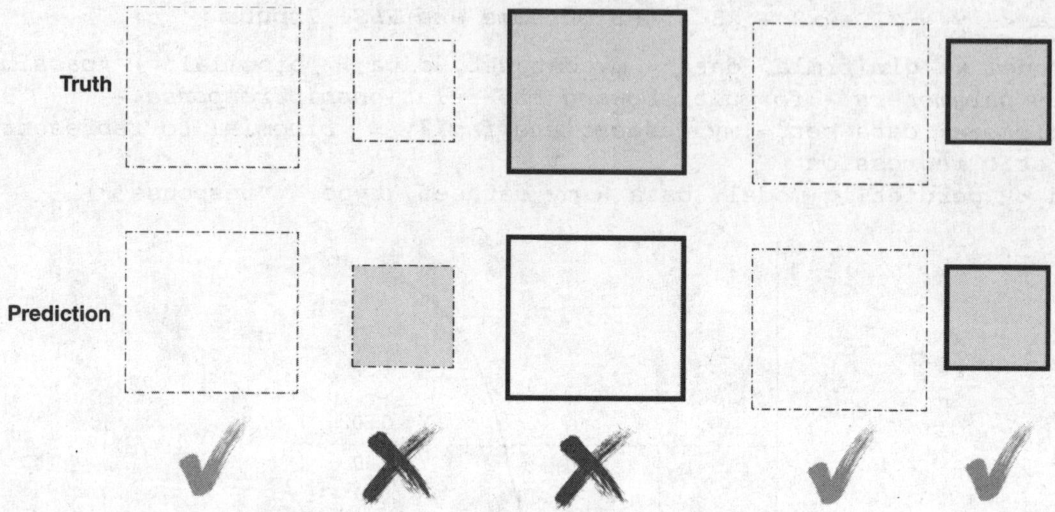

Fig. 9.20 Truth and Prediction of sample 'Square'

Confusion Matrix

Assume that a classifier model has to classify a very rare medical disease *'one in a million'*. And, out of million samples, the classifier classifies all as negative, i.e., *'not sick'* including one sample which is positive but treated as negative by the model. Hence, the performance of the model is 99.99%. That means the model correctly classified 99.99% of the samples. You must be thinking that the performance of the model is very high, '99.99%', but think twice the performance is bogus as the objective of the prediction is to predict the rare medical disease and model ended up in classifying the 'positive' case wrongly as the 'negative' one.

We have a remedy to this *'accuracy measure'* limitation. We can utilize the confusion matrix that comprises of rows and columns, Fig. 9.21. Each cell of the confusion matrix represents the frequency of the instances that are classified in a certain manner. For simplicity, we will cover a binary classifier which has two classes—positive and negative. This matrix is helpful to understand the gap between the model's *actual predictions* and *expected predictions* and the name is given to reveal the fact *'how to confuse the model between the two classes and highlight the instances where one class is confused on the other'*.

		Prediction	
		P	N
Truth	p	TP (True Positive)	FP (False Positive)
	n	FN (False Negative)	TN (True Negative)

Fig. 9.21 Confusion matrix

The rows of the confusion matrix represent the predicted classes while the columns represent the actual predicted values. The first diagonal of the matrix 'True's' refers to the correctness of the model by considering the true positive and true negative cases. The other diagonal 'False's' refers to the incorrectness of the model by including the false negative and false positive cases. Following cell information is important to understand the model:

- **True positive:** Model correctly predicts the 'Yes' cases; frequency of instances that are classified as true positive, i.e., the actual labels and predicted labels are true positives.
- **True negative:** Model correctly predicts the 'No' cases; frequency of instances that are classified as true negative, i.e., the actual labels and the predicted labels are true negatives.
- **False positive:** Model incorrectly predicts the 'Yes' cases; frequency of instances that are classified wrongly as false positive, i.e., the actual labels which are negatives are classified as positives.
- **False negative:** Model incorrectly predicts the 'No' cases; frequency of instances that are classified wrongly as false negative, i.e., the actual labels which are positives are classified as negatives.

A confusion matrix provides an efficient way to tweak the output of a model by considering various possible predictions (true positive, true negative, false positive, false negative). New measures such as *precision* and *recall*, eq. (8) and eq. (9) respectively, can be used based on the confusion matrix.

$$\text{Precision} = \frac{TP}{(TP + FP)} \qquad \text{eq. (8)}$$

$$\text{Recall} = \frac{TP}{(TP + FN)} \qquad \text{eq. (9)}$$

We can create the confusion matrix for the '*square*' classification problem as shown in Fig. 9.22.

		Prediction	
		P	N
Truth	p	1	1
	n	1	2

(a)

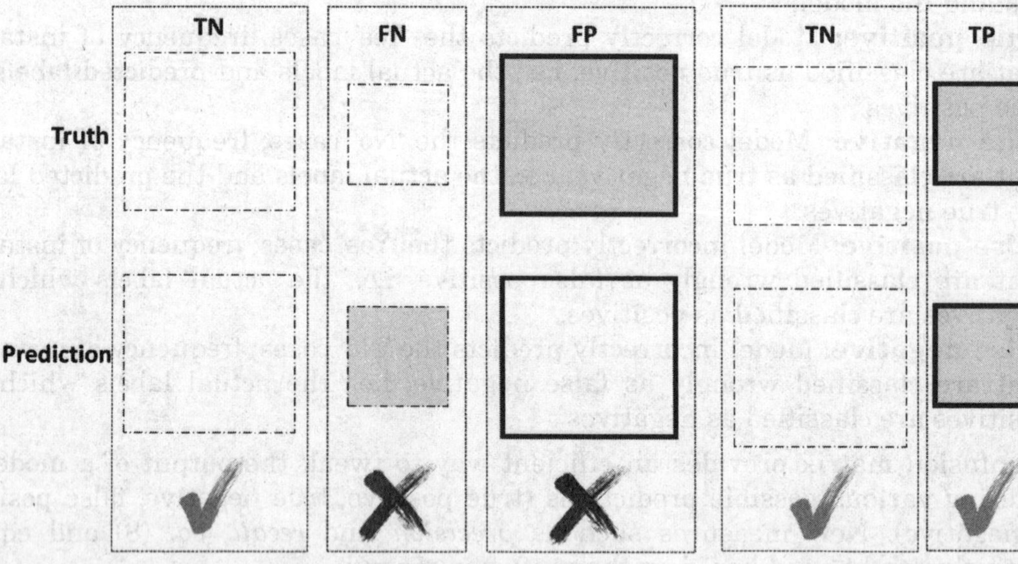

(b)

Fig. 9.22 Confusion matrix and Truth/Predictions for 'Square' example

Thus,

$$\text{Accuracy} = \frac{(TP + TN)}{(TP + TN + FP + FN)} = \frac{(1+2)}{(1+2+1+1))} = 60\%$$

$$\text{Precision} = \frac{TP}{(TP + FP)} = \frac{1}{(1+1)} = 50\%$$

$$\text{Recall} = \frac{TP}{(TP + FN)} = \frac{1}{(1+1)} = 50\%$$

In the same way, we can create a confusion matrix for the rare disease classification as shown in Fig. 9.23:

		Prediction	
		P	N
Truth	p	0	1
	n	0	999999

Fig. 9.23 Confusion matrix 'rare medical disease'

$$\text{Accuracy} = \frac{(TP + TN)}{(TP + TN + FP + FN)} = \frac{(0 + 999999)}{(0 + 1000000 + 0 + 0)} = 99.99\%$$

$$\text{Precision} = \frac{TP}{(TP + FP)} = \frac{0}{(0+1)} = 50\%$$

$$\text{Recall} = \frac{TP}{(TP + FN)} = \text{undefined [due to no coverage of +ve predictions]}$$

You can generate the probabilities into a class prediction by considering appropriate threshold for the proper cut. You can do this easily with the ifelse() function:

```
class_pred <-
  ifelse(prob_pred > 0.50,
```

```
    "pos_class",
    "neg_class"
)
```

In 'R', a contingency table can be developed by the function '*table*'. To generate more detailed results, confusion matrix comes handy.

ROC (Receiver Operating Curve)

Manually evaluating the threshold value is a hard work and, while doing so, we might encounter dozens of confusion matrices and heuristics that become difficult to handle. A systematic approach to unleash the classification threshold value is to simulate the every positive and negative, '*true/false*', and positive rate at every threshold and visualize the trade-offs. The visualization plot refers to the ROC (*Receiver Operating Curve*).

You may use the '*caTools*' package for computing ROC curves, which contains a function called *colAUC*. This function is very user-friendly and can calculate ROC curves for multiple predictors at once. You only need to calculate the ROC curve for one predictor as follows:

```
colAUC(pred_prob, actual, plotROC = TRUE)
```

The function will return a score called *Area Under the Curve* (*AUC*), and the plotROC = TRUE argument will return the plot of the ROC curve for visual inspection.

AUC (Area Under the Curve)

The classification model needs to be checked for its performance so that one can have a shift from over accurate to the actionable outcome-based model. The accuracy of the model, sometimes, is misleading due to the presence of imbalanced data sets. The 'ROC' curves are the best way to predict the positive and negative predictions and the outcome of actionable interest vs others. Let us assume that you have a data set which is categorized into two outcomes—0's and 1's. We want to know whether a given classifier model is good enough to our actionable outcome or not. For that, we can utilize the 'ROC' curve as depicted in Fig. 9.24. It shows the relationship between the percentages of the positive outcomes with the percentage of other outcomes. Now, consider that the outcomes are evenly arranged such that every alternative to 0 is the value 1 leading to the diagonal line in the 'ROC' curve. But where the data is not arranged evenly, then 'ROC' curve is not a straight line, see Fig. 9.23.

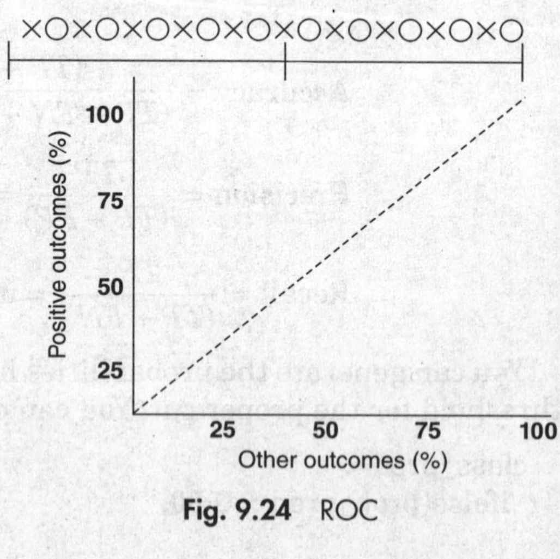

Fig. 9.24 ROC

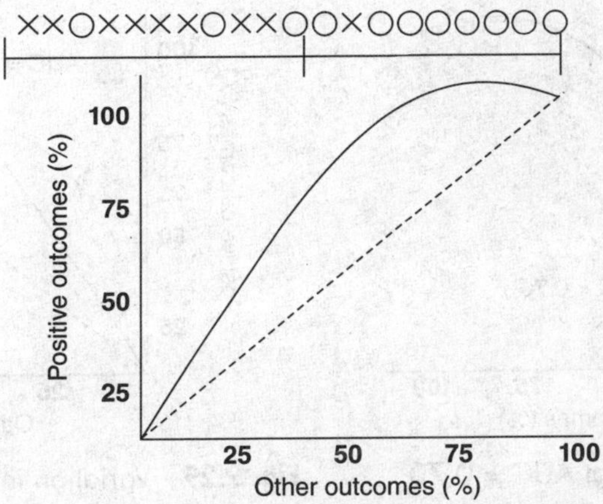

Fig. 9.25 ROC curve

The curve denotes the percentage of positive outcomes which is not *even* in the current case and best depicted by the model. To arrange the best possible curve, a term *Area Under the Curve* (AUC) is most often used.

The baseline model shows that it evenly divides the outcome values and has AUC=0.5, see Fig. 9.26. The perfect model captures the whole surface and the value of AUC=1, Fig. 9.27. Most real-world results are closer to AUC=1 and not exactly 1, see Fig. 9.28. But in some cases, the value of AUC is also misleading. In that case, one should not only look at the AUC but also at the curve that is being formed by the AUC.

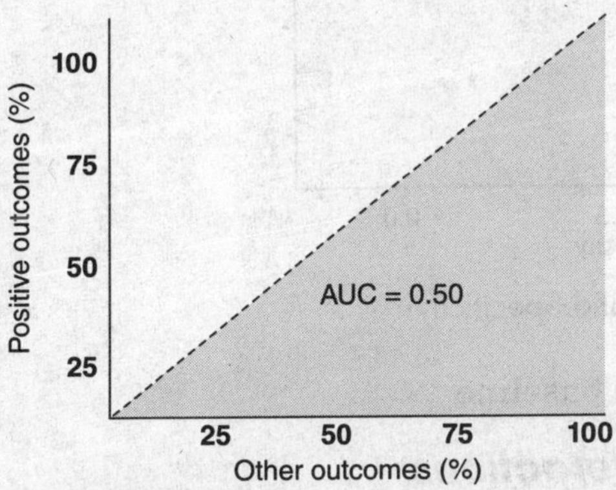

Fig. 9.26 ROC curve at AUC = 0.50

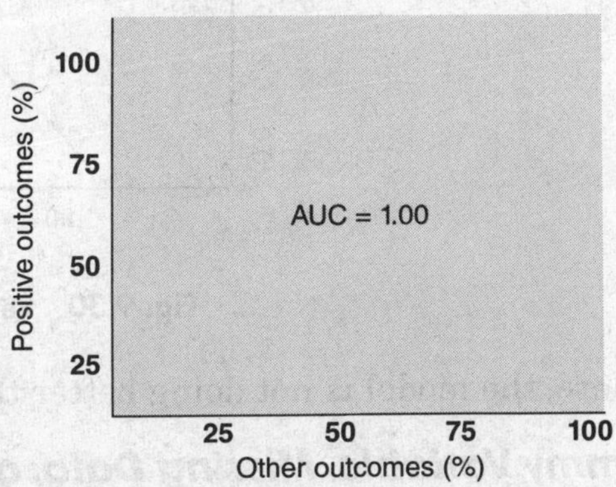

Fig. 9.27 ROC curve at AUC = 1.00

A same value of AUC can generate different curves as depicted in Fig. 9.29. We need to understand that the curve which is closer to the higher percentage of positive outcomes is chosen as the best. The ROC and AUC, both, can be used to understand the performance of the models.

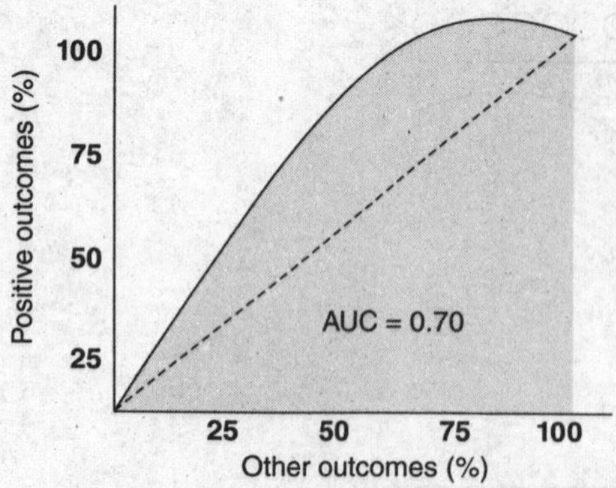

Fig. 9.28 ROC curve at AUC = 0.70

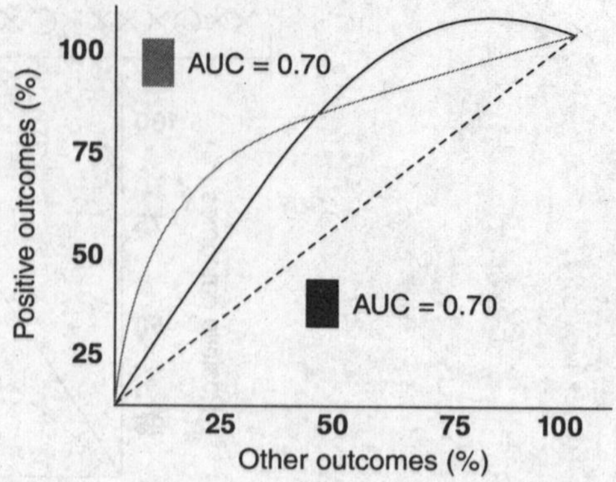

Fig. 9.29 Variation in ROC curve at AUC = 0.70

In 'R', we can use the '*pROC*' package to develop the ROC and AUC. The function 'roc' accepts two parameters—the data set and the predicted probabilities, and same can be fed to the function '*auc*' to generate the area under the curve.

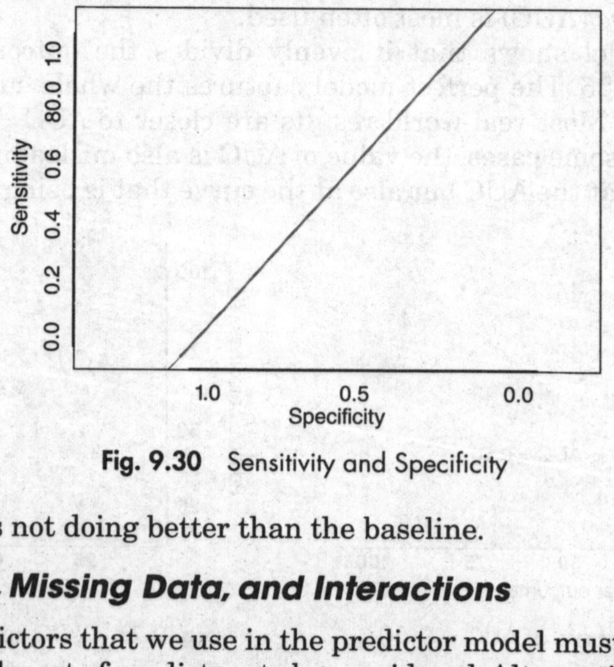

Fig. 9.30 Sensitivity and Specificity

Here, the model is not doing better than the baseline.

Dummy Variable, Missing Data, and Interactions

When all of the predictors that we use in the predictor model must be numeric, then it puts limitations on the set of predictors to be considered. Alternatively, a set of dummy variables can also be considered to include the non-numeric variables for the analysis. Similarly, missing values need to be handled so that they can also contribute to the performance of the model. Interactions among the predictors are valuable and must also be incorporated. Dummy coding is the most common method to represent the categorical data, which can be achieved in 'R' by using the *factor* function.

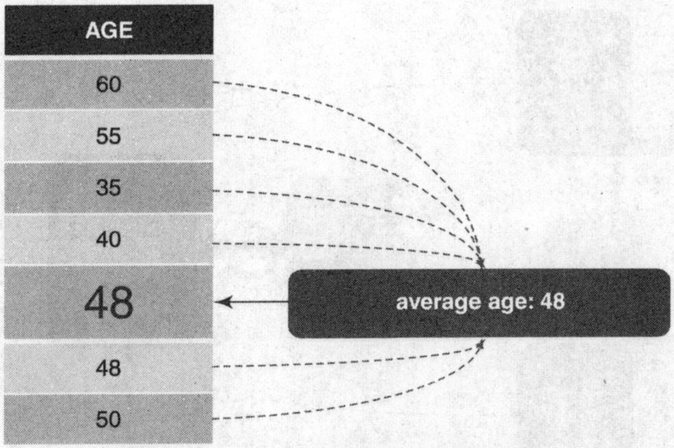

Fig. 9.31 Missing value imputation

One typical solution to fill the missing numerical value is by imputation. The average value is being put in place of the missing value.

Few predictors when combined may have different impact on the outcome as compared to the sum of their independent effects and thus planned appropriately. For example, independently obesity and drinking impacts heart disease but when combined have a more significant effect, see Fig. 9.30. But in some cases, the combination may nullify the effect. For example, independently Medicine A and Medicine B impact an individual health to survive but when combined nullifies each other effects (and may lead to death), see Fig. 9.31.

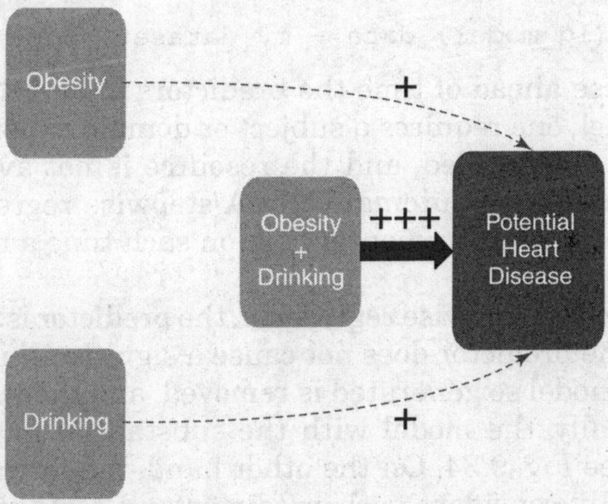

Fig. 9.32 Predictors combination outcome (obesity and drinking)

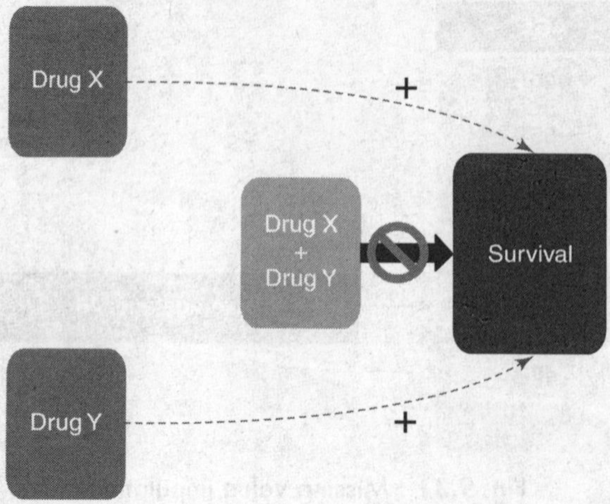

Fig. 9.33 Predictor combination outcome (Drug X and Drug Y)

In 'R', the interaction among the variables is represented by including the multiplication factor as follows:

```
frmla <- disease ~ obesity * drinking # LHS outcome and RHS: Inputs ; interaction of obesity and drinking

lg_model <- glm(frmla, data = my_dataset, data = "binomial" ) #passing three parameters - formula showing the relationship response ~ predictors; data set = my_dataset and family =  binomial to represent logistic regression

dis_pred <- perdict(lg_model, data = my_dataset, type = "response" )
```

Regression models use ahead of time the predictors to be fed into the model. Thus, to generate a good model, one requires a subject or domain expert. In some cases, such requirement might be not fulfilled, and the resource is not available; thus, one has to achieve the set of predictors automatically. A stepwise regression model produces value addition stepwise in an incremental fashion each time a new predictor is added to generate a model.

In the backward selection stepwise regression, the predictor is removed one at a time, and if the removal of the predictor does not cause a significant impact on the outcome of the model, then the model so generated is removed, and the whole process is carried for the predictors. Finally, the model with the substantial impact is considered for the further analysis, see Fig. 9.34. On the other hand, the forward selection stepwise regression incrementally considers each predictor and computes the significance of the impact until the final model is developed. The predictors are added until no new predictor is left that can cause a significant change in the prediction impact of the model, see Fig. 9.35.

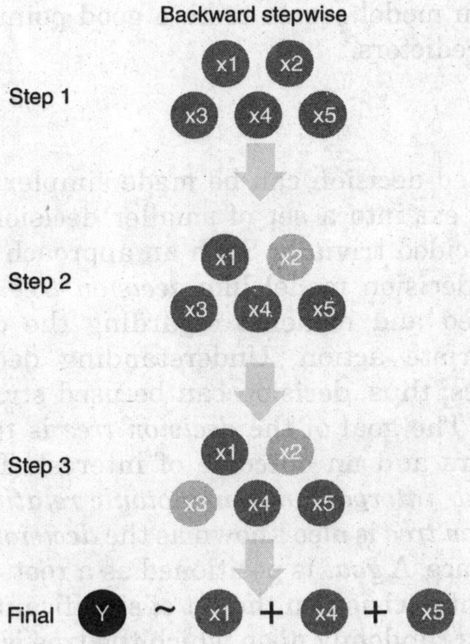

Fig. 9.34 Stepwise regression—backward

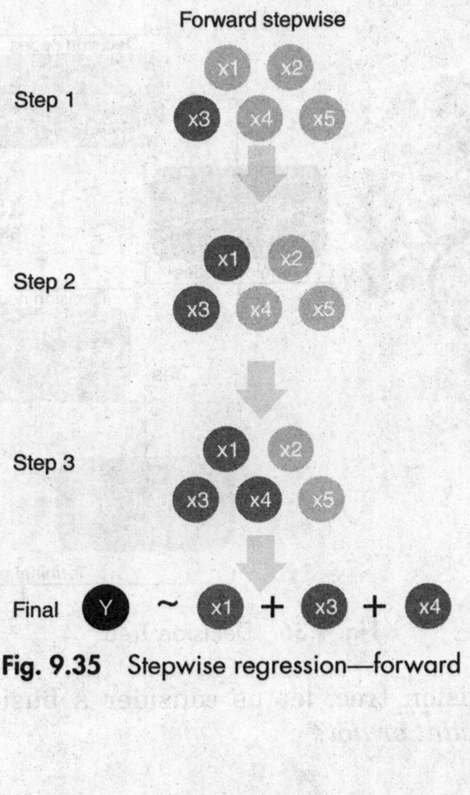

Fig. 9.35 Stepwise regression—forward

The stepwise regression model seems to be a good point to start considering and working with the set of predictors.

Classification Trees

LO 5
Comprehend classification trees and random forest

A complicated decision can be made simpler when you start breaking data in context into a set of smaller decisions until a level on which it can be decided trivially. Such an approach has given birth to a very significant decision model like *decision tree*. A set of *if-else* decisions is formulated and modeled regarding the decision tree to generate the appropriate action. Understanding decisions do not need the understanding of statistics; thus, decision can be used strategically in the business and other decision areas. The goal of the *decision tree* is to model the relationships between various predictors and an outcome of interest. The tree is well suited to *non-linear* concepts such as *intervals*, *non-monotonic relationships,* and *non-additive interactions*. A *classification tree* is also known as the *decision tree model* which depicts the decision and action space. A *goal* is positioned as a root, and then each branch out of the root is the significant decision on the set of significant predictors. One way is to choose the set of predictors randomly upon which the tree is developed, and other way is to identify which predictor is the best predictor that makes a significant impact to the outcome of interest and then select that predictor for the decision path.

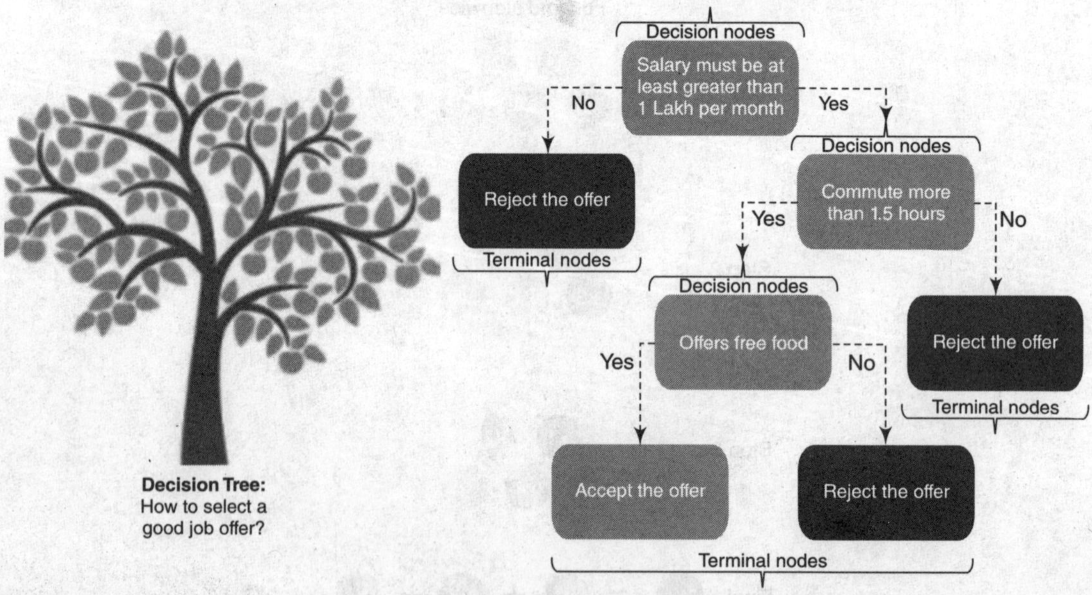

Fig. 9.36 Decision Tree

To understand the decision tree, let us consider a business process *'whether to provide a loan to an applicant or not?'*

To submit a loan application, an individual needs to fill various personal and professional information such as loan amount, salary, credit history, purpose, etc. Once the loan application is received from the customer the next task is to review and evaluate the application. The bank personnels need to understand the the profile of the loan applicant and classify him/her into potential segments of interest; for example, a defaulter or not a defaulter and accordingly process the loan application. The bank needs to run the individual's submitted information on the model that is being trained and tested on the historical data and test data for its significance to predict the outcome of interest; for example, in this case—*defaulter* and *loyal*. The decision tree inherently uses a process based on divide and conquer approach. This approach partitions the data set based on the similar value and the actionable outcome. Consider a subset of the problem where we are interested in solving the problem based on two predictors—credit score and loan amount. Figure 9.37 shows the distribution of the data points based on the predictors. While applying the decision tree approach, as shown in Fig. 9.38, we can quickly check if a partition happens on the credit score predictor, then the subsequent split-up will be on the loan amount. It can be easily understood that for an individual having a high credit score and the low loan amount is high on repaying the debt as compared to the one who has high credit score and high loan amount. The real-world decision considers large pool of predictors and a much more complicated decision tree as compared to the one that we can see in Fig. 9.37.

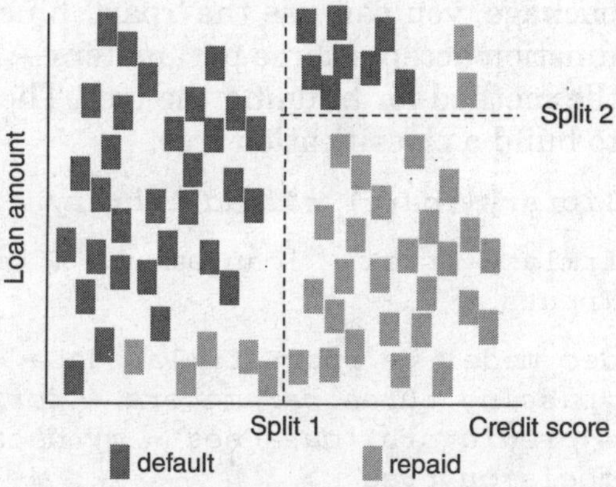

Fig. 9.37 Distribution of sample loan amount and credit score

The process to build such a tree is simple. You can use several packages to build a decision tree, but one of the most widely used packages is 'rpart'. In the 'rpart'

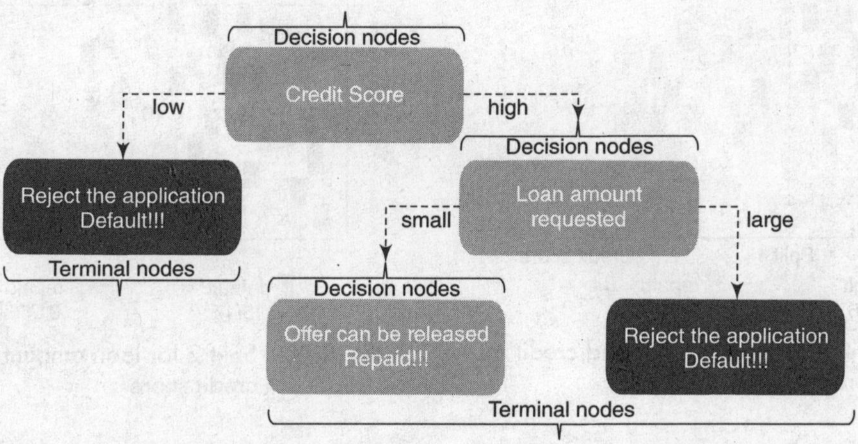

Fig 9.38 Decision tree credit score and loan amount

package, you can use the 'rpart' function to create the classification tree. The 'rpart' function accepts three parameters—the independent and predictors, the data set, and the method for building the tree. The value of 'method' as a 'class' infers the function to build a classification tree.

```
library(rpart) # load library

frmla <- risk ~ loan_amount + credit_score + x3 # LHS outcome and RHS: Inputs

dec_model <- rpart(frmla, data = my_dataset, method = "class")
#passing three parameters - formula showing the relationship response
~ predictors; data set = my_dataset and method = class to represent
decision tree
```

Later, once the model is created, it can be used to test and validate the test and validate set by using the 'predict' function as follows:

```
dec_pred <- predict(dec_model, test_data, type = "class" ) #passing
three parameters - formula showing the relationship response ~
predictors;
```

To get a robust and good performance of the classification tree model, we need to understand how the tree is growing, on what basis a split or partition is attempted, and how the tree is outgrowing. Let us consider the same example and relook it by taking into account multiple ways of splitting up the data. In the first case, the data is split up based on the credit score, see Fig. 9.39; and in the other case, it is split up considering the loan amount, see Fig. 9.40. Figure 9.39 is pure and contains good distribution of the data set; thus could be used as a potential indicator of the possible outcome of interest.

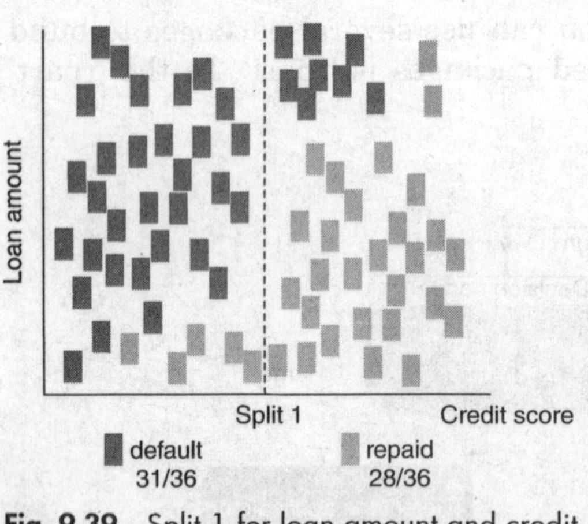

Fig. 9.39 Split 1 for loan amount and credit score

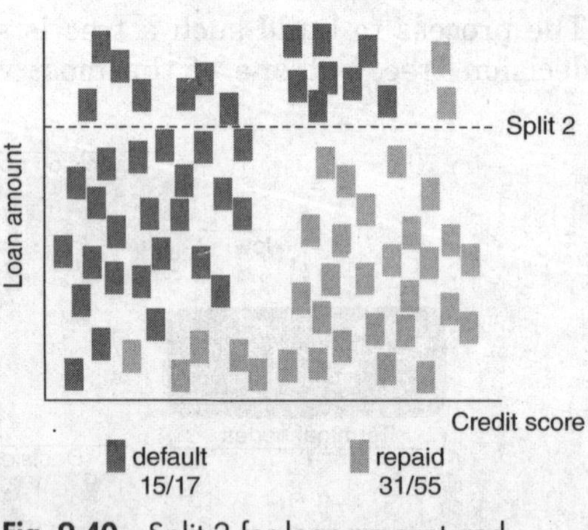

Fig. 9.40 Split 2 for loan amount and credit score

We need to take special care while considering the partition or split of the data set as it can result into an overly complex tree or a model that overfits the data set.

A classification tree grows using a *divide-and-conquer* process. Each time the tree grows larger, it splits groups of data into smaller subgroups, creating new branches in the tree. The splitting happens to create the greatest improvement in subgroup homogeneity. To make sure that the tree grows in a right manner and does not overfit the data, it needs to be pruned appropriately. We can control the tree growth in many ways, i.e., by performing pre-pruning, pruning, and post-pruning process.

Pre-pruning

One of the simplest methods to perform the pre-pruning process is to control the depth of the decision tree; accordingly, the splits of the tree are arranged. The other could be to control the size of the sample at each node to attempt a partition, see Fig. 9.39.

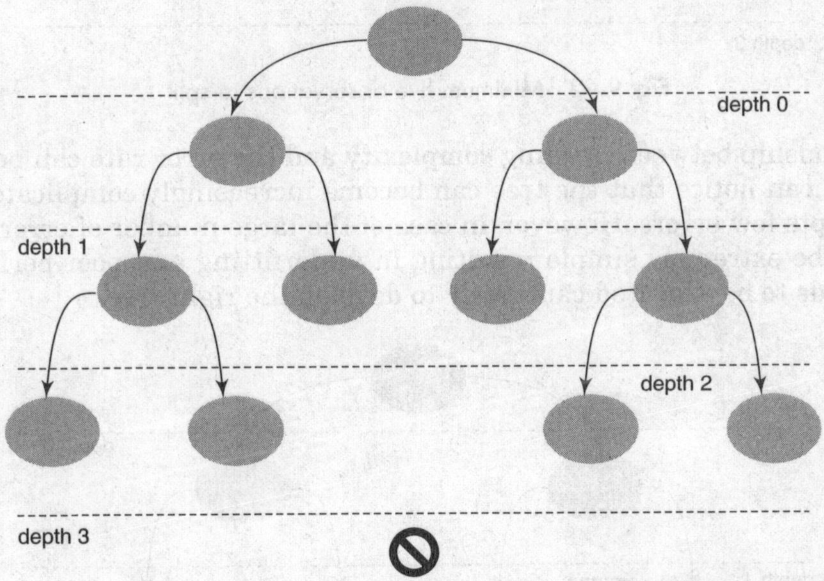

Fig. 9.41 Restriction on the maximum depth of three levels

Post-pruning

When a pre-pruning process is attempted, it limits the growth of the tree and also restricts the discovery of important and peculiar patterns. In post-pruning, our intention is to grow the tree or to say outgrow, to the maximum and then prune it to make it balanced. The sub-branches or sub-tree that do not contribute to the overall accuracy of the model or tree are removed, see Fig. 9.42.

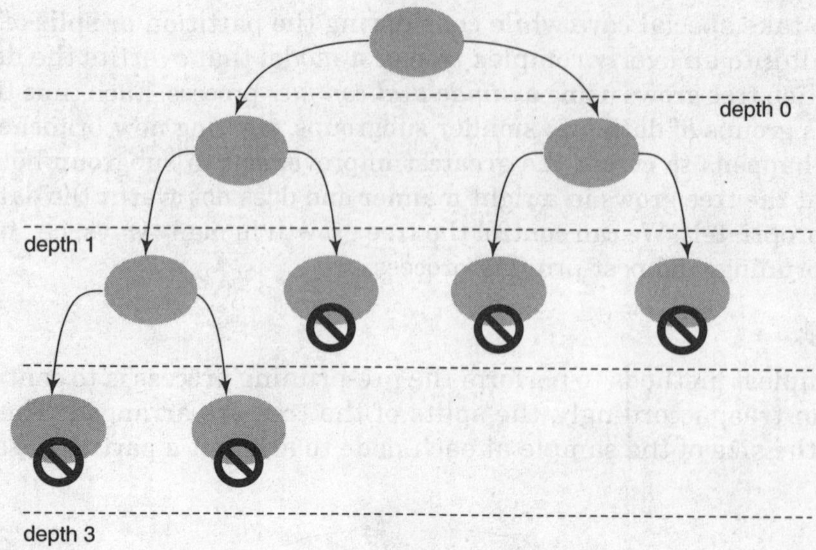

Fig. 9.42 Minimum five observations to split

The relationship between pruning complexity and the error rate can be depicted in Fig. 9.43. We can notice that the tree can become increasingly complicated when the model attempts few errors. However, in case of the large number of errors, the model turns out to be extremely simple resulting in underfitting and poor performance. A trade-off needs to be executed cautiously to develop the right tree.

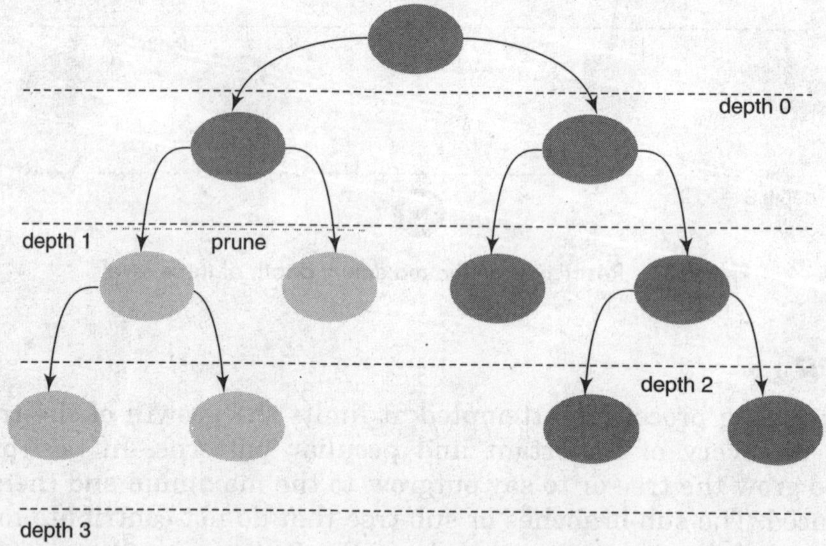

Fig. 9.43 Prune the overly complex tree

Random Forest

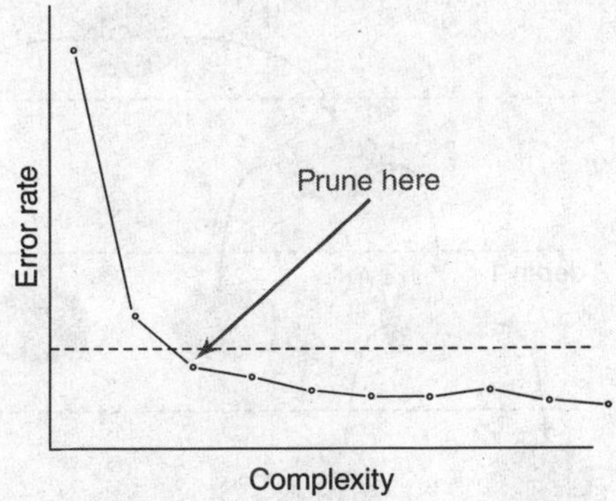

Fig. 9.44 Elbow curve

A number of classification tree model can be combined to form a decision tree forest. It is helpful in optimizing the decision as compared to one decision tree (Fig. 9.45) when we have a large and complex data set and feature set. The pool of classification models can generate many different outcomes of interest, and it is essential to understand which one is effective. A random forest is a particular class of classification that deals with the vast collection of classification models, as shown in Fig. 9.46. Each tree is generated based on the random set of data and feature set which help a classifier to diversify in generating the outcome. Consider a sports team that comprises of complementary skills to perform better. Each team member has strengths and weaknesses. A synergy of the team members results towards the performance of the overall team and not the individual sum of the performances. A similar principle, an ensemble method, drives the formation of the random forest. Thus, each classifiers vote for the outcome of interest generates the overall performance and prediction capability of the model.

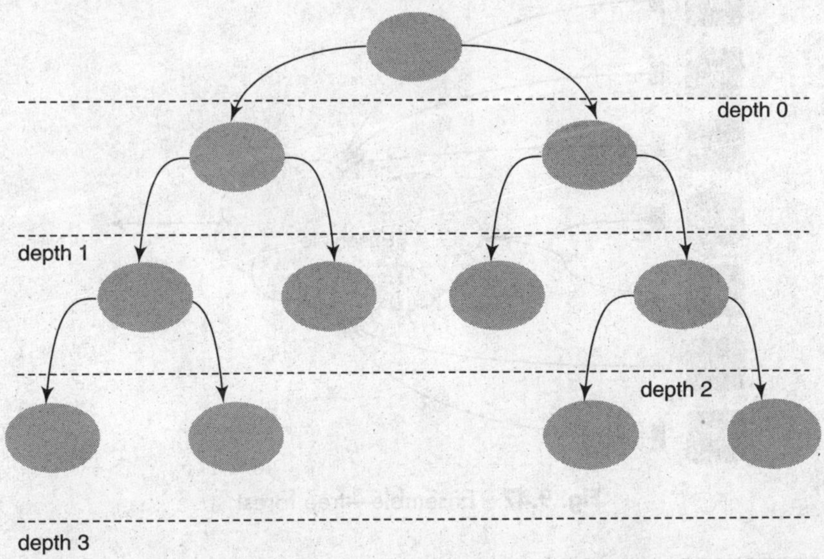

Fig. 9.45 Single decision tree might be complex

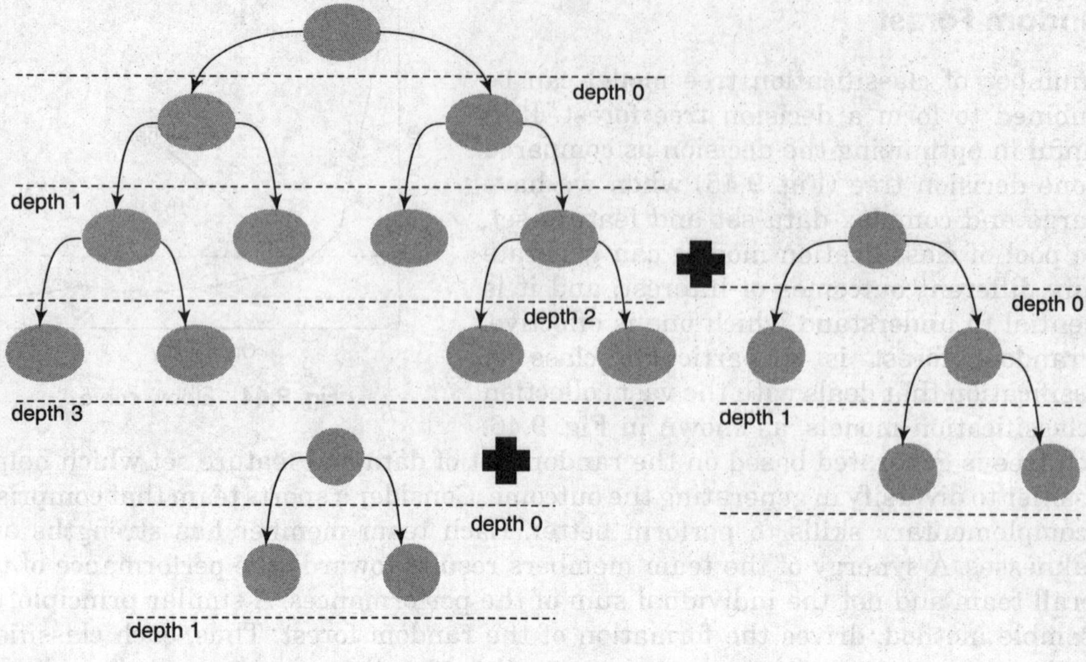

Fig. 9.46 Tree forest

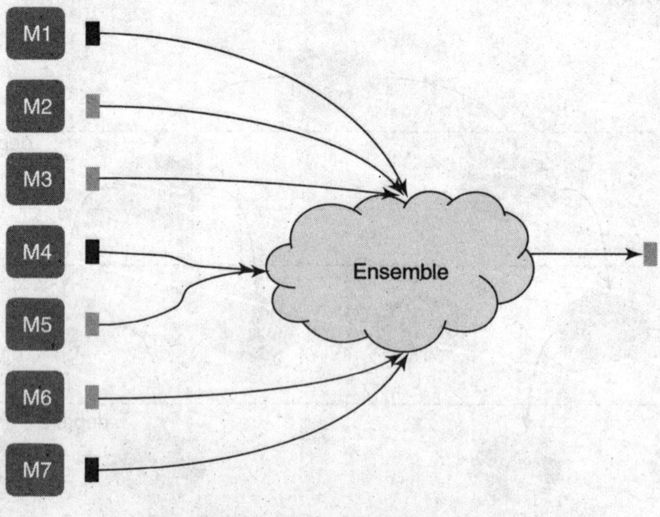

Fig. 9.47 Ensemble—tree forest

```
library(randomforest) # load library
frmla <- risk ~ loan_amount + credit_score + x3 # LHS outcome and RHS:
Inputs
```

```
dec_model <- randomForest(frmla,
                          data = my_dataset, # formula
                          ntree = 500, # number of trees in the forest
                          mtry = sqrt(p)) # number of predictors (p) per tree
risk_pred <- predict(dec_model, test_data)
```

SUMMARY

- The whole human race, as a 'learner', has evolved and continues to do so to experience and observe unseen '*world*' and '*environment*'.
- In the supervised learning, the goal is to map the input data set to the output data set through the learning algorithm by generating the set of appropriate rules. The assumption is that both the sets—'input' and 'output' data sets—are available.
- In unsupervised learning, the output data set is not provided to the learning algorithm and only input data set is being used to generate the patterns, rules, and insights.
- In the semi-supervised learning, the learning algorithm is provided with the partial data set—input and output. The goal of the learning algorithm is to generate rules, patterns, and insights where the output data set is unavailable and then use the complete output set, all together, like supervised learning.
- Regression helps to model numerical relationship within data. The regression models help to predict the value of the unseen data based on the training data.
- It is easy to perform predictions on the data set after developing the model. We can use the function '*predict*' to predict the outcome of interest. The function by default returns training data predictions.
- One major shortcoming of the linear regression model is that it is incapable to filter out the collinearity.
- Root Mean Square Error (RMSE) depicts the standard deviation of the residuals (prediction errors).
- The R^2 sometimes refers to the variance explained by the model as it includes the total sum of square (variance of the data).
- Training set and test set, both, are disjoint data sets and do not contain any common observations. Concept of training and test data is applicable only to supervised learning.
- A sampling of the data set can affect the performance of the model. Thus, we can use a method—'*Cross-validation*'—to avoid such biases of '*sampling*' and achieve a robust model.
- A same value of AUC can generate different curves. We need to understand that the curve that is closer to the higher percentage of positive outcomes is chosen as the best. The *ROC* and the *AUC*, both, can be used to understand the performance of the models.
- The goal of the *decision tree* is to model the relationships between various predictors and an outcome of interest. The tree is well suited to *non-linear* concepts such as *intervals*, *non-monotonic relationships*, and *non-additive interactions*.
- A number of classification tree models can be combined to form a decision tree forest. It is helpful in optimizing the decision as compared to one decision tree when we have a large and complex data set and feature set.

EXERCISE

Review Questions

1. Explain low bias and high variance with appropriate examples.

   Tip: Refer to the chapter to understand low bias and high variance with appropriate examples. Check the scenarios for assumptions vs sampling w.r.t. true data.

2. A same value of AUC can generate different curves. In such situations, how would you decide on the performance of your model?

   Tip: Refer to Fig. 9.27 to understand how to decide on the performance of your model.

3. Describe the way in which you approach prediction of numerical and categorical data sets.

   Tip: Refer to the chapter to understand about dummy variables, missing data, and interactions before performing prediction tasks.

4. Why the concept of pruning is important to the decision tree? Describe the situation where it is needed.

5. Describe the way to evaluate the performance of the classification models. How is it different from the regression models?

Unsupervised Learning

10

"The unsupervised learning is the way most people will learn in the future. You have this model of how the world works in your head and you're refining it to predict what you think is going to happen in the future."

—Mark Zuckerberg

Learning Objectives

On completing this chapter, you will be able to:

LO 1 Understand unsupervised learning
LO 2 Describe K-means clustering
LO 3 Apply K-means clustering
LO 4 Describe hierarchical clustering
LO 5 Apply hierarchical clustering
LO 6 Define performance measures

Fig. 10.1 Children learning through activities and games

LO 1
Understand unsupervised learning

Many times, we want to look at the useful and insightful patterns. In unsupervised learning, we are not concerned about the labels or the target outputs but we are interested in the observations. We have been programmed into grouping the similar things together by birth. Remember your first balloon that you might have received from your parents. Initially, you attributed it as a ball because of its circular dimension. But when you grew up you found that the ball and the balloon are different, even though they have circular dimensions and share somewhat similar playing/sporting abilities. Early in childhood, one learns to distinguish cats from dogs, liquid from solid, animals from plants, etc. Identification of attributes, behaviour, and characteristics is an evolutionary process. Clustering is the process by which you keep, organize, or group similar physical or abstract objects. A cluster defines the collection of objects that are similar to one another within the same cluster and dissimilar to the other objects in the different cluster.

In this chapter, we will study the requirements of the clustering process to make it operational. We will learn the computation of similarity and dissimilarity of the objects within and across the clusters. We will discuss on various techniques to develop clusters and finally elaborate the assessment of the results considering performance parameters.

Fig. 10.2 A child learning the difference between a ball and a balloon

10.1 BUSINESS USE CASE

Businesses have benefited dramatically by deploying clustering results with appropriate strategies. Some of the useful business use cases are discussed as follows.

Behavioural Segmentation

It represents the marketing strategy that is governed by the customer buying behaviour. This approach helps in forming the groups based on

- purchase history
- reviews
- activities on service solution—loyalty
- channel usage—online vs offline
- peak time and day

Categorization of Inventory

The organizations are interested in grouping the inventory to control it efficiently. The grouping can be formed by

- target sales
- region wise sale
- sale KPIs
- supply-demand metrics

Identifying Bots or Anomalies

The inclusion of social media has also increased the use of bots; for example, to use bots to increase customer reviews. The organization is also interested in understanding the anomalies, say, outrageous transactions. The grouping can be formed by

- bots activity
- potential outliers

10.2 UNLABELLED DATA

The goal of unsupervised learning is to label the unlabelled data. Table 10.1 is an example of unlabelled data set. The dataset has three features—color, shape, and size—and five observations. The label of the target or response feature is not present, and, thus, this example is well suited under the unsupervised learning paradigm. We can apply the fundamental principle of the cluster to create the label of the target or response feature—class. Table 10.2 shows the labelled data.

Table 10.1 Unlabelled data—no class label

	Features		
	Color	*Shape*	*Size (cm)*
Observations	Red	Ellipse	17
	Green	Ellipse	15.3
	Blue	Square	7
	Green	Square	11
	Blue	Ellipse	21

Table 10.2 Labelled data—class label

	Features			
	Color	*Shape*	*Size (cm)*	*Class*
Observations	Red	Ellipse	17	1
	Green	Ellipse	15.3	1
	Blue	Square	7	2
	Green	Square	11	2
	Blue	Ellipse	21	1

We have to keep in mind two primary goals for attempting the unsupervised learning problem space:

- To find the homogeneous subgroups of the objects – physical or abstract within the larger group. Consider an example where a data set size is of 70,000 people, see Fig. 10.3. Each person in the data set has some features of interest such as name, age, gender, income, education.

Fig. 10.3 Sample data depiction

Forming the subgroup on some features is easy. You may like to group these people based on education or age group, see Fig. 10.4. Other could be the range of income. But, the *name* is not a good criterion to create subgroups. The process of finding homogeneous subgroups is known as *clustering*.

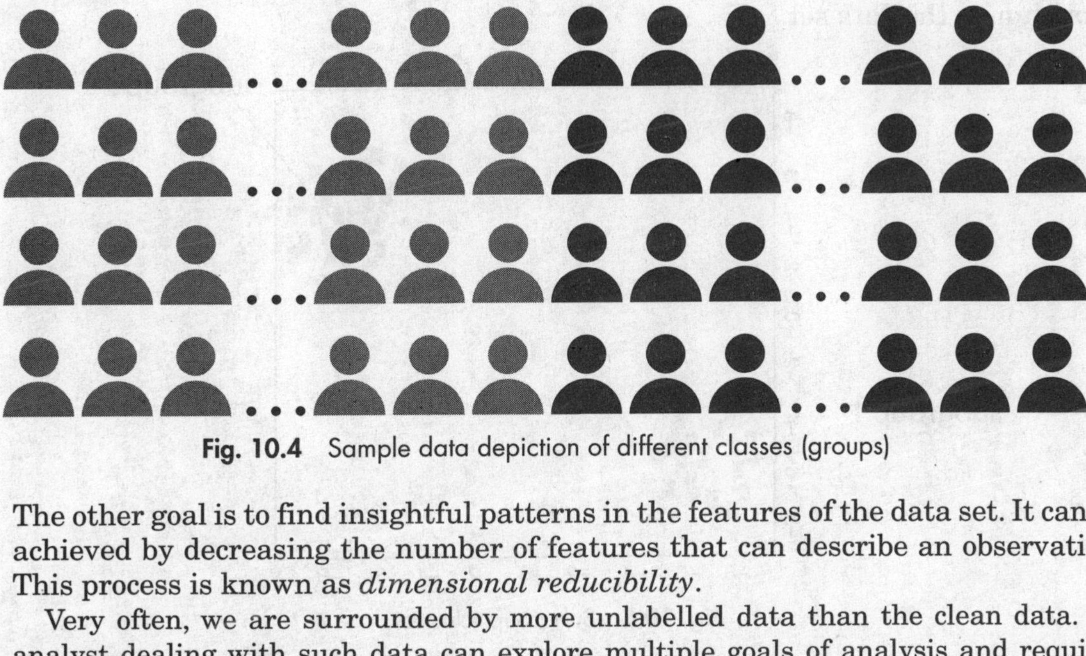

Fig. 10.4 Sample data depiction of different classes (groups)

- The other goal is to find insightful patterns in the features of the data set. It can be achieved by decreasing the number of features that can describe an observation. This process is known as *dimensional reducibility*.

  Very often, we are surrounded by more unlabelled data than the clean data. An analyst dealing with such data can explore multiple goals of analysis and requires more creativity.

10.3 K-MEANS CLUSTERING

LO 2 *Describe K-means clustering*

K-means is the most popular clustering method to form the clusters. Each cluster represents a subgroup of the data set, see Fig. 10.5. In case we are lucky, then we will get a clean *'apriori'* subgroups based data set. But in the real world, this is not the typical situation, and we have to face typically mixed or overlapped data points. It considers the number of clusters to be formed and accordingly processed each observation and placed appropriately on one of those clusters.

The '*K-means*' process requires '*apriori*' certain number of clusters. The process begins with the identification of '*k*' centroids, one for each cluster. Normally, these are placed randomly. The main purpose of placing centroids far away from each other is to create a cluster where the cognateness is minimum and distance between the clusters is maximum. In the next step, each point of the data set is then associated with one amongst these centroids. The association is accomplished based on the '*nearest neighbour*' principle. Each data point is associated with the nearest centroid. The outcome is the formation of early subgroupings. Next, the same process is repeated until there is no significant change in the centroid position or replacement in the clusters.

In 'R', it is straightforward to invoke the function '*kmeans*' to execute the '*kmeans*' algorithm on the data set.

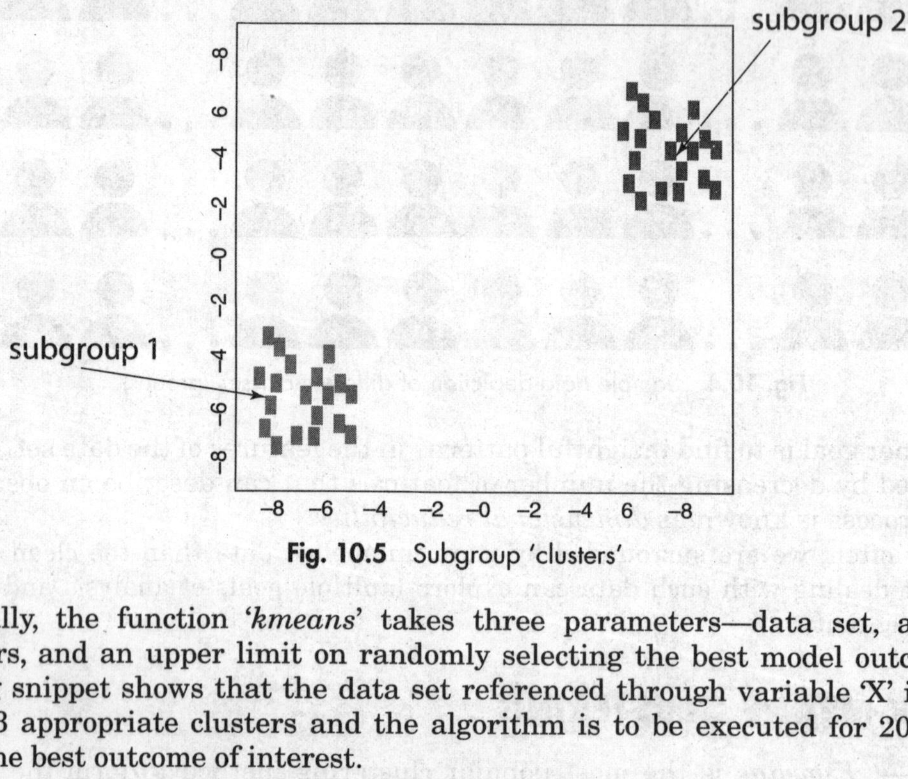

Fig. 10.5 Subgroup 'clusters'

Typically, the function '*kmeans*' takes three parameters—data set, a number of clusters, and an upper limit on randomly selecting the best model outcome. The following snippet shows that the data set referenced through variable 'X' is used to develop 3 appropriate clusters and the algorithm is to be executed for 20 times to deliver the best outcome of interest.

```
# Execute kmeans algorithm to develop 3 clusters
kmeans(X, centers = 3, nstart = 20)
```

The function '*kmeans*' has multiple components of interest and can be accessed directly by invoking the result of the '*kmeans*'.

It is better to perform useful visualization on the clustering result. You can plot the result of the '*kmeans*' cluster by coloring the cluster separately, see Fig. 10.6, by passing the cluster membership value to the *color* field as follows:

```
# plot the clusters of interest
plot(X, col = km.out$cluster)
```

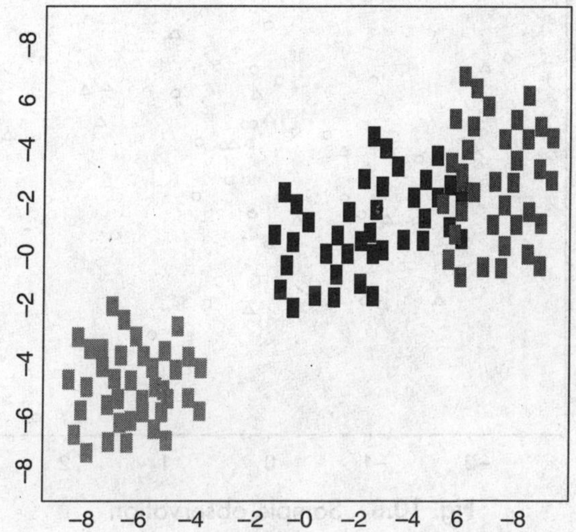

Fig. 10.6 K-means with 3 clusters

Illustration 1—K-means

LO 3 *Apply K-means clustering*

Assume that the data set sample is distributed as shown in Fig. 10.7. Following steps are executed to achieve the clusters.

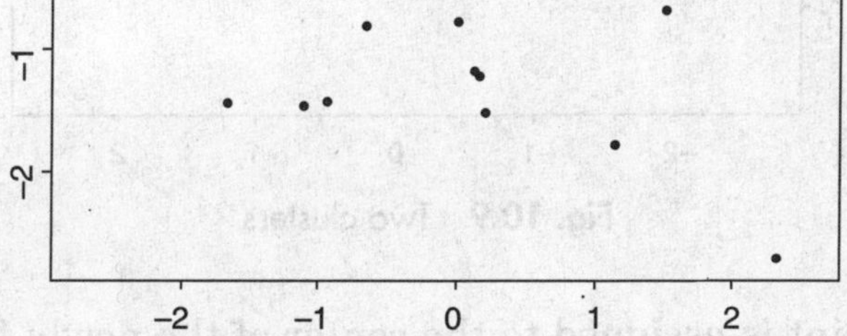

Fig. 10.7 Random data points

Step 1: Randomly assign each of the points to one of the clusters, as shown in Fig. 10.8. Assuming that we have two clusters, then each of the points is randomly assigned to each one of the two clusters.

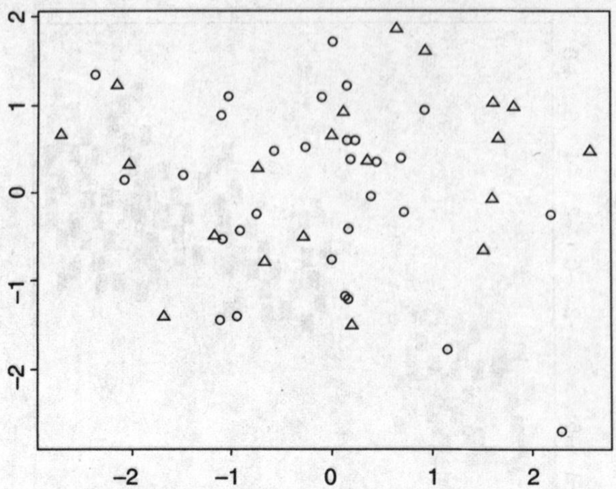

Fig. 10.8 Sample observation

Step 2: Select center of each of the two subgroups. The center of a subgroup is the average value of the distance from all the points within the subgroup, see Fig. 10.9.

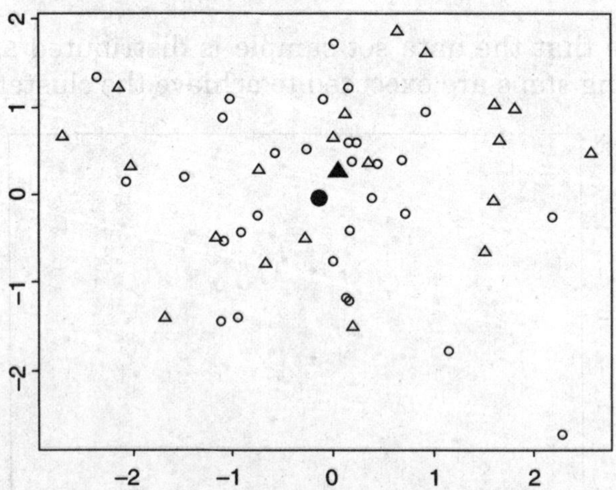

Fig. 10.9 Two clusters

Step 3: Now, each point is assigned to the center of the newly formed subgroups, as shown in Fig. 10.10. This is achieved by running the *kmeans* algorithm iteration once. We can easily see that the points cluster now have been changed.

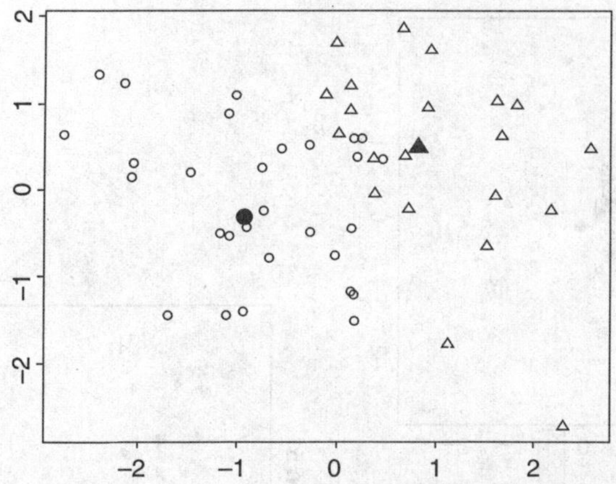

Fig. 10.10 Clusters center (reformation)

Step 4: The '*kmeans*' iteration now results in a new center position of the newly formed subgroup in the iteration 2. The process is repeated until new subgroups are stable and no further change in the subgroups is witnessed. In this case, the '*kmeans*' function does not see any further change of the observation after 5th iteration, thus, stopping further iteration of the '*kmeans*' function, see Fig. 10.11.

Step 5: Due to the presence of a random component, the '*kmeans*' outcome is selected based on multiple runs of the models. The minimum total within-cluster sum (tot. withinss) of squares represents the best result out of all possible models. The total within-cluster sum of squares can be calculated easily.

For each cluster, for each observation, we need to determine the square distance from observation to the cluster center. The distance can be Euclidean distance or any other distance measure like Manhattan distance. Finally, sum all the distances together to get the *twss* score.

K-means, by default, assumes the number of clusters to execute the algorithm; and if we are lucky, we would know up-front the number of clusters. Realistically, the condition is far away from knowing the number of clusters and, thus, we have to perform the execution of K-means 'cluster' model multiple times. Here, the rescue is to plot the number of execution results of models and then check the 'elbow' curve which indicates that the quality measures improve more slowly as the number of clusters. A cut over the 'elbow' turn is a good point to get a clue on the number of clusters. Plotting results of the different models to get an 'elbow' measure is sometimes referred to as the 'Scree Plot'. Let us assume that we have unlabelled data set and looking for the effective cut on the number of clusters. We can achieve the understanding of the number of clusters by executing various K-means models by varying the number of clusters. In 'R', we can easily perform the whole execution. Following snippet shows the part execution of the model.

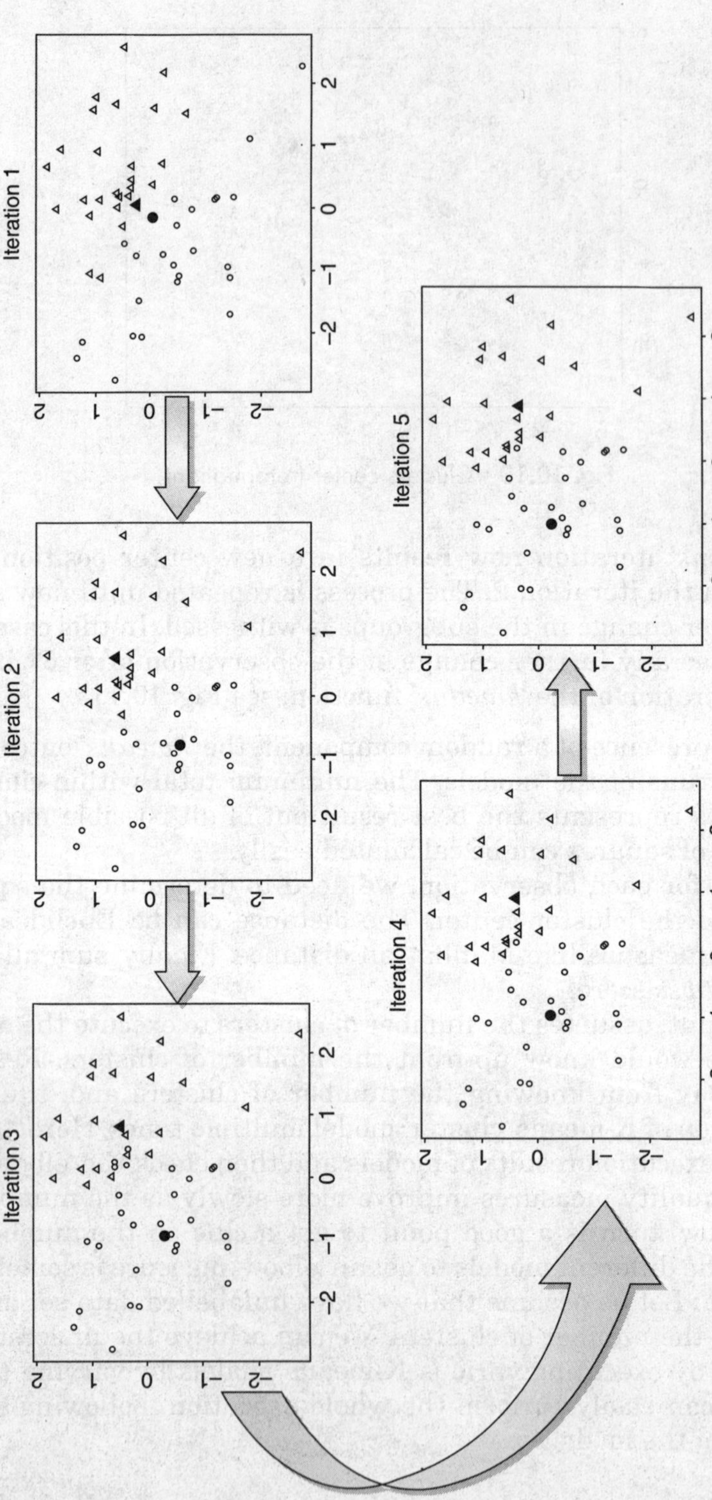

Fig. 10.11 Iterations '*kmeans*'

```
# First step: To initialize total within sum of squares error: wiss
wiss <- 0
Second step: Iteration over 15 cluster centers
#for (i in 1:15) {
  km.out <- kmeans(x, centers = i, nstart = 20)
    wiss[i] <- km.out$tot.withinss
}
# Third step: Generate the elbow effect by plotting 'total within sum of
squares vs number of clusters'.
plot(1:15, wiss, type = "b",        xlab = "Total Number of Clusters",
ylab = "Within groups sum of squares")
```

Figure 10.12 shows the elbow effect where beyond the curve, no significant change in the groups is reflected.

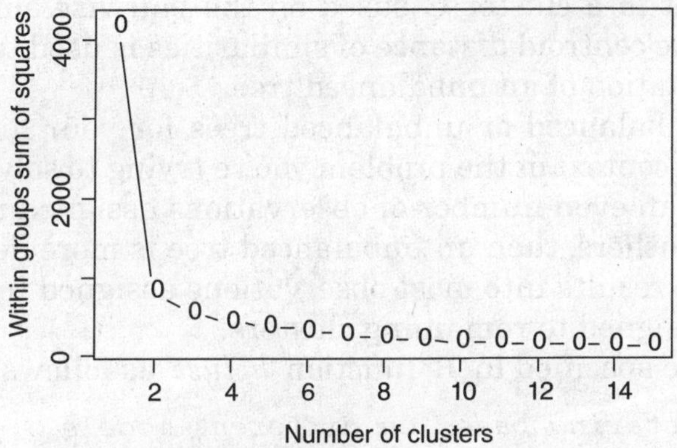

Fig. 10.12 Elbow effect—number of clusters

10.4 HIERARCHICAL CLUSTERING

LO 4 *Describe hierarchical clustering*

It is one of the predominant clustering technique which is used when the number of clusters are not mentioned *apriori*. One can achieve the hierarchical clustering by using bottom-up approach or top-down approach. In the bottom-up approach, the clusters are formed considering each point as a cluster; and in further iteration, each new closest neighbour joins to re-form a new cluster. The process gets repeated multiple times until no new changes in the subgroup formation are observed. Consider that we have five observations and, thus, initially we have five clusters. Each point represents one cluster. Next action of the bottom-up process is to join the nearest neighbour and re-form the subgroup. The clustering algorithm uses a specific rule to measure the distance and combine the nearest observations into a new cluster. In 'R', there exist four different methods by which one can achieve the similarity of the observations within the clusters:

- **Default method—Complete:** Cluster A and Cluster B are combined to result in a cluster C based on the pairwise similarity between all observations in the cluster 'A' and cluster 'B' respectively. Here, the largest distance of similarities is used to form the clusters. It results in the formation of a balanced tree.
- **Single:** Cluster A and Cluster B are combined to result in a cluster C based on the pairwise similarity between all observations in the cluster 'A' and cluster 'B' respectively. Here, the smallest distance of similarities is used to form the clusters. It results in the formation of a balanced tree.
- **Average:** Cluster A and Cluster B are combined to result in a cluster C based on the pairwise similarity between all observations in the cluster 'A' and cluster 'B' respectively. Here, the average distance of similarities is used to form the clusters. It results in the formation of an unbalanced tree.
- **Centroid:** Cluster A and Cluster B centroids are obtained, and the clusters are combined to result in a cluster C based on the pairwise similarity between two centroids. Here, the centroid distance of similarities is used to form the clusters. It results in the formation of an unbalanced tree.

Whether you want balanced or unbalanced trees for your hierarchical clustering model depends on the context of the problem you're trying to solve. Balanced trees are essential if you want an even number of observations assigned to each cluster. But if the goal is to detect outliers, then an unbalanced tree is more desirable. The pruning of an unbalanced tree results into most observations assigned to one cluster and only a few observations assigned to remaining clusters.

Each method can be specified in 'R' function *'hclust'* as follows:

```
# hierarchical clustering based on different models
  hc_complete <- hclust(d, method = "complete")
  hc_average <- hclust(d, method = "average")
  hc_single <- hclust(d, method = "single")
```

Illustration 2—Cluster by Joining Nearest Neighbour

LO 5 *Apply hierarchical clustering*

At every iteration in the process of hierarchical clustering, a new pair of the closest cluster is identified until no cluster to be formed, see Fig. 10.13.

Performing hierarchical clustering in 'R' is easy as we require only one parameter—distance between observations. Following snippet shows the working of hierarchical clustering in 'R':

```
# calculate similarity distance based on Euclidean distance "default
distance"
  dist.matrix <- dist(x) # compute distance matrix
  hc_model <- hclust(d, method = "average")
  hc_single <- hclust(d = dist.matrix)
Call:
```

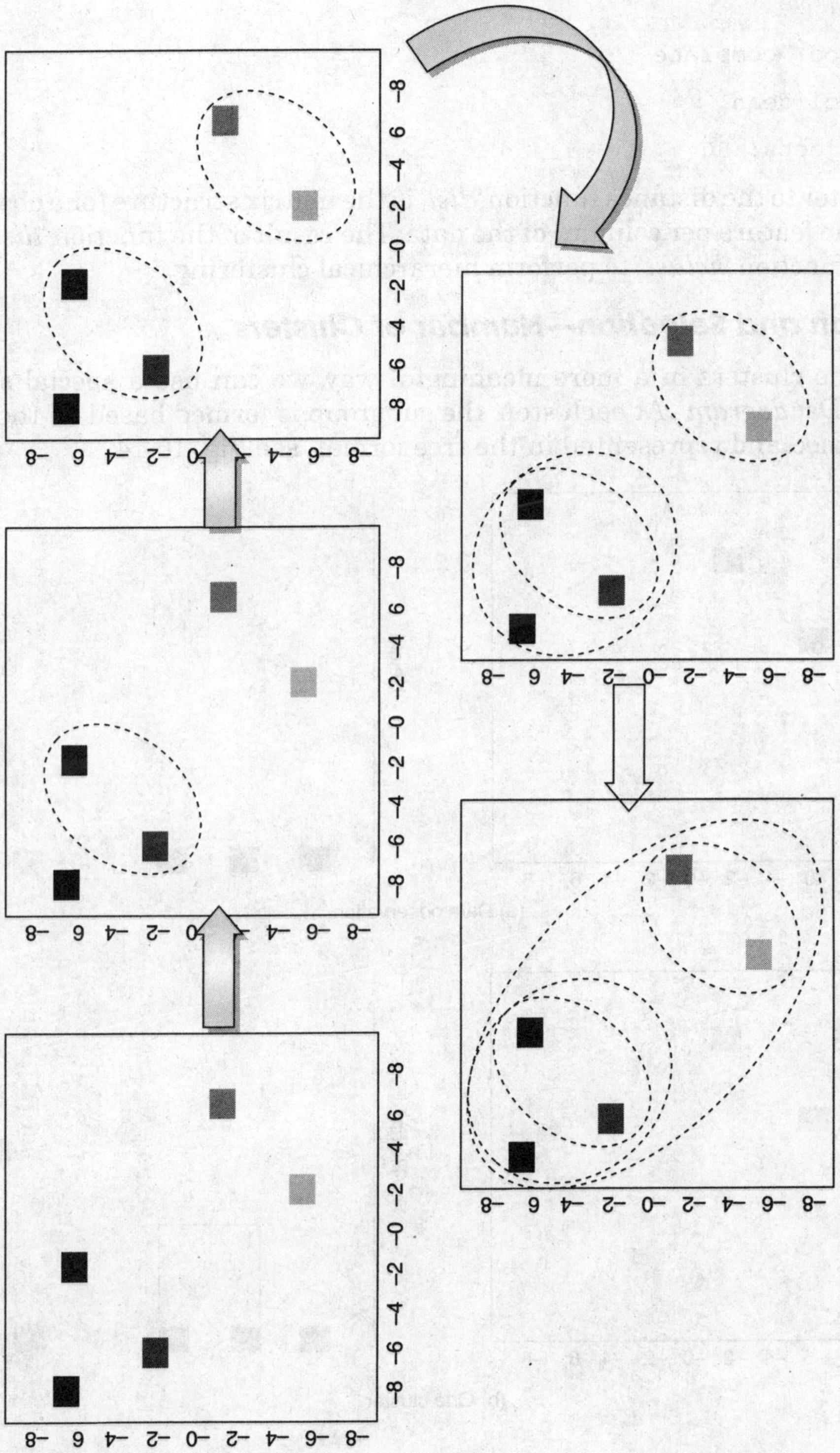

Fig. 10.13 Hierarchical clustering—nearest neighbour process

```
hclust(d = s)

Cluster method: complete

Distance: Euclidean

Number of objects: 50
```

The parameter to the distance function '*dist*' is the matrix structure (one observation per row and one feature per column) of the data. The result of the function '*dist*' is then passed to the function '*hclust*' to perform hierarchical clustering.

Interpretation and Selection—Number of Clusters

To interpret the clusters in a more meaningful way, we can use a special structure referred to as '*Dendogram*'. At each step, the subgroup is formed based on the nearest neighbour method and represented in the tree format, see Fig. 10.14.

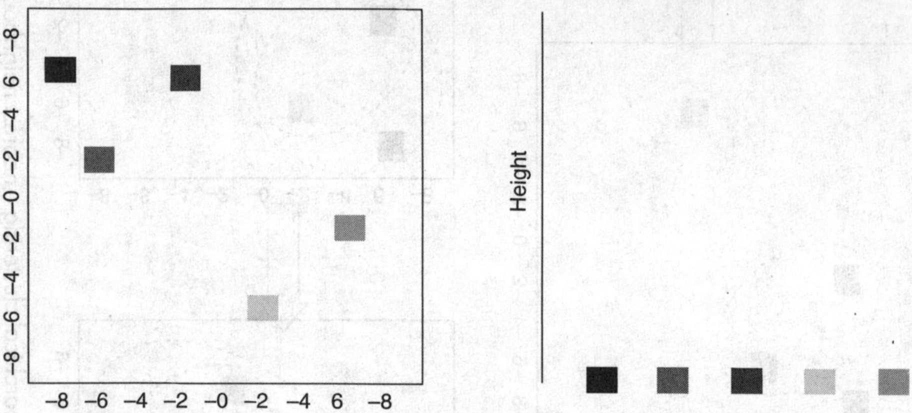

(a) Data observation

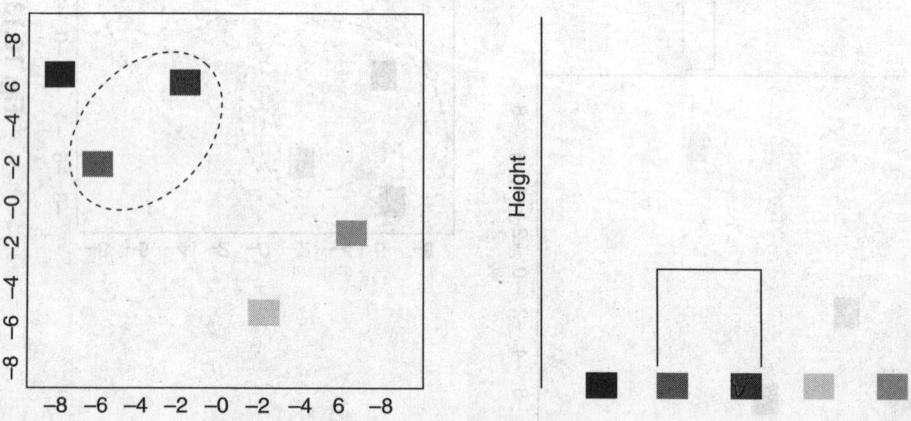

(b) One cluster

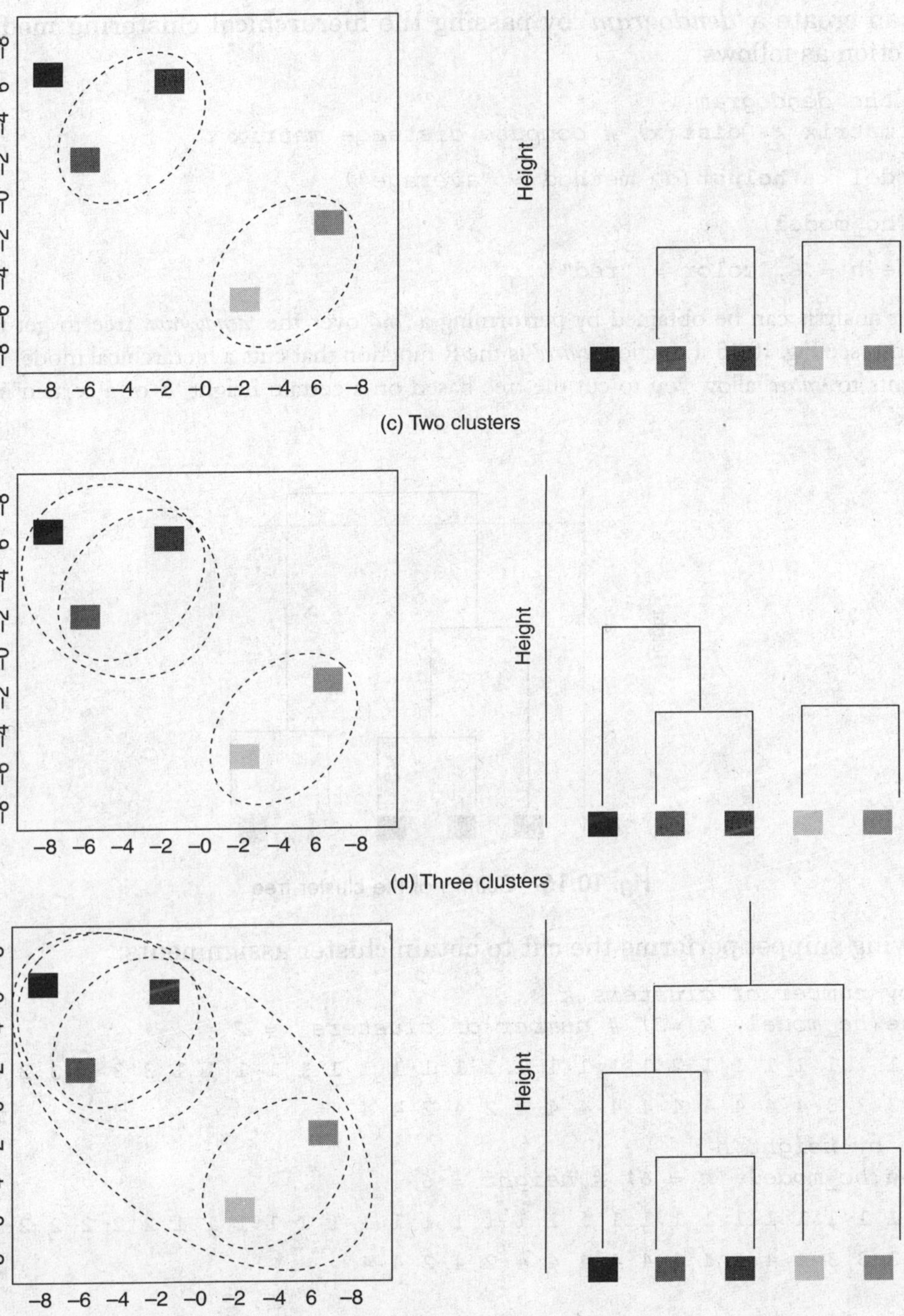

(c) Two clusters

(d) Three clusters

(e) Single cluster—process completed

Fig. 10.14 Development of 'Dendogram' tree process

You can create a '*dendogram*' by passing the hierarchical clustering model to the plot function as follows:

```
# plot the dendogram
  dist.matrix <- dist(x) # compute distance matrix
  hc_model <- hclust(d, method = "average")
  plot(hc_model)
  abline(h = 6, color = "red")
```

Further analysis can be obtained by performing a '*cut*' over the '*dendogram*' tree to get the cluster assignments, see Fig. 10.15. Function '*cutree*' is the R function that cuts a hierarchical model. The h and k arguments to '*cutree*' allow you to cut the tree based on a certain height '*h*' or a certain number of clusters '*k*'.

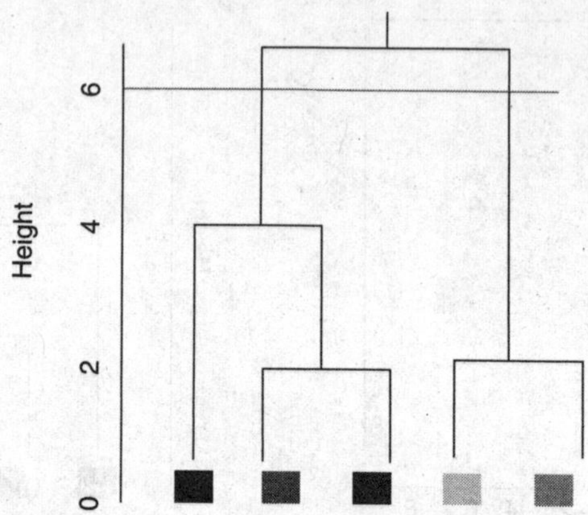

Fig. 10.15 Cutting of the cluster tree

Following snippet performs the cut to obtain cluster assignments:

```
# cut by number of clusters k
  cutree(hc_model, k =2) # number of clusters  = 2
 [1] 1 1 1 1 1 1 1 1 2 1 1 1 1 1 1 1 1 1 1 1 1 1 1 1 1 3 3 3 3 3 3
[32] 3 3 3 3 4 4 4 4 4 4 4 4 4 4 2 4 2 4 4
  # cut by height h
  cutree(hc_model, h = 6) # height = 6
 [1] 1 1 1 1 1 1 1 1 1 1 1 1 1 1 1 1 1 1 1 1 1 1 1 1 1 2 2 2 2 2 2
[32] 3 3 3 3 4 4 4 4 4 4 4 4 4 4 2 4 2 4 4
```

10.5 CAUTION

One needs to be careful while performing cluster analysis on the data set having different scales as it can cause undesirable and inappropriate results. One remedy is to scale data in such a way that the feature value will have same mean and standard deviation. It helps in achieving the appropriate distribution. To achieve proper scaling, the mean of each feature is further subtracted from the feature values and each feature value is divided by the standard deviation of the feature. One can see the normalization of the feature result into a mean of value 0 and a standard deviation of value 1. It is important to note that there is no consensus on which method produces better clusters. The job of analyst in unsupervised clustering is to observe the cluster assignments and make a judgement call as to which way provides more insights into the data.

Fig. 10.16 The 'Caution' symbol

Performance Measures

LO 6

Define performance measures

In clustering, we use distance measures to assess the performance of the clustering models. The distance matrix is comprised of two elements:

- **Similarity within each cluster:** It represents the compactness of the data points within the cluster and can be computed by the measure—within the sum of squares and diameter of the clusters. The maximum diameter is a good measure of the cluster (eq. (1)), see Fig. 10.17.

$$Dm_i = \max_{x,y \in C_i} d(x, y) \qquad \text{eq. (1)}$$

where,

x, y: data points—objects

C_i indicates cluster 'i'

d refers to distance (objects)

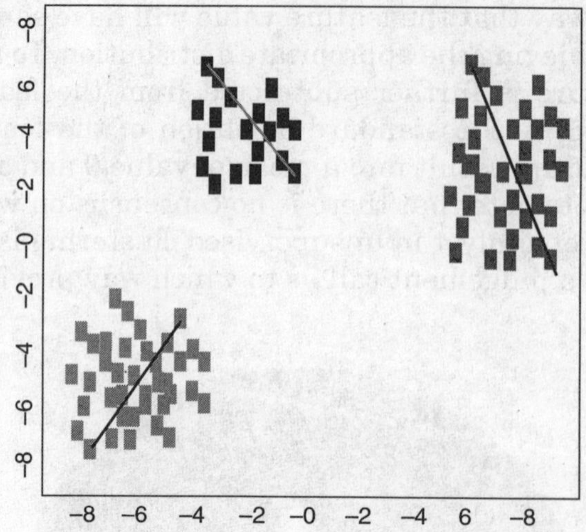

Fig. 10.17 Cluster diameter

The goal is to minimize the value of similarity measure within each cluster.

- **Similarity between clusters:** It represents the separateness of the data points within one cluster with the other clusters and is computed by the measure—between cluster sum of square (B_{ss}) and inter-cluster distance. The minimum intercluster distance is a good measure of the cluster (eq. (2)), see Fig. 10.18.

$$\delta(C_i, C_j) = \underset{x \in C_i,\, y \in C_i}{\text{Min}} \; d(x, y) \qquad \text{eq. (2)}$$

where,

x, y: data points—objects
$C_i\, C_j$ indicates cluster 'i' and cluster 'j'
d refers to distance (objects)

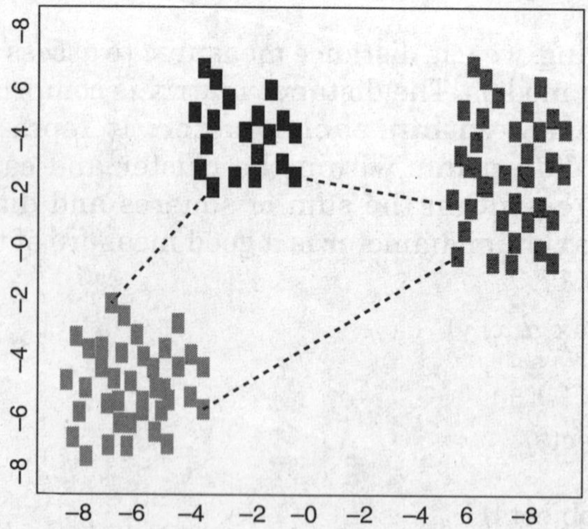

Fig. 10.18 Intercluster distance

The goal is to maximize the value of dissimilarity measure of the data points within one cluster with the other clusters.

To get an optimum '*k*', i.e., the number of clusters, to cluster the problem space of the data set, we need to understand that as we increase the value of '*k*', the measure of similarity within each cluster is decreased. At the lowest level, each data point is a cluster but we do not need such a solution. As the measure of similarity within each cluster decreases slowly with each increasing value of '*k*', the rescue is to find a value which gives us a right value for '*k*'. The expression value represents that the ratio of '*wss* / *tss*' must be less than 0.2 (eq. (3)); Fig. 10.18 shows the way to fix right '*k*'.

$$\frac{wss}{tss} < 0.2 \qquad \text{eq. (3)}$$

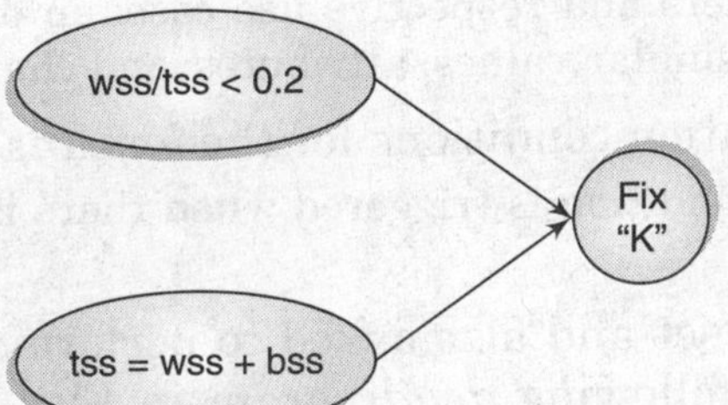

Fig. 10.19 Fix 'k'

SUMMARY

- In unsupervised learning, we are not concerned about the labels or the target outputs but we are interested in the observations.
- K-means is the most popular clustering method to form the clusters.
- K-means by default assumes the number of clusters to execute the algorithm.
- The 'elbow' curve indicates that the quality measures improve more slowly as the number of clusters.
- A cut over the 'elbow' turn is a good point to get a clue on the number of clusters.
- Hierarchical clustering is one of the predominant clustering technique which is used when the number of clusters are not mentioned *apriori*.
- There exist four different methods—complete, single, average, and centroid—by which one can achieve the similarity of the observations within the clusters.
- Balanced trees are essential if you want an even number of observations assigned to each cluster.
- To interpret the clusters in a more meaningful way, a special structure referred to as '*Dendogram*' is utilized.
- Performing cluster analysis on the data set having different scales can cause undesirable and inappropriate results.

EXERCISE

Review Questions

1. Give suitable examples of using clustering in the following sectors:
   - Airline
   - Hospitality
   - Banking
   - Education
   - Manufacturing

   Tip: Identify stakeholders and respective use cases in each domain/sector. Group the scenarios based on the similar values, attributes, and characteristics.
2. What are the termination conditions for the *kmeans* process?

   Tip: The termination condition is triggered when there is no significant change in the centroid position.
3. You are given a data set and also asked to perform the *K-means* clustering on it. You observed the following *dendrogram* in Fig. 10.20 after performing the clustering on the data set. What conclusion can you draw from the *dendrogram*?

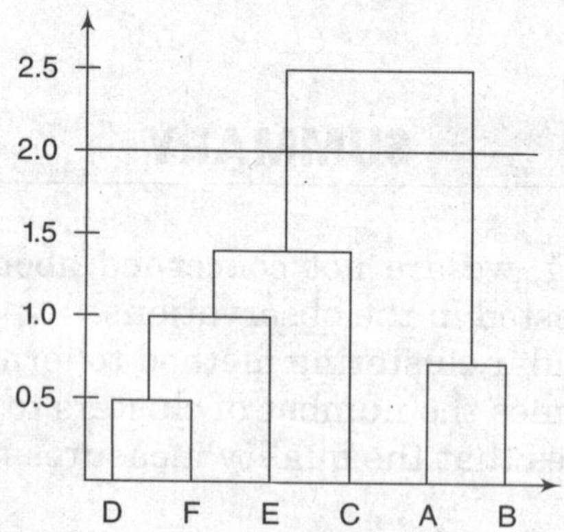

Fig. 10.20

   Tip: Conclusion could be drawn on the basis of cut, groups, and clusters.
4. Feature scaling is an important step before applying *kmeans* algorithm. What is the reason behind this?

   Tip: Non-dimensional value results into undesirable and inappropriate clusters.
5. Describe the process by which you can find the optimal number of clusters. What would be the best choice for choosing the number of clusters in Fig. 10.21? Why?

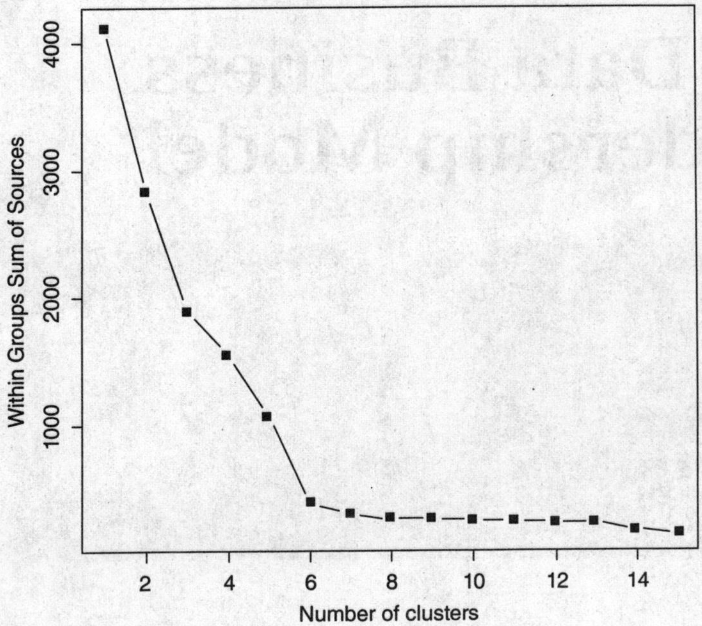

Fig. 10.21

Tip: Check for the elbow effect where beyond the curve no significant change in the groups is reflected.

Big Data Business Leadership Model

11

> *"Without big data analytics, companies are blind and deaf, wandering out onto the web like deer on a freeway."*
>
> —Geoffrey Moore, Organization Theorist and Author

Learning Objectives

On completing this chapter, you will be able to:

- **LO 1** Describe information pioneered product
- **LO 2** Explain the big data stakeholders
- **LO 3** Comprehend the big data industry
- **LO 4** Define big data management architecture
- **LO 5** Examine big data business leadership model
- **LO 6** Perform big data business leadership report-cum-analysis

LO 1
Describe information pioneered product

Attaining a big data business leadership is not easy and is full of challenges. Nonetheless, it is also achievable. We will now review the major concepts that we have covered so far; then discuss the big data business leadership model.

Fig. 11.1 Leadership in action

One of the competing strategies for a successful big data company is to establish its big data management architecture, Information Pioneered Product Pipeline (IPPP), and a value chain (IPPVC). IPPP reflects the pedagogical and mental model to understand the workflow of the information in Information Pioneered Product Value Chain (IPPVC). The pipeline shown in Fig. 11.2 can be combined with other potential IPPPs or can work in isolation to deliver the meaningful and actionable decisions.

The big data business needs to embrace fully its value chain and engage the stakeholders appropriately to develop various strategies to unleash the hidden insights. More the stakeholders get involved in the collaborative decisions, more the industry succeeds in establishing the trust and credibility network. The IPPVC, as shown in Fig. 11.3, recognizes the value activities—primary, secondary, and others required in the use of information to produce the actionable and valuable insights. The IPPVC set of primary activities refers to those activities that help the

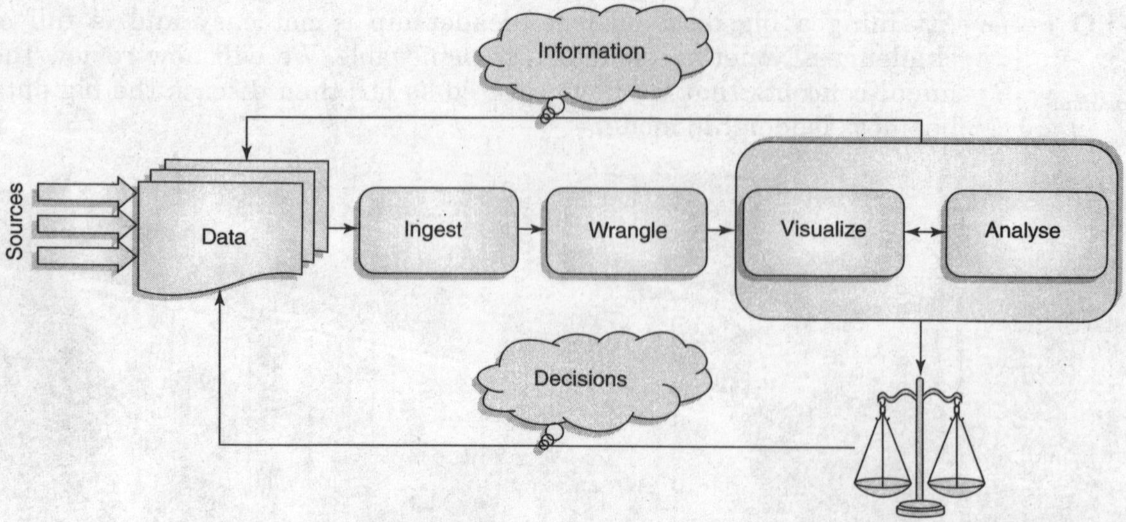

Fig. 11.2 Information pioneered product pipeline

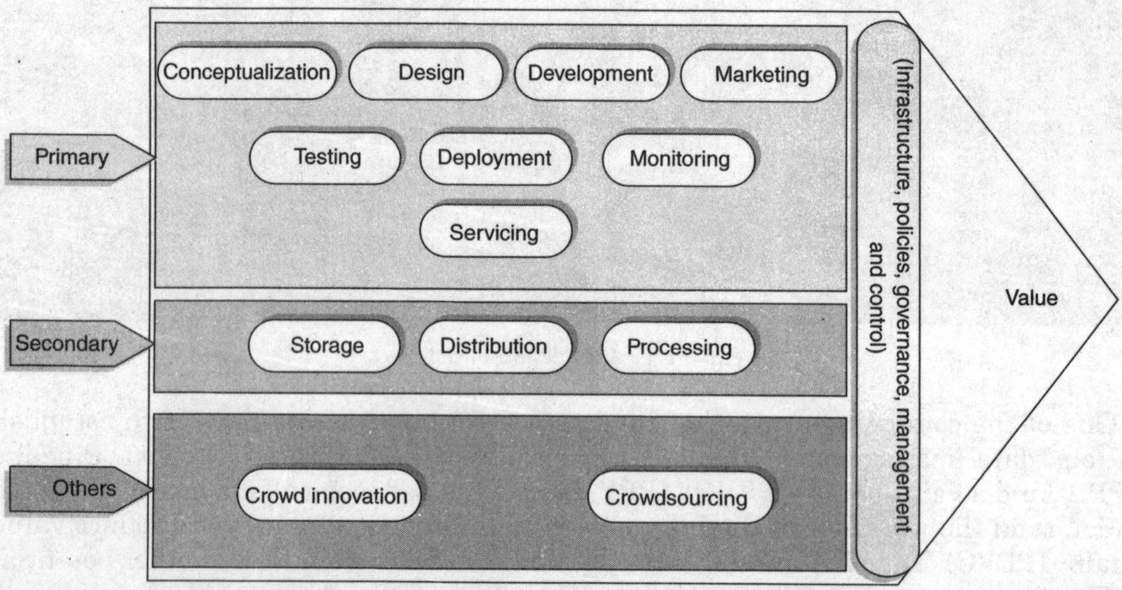

Fig. 11.3 Information pioneered product value chain

organization in conceptualizing, designing, developing, marketing, testing, deploying, monitoring, and servicing the IPP. The secondary activities are required to support the primary activities in delivering the value to the stakeholders. These include storage, distribution, and processing. The set of others activities are not enterprise-wide applicable but could be utilized for specific contextual issues; for example, crowd innovation and crowdsourcing. Organization's infrastructure, policies, governance, management, and control mechanisms drive all the activities for successful execution and accomplishments.

11.1 BIG DATA STAKEHOLDERS

LO 2 *Explain the big data stakeholders*

> There exist five power zones each representing different stakeholder—Collector, Utilizer, Generator, Regulator, and Broker.

In the hyper-connected society, the concept of power, which is more related to the dynamics of businesses, has been changing by the just mere inclusion of the networked systems. One might face a huge challenge in retaining one's own agency, i.e., knowledge and ability to act to generate potential monetization and business opportunities. The power of big data is shared among its stakeholders. Planning the appropriate level of big data, stakeholder engagement enhances the competitiveness of the industry. Normally, there exist five power zones, each representing different stakeholder—Collector, Utilizer, Generator, Regulator, and Broker, see Fig. 11.4.

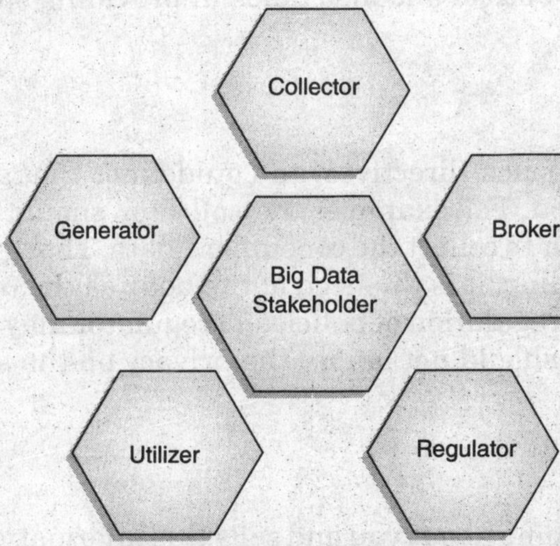

Fig. 11.4 Big data stakeholders

Collector

It determines '*what data needs to be collected*' and '*what data sources are needed to collect the data*'. It is also responsible for creating, using, and executing relevant policies to collect the data from the data sources. These data could be structured, semi-structured, or unstructured. The collector is also responsible for determining the lifetime of the data; for example, how long to store the data. The collector may or may not have a stake or any specific purpose for the collected data.

Utilizer

It is responsible for giving meaning and purpose to the collected data so that it can be used for a specific purpose. Utilizer can redefine the data set or mix it with the existing or other relevant data sets to achieve the competitive advantage. An insurance company might collaborate with a hospital for the patient data. In this way, the company can redesign or offer specific insurance schemes to the patients.

Generator

A generator is any actor that contributes to the generation of the data. This data could be generated by keeping informed the actor or otherwise. An actor knowingly or unknowingly participates in the contribution of the data. For example, Big Bazaar is a major retail store in India, which offers multiple brand products to its customers. It has several outlets across India in various cities. The customer gets very good offerings in the products with competitive pricing as well. Big Bazaar collects the customer data through customers' buying card. This card stores the transaction details of each customer who opts for the card. This huge set of data helps Big Bazaar to plan their inventory at various outlets and also helps in providing special discounts to the customers.

Regulator

It is responsible to set the rules, directives, and guidelines that govern the data policy across the data jurisdiction. For example, the collector should not violate the rules established by the regulator to collect the consumers' data. Though the regulator's work is challenging and demanding, it is the need of the hour as the technology is changing so fast as compared to the regulation of policies. A regulator may impart privacy policy on the data set but it also should not ignore the privacy on the aggregated set of data sets.

Broker

The one who knows everything about you and sells this information to the one who pays more to it is referred to as *broker*. The organization has to look at the procedures and processes to interact and involve the brokers for supplying the relevant information.

11.2 BIG DATA INDUSTRY

LO 3 *Comprehend the big data industry*

The perspective of looking at big data as a 'big data industry' helps organizations and businesses to identify any systemic risks in current big data practices. It enables one to look at its big data as a part of a system that includes other stakeholders of big data, processes, and norms to work with the data. In Fig. 11.5, the firm that is dealing with the big data

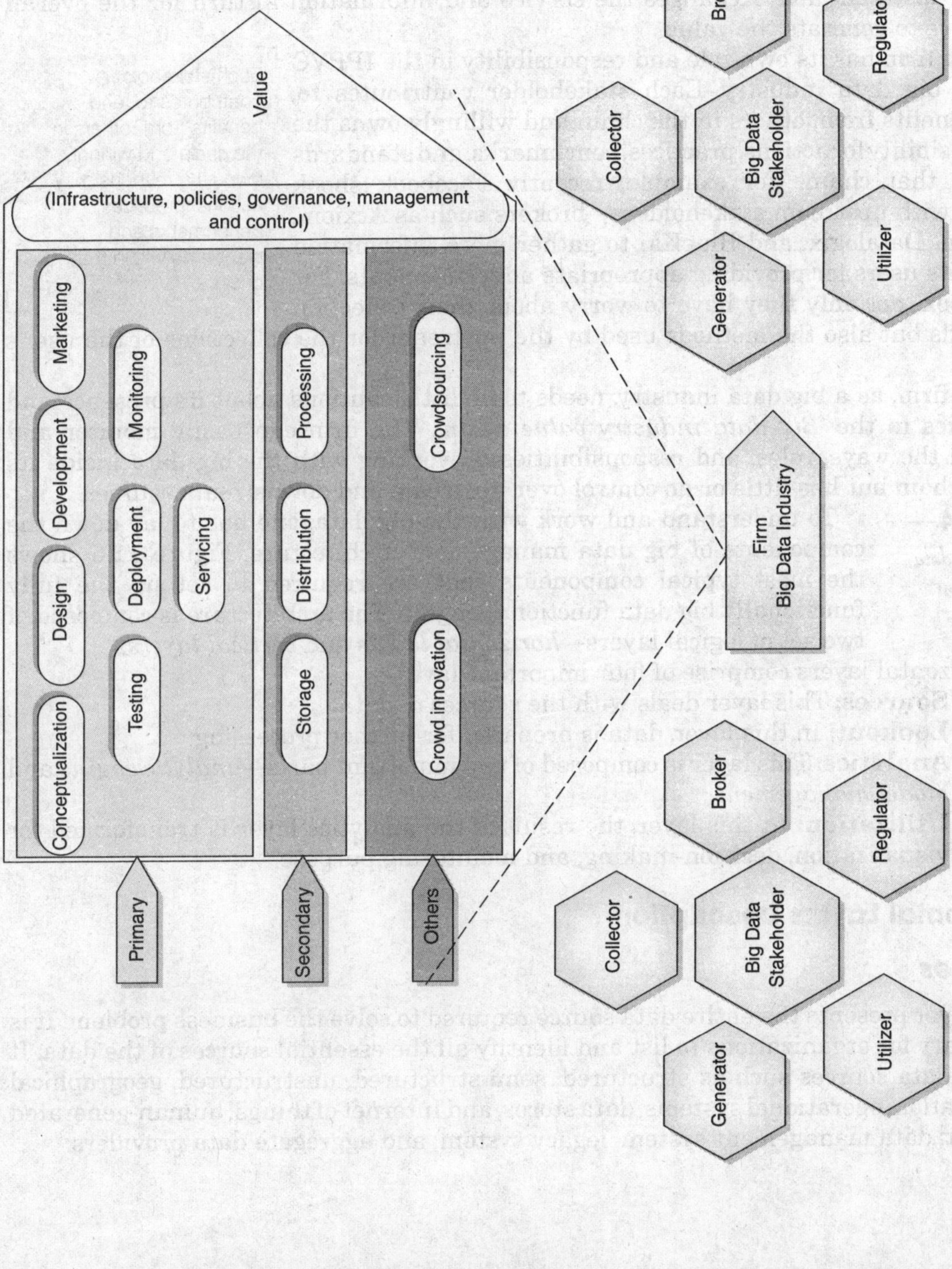

Fig. 11.5 Big data industry value chain

can be any stakeholder amongst the big data stakeholders. In the downstream, the firm, as a big data industry, connects with the bidirectional flow of services and information with the other stakeholders. Similarly, it connects the other stakeholders in the upstream and exchanges the service and information in turn for the overall objective to generate the value.

Each firm has its own role and responsibility in the IPPVC of the big data industry. Each stakeholder contributes to, and benefits from, others in the chain and willingly owns the responsibility for actions, practices, benchmarks, and standards within that chain. For example, recently Facebook shook hands with upstream stakeholders—brokers such as Acxiom, Epsilon, Datalogix, and BlueKai to gather more information about its users for providing appropriate advertisements. For Facebook, not only they have to worry about their collection methods but also the methods used by the upstream for the collections of the user's data.

> Each stakeholder contributes to, and benefits from, others in the chain and willingly owns the responsibility for actions, practices, benchmarks and standards within that chain.

The firm, as a big data industry, needs to be little cautious about its presence and activities in the '*Big data industry value chain*'. The firm can easily monitor and control the ways, roles, and responsibilities of working with the big data inside its value chain but has little or no control over upstream and downstream sources.

LO 4
Define big data management architecture

To understand and work with the big data, one has to lay down the components of big data management architecture. Figure 11.6 shows the most typical components that are required to set up the fully functionally big data functional engine. The architecture is composed of two set of logical layers—*horizontal layers* and *vertical layers*.

Horizontal layers comprise of four important layers:

1. **Sources:** This layer deals with the sources of data.
2. **Lookout:** In this layer, data is prepared for further processing.
3. **Analytics:** This layer is composed of two important parts—*analytic engine* and *model management*.
4. **Utilization:** In this layer, the result of the analytics layer is transformed for visualization, decision-making, and monitoring purpose.

Horizontal Layers Description

Sources

This layer presents the entire data source required to solve the business problem. It is necessary for organizations to list and identify all the essential sources of the data. It covers data sources such as structured, semi-structured, unstructured, geographical information, operational systems, data stores, and Internet of things; human-generated content; data management system, legacy system, and aggregate data providers.

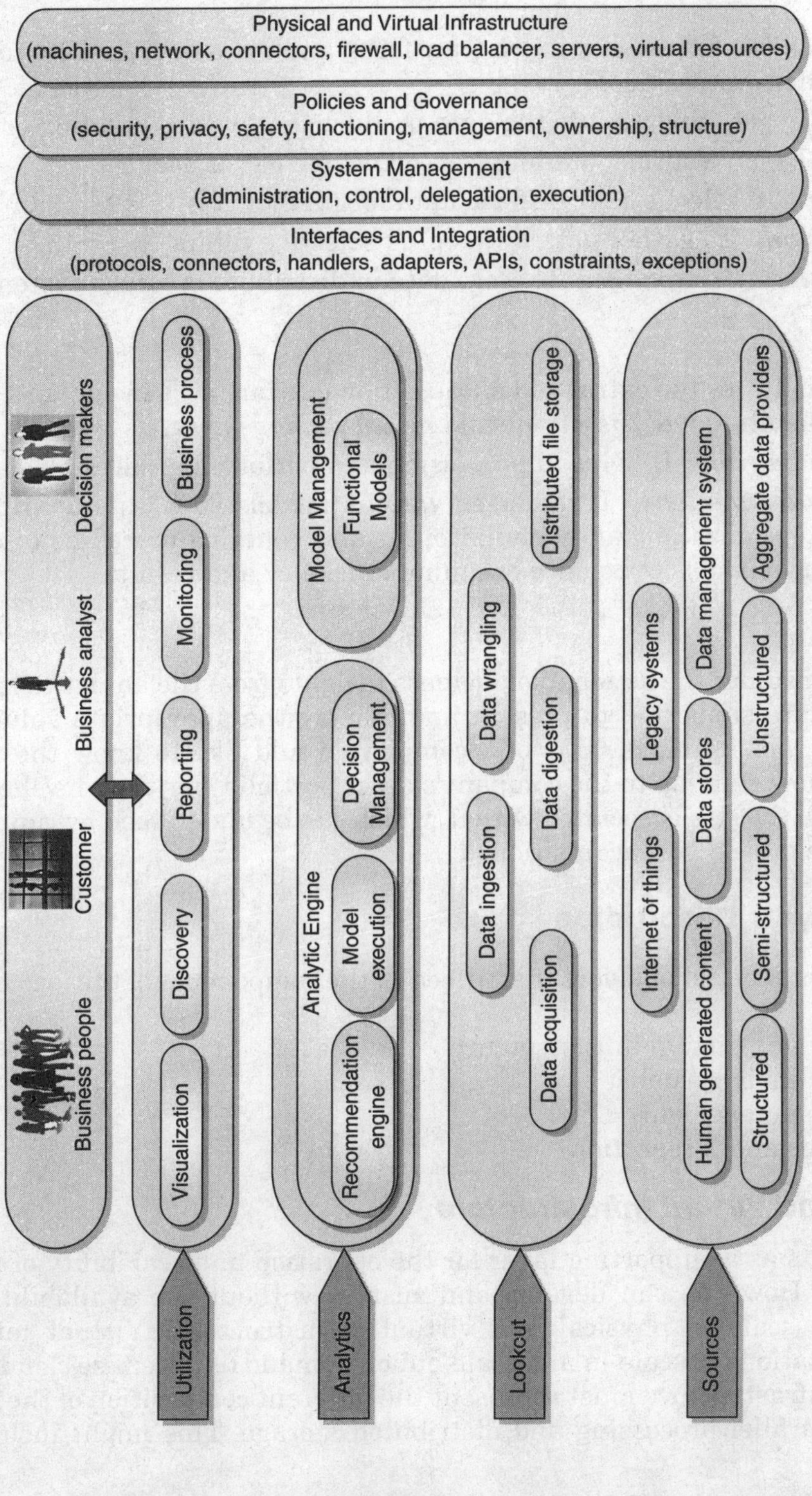

Fig. 11.6 Big Data Management Architecture

Lookout

This layer facilitates to load, convert, transform, and store the raw data to meaningful data for further processing.

- ***Ingest*** To get the data into the data product that we are building or using
- ***Digest*** To convert the data into the correct format of usage
- ***Wrangle*** To select and transform data for further analysis
- ***Acquisition*** To gather data by keeping selective filters
- ***Distributed file storage*** To store data in distributed storage system like HDFS

Analytics

This layer facilitates the extraction of the actionable business insights. It is composed of two components—*analysis engine* and *model management*.

- ***Analysis engine*** It helps in processing and performing the analysis.
- ***Model management*** It manages various models such as statistical, machine learning, optimization, and simulation. It also contains processes to manage and control such models to achieve optimum efficiency and results.

Utilization

This layer consumes the actionable business insights from the analytics layer. Various applications are supported to present and display the appropriate value to various stakeholders. For example, CEO of a company would like to know the relevance of acquiring a new start-up to the company's asset portfolio. For that, he/she might have to understand the risk associated with it, which can be understood by running the risk model for the prospective acquisition.

Vertical Layers Description

This represents the set of layers that affect all the components of the logical horizontal layers.

1. Physical and virtual infrastructure
2. Policies and governance
3. System management
4. Interfaces and integration

Physical and Virtual Infrastructure

This layer acts as a supporting layer for the operation and scalability of the big data architecture. How one can develop and sustain without the availability of robust, reliable, and scalable physical and virtual infrastructure? Virtual infrastructure helps organizations to scale-in and scale-out on demand (on-premise cloud/off-premise cloud). The infrastructure must represent the different composition of the components to support parallel processing and distributed storage. This might include efficient management and usage of machines, network, connectors, firewall, load balancer, servers, and virtual resources. This layer should also support redundancy to provide timely availability of the resources. Your company can augment internal IT growth by leveraging the benefits of external cloud infrastructure.

Policies and Governance

It refers to the set of rules, guidelines, and decisions to govern, control, manage, own, and disseminate processes, data, and information. Every company must elaborate the policies to protect sensitive and confidential data. The data that come from different sources; for example, Facebook data, that might contain sensitive information about the identification of the user, must be masked before you store, move, and process it without revealing such details. You must also adhere to the compliance and privacy policy of the data. For example, in health industry where big data applications are used to maintain patient's demographics related to patient's needs, training regimes, etc., details should be made available to only those who have the authority to access such information, without compromising on the privacy of the patients. Various policies, rules, and guidelines must be developed for security, privacy, safety, functioning, management, ownership and structure of data, processes, and organization.

System Management

It deals with the management of various systems that pan across completely big data ecosystem for its effective functioning. Some of the key measures that organization needs to manage are as follows:

- logs coming from machines, applications, and people interaction to different systems and devices
- monitoring, tracking, and notifying resources
- key performance indices
- reporting and analytic solution
- development of models followed by testing, executing, deploying, and operationalizing it enterprise wide
- Service Level Agreements (SLAs) and Quality of Services (QoS)
- storage, scalability, capacity, and performance
- processes, systems, recovery, and remedies; management of clusters, virtual machines, and networks; management of various policies

Interfaces and Integration

One needs data from various sources and to do so various open application-programming interfaces are required. These APIs help to pull the data for further processing. For example, a social media company would be interested in understanding the sentiments of people on Twitter; and for that, it needs the 'tweets' for certain period. To fetch the 'tweets', it needs to use Twitter API, which facilitates the company to pull all the relevant data, may be based on some hashtags. This layer facilitates other layers for the integration of data by providing relevant adapters, accelerators, connectors, APIs, and wrappers.

> "*Anyone can hold the helm when the sea is calm.*"
>
> —Publilius Syrus

11.3 BIG DATA BUSINESS LEADERSHIP MODEL

LO 5 *Examine big data business leadership model*

The businesses are demanding more value out of their businesses to attain a competitive edge. Most of them do not know from where to start. Only a few of them have begun their journey to achieve the big data leadership. Nonetheless, the recent surge in big data ecosystem and landscape has left the businesses wondering '*how to develop the insights, best practices, and data leadership*'. Some industries are acquiring technical skills set at their workplace to harness big data analytic projects. While, some other sectors are focusing on building technological and infrastructure capability by including a portfolio of big data ecosystems—Hadoop, Spark, MapReduce, YARN, Pig, HIVE, NBASE, Cassandra, R, Python, etc.

A select few industries have top leadership agenda '*to embrace analytic insights into their whole business ecosystem by integrating big data ecosystem and landscape to generate further businesses and monetization opportunities*'. The big data analytics business leadership model is shown in Fig. 11.7. The model is not prescriptive in nature and rather be treated as a maturity framework which can be customized and tailored as per the need of the industry.

Typically, an organization can find itself to be in one amongst the following 7 phases of the big data business leadership model:

1. Nascent
2. Pre-adoption
3. Early-adoption
4. Democratization
5. Operationalization
6. Transformation
7. Leadership

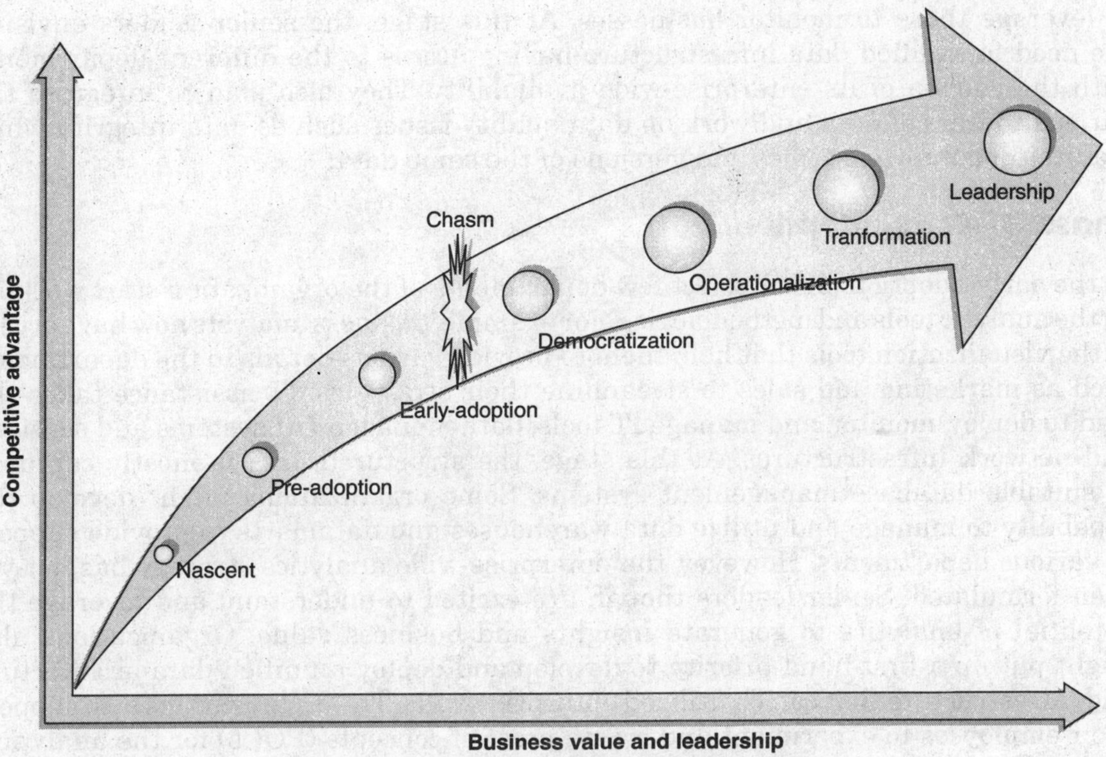

Fig. 11.7 Big Data Business Leadership Model

Phase 1—Nascent

In the nascent phase, organizations are not at all data-driven. The leaders do not see analytic or big data as an asset to the organization but they seem to be interested in understanding the value system and benefits. Only a few departments of the organization have access to some basic softwares to manage their business processes. For example, account department uses spreadsheets to manage the payroll service. There is no enterprise-wide solution to drive business processes or decisions. Only handful of employees regard analytics and big data as an opportunity to achieve competitiveness. Typically, most of the departments do not have direct access to the organization's data, and, thus, it takes time for each department to make appropriate decisions.

Phase 2—Pre-adoption

In the pre-adoption phase, an organization witnesses the employees' interest in analytics related topics. Some departments have access to the necessary tools and infrastructure to expedite processes, manage tasks, and monitor the progress. Basic business intelligence and reporting infrastructure are available for the decision makers to leverage those to monitor businesses. At this stage, the senior leaders envision the need for unified data infrastructure having access to the different departments with the agenda of its enterprise-wide availability. They also plan to integrate the various sources of data and work on data quality issues such as data integrity while maintaining multiple copies and versions of the same data.

Phase 3—Early-adoption

In the early-adoption phase, select few departments of the organization start working on the analytic tools and methodologies. For example, business analysts now have access to the visualization tools that help them to provide various details to the departments such as marketing and sales to streamline their strategies. IT assistance takes the lead to deploy, monitor, and manage IT tools, data management systems and services, and network infrastructures. At this stage, the structured data is mostly captured in suitable database management systems. Some organizations might develop the capability to manage and utilize data warehouses and datamarts to provide support to various departments. However, the enterprise-wide analytics strategy has not yet been formulated. Senior leaders though are excited to understand and leverage the potential of analytics to generate insights and business value. Organizations also might put up a first-hand priority to develop and deploy a unified data architecture and infrastructure that can be utilized enterprise-wide. The organizations also support their employees to experiment and create proof-of-concepts (POCs) for the analytics-driven projects.

Phase 4—Democratization

In the phase of democratization, organization develops the data-driven ecosystem and makes it available to all the stakeholders to make the best out of it. The departments no longer work in silos, and they have access to the big data and analytics technologies. The employees and staff are also trained in various skills set related to data science, data visualization, data management, data strategies, data governance, analytics projects management, and data-driven decision making. Leaders understand the know-how of the analytics projects and prepare their team to work accordingly. Organizations continuously harness data management architecture, information pioneered product pipeline and a value chain to develop 'collaborator- driven' decision making. They have access to internal and external, structured and unstructured data coming from omnichannels. The key and core processes are automated to get deep insights. The employees and staff get the benefits as they all can focus on more valuable services and offerings. At this stage, organization also observes a tip pining point, chasm, which helps it to operationalize the analytics culture, processes, and models across the organization and its value chain; transform its core business and identify new business models, markets and segments; and attain the big data leadership.

Phase 5—Operationalization

In the operationalization phase, organization operationalises the [big data and] analytics culture, processes, and models across the organization and its value chain. All its leaders, employees, staff, and key stakeholders all become adept at using analytics to augment their decision-making and handling of different workflows and tasks. At this stage, organization also envisions the new product, service, and solutions to contribute to the business portfolio as new source of revenues. For example, cross-selling the insights of the data gathered to the third party. The outcome of the analytical processes, models, and strategies are no longer available to only senior leaders but the front line managers and other stakeholders get the benefits in producing improved decision making. One can also perform real-time analytics and execute predictive and prescriptive models appropriately. For example, a check-out counter manager gets a recommendation to offer discounts dynamically to customer's basket billing based on weather condition, the day of the week, customer basket, product portfolio, customer segmentation, product reviews, customer reviews, etc., and, thus, expose decision making at the frontline. The power of big data is shared among its stakeholders. Senior leaders plan to engage big data stakeholder to improve the competitiveness of the industry. The firm that is dealing with the big data can be any stakeholder amongst one of the big data stakeholders. At the downstream, this firm, as big data industry, connects with the bidirectional flow of services and information with the other stakeholders. Similarly, it connects the other stakeholders in the upstream and exchanges the service and information in turn for the overall objective to generate the value. The organization clearly lays down the components of big data management architecture.

Phase 6—Transformation

In the transformation phase, organization excels in the analytical and data-driven decision making. Every facet of the organization is transformed—the organization's culture, workforce, governance, policies, ecosystems, and most importantly underlying value chain and value system. The organization is ready to change its core business; for example, by transforming product focus *per se* to 'BaaS' (business-as-a-service). A house construction industry instead of providing houses to people might sell '*happy living*' or a company which exposes its complete value chain to the third party so gets value-added service, new market, and solutions. At this stage, the organization enters a new market, segments, and new businesses.

Phase 7—Leadership

In the leadership phase, the organization sets the benchmark by establishing enterprise-wide big data architecture, portfolios, and culture. Each organization is different as it is affected by many factors in the context such as circumstances, culture, market, organization size, economic conditions, purpose, capabilities, and vast array of other elements. Thus, one size fits all does not make any sense and organization needs to develop core strategies in align with its value system. The best practices are transformed and benchmarks are developed in align with the value system.

LO 6 *Perform big data business leadership report-cum-analysis*

The following table provides assessment report-cum-analysis to get quick insight for attaining big data business leadership.

Table 11.1 Big data business leadership report-cum-analysis

What is your business mission?
What are your business strategies to achieve business mission?
How big data business enables your business strategy?
Which big data business scenarios are prevalent?
How can you use big data ecosystem to execute your business scenario?
What business context do you want to address?

(Contd.)

Which type of IPPP is involved in the delivering the value?
What is your information pioneered product value chain?
What type and dimensions of data will be stored and analysed?
Do you prefer to use proprietary components for achieving goals or utilize open source offerings?
Is the potential big data ecosystem flexible enough for all your use cases?
Do you want to integrate any existing tools with big data ecosystem? If yes, what are those and can those be integrated with it? What is the effort required?
Is there any requirement of management tools?

(*Contd.*)

Does the potential big data management architecture allow to change your core business models?
Which stakeholder's inclusion is needed in the value chain?
Does the potential big data ecosystems and unified architecture consider your future needs?

SUMMARY

- Attaining a big data business leadership is not easy and is full of challenges.
- One of the competing strategies for a successful big data company is to establish its big data management architecture, information pioneered product pipeline (IPPP) and a value chain (IPPVC).
- The big data business needs to embrace fully its value chain and engage the stakeholders appropriately to develop various strategies to unleash the hidden insights.
- In the hyper-connected society, the concept of power, which is more related to the dynamics of businesses, has been changing by the just mere inclusion of the networked systems.
- The perspective of looking big data as a 'big data industry' helps organizations and businesses to identify any systemic risks in current big data practices.
- To understand and work with the big data, one has to lay down the components of big data management architecture.
- The big data analytics business model enables industry to develop its own big data journey—pathway; assess its status-quo; measure competency and competitiveness; and develop and execute strategies to unleash the big data leadership.
- The big data business leadership has 7 phases—*Nascent, Pre-adoption, Early-adoption, Democratization, Operationalization, Transformation. and Leadership*.

EXERCISE

Review Questions

1. Identify the big data management architecture, information pioneered product pipeline, and a value chain of the industries for the following sectors:
   - Airline
   - Hospitality
   - Banking
   - Education
   - Manufacturing

   Tip: Use the artefacts of big data solutions to identify the details for the different sectors. Refer to Figs 11.2, 11.3, and 11.6.
2. Explain the involvement of big data stakeholders in the value chain of the industries for the following sectors:
   - Airline
   - Hospitality
   - Banking
   - Education
   - Manufacturing

   Tip: Use the artefacts of big data solutions to identify the details for the different sectors. Refer to Figs 11.4 and 11.5.
3. Explain the importance of '*Big data business leadership model*'. Why it is necessary for an industry to leverage the model?

   Tip: The '*Big data business leadership model*' is the maturity model that will enable industry to develop its own big data journey—pathway; assess its status-quo; measure competency and competitiveness; and develop and execute strategies, to unleash the big data leadership.
4. Justify the statement: '*In the hyper-connected society, the concept of power, which is more related to the dynamics of businesses, has been changing by the just mere inclusion of the networked systems*'.

   Tip: One might face a huge challenge in retaining one's own agency, i.e., knowledge and ability to act to generate potential monetization and business opportunities. The power of big data is shared among its stakeholders. Planning the appropriate level of big data stakeholder engagement enhances the competitiveness of the industry. Normally, there exist five power zones each representing different stakeholder—Collector, Utilizer, Generator, Regulator, and Broker.
5. You can select any industry for the following sector:
   - Airline
   - Hospitality
   - Banking

- Education
- Manufacturing

Assess the status-quo of the industries based on the '*big data business leadership model*'.

Tip: Typically, an organization can find itself to be in one amongst the 7 phases of the big data business leadership model.

1. Nascent
2. Pre-adoption
3. Early-adoption
4. Democratization
5. Operationalization
6. Transformation
7. Leadership

Refer to Fig. 11.7.

Big Data Glossary

World Wide Web (WWW)	WWW during 1993, hosted and served around 50 web pages. Today, it is very difficult to measure the full coverage of its density. Roughly, the size of the indexed WWW is around 45 billion pages as of 24th April 2017 (Source: http://www.worldwidewebsize.com/). It is the single largest and most widely used source of information, with nearly 3.2 billion users (Wikipedia, 2015).
Big data volume	It represents the scale of the data. According to big data infographic 2015, by Ben Walker at Vouchercloud, it is estimated that 2.5 Quintillion bytes are created every day. He also suggests that 'around 216,000 Instagram posts are posted every minute, 204,000,000 emails are sent in a minute, around 12 hours of footage is uploaded to YouTube and 277,000 tweets are posted on Twitter per minute.' The data size is huge.
Big data variety	Big data can be of any type. It can be structured data, unstructured data, and semi-unstructured data. Structured data are specified by rules or predefined format, can be like the relational data stored in the relational database. Unstructured data does not have a data model or any defined proper format. It includes books, journals, documents, metadata, health records, audio, video, analog data, images, files, and unstructured text such as the body of an e-mail message, web page, or word-processor document. Semi-structured data model is the model behind the Web. Mostly, they are arranged in the tree format.
Big data velocity	In massive and critical applications, sometimes, even a 1-minute delay is dangerous. Velocity refers to the speed of the data. IBM suggests that 'For time-sensitive processes, like catching fraud, big data must be used as it streams into your enterprise to maximize its value.'

Big data veracity	Data normally does not come clean. Typically, the biases, noise, and abnormality associated with it refer to veracity. One of the biggest challenges for the big data team is to store, mine clean, and process data for further analysis.
Big data valence	In big data, valence represents the interconnectedness of the data. The complexity of the analysis increases with more connections. In the real world, this works in a very handy fashion. More you establish relationships and connections among the set of data, more complex and meaningful is the relationship model.
Big data value	The real benefit of the mashup of five Vs comes to realization only if the true value is the outcome. Are you able to decide on the development of new product line, economized measure, or an opportunity for acquisition based on the actionable insights from your data?
Big data collector	It determines '*what data needs to be collected*' and '*what data sources are needed to collect the data*'. It is also responsible for creating, using, and executing relevant policies to collect the data from the data sources. The collector is also responsible for determining the lifetime of the data; for example, how long to store the data. The collector may or may not have a stake or any specific purpose for the collected data.
Big data utilizer	It is responsible for giving meaning and purpose to the collected data so that it can be used for a specific purpose. Utilizer can redefine the data set or mix it with the existing or other relevant data sets to achieve the competitive advantage.
Big data generator	A generator is any actor that contributes to the generation of the data. This data could be generated by keeping informed the actor or otherwise. An actor, knowingly or unknowingly, participates in the contribution of the data.
Big data regulator	It is responsible to set the rules, directives, and guidelines that govern the data policy across the data jurisdiction. For example, the collector should not violate the rules established by the regulator to collect the consumers' data. Though the regulator's work is challenging and demanding, it is the need of the hour as the technology is changing so fast as compared to the regulation policies. A regulator may impart privacy policy on the data set but it also should not ignore the privacy on the aggregated set of data sets.
Big data broker	The one who knows everything about you and sells this information to the one who pays more to it is referred to as *broker*.

Big data industry	Big data industry, as a perspective for the organization, enables one to look at its big data as a part of a system that includes other stakeholders of big data, processes, and norms to work with the data. The IPPVC, as a big data industry, can be analysed, both, by the downstream distribution and use of big data as well as by the upstream sourcing
Big data ethical framework	This framework will help you and your organization to unfold ethical inquires, decision points, and ethical actions in align with the core value system to develop and manage products and services utilizing big data technologies. The framework provides you a set of tools to get very specific about your values in align with your specific context of interest. It provides you a starting step, a platform to perform ethical inquiries, and take tactical actions.
Big data audit	One of the key aspects of evaluating organization's current practices of dealing with the data is to perform routine data practices audits. A specialized team having the understanding about organization's values system, data handling practices, benchmarks, and standards must work with all the stakeholders of the business. The team, further, must recommend the findings of their audit to the leadership on a routine basis so as to consider the execution of any suitable strategy in case of need.
Ethical inquiry	Ethical inquiry helps organizations to strengthen their philosophical thinking and inquiry. This inquiry, in turn, breaks the barriers for growth and success, thereby creating a sustainable and ethical culture. Ethical inquiry, in relation to big data, will help the organization to evolve big data technology and transform it into a powerful, effective, and robust set of tools that can help us live better—ethically and sustainably.
Information Pioneered Product (IPP)	Any product that combines the capability of incorporating data and intelligent processes to generate meaningful and valued actionable decisions and associated information is called *IPP*. It is self-adapting, derives its value from the information which in turn generates more associated information and actionable decisions that led to refuel its engine or used to generate new information pioneered product.
Information Pioneered Product Pipeline (IPPP)	It reflects the pedagogical and mental model to understand the workflow of the information in IPP. The pipeline can be combined with other potential IPPPs or can work in isolation to deliver the meaningful and actionable decisions. In a typical analytical drive situation, decisions and other relevant information that has emerged out of the whole process is finally fed into the IPPP.

Information Pioneered Product Value Chain (IPPVC)	The IPPVC recognizes the value activities—primary, secondary, and others required in the use of information to produce the actionable and valuable insights. The IPPVC set of primary activities refers to those activities that help an organization in conceptualizing, designing, developing, marketing, testing, deploying, monitoring, and servicing the IPP. The secondary activities are required to support the primary activities in delivering the value to the stakeholders. These include storage, distribution, and processing. The set of others activities are not enterprise-wide applicable but could be utilized for specific contextual issues; for example, crowd innovation and crowdsourcing.
Fault tolerance	Failure of a component should not result into failure of a system. Thus, system can go to a degradable performance (gracefully) stage but should not go off. Once the component recovers, it should be able to rejoin the system to achieve the same level of performance before the failure.
Recoverability	No system is ideal, but that does not mean a failure of a component or a system result into a loss of data. Distributed system provides policy to handle such event and recover data in case of any failure.
Consistency	The components perform multiple jobs towards the final goal of the workflow. Failure of one job should not affect the overall goal and performance of the workflow.
Transparency	It deals with one unified system concept instead of multiple components.
Hadoop node	A node is a commodity computer machine that can process and store data.
Hadoop cluster	A cluster in the Hadoop environment is a collection of nodes that provides the facility of computation and storage of data. Hadoop cluster typically comprises of Master node and Slave nodes, where Master node controls the storage and processing of the data while each slave node processes the data. Processing is done near the data such that it results into low I/O costs.
Workflow	A workflow is the collection of sequence of actions to be executed for the overall computation. A workflow typically comprises of multiple jobs in a cluster. Jobs are further broken into multiple tasks where each cluster node performs the task on a single block of assigned data.
Ambari	It comprises of tools to administer Hadoop. It provides services to install, monitor, and maintain Hadoop cluster. Service to add and remove slave nodes are also included in the tool set.

Avro	It is a framework that supports efficient serialization to transform data into a compact binary format that could be transmitted or exchanged over the network.
Flume	It is a data flow service, which provides aggregation, collection, and movement of large volumes of log data into Hadoop.
Hue	It is an interface that facilitates administration of Hadoop with handy GUI tools for browsing files, issuing Hive and Pig queries, and developing Oozie workflows.
Mahout	It is a library that provides collection of machine learning statistical algorithms. These algorithms were implemented in MapReduce and can run natively on Hadoop.
Oozie	It is a workflow management tool to schedule and chain together Hadoop applications.
Pig	It is a platform to analyse very large data sets that run on HDFS. It abstracts MapReduce programs by supporting an infrastructure layer consisting of a compiler to generate sequences of MapReduce equivalent programs.
Sqoop	It is a tool to collect, aggregate, and move large amounts of data between relational databases and HDFS.
Zookeeper	It is a simple interface to the centralized coordination of services (such as naming, configuration, and synchronization) used by distributed applications.
Hadoop pseudo–distributed mode (single node)	A Hadoop distribution deployment where all the Hadoop services, including the master and slave node services, run on a single machine is referred to as *pseudo-distributed node*. This kind of environment is best to quickly experiment and prototype the jobs, tasks, and workflows. Here, one need not worry about the cluster-centric services and management.
Hadoop fully-distributed mode (a cluster of nodes)	A cluster-node Hadoop distribution deployment is referred to as running, both, the Hadoop master and slave services on a cluster of computers. This mode is more suitable for production and development clusters.
Hadoop master node	It is the entry point to access the cluster. It runs coordinating services to manage, control, access, and drive the cluster. Without *master*, distributed storage and computation will not happen.

Hadoop worker node	The cluster is built of worker nodes. Nodes of this type accept variety of tasks from the '*master*'—either to store or retrieve data or to execute any particular application. A distributed computation is achieved by parallelizing the computation of the tasks across worker nodes. Worker nodes implement, both, the HDFS and YARN worker services.
YARN Resource Manager (master)	It is responsible to allocate and monitor resources (e.g., physical assets such as memory and processor cores) for the cluster and make those available to applications.
YARN Application Master (master)	It is responsible to control and monitor a particular application being run on the cluster as scheduled by the Resource Manager.
YARN Node Manager (worker)	It is responsible to manage, control, and execute various processing tasks on the nodes in a cluster. Not only this, it also monitors the health and status of each tasks. Each task requires a resource for its execution; thus, client must request set of resources from the *Resource Manager*, which assigns an application-specific *Application Master* for the duration of the job.
Data stock	It specifies the way in which data is arranged, controlled, accessed, and managed by the software system and technologies.
Navigational databases	Navigational databases are based on the design and model of a network of interrelated things proposed by Charles Bachman. The Bachman design, typically, provides the starting-point for navigating the data that is connected to the network or graph like fashion.
Relational databases	Edgar Codd, the researcher of IBM's San Jose, California, presented series of papers on the relational model of the data. The model proposes an entirely different approach to structure the data. He proved that while adhering to the implementation details of the navigational databases, the relational model can support intuitive declarative language to be working on the data.
Object-oriented databases	An object-oriented database represents the information in the form of objects. The term 'object' came from the object-oriented paradigm. The object contains feature and behaviour in an encapsulated way. The object database technology provides an easy way to deal with complex data and perform operations by leveraging the relationships among different objects by the pointers that are the links to establish relationships.

Multi-dimensional databases	Multidimensional database provides a multidimensional view of the data. The multidimensional model supports the slice and dice view of the data. Data is arranged in the form of cubes and can be vertically and horizontally cut across layers or dimensions and used for various analysis. Each cell of the multidimensional cube contains the aggregated results of the elements along each of its dimensions.
NoSQL databases	New databases came into existence with the new millennium and the explosion of Web content. The underlying philosophy of NoSQL is of '*task-oriented*' database management systems. Thus, depending upon the task at hand, NoSQL provides an appropriate solution to approach the task. Though relational database seems to be a powerful tool to deal with the data with the relations, it fails to embrace some particular kinds of relations such as key-value pairs, or graphs and some usage patterns like extremely large-scale storage. NoSQL initially subscribed to the notion 'Just Say No to SQL', but nowadays we treat it as 'Not Only SQL'.
Key-value store	It represents the simplest family of the NoSQL database systems. The simplicity lies in the fact that any data may be retained as a key-value pair without worrying of the schema. In a key-value store, key and values are aligned with an inherently schema less data model where a row forms a key and value. A key is an identifier and value can take any type from an integer to a large data string.
Column family store	This kind of database includes the sparsely populated table structure as column families.
Document store	It represents one of the popular and well-known type of NoSQL, which stores the content such as Web content in the document category. It has a comprehensive set of offering that relies on a set of similarly encoded and formatted documents to improve efficiencies. Document represents a semi-structured unit of information.
Graph databases	Graph structure represents the information in the form of a collection of entities and their relationships. It is a robust data structure and apt for storing complex structures such as web pages links. Graph databases leverage the concept of graph structures to store data and perform operations on it.

Transaction	A transaction refers to a unit of work, any change in the status of database, which is achieved within the database independent of other transactions. Two main purposes related to the database transactions are as follows: • Database consistency needs to be intact in case of any failure of the transactions • Isolation needs to be achieved during concurrent transaction to access the database
ACID	For a database transaction to be ACID compliant, it must adhere to • *Atomicity*: Every transaction must adhere to its completeness. The transaction must completely succeed or fail. Partial completion is not allowed. • *Consistency*: The status of the database at no point be invalid; thus, during transaction, the database progresses from valid state to another state. • *Isolation*: The database [client] transaction must execute in isolation to other [client] transaction. • *Durability*: The result of the transaction must persist and should be available as per the valid status of the transaction.
CAP	The CAP theorem proposed by Brewer suggests that the system has to choose any two properties among consistency, availability, and partition tolerance. • *Consistency*: It refers to the synchronization between different copies of the same piece of data. Here, it reflects that every read of the data receives the most recent write or an error. • *Availability*: It means the data is available all the time. It means that every request receives a non-error response with no guarantee of the recent write on the data. • *Partition Tolerance*: It means the system operates despite any message being dropped by the network between the nodes.
BASE	BASE (Basically Available, Soft state, Eventually consistent) signifies the following: • *Basically Available*: It guarantees the availability of the systems for querying for all the users. • *Soft state*: It promises a change in the value that is stored in the system. • *Eventually consistent*: It represents the gradual progress of the system's state across all the nodes.

Enterprise Data Warehouse (EDW)	The EDW solutions that are based on multidimensional structure provide processing and analysis at scale.
HQL	Hive Query Language (HQL) looks similar to the other traditional database SQL language, and, thus, who so ever has earlier worked with the SQL has an edge working with HiveQL. However, there exist several fundamental differences between traditional SQL and HiveQL regarding functioning and overall service. Hive is based on Hadoop, which is intended for distributed storage and distributed processing targeting long sequential or batch scans.
Hive CLI	It is a command line interface that provides an interactive way to the user to deal with queries and administrative commands. The CLI comes handy when one would like to perform quick interactive query and command. Generally, few test queries need to be run before making it a production level suite, which is well handled by Hive. Hive's native installation has CLI to interact with Hive and run HiveQL statements.
Data lookout	It facilitates to load, convert, transform, and store the raw data to meaningful data for further processing. It supports • getting the data into the data product that we are building or using. • converting the data into the correct format of usage. • selecting and transforming data for further analysis. • gathering data by keeping selective filters. • storing data in the distributed storage system (like HDFS)
Data ingestion	Data ingestion brings data into data processing system. It includes a wide variety of tasks to be accomplished to prepare data for processing.
ETL	Extract-transform-load (ETL) is a process to extract data from operational systems, transform it to the compatible format, and load the data into the analytical systems.
Sqoop	Sqoop stands for *SQL for Hadoop*, and it is primarily the best tool for data import and export from/to relational systems. It is created by Cloudera and recognized as one of the prime Apache open-source projects. The Sqoop is designed for efficiently transferring data from relational systems such as MySQL or Oracle to Hadoop data store including HDFS, HBase, and Hive. It uses MapReduce to provide the functionality of data import and export.

Flume	It provides the functionality of placing a high volume of streaming data to Hadoop. It is best used for those business cases where a high volume of streaming data is needed for further analysis. The data is written '*as-is*' to the Hadoop, and no particular batch application is written to collect and store the data into Hadoop or any other Hadoop's data sink options such as Hive, HBase, etc.
Regression	Regression helps to model numerical relationship within data. The regression models help to predict the value of the unseen data based on the training data.
Receiver Operating Curve (ROC)	It refers to a systematic approach to unleash the classification threshold value by simulating the every positive and negative, '*true/false*', positive rate at every threshold, and visualize the trade-offs. The visualization plot refers to the ROC.

Bibliography

- Abadi, D. (2012). *Consistency tradeoffs in modern distributed database system design: Cap is only part of the story*. Computer, 45 (2), pp. 37–42.
- Abadi, Daniel J; Madden, Samuel. (2008). *Query execution in column-oriented database systems*. Massachusetts Institute of Technology, Cambridge, MA.
- Abbott, Dean. *Applied Predictive Analytics: Principles and Techniques for the Professional Data Analyst*. Wiley.
- Agrawal, D; Das, D; El Abbadi, A. (2011). *Big Data and Cloud Computing: Current State and Future Opportunities*. Proc. of EDBT.
- Aiden, E; Michel, J B. (2013). *Uncharted: Big Data as a Lens on Human Culture*. New York: Penguin.
- Amazon. (Apr, 2012). *Amazon dynamodb*. Retrieved Jul 27, 2017 from http://aws.amazon.com/dynamodb/.
- Andrejevic, M. (2014). *Big data, big questions: The big data divide*. International Journal of Communication 8(0), p. 17.
- Apache. (Apr, 2012). *Apache couchdb*. Retrieved Jul 25, 2017 from http://couchdb.apache.org/.
- *Apache Sqoop*. (2013). Retrieved Aug 2, 2017 from http://sqoop.apache.org/.
- Barlow, Mike. *Real-time Big Data Analytics: Emerging Architecture*. O'Reilly Media.
- Barocas, S; Nissenbaum, H. (2014). *Big data's end run around procedural privacy protections*. Communications of the ACM 57(11), pp. 31–33.
- Bassett, EH; O'Riordan, K. (2002). *Ethics of internet research: Contesting the human subjects research model*. Ethics and Information Technology 4(3), pp. 233–247.
- Batini, C; Lenzerini, M; Navathe, SB. (1986). *A comparative analysis of methodologies of database schema integration*. ACM Computing Surveys 18(4), pp. 323–364.
- BBVA Innovation Center. *Ebook: Data (Innovation Trends Series)*. BBVA Innovation Center.
- Beeger, B. (2013). *Internet Dergläserne Mensch*. Retrieved May 27, 2017 from http://www.faz.net/aktuell/wirtschaft/internet-der-glaeserne-mensch-12214568.html?printPagedArticle¼true.
- Bengfort, Benjamin; Kim, Jenny. *Data Analytics with Hadoop: An Introduction for Data Scientists*. O'Reilly Media.

- Bengfort, Benjamin; Kim, Jenny. *Data Analytics with Hadoop: An Introduction for Data Scientists*. O'Reilly Media.
- Berman, J J. (2013). *Introduction, in: Principles of Big Data Morgan Kaufmann*. Boston, pp. xix–xxvi.
- Bernstein, P A; Halevy A Y; Pottinger R A. (2000). *A vision for management of complex models*. SIGMOD Rec 29(4), pp. 55–63.
- Birman, Kenneth P; Freedman, Daniel A; Huang, Qi; Dowell, Patrick. (2012). *Overcoming CAP with consistent soft-state replication*. Computer, 45(2), pp. 50-58, 10.1109/MC.2011.387.
- Boyd, D; Crawford, K. (2012). *Critical questions for big data*. Information, Communication and Society 15(5), pp. 662–679.
- Calo, M R. (2013). *Digital Market Manipulation*. The George Washington Law Review, 82(4), pp. 995–1051.
- Capriolo, Edward; Wampler, Dean; Rutherglen, Jason. *Programming Hive*. O'Reilly.
- Capriolo et al. *Programming Hive*. O'Reilly.
- Chang, F; Dean, J; Ghemawat, S; Hsieh, W; Wallach, D; Burrows, M; Chandra, T; Fikes, A; Gruber, R. (2008). *Big table: A distributed storage system for structured data*. ACM Transaction of Computer Systems (TOCS), 26(2), p. 4.
- Chen, Liu; Ko, Junghyun; Yeo, Jeongmo. (2015). *Analysis of the Influence Factors of Data Loading Performance Using Apache Sqoop. KIPS Transactions on Software and Data Engineering*.
- Chen, Y; Alspaugh, S; Katz, R. (2012). *Interactive analytical processing in big data systems: a cross-industry study of MapReduce workloads*. Proc. VLDB Endow., 5, pp. 1802-1813.
- Crawford, K; Schultz, J. (2014). *Big data and due process: Toward a framework to redress predictive privacy harms*. Boston College Law Review 55(93).
- Davis, Kord; Patterson, Doug. (2012). *Ethics of Big Data*. O'Reilly Media.
- Dean, J; Ghemawat, S. (2008). *MapReduce: simplified data processing on large clusters*. Commun. ACM, 51, pp. 107–11.
- Dean, J; Ghemawat, S. (2008). *MapReduce: Simplified Data Processing on Large Clusters*. Communications of the ACM 51(1).
- Dittrich, J; Quiané-Ruiz, J A; Jindal, A; Kargin, Y; Setty, V; Schad, J. (2010). *Hadoop++: Making a Yellow Elephant Run Like a Cheetah*. PVLDB 3(1).
- Divakar, Mysore; Shrikant, Khupat; Jain, Shweta. *Big data architecture and patterns, Part 3: Understanding the architectural layers of a big data solution*. Retrieved April 26, 2017 from https://www.ibm.com/Learn/Big_data_and_analytics.
- Dove, ES; Townend, D; Meslin, E M; et al. (2016). *Ethics review for international data-intensive research*. Science 351(6280), pp. 1399–1400.
- Dwork, C. (2011). *A firm foundation for private data analysis*. Communications of the ACM 54(1), pp. 86–95.
- Fan, Kai. (2010). *Suvey on Nosql*. Programmer, 6, pp. 76–78.
- George, L. (2011). *Hbase: The Definitive Guide*. O'Reilly Media, Inc., Sebastopol, CA.

- George, Lars. *HBase: The Definitive Guide*. O'Reilly.
- Gray, Katie. (Nov 18, 2010). *Why We Love HBase*. StumbleUpon Official Blog. [accessed 25 Aug 2017]
- Hacigumus, H; Iyer, B; Mehrotra, S. (2002). *Providing Database as a Service*. Proc. of ICDE.
- Harrison, G. (Jun 13, 2010). *Consistency models in non-relational databases*. Retrieved Jul 27, 2017 from http://guyharrison.squarespace.com/blog/2010/6/13/consistency-models-in-non-relational-databases.html.
- Hartman, Bruce. *Big Data is Watching You!: A comic dystopia*. Swallow Tail Press.
- Helland, P. (June, 2011). *If You Have Too Much Data, Then 'Good Enough' Is Good Enough*. Communications of the ACM, 54(6), pp. 40–47. Retrieved Aug 13, 2017 from http://m.cacm.acm.org/magazines/2011/6/108666-if-you-havetoo-much-data-then-good-enough-isgood-enough/fulltext.
- Herodotou, H; Lim, H; Luo, G; Borisov, N; Dong, L; Cetin, F B; Babu, S. (2011). *Starfish: A Self-Tuning System for Big Data Analytics*. Proc. of CIDIR.
- Himel, Alex. (Mar 15, 2011). *Building Realtime Insights*. Facebook Engineering note.
- Hoffman, S. (2013). *Apache Flume: Distributed Log Collection for Hadoop*. Packt Publishing Ltd., Birmingham, UK.
- Hoffman, Steve. *Apache Flume: Distributed Log Collection for Hadoop*. PACKT.
- Hurst, Nathan; *Visual Guide to NoSQL Systems*. Retrieved Jul 27, 2017 from http://blog.nahurst.comlvisual-guide-to-NoSQL-systems/.
- Hurwitz, Judith; Nugent, Alan; Halper, Fern; Kaufman, Marcia. *Big Data for Dummies*.
- Jiang, D; Ooi, B C; Shi, L; Wu, S. (2010). *The Performance of MapReduce: An In-depth Study*. PVLDB 3(1).
- Khurana, Amandeep. (Oct, 2012). *Introduction to HBase Schema Design* 37(5).
- Lee, H J. (2012). *Nosql benchmarking*. Retrieved Aug 2, 2017 from http://www.cubrid.org/blog/dev-platform/nosql-benchmarking/.
- Leonard, Andrew. (Feb 1, 2013). *How Netflix is Turning Viewers into Puppets*. Retrieved July 27, 2017 from http://www.salon.com/2013/02/01/how_netflix_is_turning_viewers_into_puppets.
- LinkedIn. (Apr, 2012). *Project Voldemort*. Retrieved Jul 20, 2017 from http://project-voldemort.com.
- Loukides, Mike. *What Is Data Science?*. O'Reilly Media.
- M. Seeger, S. (2009). *Ultra-Large-Sites Key-Value stores: a practical overview*. Comput. Sci. Media.
- Maheshwari, Anil. (2017). *Data Analytics Made Accessible*.
- Maheshwari, Anil. *Big Data Essentials*. Wiley.
- Marr, Bernard. *Big Data in Practice: How 45 Successful Companies Used Big Data Analytics to Deliver Extraordinary Results*.
- Mayer-Schönberger, V. (2011). *Delete: The Virtue of Forgetting in the Digital Age*. New Jersey: Princeton University Press.

- Mayer-Schönberger, V; Cukier, K. (2013). *Big Data: A Revolution That Will Transform How We Live, Work, and Think*. New York: Houghton Mifflin Harcourt.
- McAfee, A; Brynjolfsson, E. (2012). *Big Data: The Management Revolution*. Harvard Business Review, Oct.
- McAfee, Andrew; Brynjolfsson, Erik. (2012). *Big Data: The Management Revolution*. Harvard Business Review.
- Meyer, M N. (2014). *Misjudgements will drive social trials underground*. Nature 511(7509), pp. 265–265.
- Mitra, P; Wiederhold, G; Kersten, M. (2000). *A graph-oriented model for articulation of ontology interdependencies*. In: Proceedings of the conference on extending database technology 2000 (EDBT'2000), Konstanz, Germany.
- *MongoDB Forbes Case Study*. Retrieved Jul 27, 2017 from http://www.10gen.com/customers/forbes.
- Morozov, E. (2013). *To Save Everything Click Here*. London: Penguin.
- Mundkur, P; Tuulos, V; Flatow, J. (2011). *Disco: a computing platform for large-scale data analytics*. In: Erlang'11: Proceedings of the 10th ACM SIGPLAN workshop on Erlang, New York, NY, USA, ACM, pp. 84–89.
- Ng, Annalyn. *Numsense! Data Science for the Layman: No Math Added*.
- Nussbaumer Knaflic, Cole. (2015). *Storytelling with Data: A Data Visualization Guide for Business Professionals*. Wiley.
- Owen, S; Anil R; Dunning, T; Friedman, E. (2011). *Mahout in action*. Manning Publications Co.
- Patil, DJ. *Data Driven*. O'Reilly Media.
- Pierce, George W. (2013). *The Songs of Insects: With Related Material on the Production, Propagation, Detection, and Measurement of Sonic and Supersonic Vibrations*.
- Pierson, Lillian. *Data Science for Dummies*. Wiley.
- Pritchett, D. (2008). *BASE: An acid alternative*. ACM Queue, pp. 48–55.
- Rao, Purba Halady. *Business Analytics: An Application Focus*. PHI Learning.
- Rees, R. (Sep 27, 2010). *NoSQL, No problem: An intro to NoSQL Databases*. Retrieved Jul 29, 2017 from http://www.thoughtworks.com/insights/blog/nosql-no-problem-intro-nosql-databases.
- Richards, N M; King, JH. (2014). *Big Data Ethics*. Wake Forest Law Review (23).
- See "Apache HBase Book External APIs" in the *Apache HBase Reference Guide*.
- See "Data Model: Rows" in the *Apache HBase Reference Guide*.
- See "Namespace" in the *Apache HBase Reference Guide*.
- Sheth, A P; Larson, J A. (1990). *Federated database systems for managing distributed, heterogeneous, and autonomous databases*. ACM Comput Surv 22(3), pp. 183–236.
- Shoshani, Arie; Rotem, Doron; *Scientific Data Management: Challenges, Technology, and Deployment*. Chapman & Hall/CRC.
- Siegel, Eric. *Predictive Analytics: The Power to Predict Who Will Click, Buy, Lie, or Die*. Wiley.

- Subramaniam, S; Gunopulos, D. (2007). *A survey of stream processing problems and techniques in sensor networks in Data Streams*. Springer US, pp. 333–352.
- Taylor, R C. (2010). *An overview of the Hadoop/MapReduce/Hbase framework and its current applications in bioinformatics*. BMC Bioinf., 11, p. S1.
- Thaler, Richard H; Sunstein, Cass R. (2009). *Nudge: Improving Decisions About Health, Wealth, and Happiness*. Richards, supra note 8, pp. 1955–56.
- *The NSA files*. World News, the Guardian. Retrieved May 29, 2017 from http://www.theguardian.com/world/the-nsa-files.
- Ting, Kathleen; Cecho, Jarek Jarcec. *Apache Sqoop Cookbook*. O'Reilly.
- Villars, R L; Olofson, C W; Eastwood, M. (2011). *Big data: what it is and why you should care*, White Paper, IDC, MA, USA.
- Wang, Chengwei; Schwan, Karsten; Talwar, Vanish; Eisenhauer, Greg; Hu, Liting; Wolf, Matthew. *A flexible architecture integrating monitoring and analytics for managing large-scale data centers*, Proceedings of the 8th ACM international conference on Autonomic computing, June 14–18, 2011, Karlsruhe, Germany [doi>10.1145/1998582.1998605].
- Wen, H. (Jun 11, 2012). *Big ethics for big data*. O'Reilly Radar. Retrieved Jul 29, 2017 from http://radar.oreilly.com/2012/06/ethics-big-data-businessdecisions.html.
- Wessing, Taylor. *The Ownership of Big Data*. Retrieved May 29, 2017 from https://united-kingdom.taylorwessing.com/globaldatahub/article_big_data_ownership.html.
- White, T. (2009). *Hadoop: The Definitive Guide*. O'Reilly Media, Sebastapol, CA.
- Zhang, Arthur. *Data Analytics: Practical Guide to Leveraging the Power of Algorithms, Data Science, Data Mining, Statistics, Big Data, and Predictive Analysis to Improve Business, Work, and Life*.
- Zikopoulos, Paul; Chris. (2011). *Eaton Understanding Big Data: Analytics for Enterprise Class Hadoop and Streaming Data*. McGraw Hill.
- Zwitter, A. (2014). *Big data ethics*. Big Data & Society 1(2): 2053951714559253.

Weblinks

- http://history-world.org/Industrial%20Intro.htm [accessed April 26, 2017]
- https://www.brainyquote.com/quotes/topics/topic_architecture.html [accessed April 26, 2017]
- http://www.worldwidewebsize.com/ [accessed April 26, 2017]
- https://Wikipedia.com [accessed April 26, 2017]
- http://www.worldwidewebsize.com/ [accessed April 26, 2017]
- http://Cisco.com [accessed April 26, 2017]
- https://iapp.org/news/a/with-big-data-and-privacy-what-should-the-regulators-know/ [accessed May 17, 2017]
- http://www.npr.org/sections/alltechconsidered/2016/07/11/485571291/firms-are-buying-sharing-your-online-info-what-can-you-do-about-it [accessed Jul 15, 2017]

- http://www.newsweek.com/secretive-world-selling-data-about-you-464789 [accessed Jul 15, 2017]
- http://www.nytimes.com/2012/02/19/magazine/shopping-habits.html?pagewanted=1&_r=1&hp [accessed May 26, 2017]
- https://united-kingdom.taylorwessing.com/globaldatahub/article_big_data_ownership.html [accessed May 29, 2017]
- http://goo.gl/uhhZhz [data chirps: [accessed Aug 25, 2017]

Index

A

B

C

D

E

F

G

H

I